Archaeology and the Galilee

Texts and Contexts in the Graeco-Roman and Byzantine Periods

SOUTH FLORIDA STUDIES IN THE HISTORY OF JUDAISM

Edited by
Jacob Neusner
William Scott Green, James Strange
Darrell J. Fasching, Sara Mandell

Number 143
ARCHAEOLOGY AND THE GALILEE
Texts and Contexts in the
Graeco-Roman and Byzantine Periods

by
Douglas R. Edwards
C. Thomas McCollough

ARCHAEOLOGY AND THE GALILEE

Texts and Contexts in the
Graeco-Roman and Byzantine Periods

by

Douglas R. Edwards
C. Thomas McCollough

Scholars Press
Atlanta, Georgia

ARCHAEOLOGY AND THE GALILEE

Texts and Contexts in the Graeco-Roman and Byzantine Periods

by
Douglas R. Edwards
C. Thomas McCollough

Publication of this book was made possible by a grant from the Tisch Family Foundation, New York City. The University of South Florida acknowledges with thanks this important support for its scholarly projects.

Library of Congress Cataloging in Publication Data
Archaeology and the Galilee : texts and contexts in the Graeco-Roman
    and Byzantine periods ; [edited] by Douglas R. Edwards, C. Thomas
McCollough.
        p.   cm. — (South Florida studies in the history of Judaism ;
no. 143)
    Includes bibliographical references and indexes.
    ISBN 0-7885-0333-2 (cloth : alk. paper)
    1. Galilee (Israel) —Antiquities. 2. Galilee (Israel)—History.
3. Excavations (Archaeology)—Israel—Galilee.   I. Edwards, Douglas
R.   II. McCollough, C. Thomas.   III. Series.
DS110.G2A84   1997
933—dc21   97-27123
                                                     CIP

Printed in the United States of America
on acid-free paper

Table of Contents

Acknowledgments

The inception of this book on archaeology and the Galilee came in the summer of 1993 as we worked with the University of South Florida Excavations at Sepphoris expedition led by James F. Strange. That summer marked Jim's twenty fifth year of archaeological excavations. Since both of us had cut our archaeological teeth under the tutelage of Jim it seemed natural to propose a volume written by his colleagues that delved further into many of the areas dear to his own thought. This volume could not have been accomplished without the expertise, insights, and patience offered by the Israeli and American scholars who dedicated a good deal of their time over the subsequent years revising, editing, and polishing excellent contributions. Our respective secretaries, Patsy McAfee at Centre College and Carol Avery at the University of Puget Sound, have our deep appreciation. Without their countless hours of editing, typing, and computer expertise this work would not have seen the light of day. Our families also have our gratitude for allowing us the many hours necessary to complete this project. We dedicate this book to the person who inspired it in tribute to his more than twenty five years of excavation in Galilee.

To James F. Strange, mentor, colleague, and friend.

Douglas R. Edwards
C. Thomas McCollough
June, 1997

1

Archaeology and the Galilee: An Introduction

Douglas R. Edwards and C. Thomas McCollough

Archaeological and literary research on the Galilee has exploded in the last two decades with increasing methodological and interdisciplinary sophistication.[1] The work of American archaeologists James F. Strange and Eric M. Meyers and the increased activity by Israeli scholars have played a vital role in that expansion. Galilean studies now cross disciplinary lines. No longer is archaeological work of interest simply to a few specialists. Scholars working on areas as diverse as the quest for the historical Jesus, gender roles in antiquity, the formation of the Talmud, and the import of the Hellenistic, Roman, Byzantine or Islamic empires benefit from the current proliferation of material evidence from sites and surveys.

The studies in this book, many by persons long associated with Galilean archaeology, reflect the current trend to move archaeological data from the descriptive work so critical to archaeological analysis toward a dialogue with those who interpret the narrative worlds of ancient texts.[2] Many of the contributors strategically replace an interpretive world based on privileged texts or "true, factual" archaeological data with an integrated, synthetic interpretation that draws on the best of both disciplines. The results are an impressive array of illuminating, challenging, and sometimes contradictory perspectives that should significantly impact ongoing discussions of Galilee in Late Antiquity.

HELLENISTIC AND ROMAN GALILEE

The Hellenistic and Roman periods in Galilee present a host of issues for those engaged in historical and archaeological studies. The complexity of Judaism, the interactions of those in Galilee with Greek and Roman centers of power, the rise of the Jesus movement, the varied role of women, the rise and fall of Herodian power, an increasing military presence, the expansion of villages and urban areas are among the arenas confronting the historian of Galilee. Archaeology enables interpreters to reconstruct more completely the local and regional framework in which such events took place. The historical and archaeological studies in this volume endeavor to discern more fully the unique local and regional economic, demographic, social, political, and ideological threads that compose the "webs of power"[3] binding ancient Galilean society.[4]

A scholarly crux among scholars is the impact of imperial or Roman power on Galilee. The debate often centers on the nature of urban/rural relations, the nature and character of an "urban overlay," whether the economy functions as a market or a taxation/tribute system, or the influence of Graeco-Roman culture on the inhabitants of Galilee. Several writers address these conundrums. Marianne Sawicki challenges interpreters to discern the implied world of the explicit artifactual remains. Her focus on the much-neglected arena of gender addresses how gender categories intimately relate to the division of labor and power in the ancient world.[5] Roads, water systems, and other forms of Roman intervention define how the landscape is conceived and recreated and reformed (cf. McCollough/Edwards). Her lucid description of the strategies employed by colonizers and colonized presents a finely nuanced approach toward understanding town/country, urban/rural, elite/peasant interactions.

Several New Testament scholars have posited a world dominated by imperial power, urban/rural conflict, taxation and tribute, and oppressed peasants.[6] Eric Meyers, an archaeologist with over 25 years of excavation experience in Galilee, argues that first-century Galilee is Jewish without the extensive Graeco-Roman traditions that influenced outlying areas such as Scythopolis and Acco/Ptolemais. He further argues that no great tension existed between urban and rural areas (a point emphasized also by D. Groh) and that Galilee was not isolated economically although it maintained a distinctive cultural character. Meyers also concludes that trade was an important aspect of the Galilean economy, which was not simply based on taxation and tribute.[7]

Dennis Groh and J. Overman critique Marxist models that purport an innate tension between town and country, a tension often existing more in the model than in the *realia* or even, as Overman argues, the narrative worlds.[8] Overman challenges J. Crossan and R. Horsley, whose paradigm of a peasant agrarian existence being disrupted by Roman imperialism and Judean politics Overman believes is based on a flawed model of colonialism. Both interpreters, he argues, improperly use perceived peasant societies and revolts in early Medieval Europe to develop their model of peasant society in the first century. Such reconstructions, he argues, are inadequate at best and outright wrong at worst. Drawing on the work of Yves-Marie Brece, Overman notes that most accounts of peasant rebellion in the Medieval period were actually mythological themes developed around small innocuous events, rather than reflections of actual major peasant uprisings. Tax resentment does not necessarily lead to tax resistance, but rather provides the impetus for certain myths arising from those few who might have resisted. Overman also criticizes the over-reliance on Josephus's portrayal of events in Galilee, arguing that Josephus reports little more than propaganda, either for the Flavians or for his own particular concerns.

Sean Freyne addresses the vexing problem of reconstructing relations between town and country in Galilee by arguing that tensions did exist between town and country. In the first century, such tension occurred in part due to Herodian imposition of an alien value system. The tension, however, was based on historical circumstances, not

innate hostility. He challenges the notion of "urban overlay" as proposed by Strange and suggests that no simple adaptation of Roman values and culture occurred. Trade patterns need not reflect any cultural continuum. Rather, Roman values and culture created resistance that organized itself along various lines, a position with some affinities to Sawicki's study.

Scholarly perceptions of the ancient road systems in lower Galilee has played a significant role in current interpretations of the landscape. Jim Strange argues persuasively that the ancient complex of road systems discovered in lower Galilee make obsolete current maps of Galilee that depict Galilee as isolated, having no network of roads and by implication no significant trade or interaction between locales and regions. The actual road network of Galilee suggests an intricate network of roads connecting urban and rural areas.[9] Pottery from manufacturing centers such as Shikhin and Kefar Hananiah, was exported both locally and regionally, a method of distribution, Strange argues, that should be extended to other agricultural and industrial products. The Galilean landscape crisscrossed by a maze of roads, some with an imperial stamp (as Sawicki articulately argues), made trade and presumably cultural interchange more prolific than previously assumed (cf. Fradkin).

Roman and Herodian imprints on the land are addressed by McCollough and Edwards, who argue that a monumental road with large pavers found at Sepphoris was built in the mid-second century C.E. and probably during the reign of Hadrian. The road was influenced by a Roman military presence to the south of Sepphoris following the 66-70 C.E. revolt. The date of the monumental road corroborates Eric Meyers' argument that increased building activity occurred in the Galilee, especially in lower Galilee and especially at Sepphoris, during the late-first and into the second century. Edwards and McCollough, however, also found that the monumental road follows an earlier road from the late Hellenistic/early Roman period. This road probably dates to the reign of Herod Antipas, and indicates that Antipas follows a grid pattern as he builds the eastern side of Sepphoris. This appears to support the acquisition of an "urban overlay" as proposed by Strange. Still debated is the extent and date of such an "urban overlay." Weiss and Netzer, for example, argue that Herodian activity did not include the building of the theatre; Strange argues that Herod Antipas did build it. Those questions will not be more fully answered until the final publications of the various teams excavating Sepphoris are available.

Arlene Fradkin brings hard science to bear on the issue of local and regional trade in Galilee. Fradkin offers conclusive evidence of trade at Sepphoris of fish and molluscs whose origins come from the Mediterranean Sea, the Nile, the Sea of Galilee, and the Jordan River. She demonstrates that Sepphoris was part of a much larger network, that extended beyond trade in pottery[10] and lamps. Now we have perishable food items showing such interaction. Clearly, Sepphoris was no isolated territory in regards to the trade of fish and molluscs. Fradkin's study also makes clear how important it is to record seemingly innocuous bones with careful attention to their context.

Jim Strange's most provocative discussion centers on what archaeological evidence can tell about ethnic and local identities. What would a visitor to Galilee see that was Jewish (cf. Sawicki)? Jewish identity was largely an internal and private affair, he concludes. No first-century public spaces that looked "Jewish" existed. Eshel, who also addresses how one identifies something Jewish, argues that some installations called "miqvaot" or ritual bathing pools are often not, especially at Sepphoris. Critical here is how strict persons in antiquity were in assigning a prescribed form of miqveh to the various types of water installations or pools found at Sepphoris. Are later stipulations of what constituted a "ritual" pool applicable to earlier periods? Eshel raises issues that will necessitate renewed discussions of these complexes (cf. Sawicki). Eshel (and Sawicki) will force further consideration of how one moves from identifying the obvious function of a structure to hold water to something which serves a ritual function or a symbol of resistance.[11]

Eshel's interpretation revolves in part on the fluidity of tradition. Should fourth century and later texts determine second and third century complexes? Groh argues in the affirmative. He challenges interpreters to use later material remains to illuminate the first-century world, especially because the first-century archaeological remains have been disrupted by later building periods. Groh argues for a degree of continuity in material culture that continues through the third and into the fourth centuries. This important critique should force interpreters to observe certain conservative trends in the material culture long overlooked or downplayed. The danger, of course, and one which is best met by careful analysis of each situation is that one imposes a second or third-century world view onto the first century (cf. Strange).

Mordechai Aviam's report on a second-century B.C.E. fortress siege complex offers exciting and new evidence for events preceding the establishment of the Herodians in Galilee. Archaeological evidence for this period in Galilee has been relatively sparse. Aviam argues that the site was a stronghold by Marion who controlled Tyre and who was defeated by Herod the Great. He also posits this fortress as the location of a battle by Herod against rebel forces who were ultimately defeated at Arbel. Many have argued that Josephus's account of the Galilean resistance to Herod has been overstated, a perspective suggested by the paucity of archaeological evidence. Aviam argues that this site represents the first concrete archaeological evidence for such resistance.

Lucille Roussin examines how zodiac mosaics found in Galilean synagogues elucidate the diverse practices of Galilean Judaism. Moreover, Roussin proposes that the zodiac, and the figure of Helios in the zodiac, do not copy pagan models. Rather, the mosaic deliberately presents information to congregants using strategies common among Jewish groups who draw on magic, astrology, and angel worship, strategies also apparent in the lead amulets found at Sepphoris and discussed by McCollough and Glazier-McDonald. Some in the Jewish congregations, Roussin contends, apparently acknowledged Helios as a form of minor deity. Beginning with the panel furthest from the *bema*, there is a thematic progression from the earthly realm to the Helios figure (who represents the celestial realm) to the highest realm, the seventh heaven as represented by the Torah shrine, the symbolic residence of Yahweh. This theological emphasis, Roussin argues, explains the absence of zodiac imagery use by contemporary Christians in Palestine.

Longstaff and Hussey's article is provocative as much for what it does not show as for what it does. They demonstrate how the fluctuation of environmental activity may have had great consequences for the economy and ecology of the region around Sepphoris. This careful analysis of pollen from Sepphoris, however, does not show nor does it purport to show when these events took place. Again, we lack enough archaeological evidence. Their prescription for how archaeologists could attain paleo-environmental data and how it could impact analysis of cultural change in the Galilee should serve as a beacon for further studies in this area.

LATE ROMAN AND BYZANTINE GALILEE

Over the past 20 years, the archaeological evidence recovered and analyzed by the expeditions led by James Strange and Eric Meyers on the synagogues and villages of Northern Galilee contributed substantially to the transformation of our understanding of Galilee in the late Roman and Byzantine periods.[12] The transformation that these excavations both encouraged and reflected is perhaps best summarized in Dennis Groh's article, "Jews and Christians in Late Roman Palestine: Toward a New Chronology."[13] Groh, who has worked with Meyers and Strange, pulled together archaeological evidence with new analytic approaches and revealed just how dramatic a shift was being forced in historical awareness. As he pointed out, the shift from empire wide to regional studies, which parallels a shift in archaeology from the great cities and the elite to the towns/villages and the common people resulted in a significant modification of the picture of Late Roman and Byzantine Palestine. The image of crisis and decline was replaced by one of "renaissance of town and village life in the Holy Land."[14] Moreover, the new evidence forced greater care to be taken in differentiating not only between regions but also within regions, "Rather than speaking about "the Galilee" and "the Golan" we must now discuss the two Galilees and the two Golans. People worshipped, worked, and shopped (traded) in different ways, in diverse architectural structures, in various languages in each of the subregions of the country."[15]

In the article on Sepphoris by the Israeli archaeologists Zeev Weiss and Ehud Netzer, we are given striking evidence of a city of the lower Galilee which suffered dramatically from earthquake and revolt in the late fourth century only to begin rebuilding and expanding in the fifth and sixth centuries. By cannibalizing earlier structures (e.g., the theater) and building over preexisting foundations, the population of Byzantine Sepphoris transformed the space. For the most part, these were not monumental structures (although the Nile Festival building certainly approaches monumental dimensions) like those of the Roman period but this does not necessarily signal economic distress. Rather, a "new aesthetic" and a changed perception of the urban space dictated design and use. As H.P. L'Orange described this "new aesthetic" the parts are subordinated to the whole as new buildings emerged from prior structural elements.[16] Thus while close inspection of the later structures may reveal unevenness in appearance and symmetry this does not necessarily signal inability or insufficient funding. Moreover, the evidence of a shift of building emphasis from acropolis to the flank of the city, suggests a shift in perception of the place in the *polis*. In the later city, neighborhood may be taking on increasing importance for expressing urban identity. The excavations of Weiss and Netzer have given us not only our first archaeological evidence of the construction of a church (ca. late 5th century) but also evidence that the bishop of the Church (Eutropius) invested in the neighborhood by paving the sidewalks with mosaic.

While the Christian community was building and defining its neighborhood, the Jewish community was in the midst of constructing a synagogue 175 meters to the north. The floor of the synagogue was decorated with a zodiac scene similar to other synagogue floors recovered in Israel dating to this period. As Weiss and Netzer point out, such a structure not only indicates something of the location and the ongoing viability of the Jewish community in Byzantine Sepphoris, but also the persistence and extent of the penetration of Hellenism.

Between the synagogue and the church, the excavations of the University of South Florida under the direction of James Strange, have uncovered a large basilica building with early Roman foundations. This building, whose floors were also covered with ornate mosaics, suffered extensive damage in the late fourth century. In the period that followed a portion of the building continued to serve a commercial or public role while other parts were used for building materials or transformed into neighborhood industry and bath space. All of which reinforces Groh's (and L'Orange's) point that Galilee in the Late Roman and Byzantine eras remained economically and culturally viable and dynamic. The material remains of Galilee in the late Roman and Byzantine eras present to the archaeologist and those interested in the history and religions of the region a set of material data that demands an analytic framework which is prepared to honor a complex set of variables.

The article by Tom McCollough and Beth Glazier-McDonald on the amulet recovered at Sepphoris offers an example of archaeology using its data to espy the convictions and concerns of the 'common person' of the Late Roman and Byzantine periods. This period witnessed a thriving trade in such magical devices. They were employed to protect the wearer from disease or curse an enemy or even capture the attention of a lover. The amulet maker employed incantations and symbols drawn from a wide spectrum of religious and magical formulas, to the distress of leaders of religious communities. And despite efforts on the part of these leaders to thwart or at least regulate the use of such implements, amulet use and its free employment of words and symbols continued unabated. As Ramsey MacMullen has observed, "the number of amulets...is testimony to the tenacious conservatism characterizing beliefs in the supernatural... As Celtic, a language living only among the poor and the isolated, found its way into books in the form of an incantation, so the last inscriptions in Phrygian, of the third century are predominantly curse formulas...Archaeologists working with a totally different kind of evidence report parallel findings. The dominant culture of the empire exerted its strongest influence on the material plane, while unmaterial aspects such as cults and superstitions remained less affected."[17]

It is at this point that the archaeological record has opened new windows and forced new historical constructs that we see the convergence of Jacob Neusner's scholarship with the study of the material culture. Neusner's translations and critical studies of the formative texts of rabbinic Judaism have at once thrown open the world of the rabbinic literature and at the same time made clear the need for a reassessment of the present state of scholarship. His critique of Peter Schäfer's work shows just how important is the need to move the scholarly trajectory off the track of reading these texts as historical records and in the direction of texts as literary compositions with their own logic and ideology. We can no longer peer through the rabbinic texts hoping to catch sight of the world of ancient Judaism as it unfolded in Galilee in late antiquity. The thickness of the text as text makes such a task extraordinarily difficult if not impossible. Hence, this makes even more critical the full range of the material culture in reconstructing Judaism in Galilee.

The archaeological record of Galilee is of course far from complete. The material collected so far should serve more as a set of indicators rather than conclusive findings. The direction indicated is, however, one which is at once both exciting and demanding. It opens the doors of understanding much more widely, letting in the "the voices of people who speak so softly because of the passage of time and their own low station."[18] It rejects easy generalizations and requires integrating the evidence gleaned from the cities with that of neighboring towns and villages. Moreover, it is a direction which demands more from the archaeologist as he or she must take into account and be prepared to respond to questions coming from colleagues in fields such as social and economic history, anthropology, classics, and religious studies.

James F. Strange as scholar and teacher has throughout his career been aware of such demands. For those of us who have followed him into the field and read his scholarship, we have been tutored in the art of interpretation as much as in the careful recovery of the material culture of the ancient people of Galilee. The work which follows is a tribute to him and we hope an inspiration to stay the course.

NOTES

[1] Witness the plethora of books on the historical Jesus that purport to integrate archaeology and text. See also the forthcoming volume edited by Eric Meyers from the Second International Conference on Galilee held at Duke in January, 1997. Connected with the conference was an outstanding exhibit on Sepphoris, which is beautifully presented in *Sepphoris in Galilee: Crosscurrents of Culture*, ed. Rebecca Nagy, et. al., North Carolina Museum of Art (Winona Lake, Indiana: Eisenbrauns, 1996).

[2] See David B. Small (ed.), *Methods in the Mediterranean: Historical and Archaeological Views on Texts and Archaeology* (Leiden, New York, and Cologne: E.J. Brill, 1995).

[3] A term coined by Simon Price, *Rituals and Power: The Roman Imperial Cult in Asia Minor* (Cambridge: Cambridge University Press, 1984).

[4] See F. Millar's call for careful regional studies; F. Millar, *The Roman Near East 31 B.C.-A.D. 337* (Cambridge: Cambridge U.P., 1993). See also John Bintliff, "Regional Survey, Demography, and the Rise of Complex Societies in the Ancient Aegean: Core-Periphery, Neo-Malthusian, and Other Interpretive Models," *Journal of Field Archaeology* 24 (1997) 1-38; S. Alcock, *Graecia Capta: The Landscapes of Roman Greece* (Cambridge: Cambridge U.P., 1993); G. Barker and John Lloyd (ed.), *Roman Landscape. Archaeological Survey in the Mediterranean Region.* (London: British School at Rome, 1991).

[5] See Dale Walde and Noreen D. Willows (eds.), *The Archaeology of Gender: Proceedings of the 22nd Annual Chacmool Conference* (Calgary: University of Calgary Press, 1991).

[6] As articulated by the two principal representatives of this position, R. Horsley, *Archaeology, History, and Society in Galilee: The Social Context of Jesus and the Rabbis* (Valley Forge; Trinity Press International, 1996) and J.D. Crossan, *The Historical Jesus: The Life of a Mediterranean Jewish Peasant* (San Francisco: Harper Collins, 1991).

[7] A point argued further in his debate with Richard Horsley. E. Meyers, "An Archaeological Response to a New Testament Scholar," *Bulletin of the American Schools of Oriental Research* 297 (1995) 17-26.

[8] A number of anthropologists, archaeologists, and historians have begun to assail the premise that urban centers exploited rural areas. See the studies in Glenn M. Schwartz and Steven E. Falconer (eds.), *Archaeological Views From the Countryside: Village Communities in Early Complex Societies* (Washington D.C.: Smithsonian Institution Press, 1994). No one puts it more succinctly than John Lloyd."...it would seem increasingly difficult to retain the view, still widely held, that the typical Roman town was a collection of amenities for the rich and their retainers, sucking in wealth from the countryside and returning to it very little. The sheer quantity of sites in the remoter countryside with centrally manufactured objects-- tools and other metal works, amphoras, millstones, pottery, some of them imports from overseas--suggests a more vigorous economic role for the town and the large village, in trade and quite possibly in manufacture too." In "Archaeological Survey and the Roman Landscape: Forms of Rural Settlement in the Early Roman Empire," in G. Barker and John Lloyd (eds.), *Roman Landscapes: Archaeological Survey in the Mediterranean Region* Archaeological Monographs of the British School at Rome 2 (London: British School at Rome, 1991) 238.

[9] Now compare Ze'ev Safrai. *The Economy of Roman Palestine* (London & New York: Routledge, 1994) 47, 224-290.

[10] David Adan-Bayewitz, *Common Pottery in Roman Galilee: A Study of Local Trade* (Ramat Gan: Bar Ilan University, 1993).

[11] For a discussion regarding the difficulty of locating symbolic and ideologically latent features, see C. Renfrew and P. Bahn. *Archaeology: Theories, Methods, and Practice* (New York: Thames and Hudson, 1991).

[12]See for example, E. Meyers, J. Strange, C. *Meyers, Excavations at Ancient Meiron. Upper Galilee, Israel 1971-72. 1974-75, 1977* (Cambridge, MA: American Schools of Oriental Research, 1981) E. Meyers, A. Kraabel and J. Strange, *Ancient Synagogue Excavations at Khirbet Shema. Upper Galilee, Israel. 1970-72.* Series: Annual of the American Schools of Oriental Research, 42 (Durham, NC: Duke University Press, 1970).

[13]*Biblical Archaeologist* 51.2 (1988) 80-96.

[14]Ibid., 92.

[15]Ibid.

[16]H.P. L'Orange, *Art Forms and Civic Life in the Late Roman Empire* (Princeton: Princeton University Press, 1965).

[17]R. MacMullen, *Enemies of the Roman Order* (Cambridge, MA: Harvard University Press) 245-246.

[18]D. Groh, "Jews and Christians in Late Roman Palestine" *Biblical Archaeologist* 51.2 (1988) 91.

2

Spatial Management of Gender and Labor in Greco-Roman Galilee

Marianne Sawicki
Midway College

The generosity of the Galilee has funded the cultural and the economic life of the world for millennia. Its material exports since ancient times have included wheat, olive oil, salt fish, textiles, and many other good things. Among its textual exports are the Mishnah, most of the Jesus stories, some of the Baha'i scriptures, and the earliest notation (perhaps) of the phrase "house of David."[1] Galilee has given archaeologists one of the oldest recognizably human skulls, along with treasures ranging from pollens of Neanderthal funeral wreaths to metalwork, weapons, ceramics, mosaics, and coins.

Galilee gives because somebody wants to take. How archaeologists partake of the legacy of the Galilee is the question discussed in this chapter.[2] Historical archaeology, as a discipline, skillfully correlates information extracted from two kinds of evidence: *physical* remains, and *textual* remains. The key to understanding what Galilee gives us is getting the right grip on the relationship that may exist between those two: the texts, and the other artifacts.

Let's begin by orienting our inquiry toward the one artifact that the Galilee *cannot* export, its own landscape. The face of the land is sculpted with traces of ancient roadways, aqueducts, theaters, granaries, dining halls, orchards, homes, basilicas, synagogues, and factories. Along this cultural and economic landscape moved things, people, and ideas. Galilee *worked*, in every period of its past, as a grand machine for channeling or withholding, con-

centrating or separating, introducing or extracting, mixing or distilling these "fluids." Galilee moved things by design, and aspects of the design can be recovered and understood from the landscape today.[3]

With Galilee in the Roman period,[4] of course, one must speak not of a single enduring design, but of the multiple partial *re*designs and repairs of a dynamic, changing, and contested system. The cultural and economic landscape was colonized by Romans, which is to say that it adapted to ideology and trade pressures from across the empire.[5] These adaptations may be read off the texts in our libraries and the trinkets in our museums; but they left a legible imprint upon the land itself as well.

The Roman period can be characterized as one in which social institutions underwent repeated ruptures through cultural and economic trauma. An evolutionary view of history is not adequate to understand such a period. Cultural systems were confronted repeatedly with novel and challenging circumstances; solutions had to be rapidly cobbled together. In other words, the flow of historical time in Jewish history had hit a series of turbulent cataracts.[6] Galilean adaptations to traumatic political and social events in the Roman period are still evident in the landscape. We can identify both imperial intrusions--for example, the rectilinear design imposed upon cities according to Roman urbanization policies--and indigenous resistances--for example, the maintenance of a separate and ritually pure water system after the aqueduct brought plentiful, wholesome, and convenient Roman water into neighborhoods of the city of Sepphoris. However, as post-colonial studies of colonialism now underway in the late twentieth century indicate, it is not always possible to distinguish cleanly between an "imperial intrusion" and an "indigenous resistance" when interpreting complex textual artifacts, especially those produced several generations after the initial colonial establishment.[7] Like the British in India in our more recent past, Roman administrators cultivated indigenous collaborators. By the time those collaborators had grandchildren, imperial institutions had became indigenized into the culture in many respects. The Roman presence, together with Hellenistic culture generally, was taken to be the natural, ordinary state of affairs, by people who "didn't see them coming."[8]

The cultural products of the people living in such a situation are inevitably hybridized. Thus the literature of Roman Palestine must be read in context of the Hellenistic canon of which it is a part.[9] This literature, foundational for Christianity and Judaism, respectively, is a literature produced in accommodation to colonization, often by the collaborating class, growing out of the fissures in society and seeking to patch them over. Like those texts, the landscape, too, was overwritten in a compromised situation.

READING

The interpretation of the social and economic landscape of colonized Galilee is characterized with increasing frequency as a task of "reading." How ought one to "read" the land and the archaeological record that it contains? How can such a reading be coordinated with our reading of the textual artifacts of colonized Galilee: the Mishnah, Josephus, inscriptions and papyri? These issues have been addressed, implicitly and sometimes explicitly, in various ways. The options for coordinated reading may be classified into three categories: reference theories, critical confrontation theories, and recursion theories.

(1) Coordination as reference. In this approach to reading Galilee, the texts are taken to refer straightforwardly to the land. They are "about" events that simply "took place" somewhere in Galilee. The texts claim correspondences to material culture insofar as they mention various items that may turn up in the earth; for example, scythes, perfume bottles, walls, coins, courtyards. Written texts are epistemologically privileged by investigators as the most reliable means of access to the realities of the past.[10] The reality of past events is dogmatically asserted through historical positivism, and their absolute determination of the textual references is assumed. Archaeology's function, on this view, is to match up written words with dusty things. It tries to corroborate and illustrate the facts already communicated in the texts. Within this category,

there is a progressive version: besides mere matchmaking, archaeology may be called on occasionally to supply information that the texts omitted, or to correct minor textual inaccuracies. There is also a more troubling form: archaeological findings are manipulated intentionally to support claims made in the texts, or to advance some social or political objective arising from the text.

(2) Coordination as critical confrontation. Here, texts and archaeological evidence are equally privileged as sources of information. Both are "to be read." Reading is understood to be a more or less straightforward decoding of information--and the same formal codes are presumed to apply to textual and material artifacts alike. Yet in addition, texts are regarded as having rhetorical and ideological capabilities that the landscape and artifacts in general lack. Thus in the standard version of this option, texts are to be read "with suspicion," that is, as potentially deceptive or ideologically bent. In contrast with texts, however, material remains are regarded as innocent, truthful, and relatively transparent. Because deposited accidentally, not purposively--or so it is presumed--their arrangement can be explained fully through identifying causal factors.[11] Nothing but the forces of geology and marketplace economics lurks behind the configuration of the landscape.[12] In this version, the material remains are summoned as irreproachable witnesses in order to disclose and impugn the tendentiousness of the texts. There is also a somewhat more critical form of this option, which recognizes that material culture was already being "read" (somehow) even by those who first built and used it. As Miriam Peskowitz insightfully remarks, "The architecture itself would have functioned as a nonwritten text that conveyed meanings about family life."[13] Wittingly or unwittingly, the builders and dwellers *somehow* shared the literacy of a spatial idiom that made possible the teaching and learning of values and behavior through architecture. But this option does not inquire further into that "somehow." It supports no "hermeneutic of suspicion" in either the ancient readings of landscape or our own historical readings of it.

(3) Coordination by recursion. With this third sort of approach, neither the texts nor the material remains are thought to communicate "innocently." Therefore both are read with appropriate hermeneutics of suspicion, and then (as in option 2) those tandem readings are critically correlated. Moreover, the interpreters' own position within a tradition, and their own susceptibility to the persuasive power of artifacts and texts, are taken into account as well. If artifacts placed in use in antiquity were already subtly persuasive and were being "read" even then, then archaeologists should examine how this "reading" happened. They should identify the specific mechanisms for the encoding and decoding of meaning *in space*.[14] Moreover, archaeologists should expect to encounter "resistive" readings of various sorts. Both texts and artifacts, particularly the landscape, can be regarded as (potentially) strategic interventions in the negotiation of social relationships, whether for the sake of maintenance or for change. We must further recognize that archaeological investigation and reporting, too, produce non-innocent textual artifacts that are strategically powerful in the service of various academic and political enterprises today. Mark Leone and his colleagues describe how artifacts are "agents": active vectors for the cultivation of virtues and viewpoints in the population.[15] There is a mild-mannered academic version of this option; it implements these insights during the investigative phase of its archaeological work but then concludes by publishing textualized "findings" in journals and books, thus underscoring its own complicity with the tradition that it is investigating. There is also an activist version that attempts to interrupt the present-day social cultivation of received values by teaching the laypeople, as consumers of archaeological displays and reports, how to discern the covert mechanisms of persuasion at work within their own civic involvements--just as they worked in the past--and how to resist those messages when appropriate.[16]

Whichever option one chooses, the very notion that the land ought to be "read" *in relation to* the reading of written texts is what sets historical archaeology apart from the other branches of the discipline.[17]

THE LITERACY OF SPACE

Greco-Roman Galilee is a rhetorically effective cultural landscape. The "reading" and the "writing" of the landscape (or rather, the continual rereading and rewriting of it) required a distinctive *literacy* of space and movement.[18] The landscape constructed and inculcated certain social realities by managing the movement of water, foodstuffs, labor, and lore (along with numerous other things). This management of flow is the mechanism through which landscape communicated, taught, persuaded, encouraged, dissuaded, inspired--in short, *was read*. *Spatial* constructions are keys to interpreting the *textual* construction of certain social realities that come down to us in our religious traditions and still are quite powerful today. Among them are two that have received increasing attention from historical archaeologists: ethnicity and gender. Let's consider these in turn.

The quest to uncover the national past is a powerful and praiseworthy motivation driving archaeology in Israel. One wants to discover Jewish cities, Jewish architectural forms, Jewish artworks and artifacts.[19] But what does "Jewish" look like in the ancient ruins? How can Jewishness be securely identified in material culture, particularly in the landscape? For archaeology these are sci-

entific questions, and not easy to answer satisfactorily. On one hand, inscribed Hebrew letters and decorative motifs such as the menorah bespeak the intention of ancient builders to construct and furnish a place "Jewishly," to house aspects of an intentionally Jewish way of life. On the other hand, in the Roman period in Galilee many Jews wrote Greek or Aramaic, used hellenized names, and behaved "Jewishly" in places adorned with secular and heathen cultural themes--places built with colonial interests in mind.[20] In fact, to "behave Jewishly" in colonized Roman Galilee must have had something to do with maintaining identity while moving through a built environment designed to gobble up indigenous culture, wealth, and labor into the imperial maw of worldwide trade. As far as we can tell, spatial isolation was *not* the strategy for cultural and religious survival chosen by the majority of colonized people in Roman Galilee; we don't find urban enclaves (ghettos), nor has anyone yet found a village unpenetrated by Greek and Roman goods and services.

What *is* found is something much more ingenious and precious. Excavators see evidence that colonized Galileans were working on the very same question that perplexes today's archaeologists--"What is it to be Jewish, really?"-- and that their efforts produced the texts and the landscape features *that produced Judaism and provided for its reproduction*. So archaeologists find "Jewishness" by finding the instrumentalities for producing it. Those instrumentalities or templates cannot be understood in a static frame. They are not determined according to some eternal and transcendent pattern. They operated across time, transgenerationally. For example, a burial inscription memorializes someone's service to the Jewish community, or the municipal archives at Sepphoris keep track of ancestors' marriage contracts; these are ways of securing Judaism in the past (i.e., the past for a first-century Galilean). When rabbinic texts specify requirements for valid marriages and for relations within marriage, they are providing for a Jewish future.[21] Backward-reaching and forward-reaching templates for *making Jewishness* can be discerned in the archaeological record, just as they can be excavated from ancient texts. Their development at just this period surely is owing to the challenge of the colonial situation, a situation in which every traditional geographical and social border was pierced.

The quest to uncover the roots of gender oppression is also a praiseworthy and powerful motivation in archaeology. Recent advances in the archaeology of gender systems are not yet reflected in the planning, reporting, or interpretation of excavations in Israel, however.[22] But Peskowitz, in her pioneering and provocative study of the co-construction of gender in rabbinic texts and in material culture, contrasts the *representation* of women's labor with the *economic realities* of women's and men's work in one trade, that of textile production. She shows how femininity was defined through the cultural icon of the good woman who spins and weaves at home; even corpses were accessorized with spindle whorls in their coffins. Peskowitz reads the spindle whorls "with suspicion"; that is, she astutely identifies their rhetorical use to assign meaning to women by connecting individuals into the symbolic system of gender at a specific location. Besides being tools, the whorls are words in a language. They are the adjective "feminine." But, as Peskowitz shows, the language that is the ancient Jewish gender system has separated economic worth from the connotation of "feminine." What is womanly is private and therefore invisible in the economy. Peskowitz terms this semantic event the "decommodification" of women's labor.[23] The power of the gender semantic is so great that it can accomplish this ironic assertion of women's economic insignificance through the very same artifact--the whorl--that produces their substantial economic contributions.

Peskowitz's reading of rabbinic *texts* is theoretically critical and sophisticated; by comparison, her reading of *materials* is still quite rudimentary. The whorl, although it functions as a physical word, takes its meaning from a *nonphysical formal system*--a symbolism of gender that is also encoded in the rabbinic texts. But surely the whorl has significance within a *physical system* as well: the imperial infrastructure that extracts wealth from Galilee by means of edifices and roads cut into the Galilean landscape. For full spatial literacy, should we not read the whorl also in terms of its material economic function? The technology of weaving appropriates women's time and labor for production of textiles for export; that is, it turns womanpower into imperial wealth as it turns fiber into thread and thread into cloth. From the perspective of spatial management, then, the tools of the textile trade bespeak the *commodification* of women's labor, because they extract the benefits of women's labor from their village kinship circles and drain it off into the imperial economy. Now the full irony of the overlay of ideology upon economic reality comes into view. The textually produced *decommodification* of women's labor, established by Peskowitz, cloaks the actual *commodification* of it required by the colonial administration.[24]

Why this cloaking? Is this a guilty denial of oppression by the oppressors: a claim that women's work is valueless, advanced by the very men who are profiting nicely from that labor?[25] How you answer will depend upon the extent of the social phenomena that you want to cover with your explanation. If you focus narrowly upon gender relations, then you have completed your work when you have described the semantic mechanisms for *rhetorically* separating women from the value of their work. You can answer yes, the rabbis are guilty. However, if you want a more comprehensive account of the interplay of ideology and space, empire and resistance, then you must press on to examine the connections between that *rhetorical estrangement* of women from labor, on the one hand, and the *material colonial extraction* of the women's labor's fruits away from themselves and their families, on the other hand. The broader inquiry will actually provide a more satisfactory answer for the narrower investigation of gender relations as well, for this reason: ancient gender relations were not a closed system, and certainly not a system running on the sheer desire for power.[26] Gender is part of the kinship system, which in traditional societies is the instrumentality for assigning personal identity and for managing labor and its fruits.[27] Constructions of gender are affected whenever there is change or traumatic disruption to other social or natural systems such as agriculture, government, the economy, the environment, and so forth.

Moreover, gender can be deliberately and skillfully manipulated to have an effect on other systems. As we shall see, in the colonial context of Roman Galilee, gender constructions left architectural traces in the landscape, and they were a vehicle for constructing Judaism.[28] Thus we do not find "women's space" or "women's work" as such in excavations. We find instead the acute salience of the question, "What is the womanly way of being Jewish; what is the manly way?" The landscape also shows us how these ways were spatially produced.

IMPERIAL INCISIONS

Across Britain the Emperor Hadrian built a wall from sea to sea; but across Galilee he built a road from port to market.[29] Because the northern hostiles wanted nothing to do with empire, Roman policy in their regard was surveillance and vigilance. Hadrian's wall was a 73-mile elevated sentry walk for keeping an eye on hostile Britons. But many Galileans by the second century saw quite clearly the advantages of worldwide trade, so Rome fortified their economic infrastructure for them. A strategic bypass along the ancient Legio-Acco road was laid down in the 120's, and it connected this major trade route to the heart of downtown Sepphoris' business district.[30] Despite these contrasts, however, the wall and the road alike were incisions that left the scars of empire.

The roads were supposed to bring the benefits of Roman civilization and commerce into the Galilean capital, and Hadrian himself arrived on them to display his person and imperial power in a highly visible visit to the city about 134 C.E. In fact, roads run both ways. The covert function of the Roman roads, and of Galilee's complex connections into Roman world markets, was to siphon wealth out of the land.[31] Roads had networked the Galilee from time immemorial, but the Romans resurfaced and graded them the better to accommodate wagons, which transport goods more efficiently than pack animals do.

More impressive even than the roads were the Roman waterworks. The establishment of Roman cities at Caesarea Maritima, Sepphoris, Tiberias, Gadara, Gaba, Hippos, and Bethsaida/Julias would require public baths.[32] Caesarea's aqueduct brought fresh water to the seaside, while at Sepphoris two main channels running westward from the reservoir likely spanned the lower city, delivering spring water there and probably to the acropolis as well.[33] Daily patronage of the baths signified the Roman way of life. We Americans lay waterpipe humbly underground; but the Romans flaunted their hydraulics with great stone arches leaping across valleys and through city neighborhoods in giant strides. Roman water at Sepphoris bounded up the hillside on huge lifting wheels, according to one source. The *visibility* of those machines was crucial to their social function; on a clear day they could be seen from as far away as the lakeside city of Tiberias.[34] Herod Antipas, raised in Rome and ruling in Galilee, was adept at the rhetorical use of water--just like his father, who for fun (and to show he had manpower and engineering to waste on fun) had built himself a little ocean in the Judean desert, filled up the toy from a branch of the Jerusalem aqueduct system, and staged mock sea battles there. The Herodium fortress, overlooking this nautical wonder, had its own independent water supply from winter rains caught in immense cisterns.[35]

Water was at once a biotechnology and a technology of time. The urban management of water permitted large concentrations of population within the cities. The skillful utilization of storm runoff and of waste water enhanced agricultural fertility and supported tree growth in and near the city, for aesthetic enjoyment and also for fuel. The practices of bathing gave structure to the Roman citizen's daily routine.[36] People spent several hours at the baths: exercizing, relaxing, grooming themselves, and doing business. Some cities had separate facilities for men and women; otherwise, women and little children generally attended the baths before noon, men between noon and nightfall. The baths were staffed by crews of personal attendants, plumbers, engineers, and maintenance specialists, working in shifts.[37] Their regular work hours and their occupational identifications organized their social identities. The workforce of the baths was only one of several industrial groups whose rhythms and methods of production were affected by the provision of Roman water. Textiles, ceramics, glassmaking, and tanning also could be upsized and regimented thanks to the availability of plentiful, reliable running water for the city workshops. In Galilee the natural passage of time is marked by the alternation of two seasons: torrential rain and baking heat. Submissive to this divine time, traditional urban water systems had caught winter rainwater in copious cisterns, to be lifted out by hand or by animal power for the summer droughts. But now, contrary to divine plan, the Roman aqueduct ran independently of the season through the steady inexorable earthly power of gravity.

With roads and waterlines converging upon it, the Roman city itself was designed (or, often, it redesigned an earlier settlement) to connect these channels with neighborhoods. Streets were laid out in regular grids, with drains leading off into sewers. The grids defined blocks of *insulae* or multiple-family apartment dwellings clustered around courtyards. These dwellings did not necessarily house what we would term "nuclear families" or "extended families." In fact, their physical layout itself contributed to the deterioration of traditional Galilean kinship structures as expressed in village housing patterns.

Urban dwellings, like village housing, served as workspace both for provision of food and clothing, and for craft production, agricultural processing, and business. Coworkers might live together, regardless of kinship. Traditionally in the villages, virtually all inhabitants would be at least distant cousins, each related and obligated to the others by several possible patterns of reckoning. In the city, this no longer was true--especially in Roman cities like Tiberias which had been created by the forced resettlement of people from different localities.[38] Moreover, traditional village housing was such that it could expand irregularly to accommodate family growth: a new daughter-in-law, a widow returning to her paternal home, a cousin's sons arriving to begin a business venture.[39] But with the Roman urban *insula*, there soon was no more room to grow; the walls didn't support more than two stories. The street grid had the tenements and neighborhoods tightly boxed in. New residents, whether voluntarily or involuntarily occupying urban dwellings, found that traditional kinship connections in many cases simply could not be housed there; and for lack of spatial realization these relationships became less real. As alternatives to kin ties, the city offered novel architectural expressions of social identity and cohesiveness that could be chosen as a substitute for cousins.[40] For example, the theater arranged its seating by social rank; various craft guilds sponsored their own baths; and the synagogue of one's choice might be that of one's geographical origins and/or business connections.[41]

A city like Sepphoris was designed to *be* the economic interface of Galilee with the rest of the empire. If, traditionally, goods and services had circulated regionally among the towns and villages of the Galilee (with people and produce also moving southward to Jerusalem at festival times), then Roman cities were inserted like spigots to tap into those economic cycles and drain the system. One mechanism for this was taxation. Romans taxed the agricultural produce of the land, and they taxed commodities moving along the trade routes as well. Prominent local citizens were put in charge of raising revenues both for the imperial treasury and for local civic projects; they were held responsible for this liturgy or "people's service," and whatever they could not collect they had to make up from their own resources. This requirement suppressed Galilean agricultural productivity in the third century, in at least two ways. Some landowners abandoned their fields and fled in the face of insupportable tax debt. On the other hand, land was taken out of food production and used for raising sheep for wool, textiles being a better "cash crop" than wheat and oil, and in some cases being the required form of payment in lieu of severely devalued currency.[42] This led to innovations in textile production, altering the work patterns of both women and some men.

Taxation aside, the city was designed to interrupt the traditional local cycles of production and consumption. It extracted "surplus"--a euphemism for goods and labor that previously had been tied up at the village level.[43] If we consider merely the construction and staffing activities mentioned so far, we can begin to appreciate the effect of Roman urbanization. The Romans brought with them the plans for cities; they did not bring along all the workers necessary to lay the stone pilings, stoke the furnaces of the *thermae*, launder the bath towels and weave the woolen cloaks for the infantry. Those people came into the cities to work from elsewhere in the Galilee and beyond. Significantly, they generally came *from* places where a kinship network insured that their general welfare would be provided for, *to* a place where their starving would diminish no one else's honor. They came *out of* villages where the only way for wealthy people to enjoy the prestige of their agricultural surplus was to bestow it upon their poorer relations, *into* world market centers where "surplus" grain and oil now could be liquidated and transformed into material signifiers of luxurious lifestyle. Cities made consumption conspicuous. Moreover, in the cities the workers had to use wages to purchase food and clothing in shops, which entailed transportation and overhead costs previously unknown in village production. The relative ease of transport over the Roman roads brought Galilean urban consumers into direct competition with consumers in distant parts of the empire.

A further complication for Galilee was the manifold demographic and economic impact of the destruction of Jerusalem. Before 70 C.E., while the Temple stood, a significant portion of Galilean produce went south to be sacrificed and eaten within the holy city during festivals-- mostly by Galilean pilgrims on holiday.[44] Law and custom also required that specified portions of produce had to be given to the priests, levites, and the poor. Only a few aristocratic families among the priestly and levitical castes lived year-round in Jerusalem; the others went there when it was their turn, for a week's service, about twice a year. Thus, in the absence of urban interference, tithes of pro-

duce stayed in Galilee for consumption by Galilee's local priests, levites, and poor people. Besides produce, other possessions could be dedicated to the Temple by vow, and subsequently could not be put to any other use.

This system obviously helped to concentrate surpluses locally and regionally. It was disrupted by the abolition of Temple sacrifices and pilgrimage festivals, following upon the demolition of the Temple building itself. Afterwards, priests still retained their hereditary right to receive agricultural tithes--just at a time when the roads opened up world markets for that produce while traditional strictures localizing its consumption had become impossible to observe. The wars of 66-74 and 132-135 thus had the effect of enhancing the potential economic value of priestly kinship status, even while other kinship advantages were being eroded in various ways. Many priestly families emigrated to Galilee after Jews were expelled from Jerusalem in 135, and some were wealthy enough to buy land there. Small landowners in the first and second century were willing to sell, lured by the promise of waged jobs in the cities and not foreseeing the impact of the drastic inflation of currency that would befall them after the middle of the third century.

BECAUSE IT WAS *THERE*

To narrate a history is like stringing beads on a thread. The beads are "events," and the thread is our implicit belief that a gradual, forward-surging evolutionary development imparts a naturally ordered homogeneity to human time. For some aspects of the human past, that kind of narration succeeds in providing an adequate understanding. But a bead-stringing narration is not complex enough to capture the dynamic interacting processes at work in Greco-Roman Galilee. Nor can we revert to a meteorological account of abstract forces in conflict, balance, or synergy; for that would imply a more regular and predictable (even if turbulent) pattern than what the evidence actually shows us.

Before theorizing about abstract processes and forces, one should first examine whether and how such forces can have been expressed in material reality--that is, the spatial deployment of instrumentalities to impede, promote, or channel the movement of people, things, and ideas around the Galilee. Features of the landscape exhibit multiple layers of function. As we have seen, the roads, waterlines, and city grids imposed upon Galilee by Roman occupation both advertized and accomplished the Roman intention of bringing the benefits of imperial civilization into the province. But that's not all they did. Every gift had a price. Reviewing what has been said so far, Figure 1 compares the overt and covert effects of the chief elements of the Roman redesign of the Galilean landscape.

FEATURE	OVERT FUNCTION ("promise")	COVERT FUNCTION ("delivery")
roads	import blessings of empire to Galilee: lifestyle enhance-ment through exotic cultural and ma-terial goods	apply pressures of world markets; produce becomes convertible to luxury goods; food leaves Galilee; la-bor redeployed to produce cash crops and exportable goods
aqueducts	improve hygiene and comfort, promoting greater population density and interaction	support new industries as incentive for labor to move to cities from land; display Roman power over the heavens and time
grid of urban streets and *insulae*	provide new residential neighborhoods with good drainage	make kinship obligations and connections less visible and viable; geometric logic replaces logic of kin loyalties
theatres	entertain and educate city dwellers and visitors	introduce alternative cosmology and stories; assign social rank and affiliation through classified seating; promote fluency in Greek; windows on the world

Figure 1: Roman Landscape Strategy

Clearly, the material effects appearing in the wake of modifications to the landscape differed alarmingly from the social promises that those innovations embodied. But analysis of material recursivity (in the spirit of Leone, Potter, and Little's conception) does not stop with this kind of comparison of the overt and covert functions of the various spatial features of the urban landscape. It goes on to inquire how the indigenous people may have found ways to use the imperial built environment for their own purposes: *resistive* ways. Colonized people devise various strategies of resistance, ranging from outright avoidance, to restrictive regulation, to incorporation of the new features into an updated version of traditional spatial management systems. Moreover, colonized people don't always resist; they also collaborate to some extent with the colonial power.

For the collaborating class, imperial spatializations may efface the more traditional ones in part or in full. Figure 2 sketches some of the strategic indigenous responses to Roman modifications of the landscape.

This schematic comparison already suggests three principles: that indigenous responses to colonization may be multifaceted and conflicting, that the distinction between resistive and collaborative spatial responses may be a matter of degree rather than kind, and that the passing of generations may modify and redirect the strategies of resistance and collaboration. Let me explain.

Roman roads and urbanization of the Galilee insured that, from the early first century onward, residents of the villages of the lower Galilee (at least) had opportunities on all sides to participate in the culture and business of the empire.[45] Indeed, there were many incentives for them to do just that and--cumulatively, at least--the evidence is substantial for a gradual and thorough hellenization of Galilee. Yet it remained *possible* for individuals to withdraw aspects of their lives from the colonial spatializations and temporalizations produced by the Romans. How would we know whether they *actually did so*? Excavation does not succeed in uncovering individual decisions.[46] But neither can excavators infer with certitude that in the early first century, Nazareans did walk through Sepphoris because it lay along the shortest route from Nazareth to Cana. It is also possible that villagers went out of their way to walk *around* the city. In fact, the textual evidence is in keeping with such a maneuver. Gospel stories "go out of their way" to keep from mentioning Sepphoris, and this is a significant omission.[47]

FEATURE	COLLABORATIVE ADAPTATION	RESISTIVE ADAPTATION
roads, opening world markets	land put to producing wool for taxes and export	avoidance of cities by villagers when possible; flight by estate owners
aqueducts, baths, urban factories	selective patronage of baths; move to occupations in urban crafts and retail	domestic *miqva'ot* for personal and industrial use; disparagement of "nonobservant" retailers
city streets, *insulae*; theater with three-tiered cosmos and segregated seating	urbanization of the rabbinate	urban *bet midrash*: rabbinic school house re-colonizing urban space and time
Jerusalem Temple destroyed and overbuilt with a Roman temple	*miqva'ot* as defenses for hereditary right to tithes; the synagogue houses the official cult; sacrifices and localized consumption of tithed foods are abandoned	*miqva'ot* as defenses for purity of priestly kinship lines, with a view to restoring the Temple cult

Figure 2: Counter-Strategies of the Colonized Elite

At a slightly later period, roughly 70 to 200 C.E., the rabbinic movement too was based in villages and was, literally and figuratively, detouring around the Roman cities. The dispersion of rabbis among villages at this period made it impossible for them to promulgate a unified *halachah*.[48] About the year 200, Judah ha-Nasi took the revolutionary step of relocating himself and his school to the city of Sepphoris. In some respects this move was a concession to the realities of colonial existence, the inevitability of the cosmopolitan way of life. Thereafter, the Mishnah mentions rabbis in urban marketplaces and even in the baths as a matter of course. Any resistive avoidance of the city and its features has ended.[49]

On the other hand, establishing themselves and their schools in the urban environment positioned the rabbis to consolidate their authority, expand its scope, and compete with the Romans for the symbolic control of urban space and time--even while appearing to cooperate with them in the civil administration of urban affairs. Traditionally in Israelite theology, agricultural people had understood themselves to be owning and working the land in partnership with God according to the ancient Mosaic Law.[50] Now the urban streets, alleys, and *insulae* also became fields governed by Jewish law.[51] For example, while residents sharing a courtyard might not be kin, a procedure is devised through which they can constitute themselves as a single household for purposes of sabbath observance. Furthermore, the rabbis determined that aqueduct water running through a common courtyard was not owned by anyone, and so could not be lifted on the sabbath; however cistern water was private household water and so might be carried on sabbath. With a thousand little regulations like these, the rabbis took back the urban landscape. Symbolically, they re-colonized the built environment through which the Romans had first physically and psychologically colonized the land. Jews had lost Jerusalem and with it the possibility of celebrating festivals there together as one nation; but through reform of the calendar and the methods of calculating and announcing feasts, the rabbis attempted to synchronize national life. Rabbinic time resisted Roman time, not simply in the calculation of weeks and seasons, but more importantly in the manipulation of the future through the structure of finance, debts, and contracts. If you will, rabbinic Judaism mounted a gentle *urban* guerilla war against imperial space and time, from within.

The amoraim built a new kind of edifice in which to do this work: the schoolhouse or *bet midrash*. We have no specific information about the size or shape of these structures. Some supposedly were free-standing; others occupied rooms in homes or public buildings. The schoolhouse had a door and a doorkeeper, to whom students paid a daily fee for admission.[52] This architectural innovation accompanied and facilitated the codification of the

Mishnah. With it, a threshold was crossed here in several respects. The perceived competence of the rabbis was greatly expanded once it was housed in the urban *bet midrash*. Before 200, as Shaye Cohen has shown, the rabbis handled cases involving primarily matters of ritual purity and holy observances. Afterwards, they also exercised competence over civil matters such as marriages, the allotment of tithes, and disputes over ownership and use of property.[53] Expertise in such business previously had been thought to reside in Jewish homes or with the elders and officers of the synagogue, whether village or urban. Thus the rabbinic schoolhouse localized and concentrated the power to manage *space*: out of it came case law governing real estate transfers, travel, the maintenance of rental property, the shipment of agricultural produce, walls, boundaries, and courtyard relations.

The *bet midrash* also produced the means to manage *time*: regulations covering sabbath and festival observances, menstrual practices, loans, marriage contracts, and damages for injury resulting in loss of future earnings. This expansion of jurisdiction and consolidation of power was achieved partly through the rhetorical construction of the rabbi as expert and guardian of Judaism, and it was signified and accomplished by enclosing "the oral Torah" in a room with a door with restricted access. It was achieved, *spatially*, at the expense of discrediting other Jewish experts (including mothers-in-law and farmers) and by gendering the voice in which the oral Torah would speak henceforth.[54]

According to Urman, the early rabbinic schoolhouse was architecturally separate from the synagogue as well as ideologically at odds with it.[55] Only gradually would the two institutions merge. In the Roman period, Judaism does not yet express itself in the familiar European package where a synagogue is an institution with a rabbi, a study room, a prayer hall, and a *miqveh*.

WATER AS RHETORIC

Like the *bet midrash*, the *miqveh* or ritual bath has an architectural history independent from that of the synagogue and shaped in part by Roman colonization. Also like the schoolhouse, the *miqveh* was to become a rhetorically powerful gendered space and an instrumentality for constructing gender relations in Judaism. The *miqveh* marked the taming and urban housing of a practice that otherwise was accomplished in wild water--the sea, a river, or a spring.[56] The evolution of the *miqveh*, in form and use, can be read in part as evidence of resistance to Roman urban lifestyle, in part as an ingenious adaptation to it.

The basic function of the *miqveh* is to restore cultic purity to things and persons that have lost it, that is, lost eligibility to participate in certain activities in certain places and/or with certain categories of people. Biblical requirements (Leviticus 11-15) were elaborated in the Second Temple period to specify the design of the tank and the amount and kind of water needed for the bath. Reich found that stepped pools appear in great numbers in domestic contexts in and near Jerusalem, beginning in the middle of the second century B.C.E.[57] He has also reported on larger water installations in industrial contexts that seem to have been used to insure the purity of oil or wine bottled for consumption in the holy city during festival times or by the resident priestly aristocracy. Like Jerusalem itself, these industrial *miqva'ot* derive their economic significance from their cultic significance.[58] They assert that purity regulations could be followed, and in fact have been followed, in the preparation of the product.

The overriding considerations in the design of the ritual bath are the kind of water supply that it uses and the way in which that water is retained. The *miqveh* should be supplied directly from the divine hand--from rain, spring, or stream--without the intervention of any human instrumentality except that which passively catches and retains the water in a supply tank or in the bath itself. (In other words, Roman aqueduct water won't do.[59]) Obviously, such a requirement is meaningful only to the extent that there are indeed other varieties of water available. While water engineering at places like Megiddo and Jerusalem predates the Roman aqueducts by many centuries, nevertheless it is the hubris of Roman hydraulics to which the *miqveh* practices become the counter-colonial alternative.[60] The urban *miqveh* simulates indoors a little of the wild, divinely managed hydraulics of the countryside--after the countryside has been subdued by gentile invaders and has had its substance tapped by their cultural practices and their global markets.

Aside from their uses for expressing personal piety and for contradicting the secularizing rhetoric of Roman water architecture, the *miqva'ot* served a practical economic function.[61] *Miqva'ot* enhanced the marketability of agricultural products and they figured into a system of managing labor. Reich suggests that workers at the bottling plants near Jerusalem were recruited from the doubtfully observant *'ammei ha-aretz* and were required to bathe when they arrived for work each morning in order to ensure their ritually correct status. The large, "industrial strength" pools excavated at several sites could accommodate this use.[62]

The pools excavated at Sepphoris are smaller and occur in residences in the upper city.[63] They came into use in Herodian times, contemporary with (or soon after) the founding of a nearby water-filtration installation that presumably was fed by the aqueduct and its lifting wheels.[64] These houses were served by municipal drains and likely had aqueduct water. However they also had cisterns to store water collected from their rooftops during winter rains. We can no longer determine how the residents allocated their two water supplies, but there are suggestive parallels in Crouch's extensive study of water use in Greek cities. As a general rule, Crouch says, cistern water was used for household washing, for livestock, and for the needs of household industry. After use, "grey water" was not allowed to flow off into the sewers if it could possibly be reused. (Thus, Greek bathtubs do not have drains like ours, but at the foot they have little depressions in which water collects to be scooped out.) It would not be unparalleled, then, for residents of Sepphoris to have cisterns and non-drained stepped pools in their homes for use in their crafts: perhaps for textile processing and dying, ceramics, or spice and perfume preparation.[65]

On the other hand, the pools do meet the (later rabbinic) specifications for ritual baths, *miqva'ot*. If they were indeed used in a practice of frequent ritual purifications, then we must inquire into the spatial implications of this use in the urban environment of Sepphoris. There are several levels to this inquiry. First, as with the bottling plants near Jerusalem, these pools could serve to enhance the purity of a product intended for use in Jerusalem. Linens and woolens are one distinct possibility.[66] Second, the pools may be the boundary marker across which day workers must pass in order to shed the impurities of (allegedly) nonobservant village life before taking up the tasks of food preparation or craft production in the urban household. Third, the pools may be used to remove bodily impurity, particularly that accompanying menstruation. They would then form part of a technology designed to insure that heirs born in the household would escape suspicion of having been conceived unlawfully, by a *niddah* or menstruating woman. Thus they would function to maintain "Jewishness" against threats from without and from within. From without, one's cultic status could be compromised by inadvertent consumption of improperly procured or prepared food. From within, one's kinship-- and for priests, that meant cultic status and economic prospects--could be compromised by marriage to the daughter of a family that was careless in guarding the conditions under which conception was allowed to take place.[67]

Textual evidence leads us to suspect that Sepphoris in early Roman times was home to families who married their daughters into priestly lineages, with alliances enduring for many generations. In several places the Palestinian Talmud mentions that Sepphorean women were exceptionally devoted to the Temple. Moreover, the resettlement of priests in Sepphoris after the destruction of the Temple makes better sense if the priests' fathers-in-law and maternal grandparents already resided there.[68] (Their wives, at least, would be "going home.") The national hope of rebuilding the Jerusalem Temple made it very important to maintain the pure lineages of priests, insuring that there would always be a generation on hand to resume the Jewish cult. Just as the rabbis went to great trouble in the late second and early third centuries to remember and record every detail of the Temple ceremonials, they concerned themselves meticulously with guaranteeing caste status as well. Priests may not marry non-Jews, Jews of doubtful parentage, widows, divorced women, or victims of violence. The bride's family tree had to be certified free of any proscribed union for several generations back, and Sepphoris archived its marriage contracts so that bridal pedigrees could be thoroughly researched.[69]

We may then plausibly regard Sepphoris as a producer of high-caste brides. The Mishnah preserves a ruling that, when a town falls to a siege, all its women are rendered ineligible to marry priests (Ket 2:9). Sepphoris would have lost its bride crop once, in 4 B.C.E. when Varus took the city; but in the revolt of 66-74 the fathers of Sepphoris avoided another loss by making a deal with the advancing legions. Their decision is congruent with the intention to insure that there would be priests for the future, by maintaining the eligibility of Sepphorean girls to conceive and bear them--an intention also expressed in domestic ritual bathing facilities. Thus one might well say that the first stones for rebuilding the Temple were laid in the *miqva'ot* of Sepphoris.

But an economic interest surfaces here as well. Independently of any hope for restoration of the cult in Jerusalem, priestly caste status carried the right to agricultural tithes--a steady income that was sheltered from Roman taxation and protected from erosion by inflation of the coinage. Rome opened access to distant markets for priestly families if they received more Galilean produce than their households could consume. Such families needed the right kind of brides if they wanted to maintain their entitlement to those tithes transgenerationally. Galileans were loyal to the religio-national tithing system and willingly gave portions of their produce to priests--provided the lineage of the priests was securely established. Thus priests' access to tithes ultimately depended upon their ability to mount a rhetorical defense of their caste status, especially their vulnerable matrilines. That defense was in part spatially and architecturally accomplished.

We see, then, that alterations to the landscape introduced by the Romans evoked various collaborative and resistive responses from the indigenous leadership of occupied Galilee. Those responses, in turn, altered the social realities of labor and gender management in the region. Once again, this can be indicated in schematic form (figure 3) and then discussed more fully.

FEATURE	LABOR DISPLACEMENT	GENDER DISPLACEMENT
roads, opening world markets	farms sold to absentee landlords; migration to cities; waged labor competes with distant markets for food	women and children tend fields in men's absence; women visit city for jobs or to sell produce and cloth; material "commodification" and symbolic "decommodification" of women's labor
aqueducts, baths, factories	urban employment opportunities in service and manufacturing	increased social and industrial contacts among non-kin women
theater with classified seating; urban synagogues	craft and geographical affiliations strengthened; kin identification weakened	women consume culture and religious discourse on an equal footing with men
urban rabbinic *bet midrash*	students leave home, take menial jobs to afford admission, and claim the tithe for the poor	"Judaism" becomes an expertise assigned to men; women lose competence in the ritual technologies of space and time
domestic *miqveh*	a threshold between "Jewish" urbanites and the "nonobservant" *'ammei ha-aretz* who work for them, assigning oppositional identity to each	the "threat from within" to caste status is foregrounded by this attempt to reduce it; basis of negotiation within marital sexuality

Figure 3: Spatial Impacts on Labor and Gender Systems

Archaeology in Israel has not yet collected the kind of physical evidence that would confirm our hypothesis: that connection with imperial world markets, through Roman cities and roads, encouraged Galilean farm laborers to move to urban jobs, producing the kinds of social displacements experienced today in similar situations in Appalachia, Latin America, and many other localities.[70] Such evidence as we have comes from reading the Mishnah and the Talmuds with an eye trained in economic and business analysis.[71] The interpretive problem arising from the fact that these texts reflect and promote the interests of male household heads is increasingly recognized. Moreover, we recognize that historical events can affect different sectors of society in different but related ways. Thus in Figure 3 and in what follows, my comments are meant heuristically, to indicate the kinds of correlations that should be found when we begin to think and excavate spatially in the practice of archaeology in Israel.

The Roman alteration of the landscape increased the mobility of labor, and commodified it. Men left the land for waged jobs in the cities; they now sold their labor, and at the same time they became a market for food, clothing, and housing. Women may have done likewise. But if women stayed on the land, perhaps more hours of their days now were spent in producing crops, textiles, and crafts. They may have visited the city markets more frequently, or they may even have commuted to regular jobs there. Peskowitz has argued that women's labor was "decommodified" in the organized production of textiles, meaning that its economic value was hidden. I have suggested the opposite, because I see a larger picture in which "commodification" means the colonization of women's time. Industrialization--the reorganization of society to promote efficient production at the expense of other institutions--could now tap into the hours that traditionally had been occupied with rearing the next generation, caring for parents, producing for home consumption, and/or social interaction with kinswomen. The city's markets and industries now had the power to take those hours away from those tasks, and channel them into production for distant markets. In itself, this is neither good nor bad for women; but it constitutes a real change in the gender system of the indigenous society. As Peskowitz has shown, aspects of that system were resilient enough to keep on replicating themselves at an ideological level in the face of real and far-reaching changes in the organization of women's work lives.

A spatial analysis highlights the probable social and cultural effects of workplace proximity for non-kin women, whether in single-gender working groups or mixed. In the shop it became possible to form an identity and allegiances apart from one's family; but in an urban workplace one also lost the protection of a family. It is futile in Galilean excavations to try to identify "gendered space," if by that is meant rooms or buildings used exclusively by men or by women. While texts inform us that the rabbinic studyhouse was a men's house, we don't know what the *bet midrash* looked like, and furthermore we infer that not only women but most men as well were excluded from it. Similarly, texts inform us that the finer homes had women's apartments where men did not go; however, we also are told that old women, girls, and poor women did not have to remain inside those apartments, while male infants and little boys were at home there.

In short, architecture does not produce gender in any automatic or causal sense.[72] It supplies the game board on which people, going by the rules of gender and kinship, produce novel plays and strategies that sometimes result in alterations to the rules. The built environment provides for creative management of conflictive social relations.[73] In the Roman period, to maintain social identity amidst the spatial traumas of colonization, the gender system was both played and dynamically adjusted. Whether this meant that the burdens of colonization were alloted unequally between men and women must be decided on the basis of material evidence that has yet to be excavated.[74]

VISUALIZING THE CONTEST FOR TIME

Empire extracted more than commodities from the Galilee. It took away time as well. Economic pressures redirected work hours away from local needs, channeling them into production and service for the sake of world trade and imperial administration. But Rome tampered with time on a grander scale, too. Highly visible Roman hydraulic power took control of water away from the heavens and the seasons, harnessing it by means of reservoirs and aqueducts. In cities the markets were geared to the festivals of the pagan Roman calendar. Rome's history overwrote all others. Having a national past and a national future was an indulgence not permitted to subordinated provinces of the empire. The present exigencies of Rome's imperial programs overrode national memories and dreams. In response, Jews redesigned gender and ethnicity counter-colonially, as means to re-take a Jewish past and a Jewish future from within the midst of the colonized present. Material culture projected Jewishness and femininity into the perceived past and future, as we have seen.

The spatial shock of empire upon the people of the Galilee consisted in being forced to recognize that their region was a mere node in a worldwide network, rather than one pole of a world axis whose other pole lay just a few miles away in the holy city of Jerusalem. But Roman commerce opened a vista upon a universe, doing for the first century what Copernicus did for the sixteenth. The visual tactic of pacification that the Romans used on Galileans was not conspicuous surveillance (as in Britain), but the dissolution of viewpoint induced by exposition of obscenely huge perspectives. Time contracted into presence, and the "here" dilated. The possibility of rapid contact with very distant lands threatens your sense of who and where you are--especially if exotic people from those distant places confront you daily in the urban commercial centers, eager to buy up and carry away the fruits of your land and your labors.

We have already reviewed some rabbinic strategies for reasserting (at least symbolic) control over time and space: sabbath regulations and distances, calendrical calculations, the laws of *niddah*. But there is also a visual dimension to the counter-colonial initiatives of early Judaism. They emerge in opposition to certain technologies of visibility built into Roman cities. These Roman visual technologies regulate urban behaviors by directing people's attention to certain material and cultural contents: by *showing* them things.[75] In the theater, people see imported dramatic productions, mimes, and orators; and more importantly, they see one another seeing those cultural products. The Roman dining room, too, is C-shaped like the theater. At formal meals the diners lounging on three sides of an open space are entertained by performers brought into the space from the open fourth side.[76] (This contrasts with the older Greek dining practice, where the couches were arranged on all four sides of the room and the diners entertained *themselves* with their own conversation in that enclosed space.) Roman elite diners, like theater-goers, see one another consuming imported cultural fare. The city imposes other viewing opportunities as well: the colonnaded avenue for strolling and people-watching, and of course the markets and the baths. Visual intimacy with the bodies of strangers gave Jews a new experience of their circumcision--a bodily mark which traditionally had become visible only within the family circle at moments of celebrating kinship, family, procreation, and the future.

This visual colonization, enforcing alien perspectives on the far-off and the intimate, was not operative everywhere in the Roman city. Some spaces were closed to vision from and of outside: the hippodrome, the residential courtyard,[77] the industrial workshop, the rabbinic schoolhouse,[78] the cistern, the *miqveh* and its private water supply. Or more exactly, those spaces were visually closed while being pierced and tapped ideologically, economically, or socially, in intentional ways.

It is significant, then, that the architecture of the urban synagogue in the Galilee develops as an open C-shaped space where people can see and be seen, rather than as a visually closed but pierced space. By late Roman times, synagogue buildings are designed to focus the reflection of people who place themselves around three sides of the room, to let them see one another seeing, and to make a cultural content available to them. What occupies the fourth wall is the Torah niche and the *bema* for reading and preaching. Thus architecturally the Torah and its interpretation are positioned as "conversation partners" with the people in a closed circle.[79]

However, analogous to the Roman theater and *stibadium*, the synagogue also becomes a C-shaped space that produces vistas and dispenses cultural messages. The arc of the seating opens toward Jerusalem; and set into the floor at the focus of the seating, there are sometimes found zodiac mosaics.[80] The zodiac presents reality in the broadest vista that it can possibly have: the stars in the heavens. This design--imported from beyond the Roman Empire (Babylonia)--reasserts divine order through a stable mapping of the seasons and their cycles of agricultural production. The usual layout of a zodiac synagogue floor is a circle inscribed in a square. The circle encloses the pictures of the twelve star signs. The four corners outside it are occupied by female figures and fruits, which have been associated with four seasons.[81] The deity is represented in a smaller circle at the hub of the wheel with the figures of the star signs around him, either feet in or feet out.[82] Time stands still on the floor as people gaze at it; time supports them as they walk across it.

This imaginative mapping achieves its stability by preserving the naturally differentiated annual phases of time-- and by naturalizing the civil calendar's cultural periodization of them. The zodiac's principle for organizing the year is sidereal, just as in the Roman and Byzantine civil calendar.[83] Thus the zodiac floor mosaic accommodates Jewish life to Roman time. But it does more. Spanning this floor, the synagogue building effectively traps secular imperial time with walls, contains it within the living circle of Jewish Torah reading, and makes it support Jewish business and community affairs.

The *architectural* co-opting of imperial time by the synagogue community and its mosaic floor contrasts with the rabbis' attempt to assert *liturgical* time control. Because lunar time cannot perfectly match solar/sidereal time--for full moon occurs every 29½ days--the religious year had to be adjusted occasionally to keep the festivals aligned with the agricultural seasons. In the Second-Temple period this had been done by intercalation; that is, the authorities in Jerusalem would sometimes have to add an extra month in the spring to slow down the religious year. Subsequently the rabbis took over the management of religious time through the calculation of the festival calendar. Imperial administrators recognized the subversive potential of an indigenous alternative calendar, and during fourth-century persecutions the practices of calculating holidays and inserting the springtime leap month were suppressed.

Controlling the annual holiday calendar was a rabbinic strategy of resistance to the Romanization of time. In comparison, mosaic visualizations of time and deity upon the synagogue floors were also defiances of Roman time, even when in the mode of accommodating secular solar/sidereal months to religious lunar months, as we see at Sepphoris. Which strategy was the more "Jewish"? Do synagogue mosaics profane the sacred--as some of the rabbis grumbled--or do they decolonize and sanctify worldly reality? For the "spatial Torah" observed by the community that walks on time, such boundaries are permeable interfaces, reflecting the community's urban colonial experience.

SUMMARY

Using a recursive strategy, we have read features of the Galilean landscape as strategic interventions comprising the complex reciprocal negotiation of colonization and resistance during Greco-Roman times. Imperial economic pressure was brought to bear through elements of the built environment such as roads, insular high-density urban housing, civic architecture, and aqueducts. Besides siphoning wealth out of the Galilee, these structures destabilized the indigenous management of labor and production through kinship networks, and played havoc with the spatial and seasonal symbolism of Jewish religious culture. Jewish architectural innovations that emerged at this era in the land of Israel--the *miqveh*, the urban rabbinic house of study, the synagogue zodiac--should be read as adaptations offering symbolic resistance to the incursions of empire.

NOTES

[1] See A. Biran and J. Naveh, "An Aramaic Stele From Tel Dan," *Israel Exploration Journal* 43 (1993) 81-98; and P. Davies, "'House of David' Built on Sand: The Sins of the Biblical Maximizers," *Biblical Archaeology Review* 20/4 (1994) 54-55.

[2] Research reported here was supported in part by a grant from the Society of Biblical Literature for field work in Israel with the University of South Florida Excavations at Sepphoris. Joshua Schwartz and Dennis E. Groh kindly read earlier versions of the chapter and offered valuable criticisms. While writing in 1994 I enjoyed the hospitality

and support of the Center for Philosophy of Religion at the University of Notre Dame.

[3]Such a design, insofar as it cannot be merely *explained* as optimally efficient adaptation to the natural ecology, needs to be *interpreted*. For discussion of how a landscape may be read as a historical document disclosing purposive action, see P. Lewis, "Common Landscapes as Historic Documents," in *History From Things: Essays in Material Culture*, ed. S. Lubar and W. Kingery (Washington: Smithsonian Institution Press, 1993) 115-39. By "cultural landscape," Lewis designates "everything that humans do to the natural earth for whatever purpose but most commonly for material profit, aesthetic pleasure, spiritual fulfillment, personal comfort, or communal safety" (p. 116).

[4]The Roman period dates from Herod the Great, who came to power in 37 B.C.E., through the middle of the fourth century C.E. The language of imperial business and government throughout this period was Greek.

[5]In terms of investigative method, then, the Galilean landscape cannot adequately be read and understood in the ways that have been proposed by archaeologists working at *non*-colonial sites. Compare, for example, "the interactive model" of D. Sanders, "Behavioral Conventions and Archaeology: Methods for the Analysis of Ancient Architecture," in *Domestic Architecture and the Use of Space: An Interdisciplinary Cross-Cultural Approach*," ed. S. Kent (New York: Cambridge University Press, 1990) 43-72. To the two determinative factors that Sanders considers--environment and behavior--archaeologists of Galilee must add a third: the intervention of imperial policy.

[6]I have in mind events occurring in the wake of Alexander's conquest; and more specifically, the Romanization during the reign of Herod the Great, the brief revolt that followed his death, and the violence of its suppression. Demographic shifts were occasioned by the establishment of cities such as Tiberias, Caesarea, and Bethsaida/Julias on Lake Kinneret, and by the influx of refugees after the destruction of the Jerusalem Temple in 70 and the banishment of Jews from the holy city in 135. The third century brought drought, famine, plague, and monetary inflation.

[7]Rather, the situation of contact between colonizer and colonized is better described in categories of "intimate violence"; see S. Suleri, *The Rhetoric of English India* (Chicago: University of Chicago Press, 1992). On the special problems of the "archaeology of contact," see J. Levy and C. Claassen, eds., "Engendering the Contact Period," in *Exploring Gender Through Archaeology*, ed. C. Claassen (Madison: Prehistory Press, 1992) 111-26; see also the papers in *The Archaeology of Contact: Processes and Consequences*. Proceedings of the 25th Annual Chacmool Conference, ed. B. Kuhle and K. Lesick

(Calgary: The Archaeological Association of the University of Calgary, forthcoming).

[8]As Buttigieg and Bové remark in their interview with Edward Said, indigenous children grow up believing that the elite colonial personnel *were there first* and possess the finer material and spiritual culture. See J. Buttigieg and P. Bové, "An Interview With Edward W. Said," *Boundary 2* 20 (1993) 12. Imperial culture and institutions affect people differently according to their economic status, but no child is untouched. Roman contact was neither the first nor the last encounter with cultural and economic imperialism that people of the Galilee would have.

[9]This is recognized by most interpreters of Josephus and the New Testament, which are Greek texts. However the Mishnah also is the literature of a colonized and compromised people. It displays Greek loanwords and patterns of argumentation, assimilates Jewish customs to Roman laws, and presumes that Greco-Roman lifestyle accessories and housing patterns are in place. For discussion of how to read literature from colonial "contact zones," see M. Pratt, *Imperial Eyes: Travel Writing and Transculturation* (London: Routledge, 1992); see also S. Suleri, *The Rhetoric of English India*.

[10]This prejudice is described and criticized by Benjamin G. Wright III, who terms it the "interpretive hegemony" of texts over the physical remains. Wright invites the reader to suspend the hegemony of the rabbinic version of Galilee in order to take a fresh look at the archaeological evidence for the forms and possible functions of stepped pools in the land of Israel. See B. Wright, "Jewish Ritual Baths--Interpreting the Digs and Texts: Some Issues in the Social History of Second Temple Judaism," in *The Archaeology of Israel: Constructing the Past, Interpreting the Present*, ed. N. Silberman and D. Small (Sheffield: Sheffield Academic Press, forthcoming).

[11]This is termed the physical-recording connection by L. Patrik, "Is There an Archaeological Record?" *Advances in Archaeological Method and Theory* 8 (1985) 27-62. Patrik regards the configuration of the earth as *an effect* that, upon scientific scrutiny, discloses what has caused it. She contrasts with this the symbolic-recording connection, through which the configuration of the earth is *a sign* that communicates some purpose accounting for its placement.

[12]Indeed, one may find accidentally deposited (and therefore trustable) information even within texts, encoded there by processes akin to Patrik's physical-recording connection. Thus historians may make reliable inferences based on the assumptions about society that underlie rabbinic legal reasoning, without necessarily presuming that the social relations legislated by the rabbis ever were realized. For example, houses must have had courtyards; otherwise there would be no rabbinic case law about conflicts among neighbors over their management. See M. Good-

man, *State and Society in Roman Galilee A.D. 132-212* (Totowa, NJ: Rowman & Allanheld, 1983).

[13]M. Peskowitz, "'Family/ies' in Antiquity: Evidence from Tannaitic Literature and Roman Galilean Architecture," in *The Jewish Family in Antiquity*, Brown Judaic Studies 289, ed. S. Cohen (Atlanta: Scholars Press, 1993) 33. However Peskowitz does not elaborate upon the mechanism by which the architecture taught its inhabitants to be a family. We must look to recursion theories for that, and, I argue, to a theory of spatial management.

[14]And also in spatialized *time*, as will become clear below. Time is spatialized by calendars and also by the academic discipline of "history" as it constructs its object.

[15]The term *recursive* is used by Leone, B. Little, P. Potter, and their colleagues. Potter writes that "the recursive quality of material culture is the capacity of objects to teach their users ways of thinking and behaving." See P. Potter, "Critical Archaeology: In the Ground and on the Street," *Historical Archaeology* 26 (1992) 117. Leone says that "using things substantiates and reproduces all the same social actions that went into the artifact in the first place. Just as language reflects and in use creates, so things that are made reflect but also substantiate and verify, and thus reproduce the processes that led to making them." See M. Leone, "The Productive Nature of Material Culture and Archaeology," *Historical Archaeology* 26 (1992) 131. See also P. Shackel and B. Little, "Post-Processual Approaches to Meanings and Uses of Material Culture in Historical Archaeology," *Historical Archaeology* 26 (1992) 5-11. Compare Elaine Scarry's phenomenological account of how creativity redounds from the artifact to act upon its creator; see E. Scarry, *The Body in Pain: The Making and Unmaking of the World* (New York: Oxford University Press, 1985).

[16]In Leone's program there is a phase called "Archaeology in Public" (or "on the street") that is designed to raise the consciousness of tourists about these factors; see Potter, "Critical Archaeology: In the Ground and on the Street," 117-29. Leone's and Potter's site--Annapolis, MD, and its historic Statehouse--was progressively redesigned in step with political changes during the American colonial and republican periods. The city is closely linked with foundational narratives of the state of Maryland and of the United States--narratives which are both sacred to the site's visitors and taken for granted by most of them. Potter found that exposure to the archaeology and to the critical theory behind it largely failed to unseat the preconceptions of tourists in Annapolis. The discouragingly limited success of this phase of the project was regarded by the investigators as an important part of their data that must be reported. I know of no comparable initiative for assessing the audience impact of the archaeology of Greco-Roman Palestine.

[17]Developments in archaeological theory and methods are discussed in S. Dyson," From New to New Age Archaeology: Archaeological Theory and Classical Archaeology--A 1990's Perspective," *American Journal of Archaeology* 97 (1993) 195-206; see also M. Sawicki, "Archaeology as Space Technology: Digging for Gender and Class in Holy Land," *Method & Theory in the Study of Religion* 6 (1994) 319-48. Roughly speaking, the three options for coordinated reading of text and landscape, discussed above, correspond to three theoretical approaches to archaeology in general. Classical archaeology assumes that texts refer to the earth; "the new archaeology" confronts texts with what is deduced scientifically from the earth; and postprocessual archaeology discerns recursive relations between texts and things, both "then" and "now."

[18]Elsewhere I have characterized this competence as a technology for management of space, and have pointed out that the ancient landscape productions now interact with the spatial manipulations entailed in archaeological excavation, reporting, and interpretation. See M. Sawicki, "Archaeology as Space Technology"; see also M. Sawicki, "Caste and Contact in the Galilee of Jesus: Research Beyond Positivism and Constructivism," in *Galilean Archaeology and the Historical Jesus: The Integration of Material and Textual Remains*, ed. R. Horsley and J.A. Overman. Philadelphia: Trinity Press International, (forthcoming).

[19]For example, preliminary reports and discussions of the city of Sepphoris assert that it was certainly a Jewish city; see E. Meyers, "The Challenge of Hellenism for Early Judaism and Christianity," *Biblical Archaeologist* 55/2 (1992) 84-91. Standard scholarly studies of Roman Galilee take it for granted that the categories "Jew" and "gentile" are discrete and mutually exclusive. Yet, even with that assumption in place, they demonstrate the multicultural complexity of Palestine in that period. See J. Jeremias *Jerusalem in the Time of Jesus: An Investigation into Economic and Social Conditions During the New Testament Period*, trans. F. and C. Cave (Philadelphia: Fortress Press, 1969); and S. Freyne, *Galilee From Alexander the Great to Hadrian 323 B.C.E. to 135 C.E.: A Study of Second Temple Judaism* (Wilmington: Michael Glazier, 1980). For evidence and arguments that "gentiles" lived in various degrees of association with the Jewish community, see S. Cohen, "Crossing the Boundary and Becoming a Jew," *Harvard Theological Review* 82 (1989) 13-33. Cohen suggests that someone not of Jewish birth who nevertheless followed sabbath practices and participated in Jewish holiday observances in a Roman city might be considered a Jew *ipso facto* by his neighbors and perhaps by himself. If the criteria for defining whether *a person* was Jewish are subject to dispute, then it

is difficult indeed to determine whether and how a city, a house, or an artifact could be recognized as "Jewish."

[20]The methodological difficulties in identifying artifacts and structures as "Jewish" are examined in L. Rutgers, "Archaeological Evidence for the Interaction of Jews and Non-Jews in Late Antiquity," *American Journal of Archaeology* 96 (1992) 101-18. Ross Kraemer discusses the difficulty of interpreting the term "Jew" in ancient inscriptions (although she begs the question of how an investigator decides *which* inscriptions ought to be included in one's sample of "Jewish inscriptions"); see R. Kraemer, "On the Meaning of the Term "Jew" in Greco-Roman Inscriptions," *Harvard Theological Review* 82 (1989) 35-53. Byron R. McCane found that there is no reliable way to distinguish between Jewish and Christian burials in the Roman period; see B. McCane, "Jews, Christians, and Burial in Roman Palestine (Israel)" (Ph.D. diss., Duke University, 1992). The state of the question was summarized in an exchange from April 24 to May 5, 1994, on the electronic discussion list IOUDAIOS-L, archived at Lehigh University. The consensus in that exchange was that the visibility of expatriate Jews in communities throughout the empire is attested by the evidence of textual references to: their taxability, their expulsions from Rome, their ability to locate one another when traveling to distant cities, and "circumcision, in an environment in which public bathing was a routine necessity." But people in Roman baths did not bathe nude like the Greeks, according to F. Yegül, *Baths and Bathing in Classical Antiquity* (New York: The Architectural History Foundation, 1992). In any case, whatever made living Jews visible *to one another* is no longer visible *to us* in the archaeological record.

[21]For an exhaustive structural analysis of the way the Mishnah reckons kinship, see P. Flesher, *Oxen, Women, or Citizens: Slaves in the System of the Mishnah* (Atlanta: Scholars Press, 1988); for an alternative scholarly approach, compare J. Jeremias, *Jerusalem*, 270-358. Shaye J.D. Cohen discusses rabbinic caste laws and offers convincing evidence that the principles for assessing Jewish identity and caste were adjusted by the framers of the Mishnah after the example of Roman laws determining personal status and inheritance; see S. Cohen, "The Matrilineal Principle in Historical Perspective," *Judaism* 34 (1985) 5-13; and "The Origins of the Matrilineal Principle in Rabbinic Law," *AJS Review* 10 (1985) 19-53.

[22]I have argued elsewhere that this is owing to the academic disciplinary isolation of biblical archaeology from both historic and prehistoric archaeology in general and from theoretical advances in the archaeology of the Americas in particular; see M. Sawicki, "Archaeology as Space Technology." Yet some significant investigations of gender in ancient Israel have appeared. For the early

Israelite period, Carol Meyers synthesizes a remarkable portrait of Hebrew women by correlating biblical texts with evidence in published excavations; see C. Meyers, *Discovering Eve: Ancient Israelite Women in Context* (New York: Oxford University Press, 1988). Judith Romney Wegner examines the textual evidence of the Mishnah to uncover attitudes toward women and strategies for their management; see J. Wegner, *Chattel or Person? The Status of Women in the Mishnah* (New York: Oxford University Press, 1988). Miriam Peskowitz is the first to correlate material culture (from both published and unpublished finds) with a critical feminist investigation of textual constructions of gender; see M. Peskowitz, "'The Work of Her Hands': Gendering Everyday Life in Roman-Period Judaism in Palestine (70-250 C.E.), Using Textile Production as a Case Study" (Ph.D. diss., Duke University, 1993). Contemporary questions in family studies are applied to the interpretaton of evidence from the Greco-Roman world in S. Cohen, ed., *The Jewish Family*. Tentative interpretations of certain excavated rooms as gendered space were proposed by Bonnie Magness-Gardiner in "Tell el-Hayyat: Spatial Analysis of Pottery in Domestic Units" (paper presented at the annual meeting of the American Schools of Oriental Research, Washington, 1993). She analyzed the spatial distribution of implements and of floral and faunal remains with a methodology similar to the "task differentiation approach" first devised by Janet D. Spector in her work on Native American sites; see "Male/Female Task Differentiation Among the Hidatsa: Toward the Development of an Archaeological Aproach to Gender," in *The Hidden Half: Studies of Plains Indian Women*, ed. P. Albers and B. Medicine (Washington: University Press of America) 77-99. A comparable reading of an eighth-century B.C.E. structure was offered by Paul F. Jacobs in "The Shrine Room at Halif, Judahite Religion, Engendering Archaeology," (paper presented at the regional meeting of American Schools of Oriental Research, Atlanta, 1994). Unfortunately, the "task-differentiation approach" has certain unresolved methodological difficulties, including how to tell which tasks were women's tasks, and how to tell that the tasks were actually done in the place where the tools and remains finally ended up. See the discussion in S. Kent, "Activity Areas and Architecture: An Interdisciplinary View of the Relationship Between Use of Space and Domestic Built Environments," in *Domestic Architecture and the Use of Space: An Interdisciplinary Cross-Cultural Approach*, ed. S. Kent (New York: Cambridge University Press, 1990) 1-8; see also A. Yentsch, "Engendering Visible and Invisible Ceramic Artifacts," *Historical Archaeology* 25 (1991) 132-55. By comparison, the fanciful reconstruction of a Byzantine-era dwelling at Qatzrin in the Golan--the so-called house of Rabbi Abun--has been guided by gender stereotype, nostalgia, anachronism, and unwarranted assumptions about the patrilocality and patriarchy of family units; see A. Killebrew and S. Fine, "Qatzrin: Reconstructing Village Life in Talmudic Times," *Biblical Archaeology Review* 17 (1991) 44-56.

[23]See Peskowitz, "`The Work of Her Hands'," 94-102.

[24]The term "colonization" is used here in its modern political and economic sense, not in its ancient honorific sense, of course. The cumulative effect of Roman colonization upon the wellbeing of the people of the Galilee remains to be securely established. Douglas R. Edwards argues that imperial contact brought benefits to the Galilee commensurate with the wealth that was extracted, at least during the first century; see D. Edwards, "The Socio-Economic and Cultural Ethos of the Lower Galilee in the First Century: Implications for the Nascent Jesus Movement," in *The Galilee in Late Antiquity*, ed. L. Levine (New York: The Jewish Theological Seminary of America, 1992), 53-73. However, *textual* evidence for the second through the fourth centuries indicates that imperial pressures at that time promoted raising cash crops for export, flight from the land, and starvation, according to D. Sperber, *Roman Palestine 200-400: The Land. Crisis and Change in Agrarian Society as Reflected in Rabbinic Sources* (Ramat-Gan: Bar-Ilan University, 1978), and *Roman Palestine 200-400: Money and Prices*, second edition, (Ramat-Gan: Bar-Ilan University, 1991). But the *physical* evidence, including floral and faunal materials, that could clarify this picture has yet to be dug.

[25]The phenomenon of "dubeity" is described in post-colonial studies as "a mode of cultural tale-telling that is neurotically conscious of its own self-censoring apparatus"; see Suleri, *The Rhetoric of English India*, 3. The rhetorical cloaking of the value of women's work would be an instance of dubeity if the male producers of this rhetoric--the rabbis--could be viewed as women's oppressive colonizers. This may indeed fit the situation in cases where an orphaned girl was required to work to support her brother's studies with his rabbi; see Peskowitz, "`The Work of Her Hands'," 140-49.

[26]The assumption that human relations can be reduced to struggles for power underlies programs of cultural analysis inspired by the work of Michel Foucault. They rest on a twofold fallacy: that a desire for power accounts for itself, and that the many things that human beings desire all are reducible to power. On the contrary, while negotiation for power *can* be an aspect of gender, gender systems can and do express many other kinds of quests as well. Desire for power is not self-evidently the ultimate explanation of all social transactions.

[27]Christine Ward Gailey asserts two universal principles about gender as understood in the social sciences: "It is not identical with sex differences, and . . . it provides a basis for a division of labor in all societies"; see C. Gailey, "Evolutionary Perspectives on Gender Hierarchy," in *Analyzing Gender: A Handbook of Social Science Research*, ed. B. Hess and M. Ferree (Beverly Hills: Sage Publications, 1987), 37. In traditional (i.e., non-state) societies, kinship assigns the benefits of each person's labor to someone else, according to complex cultural patterns; it also assigns responsibility for the welfare of each person to someone else. Gailey explains: "The dissolution of kinship is one of the hallmarks of capitalist relations. . . . For capitalist relations to emerge, people have to be defined as legally free individuals; the solidarity of even a minimal kin group--the nuclear family, for instance--is called into question" (p. 62, n. 1). This insight can be adapted to illuminate Roman imperial economic alignments, which while they were not capitalist, did mobilize labor and displace wealth by means of urbanization, thereby disrupting the "social safety net" of kinship. Rabbinic reassertions of certain kin-based dependence relationships, then, can plausibly be read as calculated resistance against colonial market pressures. In that context, to criticize the rabbis for repressing individual prerogatives is to miss the point, anachronistically.

[28]Like constructors of ethnicity, these artifacts worked trans-generationally. They looked to the past, as when spindle whorls were placed in coffins to secure the femininity of the deceased, and they also looked to the future, as when prospective brides learned the use of the *miqveh*.

[29]Emperors Trajan (98-117) and Hadrian (117-138) maintained and expanded roadways that had been opened thousands of years earlier, as well as more recent military routes. See D. Dorsey, *The Roads and Highways of Ancient Israel* (Baltimore: Johns Hopkins University Press, 1991).

[30]The paved and colonnaded avenue crossing lower Sepphoris from southwest to northeast may be a spur of this route. See D. Edwards and T. McCollough in this volume. See also M. Avi-Yonah, *The Jews Under Roman and Byzantine Rule: A Political History of Palestine From the Bar Kokhbah War to the Arab Conquest* (Jerusalem: Magnes Press, Hebrew University, 1984) 36; and Dorsey, *The Roads*, 91.

[31]In what follows, I will suggest a "reading" of certain landscape features that promote or regulate movement. This kind of reading aims to illuminate "the differences between the messages on the surface of things and the models of society enacted by people's use of them; or, more colloquially, the difference between what an item of material culture promises its users and what it delivers," as Parker Potter says; see "Critical Archaeology," 117. Potter identifies this as an adaptation of the technique called "immanent critique" by the Frankfurt School. Ann Yentsch suggests that how things and people moved

across social and material borders has significance that is recoverable and readable; see A. Yentsch, "Engendering," 149-50.

[32]The practices of daily urban bathing are described by Yegül, *Baths*, and by G. Fagan, "Three Studies in Roman Public Bathing: Origins, Growth, and Social Aspects" (Ph.D. dissertation, McMaster University, 1992). There is as yet no study of Roman urban water management comparable to that on earlier Greek cities by D. Crouch, *Water Management in Ancient Greek Cities* (New York: Oxford University Press, 1993). Aqueducts in various locations throughout the empire are examined in volumes published by the Frontius Gesellschaft, *Die Wasserversorgung antiker Städte: Pergamon, Recht/Verwaltung, Brunnen/Nymphäen, Bauelemente.* Geschichte der Wasserversorgung vol. 2; and *Die Wasserversorgung antiker Städte: Mensch und Wasser, Mitteleuropa, Thermen, Bau/Materialien, Hygiene.* Geschichte der Wasserversorgung vol. 3 (Mainz: Philipp von Zabern, 1987 and 1988).

[33]Excavations of the reservoir and water lines continue under the sponsorship of Tel Aviv University. For preliminary information and maps, see T. Tsuk, "The Aqueducts to Sepphoris," in *The Aqueducts of Ancient Palestine: Collected Essays* [Hebrew], ed. D. Amit, Y. Hirschfeld, and J. Patrich (Jerusalem: Yad Izhak Ben-Zvi, 1989) 101-8 and T. Tsuk, "The Aqueducts of Sepphoris," in *Sepphoris in Galilee: Crosscurrents of Culture*, ed. R. Nagy, C. Meyers, E. Meyers, Z. Weiss (North Carolina Museum of Art, 1996) 44-49.

[34]Ecclesiastes Rabbah 12:6. No remains of these lifting wheels have yet been found, however.

[35]The huge pool, with an estimated capacity of 10,000 cubic meters, is described by E. Netzer, *Greater Herodium* (Jerusalem: Institute of Archaeology, Hebrew University, 1981) 10-30. See D. Small, "Late Hellenistic Baths in Palestine," *BASOR* 266 (1987) 59-74, for a discussion of the bathing installation at the fortress. Small's conclusions are to be taken with caution since all the baths in his sample were built by Herod or his family--whose practices may not have been representative of the Judaism of their day. For example, a pool that Small interprets as a *miqveh* is read as a *frigidarium* or Roman-style cool bath by B. Wright, "Jewish Ritual Baths."

[36]And to the lives of their associates and retainers. Citizenship was extended to all free residents of the empire in 212. Recycling of waste water by Greek cities is described by Crouch, "Water Management." The Romans usually adopted what worked for the Greeks.

[37]Bath-related occupations are enumerated by Yegül, *Baths*, 46-7, who estimates that the baths of a city would employ a workforce third in size after those engaged in military administration and in construction.

[38]See Freyne, *Galilee*, 129.

[39]For references to this practice in the Talmud, see Killebrew and Fine, "Qatzrin." Traditional village housing shows the irregular patterns of organic growth, rather than conformity to a planned urban grid. Greek cities also had been established with quadrangular housing blocks; see M. Jameson, "Domestic Space in the Greek City-State," in *Domestic Architecture*, ed. S. Kent, 92-113.

[40]Depending upon whether your village cousins had been a social advantage or a liability for you, the urban options for non-kin alliances could appear either as a family-eroding temptation or as a golden opportunity.

[41]In villages, one would expect business associations and craft-guild connections to form along kinship lines. In the Roman city, that need no longer be the case.

[42]These events are documented in Sperber's two volumes on *Roman Palestine*. Ancient textual references to imperial loom shops and to imperial taxes payable in woolens woven for soldiers' cloaks and blankets are cited in Peskowitz, "`The Work of Her Hands'," 69-70, 212. Compare twelfth-century England, where "Europeans discovered how to make money reproduce itself over time" by commodifying the future through credit, loans, and trade, according to K. Biddick, "People and Things: Power in Early English Development," *Comparative Studies in Society and History* 32 (1990) 3-23. Biddick shows that this new financial expertise involved the redefinition of land as "property" and the conversion of this property from food production to wool production by agrarian lords. British people were resettled into villages to make room for herds of sheep. Wool could be sold abroad for cash to cover the escalating interest charges on loans and to pay taxes. If women did the spinning and weaving of this wool, we see here the means for separating them from the fruits of their labor.

[43]Or that had circulated among villages through city distribution centers, as Edwards suggests for the first century; see "Socio-Economic and Cultural Ethos of the Lower Galilee." The extraction and deployment of "surplus" goods and labor is the mechanism supporting the foundation of large-scale political entities--states and their empires--whether militarily, economically, or both.

[44]It may have gone in edible form, or it may have been redeemed and taken as money.

[45]The 470-square-mile region of Lower Galilee was more thoroughly in touch with imperial goods and institutions than was the less accessible and smaller Upper Galilee. This was convincingly argued by Eric Meyers, citing evidence such as the distribution count of Greek inscriptions by James F. Strange; see E. Meyers, "Galilean Regionalism as a Factor in Historical Reconstruction," *BASOR* 221 (1976) 93-101. Nevertheless, the excavation of villages and village-city connections in lower Galilee

continues. Perhaps a village without any trace of imperial contact will eventually turn up; but it seems unlikely.

[46]For example, excavations of dwelling places ordinarily cannot resolve the habitation layers finely enough to distinguish the activities of grandparents and grandchildren who may have occupied the same house. The meanings of artifacts shifted rapidly over the course of the Roman occupation, as strategies of resistance and collaboration adjusted in response to the changing situation. At Sepphoris, implements of Serapis worship turned up in the same villa with four pools that looked like Jewish ritual baths; see J. Strange, "Six Campaigns at Sepphoris: The University of South Florida Excavations, 1983-1989," in *Galilee in Late Antiquity*, ed. L. Levine, 339-55. Nearby, statuettes of Prometheus and Pan turned up in the same domestic cisterns with artifacts thought to reflect Jewish cultic intentions; see E. Meyers, E. Netzer, and C. Meyers, *Sepphoris* (Winona Lake, IN: Eisenbrauns, 1992) 23-5.

[47]Douglas Edwards, following Freyne, suggests that the people active in the Jesus movement "by-passed major urban areas such as Sepphoris and Tiberias to avoid direct confrontation with Herodian power. Nevertheless the movement took full advantage of the socio-economic and cultural networks operative in the Galilee." See Edwards, "Socio-Economic and Cultural Ethos of the Lower Galilee," 73. This view is becoming the consensus for the mid-first century.

[48]This is established by C. Hezser, "Social Fragmentation, Plurality of Opinion, and Nonobservance of Halachah: Rabbis and Community in Late Roman Palestine" (paper presented at the annual meeting of the Society of Biblical Literature, Washington, 1993).

[49]Or, perhaps it continues among desert hermits; but they left us no texts. Interestingly, some rabbis practice spatial avoidance of synagogues; or, if they visit the buildings at all, they refuse to pray there. The aspect of urban synagogue architecture that was offensive to some of the rabbis was the decorative figuration in the mosaics on the floors. See D. Urman, "The House of Assembly and the House of Study: Are They One and the Same?" *Journal of Jewish Studies* 44 (1993) 236-57; reprinted in *Ancient Synagogues: Historical Analysis and Archaeological Discovery*, Studia Post-Biblica 47/1, ed. D. Urman and P. Flesher (Leiden: E.J. Brill, 1995) 232-55.

[50]As J. Neusner argues in *The Economics of the Mishnah* (Chicago: University of Chicago Press, 1990).

[51]Of course, this did not change the streets in any physical way that we can discover through excavation today. The information comes from the Mishnah and Talmuds.

[52]This fee was to cover maintenance of the structure. The rabbi was not supposed to charge for his instruction,

and rabbis supported themselves by a variety of trades and businesses.

[53]See S. Cohen, "The Place of the Rabbi in Jewish Society of the Second Century," in *Galilee in Late Antiquity*, ed. L. Levine, 157-73; see also L. Levine, "The Sages and the Synagogue in Late Antiquity: The Evidence of the Galilee," in *Galilee in Late Antiquity*, 201-22.

[54]Practical suggestions on negotiating the ambiguities of the phrase "oral Torah" were offered by Sigrid Peterson, December 29-30, 1993, on the electronic discussion list IOUDAIOS (archived with IOUDAIOS-L at Lehigh University). She pointed out that, on some interpretations, the phrase could extend to the management of time by housewives who know, and transmit, the way to correlate seasonal meal planning with the cycle of synagogue Torah readings.

[55]Urman discusses the activities conducted in houses of study, edifices which he associates with the sages' desire to keep aloof and apart from other people; see "House of Assembly." Besides surveying the texts, Urman has excavated the only physical evidence of such an edifice found so far, in Dabbura in the Golan.

[56]Benjamin Wright, who points this out, also criticizes the reckless logic of making an inference from the *form* of a pool to its ritual *function*. See Wright, "Jewish Ritual Baths." Ritual bathing occurred elsewhere than in *miqva'ot*; while many tanks that have been labeled *miqva'ot* by archaeologists may well have had secular uses for part or all of their time in service.

[57]See R. Reich, "*Miqwa'ot* (Jewish Ritual Baths) in the Second Temple Period and the Period of the Mishnah and Talmud" [Hebrew, with English summary] (Ph.D. diss., Hebrew University, 1990) 12. Reich also surveys comparable pools from urban areas beyond the holy city and from the Roman and Byzantine periods. For discussion of agricultural *miqva'ot*, see also R. Reich, "*Miqwa'ot* (Jewish Ritual Baths) in Rural Regions in the Second Temple Period" (paper presented to the national meeting of the American Schools of Oriental Research, Washington D.C., 1993). Reich's interpretations have been critically reviewed by Wright, "Jewish Ritual Baths."

[58]In other words, pilgrims and priests were two important "markets." Each needed to procure the specially prepared foods required by religious regulations connected with the sacred space of Jerusalem and the sacred actions that were performed there; so say the texts. Some industrial *miqva'ot*--if such they be--have elaborate arrangements to guarantee that vessels and persons emerging from the purifying waters will not accidentally touch those going down to enter the bath. Thus the architecture of the tanks was *rhetorical* insofar as its very existence could persuade buyers (wholesalers and consumers) of the reliability of the bottling operation. This much is obvious, re-

gardless of the complex problems of determining exactly who were attempting to observe purity laws, in which contexts, in which eras.

[59]Aqueducts are built rivers, with ingenious devices to hold back the water, let the sediment precipitate out, regulate the rate of flow, make the water run uphill by siphon, or lift it by machine. Roman fountains and baths manipulated water with a combination of gravity and pumps, producing effects that were aesthetically pleasing and hygienically beneficial. The Jewish population could have no moral or ethical objection to the colonial manipulation of water as such. Rather, the resistance built into *miqveh* practices is symbolic in nature. Poetically it reclaims the metaphors of rain and dew, familiar in the Psalms and the Prophets as vehicles for divine providential-salvific action. Christian baptistry architecture, including water supply and handling, should also be contrasted with Roman and Jewish water architecture.

[60]For non-Roman waterworks, see *Aqueducts of Ancient Palestine*, ed. D. Amit *et al.*

[61]This is not to deny the problems of classifying certain structures exclusively as ritual baths, not the least of which is anachronistic projection of mishnaic or talmudic descriptions back into the Second Temple period. The difficulties are discussed by Wright, "Jewish Ritual Baths."

[62]See Reich, "*Miqwa'ot* (Jewish Ritual Baths) in Rural Regions." The urbanization and domestication of the *miqveh* should be seen as an adaptation responding to *urban* needs. If ritual pools are built in the countryside, this seems to have been done with a view to an urban or even an international market.

[63]In this they resemble the residential pools in Jerusalem discussed by Reich, "*Miqwa'ot* (Jewish Ritual Baths) in the Second Temple Period."

[64]This early-Roman non-residential building with eight pools might have been a nymphaeum or a secular bath, according to Strange, "Six Campaigns at Sepphoris" 347-49. Quite nearby, in the western residential district of the Sepphoris acropolis, Meyers found more than 20 tanks that he dated from the end of the Second Temple period and identified as ritual baths; see Meyers *et al.*, *Sepphoris*, 28-9. Strange reports earlier finds of four stepped pools in a nearby villa (p. 345). He has dated their first cutting and use to the first century C.E., and finds that they went out of use during or after the second century. Cisterns at Sepphoris generally went out of use in the late third or fourth century; but typically they had been converted to non-hydraulic uses well before that.

[65]Thus, the presence of a stepped undrained pool does not unambiguously identify a structure as the residence of ritually observant Jews. Moreover, two distinctive features of the domestic pools--their steps, and their narrow but deep shape--are well explained as adaptations to climatic conditions and need no special ritual motivation. In very dry weather, the low surface-to-volume ratio of a deep pool minimizes evaporation. Yet of course the water does gradually evaporate throughout the dry season, so the stairsteps are necessary to provide access to the receding surface. In other words, steps need not indicate that people intended to climb down beneath the surface to immerse themselves. Likewise, cutting the pool into bedrock and covering or sheltering it are ways to keep the water cool and reduce evaporation; they need not be interpreted as provisions for modesty while immersing.

[66]In the Infancy Gospel of James, the young girl Mary is commissioned to spin and weave tapestry for the Temple in Jerusalem. Textiles and clothing may need immersion; see Ta'anit 4.8, discussed by Peskowitz, "'Family/ies' in Antiquity," 21-3. Scribal industry is another possible use.

[67]On this view of Jewishness, women constitute the permanent threat from within that never can be completely controlled. They are capable of adultery and of menstrual malpractice, and they can subvert the proper management of the home. Kinship and caste require the import of brides in each generation; but with each bride comes the risk that a defect in pedigree will enter the patriline. Therefore bride-producers must have the means to offer rhetorical assurances--*ultimately there are no other kind*--that the girl knows how to manage a ritually pure household, wants to follow the rules of *niddah*, and will not commit adultery. These desireable (and marketable) behaviors cannot be *caused* by building walls for enclosure or baths for purification. Nevertheless, such architecture constitutes a rhetorically persuasive statement in stone that the girl has been raised right and will behave herself once married. The salience of such concerns is underscored by Ross Kraemer's suggestion that "preparing daughters for licit marriage was the focal point of mother-daughter relationships among free Jewish families"; see R. Kraemer, "Jewish Mothers and Daughters in the Greco-Roman World," in *The Jewish Family*, ed. S. Cohen, 110.

[68]As would be the case given a longstanding practice of bride-taking from the same matriline; that is, marrying boys to their maternal cousins. Such kinship strategies are pursued in numerous cultures. They have been studied ethnographically among contemporary traditional African peoples, and archaeologically through material remains in places as diverse as the colonial Chesapeake and Mesoamerica in the period of European contact. However, the archaeology of kinship requires more subtle attention to variations of stylistic elements in the material culture than is currently accorded to ceramic analysis in Israel.

[69]See S. Miller, *Studies in the History and Traditions of Sepphoris* (Leiden: E.J. Brill, 1984) 46-55. Levitical lineage was carefully guarded as well, and a pure Israelite

family tree was required for serving in many honorory civic positions, such as witnessing documents. For an exhaustive structural analysis of the Mishnaic systematization of kinship, see P. Flesher, *Oxen, Women, or Citizens.*

[70]Relevant evidence should be sought through forensic anthropology, examining human bone for traces of occupational and nutritional changes, correlated with gender. Birthrate and lifespan can also be approximated through examining bone. Floral and faunal analysis and distribution data also are needed. The possibility of spatially sensitive interpretation depends upon the willingness to pursue such evidence.

[71]For example, see Sperber, *Roman Palestine* (both volumes); Goodman, *State and Society in Roman Galilee*; Neusner, *Economics of the Mishnah*; Edwards, "The Socio-Economic and Cultural Ethos of the Lower Galilee"; and Peskowitz, "'The Work of Her Hands'."

[72]But for the contrary claim and an argument that a cultural text, expressed materially in housing design, can indeed produce or modify gendered subjectivity, see C. Baker, "'Ordering the House': On the Domestication of Jewish Sexuality" (paper presented to the national meeting of the Society of Biblical Literature, Chicago, 1994).

[73]Sociological observation of those conflicts no longer is possible; however, contemporary ethnographic studies are suggestive. For example, the potential for using the *miqveh* in power negotiations between spouses is illustrated by the practices of a twentieth-century Israeli immigrant group described by R. Wasserfall, "Menstruation and Identity: The Meaning of Niddah for Moroccan Women Immigrants to Israel," in *People of the Body: Jews and Judaism from an Embodied Perspective*, ed. H. Eilberg-Schwartz (Albany: State University of New York Press, 1992) 309-27. Wasserfall found that wives did not go to the *miqveh* unless and until "sent" by their husbands; but even if "sent," they might refuse or procrastinate. Thus either party could apply psychological pressure to the other by delaying, advancing, or even forgoing the trip to the *miqveh* that was to signal the resumption of intercourse after menstruation. Wasserfall's women respondents associated the *miqveh* with the future health and welfare of the Jewish people.

[74]Comparable questions are being asked between African American women and men as they seek to understand how the burden of slavery fell upon them and was carried.

[75]On the city as a surveillance installation, see M. Leone and B. Little, "Artifacts as Expressions of Society and Culture: Subversive Genealogy and the Value of History," in *History From Things: Essays in Material Culture*, ed. S. Lubar and W.D. Kingery (Washington: Smithsonian Institution Press, 1993) 160-81. The colonial city of Annapolis, whose landscape was redesigned in the wake of the American Revolution, is read by Leone and

Little in terms of the surveillance it offered to citizens. The "panopticon" of the dome, added to the Statehouse in the 1780's, is "an all-seeing eye of the state watching and being watched by fellow citizens" from atop a hill in the center of the city (pp. 161-2). By comparison, Roman cities built *convex mirrors*: the C-shaped orientation of the theater, the basilica, and the stibadium or Roman dining room. Each architectural form provided emplacements for individuals facing inward, toward one another.

[76]The *triclinium* floor excavated at Sepphoris is clearly designed for such a use.

[77]Cynthia Baker suggests (in "'Ordering the House'") that Roman housing design produced a "panopticon" by promoting direct visual access from the central atrium into the rooms, most of which opened onto it. Domestic surveillance thus contributed to the formation of a certain kind of subjectivity in the occupants. By contrast, she says, in the same climate traditional village houses in Palestine tended to block line-of-sight access from the courtyard into most rooms. These houses were "an-opticons," producing women as invisible subjects who, although present, could neither exert nor undergo surveillance between their courtyards and the surrounding rooms. But two archaeological difficulties confront this intriguing theory. Baker must establish that the shielded rooms were indeed *women's* rooms, and she must show that the shielding walls were not pierced by windows. The excavated ruins do not support either of those inferences. Nevertheless the approach to spatial management of visibility as a means to manage subjectivity seems sound.

[78]The cloistering of the Torah in the rabbinic study house renders it an-opticonic (if I might redeploy Baker's apt term). By hiding--or rather, by being hidden and speaking from behind a closed door--the "oral Torah" transforms the mechanisms by which its power is negotiated and applied.

[79]Unlike the schoolhouse, the synagogue belongs to both men and women. During the Second Temple period, synagogues in the Land of Israel were multi-purpose community administration and service centers. They became places for scheduled public prayers and Torah reading only gradually after the destruction of the Temple, judging from evidence and arguments presented by Urman, "House of Assembly."

[80]These startling finds have been much discussed; see R. Hachlili, *Ancient Jewish Art and Archaeology in the Land of Israel* (Leiden: E.J. Brill, 1988); and L. Ness, "Astrology and Judaism in Late Antiquity" (Ph.D. diss., Miami University, 1990), and "Astrology," *Archaeology in the Biblical World* 2 (1992) 44-54. See also Roussin in this volume.

[81]Even though Galilee has only two seasons. For whatever reason, the seasons in the mosaics sometimes are out of sync with the star signs.

[82]An exception was uncovered at Sepphoris by Hebrew University excavators in 1993. They found a synagogue zodiac from perhaps the fifth or sixth century. One of its unique features is that the deity is *not* represented as usual at the center of the circle.

[83]The twelve star signs with their Hebrew names (borrowed from Babylonian) are found at Hammat Tiberias, Bet 'Alpha, and Na'aran. Too little remains of the Huseifa and Susiya zodiacs to see how they were labeled. The Sepphoris zodiac is the first one found that explicitly correlates secular and religious time, making the liturgical lunar months fit the constellations.

3

The Clash Between Literary and Archaeological Models of Provincial Palestine

Dennis E. Groh
Illinois Wesleyan University

The upsurge of interest by New Testament scholars in understanding and integrating information from archaeology and material culture into New Testament study and research is surely one of the more exciting and promising current developments.[1] For those of us who have been hard at work at the intersection of textual and material culture of New Testament and post-New Testament Palestine for over 20 years, this offers a splendid opportunity to open discussions of how one uses this kind of evidence in the face of the formed agendas and biases of religious literary documentation. We know two things about intersections from insurance statistics: that they offer the opportunity to safely and surely go a new direction but also that *most serious accidents happen there*. In light of this opportunity to avoid some accidents and turn discussion in some new directions, I want to make four methodological observations:

1. The serious contradiction in current discussions of life in first century C. E. Galilee in which the literary texts are said to speak of unrest, banditry, and revolt, but the overwhelming weight of material culture indicates continuity and "business as usual" requires much more extensive discussion than it has received and, probably, a reexamining of the literature to show exactly what group (socially) is in crisis and exactly where (geographically) they are in crisis.

2. Twentieth century Marxist models that invent a tension between town or city and countryside have absolutely nothing to do with Palestine during any part of the common era.

3. The importation of models or theories of "power elites" developed from the study of other provinces of the Roman Empire to describe the interaction (or lack thereof) of ruling and ruled classes probably will not enlighten us about Palestine. Researchers need, instead, to discover what constitutes a "power elite" in a primarily Jewish country and context.

4. Scholars need to learn how to read and interpret archaeological evidence from the fourth century backwards to enlighten the first century C.E., since it is extremely difficult to recover first century evidence that has not been badly disturbed by Late Roman/Early Byzantine occupation or reuse.

LITERARY AND ARCHAEOLOGICAL EVIDENCES IN CONFLICT

The problem of relating the literary picture of Palestine to the archaeological evidence comes to sharpest focus in the crises of the Jewish Wars of 66-73 C.E. and 132-135 C.E. There is no doubt from the literary records (Josephus for the first revolt and Roman and Jewish sources for the Bar-Kokhba revolt) that the Jewish people underwent great and destructive defeats. But archaeological evidence for these defeats is hard to establish outside of Judaea. The Bar-Kokhba revolt was confined primarily to Judaea; but archaeological evidence from the First Jewish Revolt in the Galilee testifies to how irregularly sites there suffered from the consequences of the revolt.[2] Sepphoris, we know from literary sources, stayed completely out of both revolts; and the first century and early second century materials recovered by The University of South Florida Expedition to Sepphoris indeed indicate no warfare destruction materials in, for example, the Field I house or the theater on the acropolis.[3] There is some small evidence that there may have been destruction caused by an earthquake in 113/114 C.E.[4] But siege and post-siege destruction does not appear on the Acropolis until post-352 C.E., when Sepphoris joined with a handful of other Galilean cities in an unsuccessful revolt against Gallus Caesar.[5]

Similarly, the village of Capernaum shows no evidence of any break in the continuity of its material culture throughout the history of its occupation, as the careful Italian Franciscan excavations show.[6]

Moreover, the evidence from the local ceramic trade indicates no great interruption in the ceramic trading patterns of at least two Lower Galilean factories--Kefar Hananiah[7] and the recently discovered Asochis (Shikhin).[8] The wares of these potters not only marched through the first and early second centuries without interruption, they marched across the two Galilees from the large urban marketplace centers (*likely Sepphoris and Tiberias*) *to which they were initially brought for subsequent distribution* .[9]

None of this is to deny that some sites were truly and thoroughly destroyed in the North, as the Roman siege ramp at Jotapata and the leveling of Gamla in the Golan testify.[10] But any crisis brought on by the revolts must be evaluated in terms of their effect on people at specific locations.

We are coming to a consensus in archaeology that the Jews of Judaea bore the brunt of both revolts that changed permanently the dream of a Jewish Jerusalem, and even of a Jewish Judaea. The consequence of the disruptions of Jewish life in Judaea extend all the way to the Byzantine period in which we find the concentration of Jews in the Hebron hills, Bethlehem, and the Shephelah, but not in the immediate environs of Jerusalem.[11]

But even interpreting material culture in what we know to be the aftermath of the severe and total destruction of the Jerusalem temple and that whole quadrant of the city is exceedingly problematic. For example, we know that the loss of the temple was one of the greatest crises in Jewish history. But here, again, material culture does not always cooperate with historical traumas in exactly the ways we might predict. We are uniquely positioned to see how the fall of the temple affected at least one area of Jewish life and commerce, thanks to Varda Sussman's superb synthetic study of Jewish oil lamps of the period 70-132 C.E. The destruction of the Temple-proper gave birth to the Jewish oil lamp bearing Temple symbolism for the first time in this period between the two great Jewish wars.[12] It is just this kind of a burst of material culture that transformed Jewish cultic loyalty into new artistic and cultural forms that would have been hidden from view had we to rely on the scantiness and sorrow of the literary texts. Even in the aftermath of great crisis, people return to daily life and ordinary (or perhaps in this case, extraordinary) commerce with amazing speed and regularity. Therefore, our reading of the literary texts must not invest crises with ubiquitous long-term social effects. Judged from the standpoint of material culture, there may be great disruption at the epicenter of crisis, but quick recovery and not necessarily a long-term hangover for the average person at a brief distance from the epicenter.

Thus attempts to portray New Testament Palestine as swept by constant currents of unrest, revolt and warfare[13] must be moderated by precise notations of evidence from "where" geographically and socially the crisis struck and sobered by the testimony of the material culture as to how quickly the average person needs to put life back together again.

CITY AND COUNTRYSIDE

One of the greatest contributions to the establishment of social and economic history as a legitimate concern of historians resulted from the Russian Revolution. Ironically, the most significant contributions to theories of social change and turmoil were initially made not by Marxist historians but *by anti-Marxist historians*--those scholars driven out of their native Russia by the Reds. Unfortunately, the anti-Marxists were shaped in the same crucible as their enemies and carried their experiences of the Russian Revolution into their studies of the ancient world. Thus M. Rostovtzeff, the dean of social and economic historians, saw the same dynamics he had witnessed in his youth being recreated in the Roman Empire: the conflict between the oppressive and self-centered aristocracy of the cities and towns and the peasants of the countryside. The urban lower-classes allied with the rural peasantry to squeeze off and finally bring down urban life.[14] It was a grand theory and brilliantly supported, but *simply wrong*. It brought to the ancient world, not only a modern theory of economics, but also a modern situation of huge *industrial* cities, in which the urban lower classes were cut off from their roots and "alienated" by the impersonal world of the city.

North African studies put such a rural/urban, upper class/lower class, theory to the test in the Donatist Controversy of the fourth century. At first W.H.C. Frend thought he had found his model for the explanation of the North African ecclesiastical schisms of the various Donatist and Catholic groups.[15] But the highly critical revisiting of that same ground by H.P. Brisson[16] not only disproved the theory, but caused Frend to reevaluate his position on it.[17] Unfortunately, the news did not reach New Testament studies in time to stop the importation of this same flawed theory into Palestine.

The urban/rural situation in Palestine is an exceedingly complex one; but it is definitely not one that should be characterized by urban/rural or city aristocracy/rural peasantry clashes. We are poorly informed about the exact relationship between the city (*polis*) and the village (*kome*) for Palestine. To begin with, Palestine of the first century C.E. is a country with a "mixed" constitution to the First Revolt--both a kingly and a Hellenistic city-based organization.[18] Josephus gives us extensive information about what places are termed *poleis*, but the information is, again, quite complicated. In its more technical sense of a constituted legal entity, a *polis* has a council of leading citizens *(boule),* some autonomy, and a territory of hinterland to administer. Jerusalem seems to have been the clearest example of such a *polis* from both Jewish and Roman sources.[19] Josephus mentions the existence of a *boule* in conjunction with other sites, but he also uses the term *polis* with a stunning imprecision. His basic meaning for the term involves the large size of such an urban entity, though whether any of the sites he designates *poleis* rest their title back on official Hellenistic political charters remains hidden.[20]

In any event, we need to remind ourselves that large urban centers of the kind that other provinces can boast remain quite scarce in Israel, which, throughout the C.E. centuries was primarily a country of small towns or villages. Lower Galilee can boast only Sepphoris and Tiberias (after 19 C.E.) as large *poleis*. And Upper Galilee (*Tetracomia*) has not a single *polis*. Its closest urban trade-connection is not even with Caesarea Maritima, but with distant Tyre to the North and West as the preponderance of Tyrian coins at Meiron and Gush Halav have shown.[21]

Moreover, we do not know exactly to what we are referring when we speak about a "city territory." We do know that at the ground level of daily life people did not pay particular attention to political boundaries, as we can see by the expanding and contracting boundaries of Galilee throughout the ancient centuries. One example may suffice: although Josephus does not include the Golan within the boundaries of Galilee, his command as General of the Galilee clearly includes Gamla.[22]

The evidence of material culture recovered from archaeology indicates a *symbiosis* between city and village and not a tension between them. Unlike the modern industrial world, industry was located primarily in the villages and not exclusively in the nearby cities. The rural villages brought goods and products to trade and sell in the cities and went there to employ specialists which the small village could not provide with enough work. Villagers arrived in the towns with something to sell and not as a disinherited proletariat looking for work.

At Sepphoris, for example, much of the pottery used there in the first century was made in the Galilean village of Kefar Hananiah.[23] The source of some forty-five per cent of Sepphoris' pottery repertory, including some of its most characteristic first century forms, and the source of the majority of storage jars found in the Galilee remained a mystery until Strange, Longstaff, and I located the pottery factory that produced them at nearby Asochis (Talmudic Shikhin), on a previously unexplored and unnamed ridge at the south end of the Beit Netophah Valley.[24] However we wish to interpret such trade links, our interpretations must surely include the close interdependency of city and village to each others' mutual benefit. And it is precisely this mutual benefit between city and hinterland that has been emphasized in recent studies of city/countryside relations in the Near East in late antiquity. Commenting on the results of Georges Tate's *Les Campagnes de la Syrie du Nord I* (1992), Clive Foss has written:

> the location of the limestone hills at the centre of one of the densest concentrations of cities of the empire shows that city and village worked together, with the city providing an essential market where the villages could sell their products and buy what they needed.

> Tate points out that the peasants formed the vast majority of the population everywhere, and concludes with the paradox that the countryside did not suffer oppression by the cities, but that the cities would have been in a stronger position had they been able to exercise firmer control over the countryside, and extract a greater proportion of its surplus. If ancient society reached a dead end, it was not because of a mentality that favored aquisition over production, but because the peasants had no technical means of increasing their production and thus petrified their surpluses in stone, leaving the ruins that still stand.[25]

This issue of the distribution, or lack of distribution of power, introduces my next point.

POWER ELITE AND PEASANT

It is extremely difficult, if not impossible, to find in Palestine traces of the concentration of enormous wealth and power in the hands of the aristocratic few, with the corresponding social distance between rich and poor, so characteristic of other provinces of the empire. The Herodian circle could certainly boast such wealth--as Herod's fortress-palaces in the Judaean desert and his winter palace at Jericho amply testify.[26] The patrician and priestly circles that centered around the royal house, as witnessed by their partially excavated homes on Mt. Zion and their tombs, had great wealth as well.[27] But once outside this (short-lived) circle, we are hard-pressed to find the material vaunting of the rich, best represented by the sprawling *private* urban villas and the extensive *private* country estates, found throughout other provinces of the Empire. Even in a much later period, the fourth century C.E., when all restraint is removed from the showy greed of the *potentiores* (significantly, they were termed *honestiores* in previous centuries), the villas of the rich, such as the Patrician House at Meiron or the Late Roman Villa on the acropolis at Sepphoris are spacious and comfortable,[28] but nothing compared to finds in other provinces such as Asia Minor.

Where money was spent on luxury items (i. e., non-income producing building), it tended to be spent on Jewish public buildings for the community to assemble in--hence our growing corpus of "synagogues."[29] The twenty years I have spent in Jim Strange's company exploring Jewish village and city life in both Galilees, has reinforced this impression of a largely egalitarian society (at least in external appearance), whose wealth was founded in agriculture and small spin-off cottage industries related to it (fulling, dyeing, wine and oil processing, flax production, pottery manufacture, etc.).[30]

What historians have been able to deduce from the literary sources reinforces this picture of a largely agrarian world of farmers that worked small holdings, of shop keepers, peddlers, scholars, tanners, merchants--which occupations cut across both city-and village-dwellers, pious Jewish congregations *and* their rabbis.[31] Notions of tensions and great differences of practice between Judaean and Galilean Jews are demonstrably absent from Josephus' writings. Popular unrest based on socio-economic incompatibility of various classes in Palestine is absent, because it is irrelevant.

Moreover, thanks to the work of Daniel Sperber, we know the precise moment at which the small land holder and tenant farmer began to be pushed off the land by the wealthier class's agressive efforts at acquisition--the second half of the fourth century C.E.[32] The pain of the small-holder at precisely the mid-fourth century is probably not unrelated to the abandonment of several previ-ously prosperous villages in Upper Galilee, to the Gallus Revolt of 352, and to mid-century tax-law changes requiring payment of taxes in gold currency only.[33] However, before this period, there seems to be little evidence of grave social distance or social-warfare among the peoples of Palestine, other than the anti-Gentilism of the Jewish revolts and the standard ethnic tensions between Jew and Samaritan.[34]

Ground-breaking work here needs to be done to explore the meaning of terms (now bandied about) like "power" and "elite" in a Jewish context. What does in fact a *Jewish elite look like?* If I am right they do not resemble the Gentile elites of the Diaspora. Here the Decapolis cities (with a Palestinian Decapolis city like Scythopolis/Beth She'an being the control site) may provide the ground for answering just such a question.

THE ELUSIVE FIRST CENTURY ARCHAEOLOGICAL EVIDENCE

The previous generation of archaeologists knew very little about the Roman period in Palestine. The national interests of establishing a newly created Jewish state understandably caused archaeological work to be focused on the sites and places prominent in Hebrew Scripture, especially those dating to the Iron Age. The major discoveries in the NT/Rabbinic/Patristic Eras have mostly come in the last thirty years or so. The adaption of former tel techniques of excavation to Roman/Byzantine Period sites by both the Israeli and American Schools of Archaeology and the refinement of these advances in the "Khirbet" Method developed by Meyers and Strange have produced a huge body of data on Palestine in the C.E. centuries all the way up to the Islamic takeover (ca. 640).[35] But pure and undisturbed first century sites and materials have been hard to come by. This was not a serious problem until New Testament literary scholars and some New Testament archaeologists began to confine proper understanding of the life and material culture of the New Testament to the first century C.E. exclusively. Thus in certain textual and archaeological circles anything from earlier or later centuries seems to be regarded as automatically suspect in shedding light on the NT unless it comes from that particular and exact time-period.[36] One could almost speak of the recent re-invention of a "canonical time" to accompany a "canonical document." Thus if the church fathers of the fourth century created the concept of the first century C.E. as a special and plenary age of the Spirit, and the Deists of the eighteenth century repeated such a concept to explain why miracles no longer happened,[37] historians of our time have invested the first century evidence with a reverence and attention that neither earlier Hellenistic nor later second century C.E. evidence can share. Thus NT scholarship finds itself ideologically wedded to a depressingly small body of evidence, because the reality we have had to face in the last twenty years of discovery and excavation has been how extensive and complete were the settlement and building activities of the Late Roman and Byzantine Periods. Here I want to stress that careful stratigraphic excavation and publication has produced only two first century synagogues from the large number of Jewish public structures found throughout the Galilee and Golan.[38]

The elusive search for the first century was exactly how Jim Strange and I first met. I began working at Caesarea Maritima in the staff of the Joint Expedition in 1972. Jim Strange had written the field manual for that expedition and departed to work with Eric M. Meyers in the Galilee the previous year. One of the announced goals of the Caesarea expedition, and the goal that drew Garrett Theological Seminary's New Testament and patristics personnel into the founding expedition consortium, was to discover and plan the Herodian city. The lure of being able to uncover and study an entire Roman city planned *de novo* by Herod the Great was just too tempting to resist.

There was only one problem: that first century city was entirely overlaid and disturbed by the extensive building activities of the later Romans, especially active from the mid-third century C.E. on.

After several seasons of digging, I finally put in a probe at the base of one of the round towers identified as "Strato's Tower" at the north end of the site. Here was an obviously Hellenistic wall and tower, beautifully paralleled by a similar structure at Samaria/Sebastia; yet the earlier Italian Expedition had reported that the wall surrounding Caesarea was Late Roman.[39] But surely the first century city was to be found here! Surprisingly, the sections and pottery clearly showed a major repair of the wall to its founding precisely in the late-third/early-fourth centuries, which removed or made unreadable the wall's obviously earlier founding.

Back in Jerusalem at the end of the 1975 Caesarea season, I talked with Eric Meyers, who revealed a similar problem at his previous Khirbet Shema and (now) Meiron sites in the Upper Galilee. Eric invited me up to help Strange and him read the backlog of pottery and check the dating horizons. Out of that experience, the following year I joined together with Meyers and Strange to survey synagogue sites and Josephan fortress cities in the Galilee and Golan and to finish the Meiron site and to excavate the Gush Halav and en-Nabratein sites in subsequent years.[40] The results of our surveys and excavations revealed an enormous building-boom from the mid-third century on!

I am not trying to deny the discovery of important first century finds across the country, but simply to indicate that they are a drop in the bucket compared to the flood of evidence we have from the late-third century onward. And above all, I want to reemphasize how badly that early evidence was disturbed (with notable exceptions like those of remote Gamla and some Negev fortress sites) by the exuberant destructiveness of the Byzantines. What are we to make of this? Is all of that later evidence to be set aside, or can we find some ways to work *backwards* from later evidence to earlier time-periods?

Here I want to express directly what has been previously only implicitly said: pre-industrial material culture changes much more slowly and over a much longer time-period than political currents! The kitchen pottery which perdures in basic form for up to a century, house plans which make only small changes in their use of interior space over centuries (the Late Roman House at Sepphoris' acropolis began as a first century structure on probably the same basic plan), city streets (like the one found in Field V at Sepphoris) used for over six centuries--all indicate such slow change and long-term usefulness to ancient people. If Kitchener could write in the late nineteenth century of the large number of Galilean synagogues already known in that day "...the Jewish influence which gave rise to these buildings was both extremely local and short-lived," we now know that a 200-400 year *usage* of a particular building by a Jewish community was not at all unusual.[41] The words written by Meyers and Strange are particularly relevant here:

For all the indications of cultural diversity in late antiquity, there is a recognizable homogeneity of culture as well. It is as important to stress the forces of continuity which bind the past inextricably to the present as it is to point to the emergent forces of discontinuity which enable change to occur. It is clear to us that a genuine sense of conservatism in burial customs lingers on into late antiquity and greatly affects views of afterlife and even influences the modest nature of grave goods which are left behind. Conservatism in art goes hand in hand with a kind of self-conscious attempt to preserve Hebrew/Aramaic culture and characterizes the extreme north of Ancient Palestine. It is such a force of continuity which enables us to measure the extent to which new forces have come to dominate.[42]

I especially want us to rethink the possible usefulness of later materials in the light of the brilliant work carried out by Peter Lampe in reconstructing first century Christian Rome by working backwards from the lists of *tituli* churches of later centuries to confirm and enlighten the picture of the Roman churches in *Romans* 16.[43] What Lampe found is a fascinating continuity in the pattern of multiple, individually self-sufficient and factionalized congregations organized by the space provided by owners of private houses (or *insulae*) rooms. Lampe's argument is long, complex, and nuanced by a full sifting of the literary and archaeological evidence of the intervening centuries. Clearly, as he points out, the beginning of the third century signals a decisive change away from the use of an architecturally unmodified private house to the need for a discreet and separate cultic room.[44] But the continuity of patterns over long periods of time is what I want to emphasize here.

What Lampe has done for first century Christianity in Rome might be repeatable in Palestine, especially in the light of the excavations currently underway at ancient Sepphoris. Quite a diverse Judaism (for which we have numerous rabbinic texts) from the third-seventh centuries is coming to light. We know from rabbinic texts that there were numerous synagogues in the city in the third/fourth centuries and that some of the synagogues were organized around ethnic lines (the "synagogue of the Babylonians," for example) or place of origin (the "synagogue of the people of Gophna").[45] Currently scholars are operating under the assumption that an ethnically diverse and varied populace in the Galilean cities came about as a result of a huge influx of Judaean refugees fleeing the Bar-Kokhba revolt and its aftermath.[46] But is this the case?

In the first place, I would have expected to find much more evidence of pottery and lamps of distinctively Judaean type and manufacture among the first and second century levels in the Galilee; so one of the things that needs to be more carefully checked is this axiom which posits large population movements and, therefore, great discontinuity between the first and second centuries.

Secondly, even assuming that the case is right, and that a new factor which could lead to numerous changes was introduced into the Galilee as a result of an influx of new residents in the second century, on what basis can we assume that the new residents did not assimilate into the social patterns dictated by the material world of the city in which they settled? In short, it will be extremely important to identify the various quarters of the city, the precise locations of the synagogues, and to hypothesize about the ethnic/linguistic groups to which they belonged. With that in place, it may be possible to think backwards from the later centuries to at least peer into the patterning of citizens and congregations of the first century who stood at the very genesis of both Christianity and rabbinic Judaism. The long usage of housing thus far excavated by both the Duke/Hebrew University and the University of South Florida teams on the Sepphoris acropolis is very encouraging at this point. Needless to say we are only at our most interesting beginning points in trying to understand and reconstruct the world of the earliest Christians and first century Jews.

NOTES

[1]This very volume best attests to the new trend; but see also, S. Freyne, *Galilee, Jesus, and the Gospels. Literary Approaches and Historical Investigations* (Philadelphia: Fortress Press, 1988) 135-75; T. Longstaff, "Nazareth and Sepphoris: Insights into Christian Origins," in *Christ and His Communities. Essays in Honor of Reginald Fuller*, ed. A. Hultgren and B. Hall, *Anglican Theological Review*, Supplemental Series 11 (March 1990) 8-15; J. Charlesworth, "Archaeology, Jesus and Christian Faith," and J. Strange, "Some Implications of Archaeology for New Testament Studies," in *What Has Archaeology to Do with Faith?*, Faith & Scholarship Colloquies, ed. J. Charlesworth and W. Weaver (Philadelphia: Trinity Press International, 1992) 1-22 and 23-59 respectively.

[2]The Roman siege ramp at Jotapata (Yodefat) and the city's first century defense wall were correctly identified by the 1976 joint Garrett/Duke survey of the Galilee/Golan: E. Meyers and J. Strange, "Survey in Galilee, 1976," and A. Sundberg, Jr., "Josephus' Galilee Revisited: Akbara, Yodefat, Gamla," in *explor. A Journal of Theology* 3 (1) (1977) 9-10 and 46-51 respectively; E. Meyers, J. Strange, and D. Groh, "The Meiron Excavation Project: Survey in Galilee and Golan, 1976," *Bulletin of the American Schools of Oriental Research* 230 (1978) 1-24.

[3]Based on the Field Books for Fields I (the Late Roman house Waterman's "Basilica") and Field II (the theater) of The University of South Florida Excavations at Sepphoris, James F. Strange, Director; Dennis E. Groh and Thomas R. W. Longstaff, Associate Directors.

[4]For the Trajanic earthquake, consult K. Russell, "The Earthquake Chronology of Palestine and Northwest Arabia From the Second Through the Mid-eighth Century," *Bulletin of the American Schools of Oriental Research 260 (1985) 39-41*. Both the Field I Late Roman house and the Field II theater (see n. 3 above) show such damage: results reported by D. E. Groh in "The Gallus Revolt at Sepphoris?" (paper presented at the Sepphoris Symposium of the Annual Meeting of the American Schools of Oriental Research, Boston, MA, December, 1987). Hence, the relegation of the 113/114 C.E. earthquake to "doubtful authenticity" is simply incorrect, as is done by D. Amiran, E. Arieh, T. Turcotte. "Earthquakes in Israel and Adjacent Areas: Macroseismic Observations since 100 B.C.E," Israel Exploration Journal 44 (1994) 289.

[5]See n. 4 above and B. Nathanson, "The Fourth Century Jewish Revolt During the Reign of Gallus." (Ph. D. Dissertation. Duke University, 1981). B. G. Nathanson, "Jews, Christians, and the Gallus Revolt in Fourth-century Palestine," *Biblical Archaeologist 49 (1986) 26-36*. A recent challenge to the accuracy of the literary accounts of the revolt by J. Schaefer, "Der Aufstand gegen Gallus Caesar," in *Tradition and Interpretation in Jewish and Christian Literature: Essays in Honor of Juergen C. H. Lebram*, Studia Post-Biblica 36, ed. J. van Henten et. al. (Leiden: Brill, 1986) 184-201, does not cancel the archaeological evidence for such a revolt.

[6]V. Corbo, *Cafarnao I. Gli Edifici della Citta* (Jerusalem: Franciscan Press, 1975) 215, reported "...a natural and progressive development of the city through the entire Roman Byzantine period."

[7]D. Adan-Bayewitz, *Common Pottery in Roman Galilee. A Study of Local Trade,* (Bar-Ilan Studies in Near Eastern Languages and Literature) (Ramat-Gan, Israel: Bar-Ilan University, 1993) 236-37, 240.

[8]James F. Strange, Dennis E. Groh, and Thomas R. W. Longstaff, "Excavations at Sepphoris: The Location and Identification of Shikhin. Part I," *Israel Exploration Journal* 44 (1994) 216-27; Part II, *Israel Exploration Journal* 45 (1995) 171-87. "The Location and Identification of Ancient Shikhin (Asochis)," hypertext version by T. Longstaff, May 1994, World Wide Web (http://WWW.Colby.Edu/Rel/Shikhin.HTML).

[9]D. Adan-Bayewitz, *Common Pottery in Roman Galilee,* 232-33.

[10]See n. 2 above for Jotapata. For Gamla, see S. Gutman, *Gamla* [Hebrew] (Tel Aviv: Hakibbutz Hameuched, 1981); "Gamla--1983," in *Excavations and Surveys in Israel* 3 (1984) 26-27; "The Synagogue at Gamla," in *Ancient Synagogues Revealed*, ed. L. Levine (Jerusalem: Israel Exploration Society, 1981) 30-34 ; S. Gutman and H. Shanks, "Gamla, The Masada of the North," *Biblical Archaeology Review* 5 (1) (1979) 12-19; Z. Maoz, "The Typology of Second-Temple Synagogues," *Ancient Synagogues Revealed,* 35-41.

[11]On the overall demographic balance, see G. Alon, *The Jews in Their Land in the Talmudic Age (70-640 CE),* trans. and ed. G. Levi (Cambridge, MA and London: Cambridge University Press, 1989) 5-6, 750-57 (though in the late Byzantine Period Jewish population may have made a come-back in Jerusalem and environs). For the centers of the Bar-Kokhba Revolt, see Y. Yadin, *Bar-Kokhba. The Rediscovery of the Legendary Hero of the Second Jewish Revolt Against Rome* (New York: Random House, 1971) 18-27. Debates as to exactly which territories fell into the revolutionaries' hands continue: see L. Mildenberg, *The Coinage of the Bar-Kokhba War,* ed. P. Mottahedeh (Arrau, Frankfurt-am-Main, Salzburg: Sauerlander Verlag, 1984) and the remarks by W. Metcalf and G. Bowersock in their review in the *American Journal of Archaeology* 90 (1986) 254-56.

[1f]V. Sussman, *Ornamental Jewish Oil Lamps From the Destruction of the Second Temple Through the Bar-Kokhba Revolt* (Warminster, Eng.: Aris & Philips and the Israel Exploration Society, 1972) 16-25.

[13]Cf. R. Horsley and J. Hanson, *Bandits, Prophets, and Messiahs. Popular Movements at the Time of Jesus,* New Voices in Biblical Studies, ed. A. Collins and J. Collins (San Francisco: Harper & Row, 1988) 51, 60-61, 72-73, 232-3. The archaeological evidence on "social banditry" supports the conclusion drawn more from literary texts by Freyne, *Galilee, Jesus, and the Gospels*, 165: "We shall have to conclude then that social banditry was not at all a dominant feature of Galilean life in the first century."

[14]M. Rostovtzeff's article "Les classes rurales et les classes citadines dans le haut empire romain," in *Melanges offerts a Henri Pirenne* (Bruxelles: Vromant & Co., 1926) vol. 2, 419-34, distills the social theory that lies embedded in his magisterial *The Social and Economic History of the Roman Empire*, 2 vols., second edition revised by R. M. Fraser (Oxford: Clarendon Press, 1957).

[15]W. Frend, *The Donatist Church* (Oxford: The Clarendon Press, 1954) 7-11, 20, 32, 36-47, 52- 66, 298, 331-34.

[16]J. Brisson, *Autonisme et Christianisme dans l'Afrique romaine de Septime Severe a l'invasion vandale* (Paris: E. de Bochard, 1958) 5, 28, 413-14, particularly removed the Berber peasant background as a key factor in the schism.

[17]W. Frend, *The Donatist Church*, x.

[18]A. Kasher, "The *Isopoliteia* Question in Caesarea Maritima," *Jewish Quarterly Review* 68 (1977) 24, 26. Thus R. Horsley, "Bandits, Messiahs, and Longshoreman: Popular Unrest in Galilee Around the Time of Jesus," in *Society of Biblical Literature Seminar Papers* (Atlanta, GA: Scholars Press, 1988) 195, can consider Tiberias more a royal than a Hellenistic city; and S. Applebaum's "Jewish Urban Communities and Greek Influences," in *Judaea in Roman and Hellenistic Times. Historical and Archaeological Essays* (Leiden: Brill, 1989) 44, notes that Sepphoris was a Jewish city with a Greek constitution. Cf. also Applebaum's "Hellenistic Cities of Judaea and Its Vicinity--Some New Aspect," in *The Ancient Historian and His Materials: Essays in Honor of C.E. Stevens on His Seventieth Birthday* (Westmead, Eng.: Gregg International and D. C. Heath, 1975) 64.

[19]A. Tcherikover, "Was Jerusalem a *Polis*?" *Israel Exploration Journal* 14 (1964) 61-78.

[20]For a philological word-study on Josephus' use of *polis*, see Strange, Groh, Longstaff, "Excavations at Sepphoris: The Location and Identification of Shikhin. Part I," 222-25.

[21]R. Hanson, *Tyrian Influence in the Upper Galilee,* Meiron Excavation Project 2 (Cambridge, MA: American Schools of Oriental Research, 1980) 67-69. For the status and administrative responsibilities of Sepphoris and Tiberias as *poleis*, see M. Goodman, *State and Society in Roman Galilee, A.D. 132-212* (Totowa, NJ: Rowman and Allanheld, 1983) 129-30, and S. Cohen, *Josephus in Galilee and Rome* (Leiden: Brill, 1979) 138-39.

[22]For texts and discussion, see D. Urman, *The Golan. A Profile of a Region During the Roman and Byzantine*

Periods, BAR International Series 269 (Oxford: B.A.R., 1985) 22-24.

[23]Based on statistical analyses of pottery recovered in The University of South Florida Excavations at Sepphoris, 1983-1994.

[24]Strange, Longstaff, Groh, "Excavations at Sepphoris: The Location and Identification of Shikhin. Part I," 227.

[25]C. Foss, "The Near Eastern countryside in late antiquity: a review article," in *The Roman and Byzantine Near East: Some Recent Archaeological Research, Journal of Roman Archaeology* Supplemental Series Number 14, (Ann Arbor, MI, 1995) 221. Similarly, Carthage's place as the key city for its hinterland rested not so much on a formal, or legal, charter as on its role as the marketplace and talentbroker for the entire region: G. Schoellgen, *Ecclesia Sordida Zur Frage der sozialen Schichtung frühchristlicher Gemeinden am Beispiel Karthagos zur Zeit Terullianus,* Jahrbuch für Antike und Christentum Ergaenzungsband 12 (Münster, Westfalen: Aschendorffische Verlagsbuchhandlung, 1984) 70-88.

[26]For Herod's winter palace at Jericho, see E. Netzer, "The Winter Palaces of the Judaean Kings at Jericho at the End of the Second Temple Period," and E. Meyers, "Preliminary Report on the Joint Jericho Excavation Project," *Bulletin of the American Schools of Oriental Research* 228 (1977) 1-13 and 15-27, respectively.

[27]J. Strange, "The Art and Archaeology of Judaism," in *Judaism in Late Antiquity. Part One. The Literary and Archaeological Sources*, ed. J. Neusner (Leiden, New York, Köln: E. J. Brill, 1995) 95, makes the same point about the scarcity of such villas in ancient Palestine in discussing the patrician/priestly villa found in the Jewish Quarter. For the patrician housing and tombs, and the destruction caused to them, see *Jerusalem Revealed. Archaeology in the Holy City 1968-1974* (Jerusalem: The Israel Exploration Society, 1975) 17-20, 22-23, 44-47 (a priest's house) 54, 57; B. Mazar, *The Mountain of the Lord* (Garden City, NJ and New York: Doubleday & Co., 1975) 38; N. Avigad, *Archaeological Discoveries in the Jewish Quarter of Jerusalem. Second Temple Period* (Jerusalem: The Israel Exploration Society and The Israel Museum, 1976) 8-14; *Discovering Jerusalem* (Nashville, Camden, New York: Thomas Nelson, 1980) 83-137, and "Jerusalem. Herodian Period," in *The New Encyclopedia of Archaeological Excavations in the Holy Land*, ed. Ephraim Stern (Jerusalem: The Israel Exploration Society & Carta; New York: Simon & Schuster, 1993) 2: 729-36; Y. Shiloh, *Excavations at the City of David, I, 1978-1982. Interim Report of the First Five Seasons*, Qedem 19 (Jerusalem: The Institute of Archaeology, The Hebrew University of Jerusalem, 1984) 6 (Area H).

[28]Cf. E. Meyers, J. Strange, C. Meyers, *Excavations at Ancient Meiron, Upper Galilee, Israel 1971-72, 74-75,* *1977*, Meiron Excavation Project 3 (Cambridge, MA: American Schools of Oriental Research, 1981) 50-76 (The Patrician and Lintel Houses). For the housing at Sepphoris, see n. 45 below. Cf. also the relatively small size of even rural estates in Palestine: Y. Hirschfeld and R. Birger-Calderon, "Early Roman and Byzantine Estates Near Caesarea," *Israel Exploration Journal* 41 (1991) 81-111. The great palaces of the *honestiores* in other provinces form a great contrast to those of Palestine: D. Groh, "The Religion of the Empire: Christianity From Constantine to the Arab Conquest," in *Christianity and Rabbinic Judaism*, ed. H. Shanks (Washington, D.C.: Biblical Archaeology Society, 1992) 279-81.

[29]For recent research on synagogues, see *Ancient Synagogues. Historical Analyses & Archaeological Discovery*, 2 vols., ed. D. Urman and P. Flesher , Studia Post-Biblica 47, 1-2, ed. D. Katz (Leiden, Brill: 1995) especially vol. 1: 51-54.

[30]See M. Avi-Yonah, *The Holy Land From the Persian to the Arab Conquest (536 B.C.-A.D. 640). A Historical Geography*, revised edition (Grand Rapids, MI: Baker Book House, 1977) 200-205; Alon, *The Jews in Their Land*, 152-75.

[31]M. Avi-Yonah, *The Holy Land*, 205-206. For the absence of tensions or differences between the Judaism of Galileans compared to that of other Jewish inhabitants of the Land, see F. Malinowski," Galilean Judaism in the Writings of Flavius Josephus" (Ph. D. Dissertation. Duke University, 1973) 302-303.

[32]D. Sperber, *Roman Palestine 200-400. The Land: Crisis and Change in Agrarian Society as Reflected in Rabbinic Sources* (Ramat-Gan, Israel: Bar-Ilan University, 1978) 96-118. The fate of Palestine's small-holders contrasts markedly with those of Syria in the same time-period: cf. P. Brown, "The Holy Man in Late Antiquity," in *Society and the Holy in Late Antiquity* (Berkeley: University of California Press, 1982) 115. A typical Galilean "holding" was a field, a vineyard, and an olive grove (*Lev. R.* 30. 1) M. Avi-Yonah, *The Holy Land*, 201.

[33]D. Groh, "Jews and Christians in Late Roman Palestine: Towards a New Chronology," *Biblical Archaeologist* 51 (1988) 84.

[34]L. Levine, *Caesarea Under Roman Rule* (Leiden: Brill, 1975) 106-112; Alon, *The Jews in Their Land (loc. cit.).*

[35]See A. Mazar, "Israeli Archaeologists," 120-21; P. King, "American Archaeologists," 33-4; J. Eakens, "The Future of ` Biblical Archaeology'," 448-9, in *Benchmarks In Time And Culture*, ed. J. Drinkard, Jr., G. Mattingly, and J. Miller (Atlanta, GA: Scholars Press, 1988). For the practice of the Khirbet method, see n. 40 below.

[36]Especially important to note here are certain statements and formulations found in the Draft Statement of

the Consultation on the New Testament and Archaeology: "New Testament archaeology seeks to understand the New Testament text through the identification, analysis, and interpretation of the material context in which the New Testament originated.... The relevant time frame for this field of inquiry is generally that of the late Roman Republic and early Roman Empire.... It is generally inappropriate to infer backwards from later data to the first century." The full text of the Draft Statement is available on e-mail (strange@chuma.cas.usf.edu) and grew out of the Consultation on New Testament Archaeology, Feb. 28-29, on the campus of Pepperdine University, under a grant through the American Schools of Oriental Research provided by The Endowment for Biblical Research. The participants included: Dr. James Strange, Dr. John McRay, Dr. Richard Batey, Dr. Richard Oster, Dr. John F. Wilson.

[37] Cf. Eusebius of Caesarea, *H. E.* II. XIV. 1-4; III. XXXII. 8; II. I. 10. and Thomas Sherlock (1678-1761 C.E.), *The Trial of the Witnesses of the Resurrection of Jesus*, in *Deism and Natural Religion. A Sourcebook*, ed. with intro. by E. Waring (New York: Frederick Ungar Publishing, 1967) 105-106.

[38] D. Groh, "The Stratigraphic Chronology of the Galilean Synagogue From the Early Roman Period Through the Early Byzantine Period (ca. 420 C.E.)," in Urman & Flesher, *Ancient Synagogues*, vol. 1: 57-60, 69.

[39] A. Frova, *Scavi di Caesarea Maritima* (Milano: Istituto Lombardo--Accademia di Scienze e Lettere, 1965) 45-53.

[40] For Meiron, see n. 28 above. E. Meyers, C. Meyers, with J. Strange, *Excavations at the Ancient Synagogue of Gush Halav* (Winona Lake, IN: Eisenbraun's for the American Schools of Oriental Research, 1990). E. Meyers, J. Strange, C. Meyers, J. Raynor, "Preliminary Report on the 1980 Excavations at en-Nabratein, Israel," *Bulletin of the American Schools of Oriental Research* 244 (1981) 1-25. Meyers, Strange, Meyers, "Second Preliminary Report on the 1981 Excavations at en-Nabratein, Israel," *Bulletin of the American Schools of Oriental Research* (1982) 33-54.

[41] In Galilee, for example, where we have the greatest precision in dating synagogue structures, cf. the long history of the structures at Khirbet Shema, Meiron, en-Nabratein, Capernaum, etc. For a discussion of their dates, see D. Groh, "Judaism in Upper Galilee at the End of Antiquity: Excavations at Gush Halav and en-Nabratein," in *Studia Patristica XIX, Papers Presented to the Tenth International Conference of Patristics Studies Held in Oxford 1987*, vol. 1, *Historica, Theologica, Gnostica, Biblica et Apocrypha*, ed. E. Livingston (Leuven: Peeters Press, 1989) 62-71. The quotation cited in the text above is from H. Kitchener, "Synagogues of Galilee," *Palestine Exploration Fund Quarterly Statement* 11 (1878) 126.

[42] E. Meyers and J. Strange, *Archaeology, the Rabbis & Early Christianity* (Nashville: Abingdon, 1981) 172.

[43] P. Lampe, *Die stadtrömischen Christen in den ersten beiden Jahrhunderten. Untersuchungen zur Sozialgeschichte*, Wissenschaftliche Untersuchungen zum Neuen Testament, Reihe 2. 18 (Tübingen: J.C.B. Mohr [Paul Siebeck], 1987) 305.

[44] Lampe, *Die stadtrömischen Christen*, 310.

[45] "Synagogue of the Babylonians": *J. Sanhedrin* 10. 28a. "Synagogue of the People of Gophna": *J. Nazir* 6. 56a. For more recent discussions of the history and archaeology of Sepphoris, see: F. Manns, Un centre judeo-chretien important: Sepphoris," in *Essais sur le Judeo-Christianisme*, Studium Biblicum Franciscanum Analecta 12 (Jerusalem: Franciscan Printing Press, 1977) 165-90; E. Meyers, E. Netzer, C. Meyers, "Sepphoris. 'Ornament of All Galilee'," *Biblical Archaeologist* 49 (1986) 4-19; "Artistry in Stone: The Mosaics of Ancient Sepphoris," *Biblical Archaeologist* 50 (1987) 223-31; *Sepphoris* (Winona Lake, IN: Eisenbrauns & Joint Sepphoris Project, 1992); T. Longstaff, "Nazareth and Sepphoris;" D. Groh, "Recent Indications of Hellenization at Ancient Sepphoris (Lower Galilee), Israel," in *The Ancient Eastern Mediterranean*, ed. Eleanor Guralnik (Chicago: The Chicago Society of the Archaeological Institute of America, 1990) 39-41, Figs. 17-22; Z. Weiss, "Sepphoris," in *The New Encyclopedia of Archaeological Excavations in the Holy Land*, ed. E. Stern (Jerusalem: The Israel Exploration Society & Carta; New York: Simon & Schuster, 1993) 4: 1324-28. For the long history of the use of buildings at Sepphoris, see especially J. Strange, "Six Campaigns at Sepphoris: The University of South Florida Excavations, 1983-1989," in *The Galilee in Late Antiquity*, ed. L. Levine (New York and Jerusalem: The Jewish Theological Seminary of America, 1992) 344-349.

[46] Alon, *The Jews in Their Land*, 741.

4

First Century Galilee from Archaeology and from the Texts

James F. Strange
University of South Florida

INTRODUCTION

It is not clear that modern scholarship of Second Temple Judaism and earliest Christianity is always informed by archaeological research. This is true whether the scholar in question is discussing the geography of the First Revolt or of the Galilean background of the gospels.

In view of these perceived deficiencies, the following essay addresses certain lacunae sometimes noted in such works, namely, the local and regional trade networks of lower Galilee, some notes on ethnic identity in the material culture, and some further notes on archaeology and social realities of first century Galilee.

THE LOCAL TRADE NETWORK IN LOWER GALILEE

There was a highly developed, local trade network in Galilee upon which the citizens of Galilee transported goods and services from village to village, to town, to cities, and vice-versa. Parts of this network, in terms of the Roman road system, have been known for some time. However, we have had no archaeological method for detecting pre-Hadrianic roads until recently. Therefore, the classical maps of the Roman road system have presented no traces of any pre-Hadrianic road system.

Earlier in this century scholars worked backwards from the evidence of Roman milestones, but also from the Madaba mosaic map of the sixth century. For example, the early editions of Avi-Yonah's *Map of Roman Palestine* gave us a network that hardly seemed to allow the traveller of the first century access to Galilee.[1] This is true even in the last edition of its successor, *The Holy Land from the Persian to the Arab Conquest (536 BC - AD 640).*[2] In chapter 1 of Part III, "The Roman Road System," Avi-Yonah only shows the pre-Hadrianic roads more or less bracketing Galilee on the west at the Mediterranean coast and on the east beyond the sea of Galilee in the road from Beth Shean-Scythopolis to Damascus. There are no pre-Hadrianic roads that cross the Galilee. Indeed, even after Hadrian, according to Avi-Yonah's map, one could travel from Ptolemais-Acco inland to Tiberias, or one could travel from Legio to Sepphoris. It is no wonder that generations of scholars of the New Testament and of early Judaism grew up believing that the Galilee was more or less inaccessible.

If we turn to a more recent map, "Eretz Israel during the Hellenistic, Roman, and Byzantine Periods," which reflects the extensive knowledge of Israel Roll, we find a marked advance over Avi-Yonah's work, but a similar pattern.[3] On this map, we see that Lower Galilee is

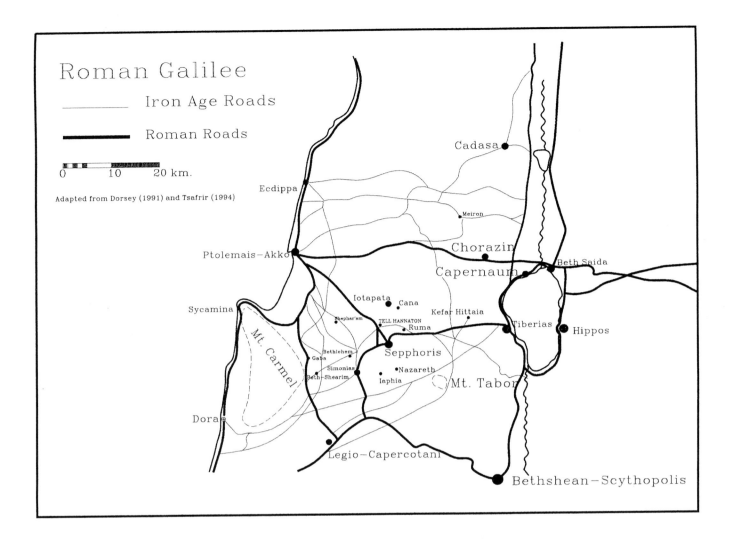

Figure 1: Roman Galilee, showing Iron Age and Roman Roads

outlined as follows: (1) a road which traverses Lower Galilee from Acco to Sepphoris and then to Tiberias. Nine milestones are shown on that map between Acco and Tiberias. (2) From Tiberias a Roman road leads south on the western shores of the Sea of Galilee and then to Scythopolis-Beth Shean. Nine milestones are shown on that map between Tiberias and Scythopolis-Beth Shean. (3) From Scythopolis-Beth Shean, a major road of the second century departs west and a little north to Khirbet Ladd. At Khirbet Ladd, this road turns southwest to Legio-Capercotani in the western Jezreel Valley. In this track of about 33.5 km a total of 15 Roman milestones have been found. (4) A major second century Roman road leads north and a little west from Legio-Capercotani to Acco-Ptolemais. Seven Roman milestones are known from this road, of which about 28 kilometers (ca. 65%) has actually been traced. (5) To the north, virtually in the border between

Upper and Lower Galilee there is now a Roman road that can be followed on the ground west from Bethsaida-Julias about twelve kilometers or nearly nine Roman miles past Chorazin. Roll proposes that this is the road that connects Bethsaida-Julias with Acco-Ptolemais another thirty-nine kilometers to the west.

Another second century Roman road virtually bisects Lower Galilee east and west. This is the road from Legio which leads northeast, then north from Legio to Simonias and then north-east to Sepphoris. Thirteen milestones have been found on that road.

One could safely object that, as far as we know, these are primarily second century C.E. roads. But are we therefore to conclude that first century Galilee possessed no means of communication apart from those that followed the same route as second century military roads?

In 1991, David Dorsey published *The Roads and Highways of Ancient Israel.*[4] Dorsey was interested in Iron Age Israel, not Roman or Byzantine Israel. Dorsey believes he can trace the route in Galilee of the two international highways of the Iron Age (1) on the coast from Yokneam to Acco, then to Achzib and Tyre, and (2) in the interior, from Mt. Tabor to Qarn Hatten (Roman Kefar Hittaia) or a point nearby, then east to the lake Chinnereth, then north to Chinnereth, Hazor, and then Abel-Beth Ma'acah. In Upper Galilee he traces seven "local and lateral roads", most of which run east and west. One of his roads runs from Acco to Tell Keisan and then southeast to Tell Hannaton (Tell Bedawiyye) at the west end of the Beit Netopha Valley, which happens to be the course of the major Roman road from Acco to Sepphoris. In other words, the Romans used a venerable track to move men and material in this area (see Fig. 1: "Roman Galilee", which contains many of Dorsey's Iron Age roads).

From Hannaton, Dorsey traces a road eastward to Rimmon and then on a gentle curve to the south and east towards the south end of the Chinneret. About four miles east of Rimmon the road also forks north to Qarn Hattin (Kefar Hittaia) and east to the lake. Despite this impressive number of Iron Age roads, Iron Age Lower Galilee is traversed by fewer roads on his maps than Upper Galilee, the opposite of what one might predict. But the point is that we have ample pre-Roman period evidence for a road system in Galilee. Even if it is not completely filled in yet, we are not in the position of positing lack of communication in either Galilee.

As a matter of fact, we can deduce by archaeological methods that an extensive, first century C.E. trade network existed that connected the villages, towns, and cities of Lower Galilee, Upper Galilee, the rift, and the Golan. Our evidence is first the tracing of the local production of ordinary pottery vessels from all of Galilee and part of the Golan Heights to ancient Shikhin, Kefar Hananiah, and Nahaf, a small village near Ramah in Upper Galilee. David Adan-Bayewitz has demonstrated by neutron activation analysis that first century pottery vessels manufactured at Kefar Hananiah were transported 24 kilometers as the crow flies from that village to Sepphoris.[5] Furthermore, 75% of the Early Roman common table wares of Sepphoris from the first century C.E. were manufactured at Kefar Hananiah. Another 15% of the common wares of Sepphoris of the first century C.E. and later were manufactured hardly 1.5 kilometers away at the ancient village of Shikhin. It is striking that the majority of the common table wares of Sepphoris were imported from a Galilean village many times further away than the nearby pottery production village of Shikhin. Furthermore, it is not merely that these wares were sold at Sepphoris. By the same neutron activation methods Adan-Bayewitz has demonstrated that these wares were sold

everywhere in Lower Galilee, Upper Galilee, and the western Golan Heights. Evidently, it was not difficult to move the village productions of Kefar Hananiah, Shikhin, and Nahaf as well as other localities to their markets everywhere within the Galilee and to the western villages of the Golan Heights.

If the manufacturers and sellers of pottery vessels transported their products to market with relative ease, then it follows that the same is true for other products. In fact, we may soon be able to demonstrate a similar success with raw glass manufacturing centers and the dispersal of their product. A Hellenistic glass production and distribution center was discovered at Tel Anafa in the east Metullah Valley. A fourth century C.E. glass production village, in western Galilee, Jalame, was given over to glass vessel production.[6] Why not other such centers in the first century C.E.?

The trade network made it possible for villages to devote themselves to a single product. We have already seen that Shikhin, Kefar Hananiah, and Nahaf were given over to the production of pottery vessels. This is both a literary and an archaeological fact. We also know from literary evidence of the fourth century and later that certain localities were still wheat production centers: the plain of Arbela and therefore the town of Arbela (y Peach 20A) and Kefar Hittaia ["Village of Wheat"] hardly five kilometers west and a little south of Arbela, Hukkok ten kilometers west of Capernaum (y Pesachim 27C), and Chorazin (b Menahoth 85A), which is about three kilometers north and a little west of Capernaum. The Jerusalem Talmud distinguishes the wheat of Sepphoris and the wheat of Tiberias (y Baba Kama 6D), which may be a contemporary, i.e., fourth century bit of common knowledge that Tiberias and Sepphoris were central markets for wheat. The same assumption informs other texts (Gen Rabba 79; Midrash Psalms XII, 53A). If we investigate with care, we may find centers for other agricultural products such as olives, barley, wine, fish, herbs, and flax, and for finished products such as cloth, clothing, dye-stuffs, basketry, furniture, breads, perfumes, and metal fittings.

We know from an unpublished archaeological survey that wine presses are to be found on many hilltops in Lower Galilee. These are basically of two types, a simple type that relies upon treading the grapes and a later type that relies upon a screw press as well as treading out the vintage. In general, we take the simple type to be earlier and the screw type to be later, i.e., Byzantine. Pottery and coin finds tend to support this chronological division.

Wine manufacture, storage, and shipment is one of the most important industries of the ancient world, as we know both from texts and from archaeological evidence from the Iron Age forward. We have the names of at least seven villages and cities that were involved in the wine industry in some fashion: Sepphoris, Tiberias, Kefar

Sogane, Sallamin, Acchabaron, Beth Shearim, and Gennesaret (Josephus, *War* 3.3.3; 3.10.8; *M. Menachoth* 8:6, y *Megillah* 72D; *Eccl Raba* 3.3, *M. Kilaim 4:4* [Salmin]; *b Abodah Zarah* 30A [Acchabaron]). Furthermore, the name of the Valley of Beth Ha-Kerem ("House of the Vineyard") and the village of the same name in that valley, implies that wine production was its major industry.

This economic analysis can be extended to include other kinds of agricultural and industrial products, but the point is that an extensive specialized agricultural and industrial production implies a vigorous trade network. That is, there can be little doubt that these products both industrial and agricultural were moved to market on well-defined if not paved roads. The publication of an extensive Iron Age road system, detected and confirmed archaeologically, seems to support the hypothesis that the trade and communication network of the Persian, Hellenistic, and Roman periods in the Galilee is at least equally important and subject to the same kind of archaeological survey and study.

One also needs to consider what some take to be merely anecdotal evidence, but which is the staple of field anthropologists, that is, the ethnographic information given by local informants, the older the better. It is possible to interview old settlers, Arab villagers, and even shepherds, and gain usable information. This was known by Gustav Dalman and others in the nineteenth and early twentieth century. When engaged in surface survey, it is invaluable to ask locals at work in the fields or tending flocks how to get from here to there. They invariably know, and often know that their grandparents took a slightly different route that is no longer usable, perhaps from earthquake damage in 1927 or for some other reason. Such anthropological data enables us to evaluate more judiciously ancient accounts that provide evidence of transportation. Pilgrim texts and traveler's itineraries of the Byzantine to the early Arab periods,[7] give us important evidence about the distance one could comfortably travel in a day on good roads, details of food and drink for the traveler, and questions of security. It is inappropriate, however, uncritically to work backwards from these texts to the first century. What one can determine is that, on the average, the fourth or fifth century traveller walked or rode about 20 Roman miles in one day, though Theophanes of Pelusium sometime between 317 and 324 C.E. traveled 40 Roman miles a day from Gaza to Tyre, presumably on horseback.[8] If we halve the previous figure to allow for poorer roads (perhaps paths) in the first century and walking instead of riding, we still find that a traveller from Sepphoris in the virtual center of Lower Galilee can travel east to the border with Tiberias, to the west to Gaba, to the north to Sogane, and to the south to Tarbenet. This traveler can reach a point anywhere within 240 square Roman miles of territory. Since the map in question gives

us about one village or other locality per six square Roman miles, then the traveler from Sepphoris has access potentially to about 40 villages one short day's journey away. If this seems high, then it must be mentioned that the 1984 Survey of Sepphoris carried out by a team under the direction of the author located several hamlets about 1.5 km from Sepphoris near the major wadis. For example, one kilometer south by southeast of Sepphoris on a small ridge there was found a set of four underground agricultural chambers. Two were originally cut as tombs and re-used for agriculture. Scattered remains on the surface suggested that a small hamlet once stood there.

Furthermore, during the summer of 1994 a team from the University of South Florida Excavations at Sepphoris walked portions of the Legio-Sepphoris road and other possible ancient regional roads around Sepphoris that do not seem to be part of the Roman imperial road system. One archaeological probe was found across a regional road near Sepphoris. This road is not part of the Legio-Sepphoris road, nor is it part of the Acco-Sepphoris road. It seems that we will eventually map scores of local routes that served the local citizens moving short distances.

Furthermore, the second century C.E. road from Legio to Sepphoris was apparently founded on a known but unpaved route that took one from Sepphoris south and a little west toward the west end of the Plain of Jezreel. In other words, the Roman engineers could see a route that took them almost to their destination at Legio. Only the first four miles of this road from Legio to Kh. Ladd seems to have been built *de novo*. Second, clearly an alternative road exists that lead past Sepphoris in the valley just to the west. This road has no milestones and is not mentioned as an alternative route in ancient texts. Yet it can be traced, with a few interruptions from modern agriculture, from a point about three Roman miles west of Sepphoris to its outlet into the Beit Netopha valley west of Shikhin, about one Roman mile northwest of Sepphoris. This road surely connected the major Roman road from Acco to Sepphoris with a cut-off, as it were, which by-passed Sepphoris and allowed the traveler access to the villages and hamlets west of Sepphoris. It seems likely that we will find similar regional roads elsewhere, if we will look. These regional roads were in place long before Hadrian and made up part of the regional network.

The foregoing analysis provides us with a picture of relative ease of travel within the Galilee. Of course, there are topographic difficulties, but few of them are barriers. Furthermore, the Galileans clearly moved their products to market, and there seems to be little reason to continue to insist that Galilee was isolated in any sense. After all, we find finished ceramic products of the first century imported from as far away as Italy in excavations throughout the Galilee.

LOCAL AND ETHNIC IDENTITY IN MATERIAL CULTURE

How would the material culture be distinctive in a way that might elicit comment on the part of a traveler? To put it another way, what would the traveler see in Galilee that he or she did not see elsewhere? What would the traveler NOT see that might seem a striking omission?

There are two answers to this question. First, that which is most visible in any village is architecture. The houses and other buildings form a pattern, which is the village or town lay-out (city planning, if you will). Excavation of about twenty sites in Galilee seems to confirm that ordinary houses are not distinctive in the Galilee. Galilean domestic architecture appears to share in the uniformity of the eastern Mediterranean. We must remember that these are owner-built homes of native materials. Since the most easily available native material is stone, then it follows that stone is what was used. Little attention was given to the exterior except to make the walls unaffected by the weather. This means extensive plastering with a lime and clay plaster, a technique that requires almost daily maintenance during the winter rains.

The point is that the traveller from some other part of the eastern Mediterranean world would not find the Galilean houses distinctive. They were rectilinear in plan, flat-roofed, and used stone and plaster to advantage. From the outside one would see virtually blank walls occasionally pierced by high, small windows and by doorways with wooden doors bolted from the inside.

Furthermore, the layout of the village or town, its city planning, does not seem to be distinctive either. It appears that the Hippodamian grid is not the norm, but villagers imposed a kind of order in the sense of blocks of houses. Probably the steep topography distorted any grid, Hippodamian or otherwise. In any case, there seems to be no reason to conclude that the traveller would be surprised by the city, town, or village planning that he or she might encounter.

The second answer is based on public architecture. The traveller sees many mausolea and memorials on approach to a major city in Turkey, Syria, or Egypt. If this is the norm, then we expect to see many mausolea lining the roads in Galilee. In this way, the traveler has a chance to see the names of the major families of the city or town displayed prominently in epitaphs. The traveller is even able to gauge the relative wealth of the families from the resources put into family mausolea.

But this picture does not seem to pertain, in the main, to the cities and towns of Galilee. Of course, mausolea and public epitaphs are known, but there is nothing to compare to Ephesus or Miletus in Asia Minor or to Timgad in North Africa. This might appear to be a striking omission to a seasoned traveler, who might even inquire about the custom whereby the locals conceal the architecture of death and burial rather than displaying it. This is at least partially true even of the great catacombs of Beth Shearim. First, we do not know that their facades stood on an ancient road. But even if they did, their architecture resembles public architecture for the living. Only the stone doors of the entries might give away their sepulcher nature to the traveller.

On the other hand, additional public buildings in various population centers would not seem to be distinctive. The building elements would be familiar, as would their plans. This is true of basilicas, theaters, city gates, forums or agora, and perhaps also for amphitheaters or circuses and hippodromes, if any Galilean examples of the latter dating from the first century C.E. shall be found.[9] The traveller might find a certain comfort in the fact that public architecture seemed altogether familiar. Public buildings in effect declared that they belonged to the broader Greco-Roman culture.

When the population in the Galilee decorated their buildings, they used recognizable Roman forms. They cut high relief floral and other decorations into the facades which resemble decorations known almost anywhere in the eastern Mediterranean. On the other hand, the low-relief geometric and floral decorations of the Second Temple do not appear in Lower Galilee - yet. The only datum that suggests a local adaption of Greco-Roman norms is that the Corinthian order of columns is not fluted. To reiterate, public buildings would impress the traveller as belonging to the eastern Mediterranean, Greco-Roman world he knew.[10]

But are there cultural artifacts that a traveller might encounter that would surprise him or her? I think the answer to this is that he or she would first have to move into private space, or near-private space, to find such surprises. For example, we all know of those structures which we identify as synagogue buildings at about twenty synagogue sites in Upper and Lower Galilee dated from the middle of the third century C.E. These buildings have one architectural feature that seems to be almost a constant; it is the habit of their builders to place a row of columns between the benches against the walls and the central worship space.

This is a most peculiar arrangement, given the habit of the Romans to place rows of columns behind the backs of gathered spectators or participants in a bouleuterion or in an ecclesiasterion, or even in a theater. The simplest explanation for why this space was organized in such a unique fashion is that the builders were copying a similar arrangement seen in the Second Temple in Jerusalem.

Josephus describes the inner courts of the temple as adorned with colonnades or cloisters. Thus the Court of Women, the Court of Israel, and the Court of the Priests would all present this feature. For example, Josephus explains that the Court of Women featured its own covered porches or cloisters. "The western part of this court [of women] had no gate at all, but the wall was built entire on that side; but then the cloisters which were between the gates, extended from the wall inward, before the chambers; for they were supported by very fine and large pillars. These cloisters were single, and, except in their magnitude, were no way inferior to those of the lower court (*War* 5.5.2)

Josephus does not describe the Court of Israel in detail except to note that there is a low wall or barrier one cubit high to separate the Court of the Priests from the people (*War* 5.5.7). However, it is reasonable to infer that it too was adorned with a colonnaded portico all around.[11] If so, then as one watched the sacred proceedings in the Court of the Priests from the vantage of the Court of Israel, one would be watching between columns (see figure 2: Plan of the Second Temple Showing Cloisters and Colonnaded Spaces).

One indicator that such a feature in synagogue buildings is to be interpreted as a re-presentation of sacred space in the Second Temple is its striking omission from several published Samaritan synagogues. This is true of at least four of the recently published synagogues - albeit of the fourth century and later - excavated within sixteen kilometers of Mt. Gerizim.[12]

Even if one objects that the Galilean synagogue buildings are third or fourth century or even later, then it must be pointed out that this architectural feature is also found in the putative first-century synagogues of Magdala-Taricheae and Capernaum, and certainly in Gamla across the lake. It also appears in the second century C.E. synagogue at Nabratein. This feature is only recognizable from inside the building. The exterior of the building would resemble Roman buildings of the period anywhere else they were seen.

This is even the case for what we identify with some controversy as Jewish ritual baths beneath the floors of houses or nearby at Sepphoris, Jotapata, Khirbet Shema, Meiron, and other Galilean sites. It would be impossible in the main for our hypothetical traveller to see one of these ritual baths, if indeed that is what they are, unless he was invited into private space. The same analysis pertains to Jewish tomb art and tomb contents. Our traveller might see a tomb facade outside some ancient city and may not be surprised. Most of the tombs identified as Jewish have blank facades or the facade is decorated with grape tendrils, Doric or Corinthian columns, or other familiar motifs. The traveller might wonder why there are no depictions of deities familiar from the Greco-Roman pantheon, depending on how strange this omission may have seemed.

Jewish tomb art and tomb inscriptions would, in the main, be encountered inside the tomb. But this is private

space, and it is hard to see why a law-abiding traveller would be entering such private space on his or her travels.

A unique item in the material culture of the Early Roman Jewish world was a class of soft, white stone vessels which appear in no less than sixty-five sites all over ancient Palestine. At least fourteen of these sites are in Upper and Lower Galilee (Gush Halav, Nabratein, Meiron, Kefar Hananiah, Capernaum, Yodfat, Jotapata, Ibelin, Kefar Kenna, Sepphoris, Reina, Nazareth, Bethlehem of Galilee, Migdal Ha-Emeq, and Tiberias). In fact, a site for the manufacture of these vessels has been found at Reina, about six kilometers north of Nazareth.[13] These vessels were evidently designed to meet the requirements of laws of purity. They seem to be distinctively Jewish, as they only superficially resemble the marble vessels well known in the Roman world. They are both hand-made and made by turning on a lathe.

Among the items hand-made from soft stone are those vessels commonly called "measuring cups" with one and sometimes two handles, and a square bowl with ledge handles under the rims. Others which were turned on a lathe include large, barrel-shaped vessels with a pedestal base and no handles and small cups or chalices with no handles. The large, lathe-turned vessels play a role in the pericope of the turning of water into wine at Cana of Galilee in John 2:6. It is interesting that this pericope is set in a Galilean site.[14]

We find these vessels in our excavations in Galilee. They appear only in Early Roman, even first century C.E., contexts. During the 1994 excavations at Sepphoris conducted by The University of South Florida Excavations at Sepphoris, we found many fragments of the lathe-turned vessels in first century contexts, and sometimes well-worn in later contexts (see figure 3).

The point of this recitation is that our hypothetical traveller of the first century would likely and mainly encounter this marker of Jewish material culture in private space. The public space where he or she might see them would be in market stalls where they were sold as an item of specialty manufacture. Thus, the traveller may not notice that there is a unique set of items in Jewish Galilee, unless he or she visits a market on market day and unless someone is selling them in that market.

Speaking of markets, and therefore of economics and the medium of exchange, it has been known for some time that the motifs on Jewish coins are, in the main, familiar to a non-Jewish audience. Therefore the usual run of coins that our traveller might handle in the towns and villages of Galilee would likely appear, more or less, ordinary to him or her. This is certainly true of the city coins of Tiberias, which honor the emperor Tiberius and feature his portrait nearly from the beginnings of minting coins in that Galilean city.[15] On the other hand, the coins of Herod Antipas, the Ethnarch of Galilee and of Perea, and the city

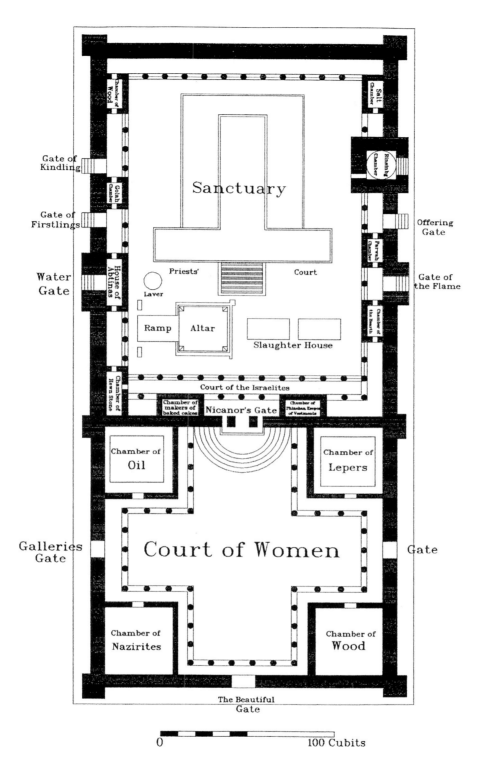

Adapted from the Atlas of Israel, 1970.

by James F. Strange, 1995

Figure 2: Plan of the Second Temple showing Colonnades and Cloisters

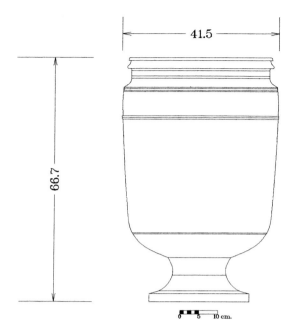

Figure 3: A Chalk Stone Vessel found in Jerusalem.
Height and diameter given in centimeters.

coins of Sepphoris and Tiberias minted by Antipas, might surprise the traveller because of the lack of a ruler's portrait on their obverse.[16] There is both familiarity and unfamiliarity in the coinage of ancient Palestine, though this is true of the entire empire.

ARCHAEOLOGY AND SOCIAL REALITIES OF FIRST CENTURY GALILEE

It was an accidental discovery at Hefzibah in the Beth Shean Valley (the eastern extension of the Jezreel) that disclosed for us a set of Greek inscriptions recording for posterity the correspondence between Antiochus III "the Great" (223-187 B.C.E.), the Seleucid Greek ruler, and a certain Ptolemaios, the *strategos* or local owner and governor of a huge estate near Beth Shean. The *strategos* was de facto, if not de jure, a despot or ruler of his estate, which included villages. It seems that the villagers worked his land and lived upon it in villages which he owned in fee simple.[17]

This Ptolemaios, then, was one of the first documented estate owners in Galilee. Such land ownership is well known in Josephus and in the New Testament, and attests to a social reality in which numbers of farmers work and live upon the lands of wealthy owners. Archaeological

surveys of the Galilee and other regions of ancient Palestine confirm that large farmhouses, presumably of wealthy land owners, dot the landscape.[18] Golomb and Kedar, in their work on ancient Galilean agriculture, have deduced five patterns of land use: strip lynchets, (geometric) enclosures, terraces, dams, and alluvial lands.[19] They give the size of enclosures as ranging from one to fifteen acres, but averaging four acres. They further suggest that this was a form of centuriation;[20] however, it is impossible to deduce which periods their classifications cover.

It is premature to make firm estimates of how much of the land was in the hands of wealthy landowners, but it is enough to be suggestive about the unfolding of social reality in the first century C.E.

From archaeological surveys in Galilee and Samaria it is possible to posit another dimension of social reality. There may be more farmers on small plots of land than those plots will support for a full year. If so, then the farmer will have to hire out to someone else at least part of the year as an agricultural laborer or as a skilled worker.

Golomb and Kedar estimate that four acres is the average size of an enclosure. If this describes the Roman period, then it may be a few acres short to support a family of six. Fiensey has calculated that a farm of 17.4 acres planted in wheat could support a family of six for one year after taxes and with one-half the field lying fallow, "a standard practice in the ancient world."[21] Other calculations have ranged from 6 to 16.8 acres as a minimum requirement.[22] The average of these estimates is 11.4 acres. But Borowski has estimated that an Iron Age farmer would leave fallow only one-seventh of his land each year in a rotation system.[23] If so, and if this practice applies to Galilee in the Roman period (a period of high crop yields according to Sperber),[24] it would reduce Fiensey's calculation of what is required to support a family of six from 17.4 acres to 10 acres. It would reduce the average of other calculations mentioned above from 11.4 acres to 6.5 acres.

This revision brings us closer to an actual observed and calculated figure from Samaria. Dar's survey of Khirbet Buraq in Samaria has suggested that 70 families farmed 445 acres, which gives us 6.3 acres per family. This plot would feed a family of six for only four months according to Fiensey, but for almost a year if we correct Fiensey's calculations with Borowski's estimates of the percentage that lies fallow. If these calculations are only approximate, they still suggest that the small land owner sometimes had to work for wages for someone else at least part of the time, or else develop a specialty on the side which could be marketed. Thus the simple designation "peasant" for this social stratum is misleading, since these people appear to have also been artisans and small entrepreneurs as well as tenants and agricultural laborers. This fact of life appears to have forced a diversification in social roles that remains largely unrecognized in modern scholarship.

Recent research into the number of people that the land can sustain with ancient agricultural methods seems to suggest that we will have to revise downwards our previous population estimates. This is true of the figures gathered by Fiensey, in the surveys of certain scholars in Israel, and of the researches of scholars in the U.S.A. and in Europe. It is difficult to say as yet what this might mean for our understanding of the New Testament and other ancient Jewish literature, but it might change our interpretation of the word "crowd" in the New Testament. It may also force us to move the decimal point to the left when interpreting Josephus' numbers.

Finally, let us turn our attention to the presence of Rome and especially the military. It seems to have been the military units that transmitted Roman cultural norms and symbols most rapidly and most immediately. It was Roman legions not engaged in battle who built roads, bridges, and even some architectural entities, such as aqueducts. The Roman legions lived off the land, and the Roman ideal of farming the land resulted in Roman officers renting farms, vineyards, and orchards in the places of their assignment.

But the main archaeological evidence for the Roman military presence in Galilee is post-Second Revolt. This evidence is in the form of Roman milestones, of which the earliest inscribed examples are Hadrianic and in Latin. The second evidence is epitaphs for Roman soldiers in Greek, which are also post-Hadrianic. The third is roof tiles of the Sixth Roman legion, which appeared to have its prime camp at Legio, but which may have had its roof tiles manufactured elsewhere in lower Galilee, specifically at Kefar Hananiah. Are we to conclude that there were really no Roman soldiers in the Galilee? It does not follow that there were *no* soldiers in Roman Galilee. If it is true that Gabinius set up a *synedrion* at Sepphoris in Galilee in 55 B.C.E. (Josephus, *Antiquities* 14.5.4; *War* I.8.5), were its judgments enforced out of sheer respect for the aristocracy which it represented? We do not yet have an early first century Latin inscription from the Galilee, such as the famous Pontius Pilatus inscription from Caesarea, but when soldier's epitaphs are found in Galilee, they are likely to be in Greek. The early epitaphs of Roman soldiers in Syria are in Greek.

CONCLUSIONS

It seems clear that archaeological evidence supports a picture of the Galilee that participates more or less completely in the Roman world of its day in public space. A trade network all the way to the level of the village supports the movement of people, goods, and services in the region. This does not tell us anything yet about private attitudes or whether the local citizenry was glad or sad about Rome's presence, whether they were rebellious or conforming. It only tells us that they played by Rome's cultural rules. They were recognizably part of the Roman empire such that our hypothetical traveler knew where he or she was in the social world we call the Roman empire.

On the other hand, it is also true that we can detect certain items of Jewish identity in private space. This seems to be the place where we should look for Jewish practice, Jewish material culture, and, therefore, recognizable Jewish values and attitudes. As archaeologists refine their methods and above all their means of interpretation of the meaning of their finds, it will be possible to construct ever more accurately this world and leave behind the speculations of those uninformed by this evidence.

NOTES

[1]M. Avi-Yonah, "Map of Roman Palestine," *QDAP* 5 (1936) 139-93 and *Map of Roman Palestine*, second rev. ed. (London, 1940).

[2]M. Avi-Yonah, *The Holy Land from the Persian to the Arab Conquest (536 BC- AD 640)*, rev. A. Rainey and C. Pfeiffer (Grand Rapids: Baker Book House, 1977).

[3]See, Y. Tsafrir and L. Di Segni with I. Roll, Map, "Eretz Israel during the Hellenistic, Roman and Byzantine

Period, 1:250,000," (Jerusalem: Israel Academy of Sciences and Humanities, 1993) and Y. Tsafrir, L. Di Segni, and J. Green, *Tabula Imperii Romani: Iudea, Palestina: Eretz Israel in the Hellenistic, Roman and Byzantine Periods. Maps and Gazetteer.* (Jerusalem: Israel Academy of Sciences and Humanities, 1994).

[4]D. Dorsey, *The Roads and Highways of Ancient Israel* (Baltimore: Johns Hopkins University Press, 1991).

[5]D. Adan-Bayewitz, *Common Pottery in Roman Galilee: A Study in Local Trade* (Ramat Gan: Bar-Ilan University Press, 1993).

[6]*Excavations at Jalame: Site of a Glass Factory in Later Roman Palestine.* ed. G. Weinberg (Columbia: University of Missouri Press, 1988). For Tel Anafa see *The New Encyclopedia of Archaeological Excavations in the Holy Land*, ed. E. Stern (Jerusalem: The Israel Exploration Society and Carta, 1993) 1: 58-61 and Sharon Herbert, *Tel Anafa I* (Ann Arbor, MI: Kelsey Museum, 1994.

[7]See J. Wilkinson, *Jerusalem Pilgrims Before the Crusades.* (Warminster: Aris and Phillips, Ltd., 1977) and L. Casson, *Travel in the Ancient World* (Baltimore: Johns Hopkins University Press, 1994).

[8]Casson, *Travel*, 191.

[9]A. Segal, *Theatres in Roman Palestine and Provincia Arabia.* (Leiden: E.J. Brill, 1995).

[10]The decorative, architectural elements found so far in the excavations at Sepphoris, Tiberias, and the Upper Galilee are in the main in high relief. But even elements in low relief do not resemble the floral and geometric, low-relief elements of Jerusalem.

[11]See J. Hurlbut and J. Vincent, *Bible Atlas: A Manual of Biblical Geography and History,* rev. ed. (Chicago: Rand, McNally and Co., 1910), 141 and M. Avi-Yonah, *The Holy Land*, 218, fig. 56.

[12]Y. Magen, "Samaritan Synagogues," in *Early Christianity in Context: Monuments and Documents,* eds. F. Manns and E. Alliata (Jerusalem: Studium Biblicum Franciscum, 1993) 38: 193-227.

[13]Y. Magen, *'Purity Broke Out in Israel:' Stone Vessels in the Late Second Temple Period* (Haifa: University of Haifa, 1994).

[14]R. Deines, *Jüdische Steingefasse und pharisäische Frömmigkeit: Ein archäologisch-historischer Beitrag zum Verstandis von Joh 2,6 und der jüdischen Reinsheitshalacha zur Zeit Jesu* (Tübingen: Mohr-Siebeck, 1993).

[15]M. Rosenberger, *City Coins of Palestine* (The Rosenberger Israel Collection). Vol. III (Jerusalem.: M. Rosenberger, 1977).

[16]See Rosenberger, *City Coins of Palestine*, 60, Y. Meshorer, *Ancient Jewish Coinage. Vol II: Herod the Great through Bar Cochba* (New York: Amphora Books, 1982), 35-41, 242-3, 279, pl. 6 and Y. Meshorer, "Ancient

Jewish Coinage Addendum, I," *The Israel Numismatic Journal* 11 (1990-91) 108, pl. 25.

[17]W. Landau, "A Greek Inscription Found Near Hefzibah," *Israel Exploration Journal* 11 (1961) 54-70.

[18]See S. Applebaum, "Economic Life in Palestine," in *The Jewish People in the First Century. Compendia Rerum Iudaicarum.* The survey comes out of S. Dar, *Landscape and Pattern: An archaeological survey of Samaria 800 BCE - 636 C.E. Oxford: BAR, 1986.*

[19]B. Golomb and Y. Kedar, "Ancient Agriculture in the Galilee Mountains," *Israel Exploration Journal* 21 (1971) 136-40.

[20]Ibid., 138.

[21]D. Fiensey, *The Social History of Palestine in the Herodian Period: The Land is Mine.* (Lewiston: Edwin Mellen Press, 1991) 94.

[22]See the table in Fiensey, *The Social History*, 94.

[23]O. Borowski, *Agriculture in Iron Age Israel* (Winona Lake: Eisenbrauns, 1987).

[24]D. Sperber, *Roman Palestine 200-400: The Land.* Bar-Ilan Studies in Near Eastern Languages and Culture (Ramat-Gan: Bar-Ilan University, 1978) 30-44.

5

Town and Country Once More: The Case of Roman Galilee

Sean Freyne
University of Dublin, Trinity College

The work of Professor James Strange has contributed greatly to our knowledge of first-century Galilee, not just as a member of the Meiron Expedition investigating the synagogues of Upper Galilee, but more recently for his ongoing work at Sepphoris. His publication[1] on the location of Shikhin (probably to be identified with Asochis of Josephus) raises the important question of town and country, a question that is crucial for understanding Greco-Roman society. For those interested in the historical Jesus and his movement this question has moved center stage, raising issues about the background of Jesus' movement and message as well as the currency of Cynic ideas in the Galilee. All of these questions are currently under continuous scrutiny with different scholars adopting different stances. The vexed question of the choice and use of sociological models is also part of the debate. Such debate makes Galilean studies today a veritable showcase of the best of contemporary academic investigation of ancient society, calling on the diverse skills of literary, archaeological, linguistic and sociological expertise of the various clienteles interested in the Galilee of the Roman period.

Within this veritable barrage of often conflicting voices, James Strange's work has, for me, always sounded a note of good sense, bringing to his undoubted skills as a field archaeologist a real understanding of life as it was lived within the everyday experience of people struggling to cope with their environment. This has inevitably meant moving away from main street Sepphoris, and thinking seriously about how life as it was lived in that quarter impacted on the wider environment of the many villages/towns whose remains, like those of Shikhin, dot the landscape of Lower Galilee.

This same topic has also been of central concern to my own study of the Galilee. It was difficult to move beyond fairly general observations when working mainly with literary sources, however, since the texts themselves only illuminated those aspects of the society that interested their authors, and then always with particular interests in view. The terminology employed by different authors admittedly raised interesting questions: why does Mark (1:38) use the rare *komopoleis* on one occasion to describe locations visited by Jesus? Both Luke and Josephus appear to have a highly flexible use of the term *polis*, the former calling such places as Nazareth and Caphernaum by that designation (Lk 1:26; 4:31), and the latter applying it to a place which he elsewhere calls *komes* (Josephus, *War* 3:129; *Vita* 395). The Jewish sources seem to have a more varied terminology - *giriah*, *'ir*, *kefar*, *'ayarah*.[2] Does this mean that the Jewish mode of settlement was different from other areas of Greco-Roman society, and if so what were the factors that brought that about?

IN SEARCH OF A MODEL

In an earlier book, I distinguished two phases of urbanization with very different impact on Galilean life, because in my view they were very different in character.[3] The first phase, that of the Ptolemaic/Seleucid period, took place in the outer circle or *galil* and was thoroughly Greek in its inspiration and intention; the second was Herodian and touched the interior of Galilee itself in the cities of Sepphoris and Tiberias. While I still maintain the difference between these two phases, archaeological evidence now indicates another element in the settlement of Galilee, namely, those places which can be attributed to the Hasmonean expansion in the late Hellenistic period, i.e. late second and early first century BCE. These foundations arguably had a more profound and lasting impact on the overall ethos of Galilee than had either of the other two phases. At least, as we shall see, that is one of the major issues at stake in this debate.

My first book, which was completed in 1978, did not include the important survey of Galilee and the Golan of the Meiron Excavation Project. That the survey had not been published at the point of the writing of my book is a fact frequently overlooked by those who criticize me for ignoring the evidence produced by the survey.[4] In retrospect what shaped my thinking most profoundly, if implicitly, was my experience of growing up in the rural West of Ireland. The area was dotted with towns of various sizes and importance, ranging from villages (usually a number of dwellings grouped around a church and or a school) to larger market and county towns, with one or two places that could have been described as cities. This environment gave me a life-long appreciation of the subtle, but real, differences that can exist between various villages despite their proximity, with the next hill, stream or valley providing the social as well as the physical boundary between various townlands. A sense of local pride, ranging from esteem earned through displays of prowess by certain individuals (even in faction fighting among different villages) to acquired skills, manual or otherwise (such as those of the *seanacha,* or story-teller), gave rise to differentiation between villages, even though all shared a sense of relative deprivation by comparison with the inhabitants of even the medium sized towns around. These were visited on market-day, for sports or other events, but there was always a sense of reserve, even suspicion among the peasants with regard to the townspeople. The social boundaries between one village and another arose and were maintained for apparently intangible reasons to do with loyalties expressed at times of political or physical crises (e.g., the bitter, post-revolution civil war of 1919-21, or the great famine of the last century), which were deeply engrained in the folk memory. Other factors such as economic stratification in terms of the quality of land owned or blood relations all played their part in this highly complex network of social relations. Despite these very real divisions the peasants had a shared sense of solidarity; if peasants are what we must call them. They maintained their rootedness to the land, even to unproductive holdings, often eking out a meager existence through subsistence farming of their own few acres, combined with seasonal labor through harvesting as hired workers on larger estates elsewhere, mostly in England. In particular, I was and am impressed by the ways in which through song, story and seasonal rituals, they were able to maintain their social and cultural identity and ancestral values, even when, for extraneous reasons, the tongue of the colonizer had become the *lingua franca.* It was this pattern of cultural resistance, despite the blandishments of outside influences that gave rise to the description of 'the bog Irish,' with their strong group and weak grid identity[5].

Far from disqualifying my hunches about Galilee, I now realize that I was operating with an implicit model that was just as feasible as any other drawn from Mediterranean cultures today in terms of a working hypothesis for discussing Galilean life. All that was missing was a critical apparatus to test the resulting picture in terms of its 'fit' with historical Galilee and, in particular, the archaeological and literary evidence pertaining to the region. In a subsequent publication I applied a model drawn from the social sciences that dealt with the cultural role of cities to the Herodian foundations of Sepphoris and Tiberias. There I relied on the literary evidence from Josephus and the Gospels.[6] This model was based on the well-known distinction of The Chicago School between the Great Tradition and the Little Tradition. The article suggests that, with respect to their hinterlands, cities can function either orthogenetically, that is, supportive of the local folk tradition, or heterogenetically, namely, in a manner that is hostile to it. According to the model, these different types of cities give rise to different kinds of personnel who are perceived differently by the indigenous folk population.[7] The model although an 'ideal type,' seemed suitable for sorting out the cultural roles of the Herodian foundations in Galilee. The conclusion was that both Sepphoris and Tiberias functioned heterogenetically as far as Galilean peasants were concerned, not because they were gentile enclaves in a Jewish hinterland (and in this they differed markedly from the Greek cities surrounding Galilee), but because, as Herodian centres, they represented an intrusion to a more traditional way of life, by a new type of Hellenised (or Romanised) Jew who was prepared to collaborate with an alien Roman system as its power-brokers.

AN URBAN OVERLAY?

This picture is undoubtedly overdrawn, as are all pictures based on ideal types. There is also the clear bias of Josephus' account to be considered and evaluated. Yet, the question remains as to the possible truth of such a depiction. It is here that James Strange's interest in urban/rural relations, from an archaeological point of view, has provided a challenge for testing, refining or rejecting previous positions. In a recent article that is highly pertinent to the present discussion he speaks of an urban overlay as a way to describe the clear signs of Roman imperial presence, which, at least on the basis of Sepphoris, reached down to the domestic level of Jewish life in the city.[8] Comparisons with other important sites such as Caesarea Maritima, Ptolemaios/Acco and Scythopolis/Beth Shean suggest to Strange that, in its architectural remains, Sepphoris was part of a wider pattern in which the city, conceived as model, can be seen as 'a conceptual artefact' of the culture as a whole. Through its buildings and other visual expressions it represents the way in which people living in that place, 'the locals', viewed the world and gave expression to those views in stone. This architectural symbolism can then be used as a gauge or yardstick to measure the degree to which Roman ideas had blended together to make a comprehensive statement within the larger framework of Roman imperial ideology, as mediated within Galilee by Herod Antipas.

In developing his argument Strange acknowledges the possible clash of Roman and Jewish cultures and the ways in which this will express itself through the different art and architectural forms: theatre, baths, hippodrome, aqueduct for the Romans and temple and synagogue for the Jews. Nevertheless, he does not see any serious conflict between the two; 'strangeness' inhibiting the graft between them is the nearest he comes to posting any real opposition. It is a matter of focusing or centering of the different symbolic expressions rather than establishing any rigid boundaries between them. Insofar as it is permissible to speak of boundaries, it is the symbolically neutral zone where forms and symbols have a more generalized meaning and are not specific to either culture. This absence of cultural conflict between Roman and Jewish cultures in Galilee was because hellenism had prepared the way for both, on the one hand providing the Romans with a suitable repertoire of symbols for its purposes, and, on the other, preparing the Jewish culture for its encounter with Rome. The process of grafting that can be perceived in Sepphoris is not confined to the city but extends well outside that setting so that it is possible to detect it in the earliest strata of the Jesus tradition, as these are represented in Q and Mark, where a strong urban overlay can also be detected in the imagery and language. Strange's account differs most pointedly from mine in that (1) he sees a real

similarity between Sepphoris and other Greco-Roman towns in Palestine, and (2) he posits a continuity between Sepphoris and the rest of Galilee in the material culture and its symbolic impact. He understands my work as espousing an isolationist Galilee, one that being free of Hellenisation is also free of urbanization, since the two go hand in hand.[9] Leaving aside the possibility that we are both misreading each other, how might one adjudicate between the two accounts and methodologically, where is the difference between us located?

TAKING A CUE FROM THE LITERARY EVIDENCE

A first answer is that we both have different starting points, he with the archaeological remains and I with the literary texts. In itself, this should not lead to such a different assessment of the overall picture provided each is open to the other discipline, as would seem to be the case. Another difference concerns the time spans within which each discipline operates. Archaeologists speak of early, middle and late Roman periods, each having as much as 100 years duration, which is not sufficiently precise for the historian seeking to differentiate between the period of Jesus in the thirties and Mark's reporting of this in the sixties. In this regard, it is noteworthy that Strange and Eric Meyers differ in their dating of the theatre at Sepphoris, the former attributing it to the period of Antipas and the latter to later in the first century, possibly even post-70.[10] This is not to suggest that the two disciplines should not seek to dialogue with each other. The temptation is for each to seek a complete picture (insofar as this is ever attainable) without having all the pieces in place or all the perspectives of the texts fully examined and articulated. Some interaction and mutual correction should be possible, even as the separate tasks are being conducted. How might such a critical co-relation be achieved?

Starting from the literary end, too little attention has been given to what can be learned from the Jewish sources, especially Mishnah and Tosefta. The fact that in their present form these are late compilations has made scholars cautious in using them for pre-70 historical reconstruction, especially following the strictures of Jacob Neusner about uncritical use by Jewish and Christian scholars of rabbinical sources.[11] When all due allowance is made for Neusner's pioneering work in deciphering the individual statement of each of these works understood as a literary production, there is no good reason for not taking seriously their description of social realia as being actual, rather than fictional, especially in regards to the size and nature of settlements. The designations *giriah*, *'ir*, *'ayarah* and *kefar*, were inherited, not invented by the Tannaim, no matter how much they used them to exploit various halakoth dealing with spatial matters.[12] A more realistic starting point for archaeologists and literary historians alike would be to accept that both the New Testament and Josephus are limited to available Greek terminology, leaving us to fit various types and sizes of settlements into one of two possible categories - city or village - on the basis of such disparate criteria as size, capacity for defense, population numbers, administrative role, etc. In our post-industrial world, a village has the slightly pejorative connotation of a place that did not have the resources or capacity to 'make it' to the status of town, and is, therefore, backward, primitive and uncultured.

This picture of the village is quite inappropriate in terms of a pre-industrial society. According to *Tosefta* Makot 3, 8 an *'ayarah* was not constructed like the large cities (*'ir*) or the small villages (*kefar*), but as cities of medium size. This distinction seems to be echoed by Josephus when on occasion he speaks of 'a village, not inferior in size to a city' (Josephus, *Antiquities* 17: 23 - Batanea and 20:130 - Lydda),and possibly also in Mark's *komopolis*. Elsewhere, *Tosefta* Eruvin (4.4f) speaks of different plans for *'irot:* rectangle, circle, semi-circle, gamma shaped, long on one side and short on the other. While this passage may have been produced in order to work out all possible permutations for fulfilling Shabbat requirements, the fact that such patterns have been detected at various excavated sites suggests that the description has basis in reality and is not a purely fictional creation. Many aspects of life within the *'irot* can be gleaned from other references: a distinction is made between private and public buildings (*T. Shev.* 8:2; Bab.Kam. 4:3; Ned. 5:5); fortification was important (*T. Arak.* 5:12; Eruv. 10:30); the location of various installations such as oil presses and tanneries as well as the burial place is stipulated (*T. Bab. Bat.* 2:8-9; 4:7-8). In addition, threshing floors, granaries and wells are all mentioned.

Even this cursory glance at village life from the literary texts suggests a place of some self-sufficiency, as far as domestic and communal life was concerned. It is a picture that has been corroborated by many different surveys and excavations at various Jewish sites both in Galilee - Meiron, Kh. Shema, Nabratein,[13] Chorazin,[14] and Kfar Hananiah[15] - and in the Golan - Qatzrin,[16] Kfar Naffakh, Na'aran, Farj and Er Ramthaniyye.[17] Not dissimilar patterns of village life have been reported from the Hauran (Auranitis) for the Hellenistic and Roman periods.[18]

Unfortunately archaeology in Egypt has, for various reasons, not been systematically conducted, even in the larger urban sites, such is the embarrassment of riches in papyri, temples, and tombs. There is, however, some information from the Fayum region which dates from the early Hellenistic period when many of the villages originated as settlements for Greek and Macedonian military colonizers, and so would correspond with the expansion of settlements in Galilee in the Hellenistic period. The papyri are invaluable in terms of understanding the organization and self-sufficiency of village life. Papyri from Karanis (one of the few Egyptian villages excavated in any detail) suggest that the inhabitants of these villages were farmers who owned their own plots of ground and the buildings, their houses, and such things as granaries, threshing floors, bakeries, potteries and a pigeonhouse. Almost half of those which could be estimated on the basis of tax records owned plots of between 10 and 39 arouras, i.e. subsistence or just above subsistence levels, and a small percentage owned larger plots of above 70 arouras requiring slave or hired labor in order to run the farm. Activities other than farming were largely of the service variety. Second century Karanis had an oil maker, a baker, retailers of wine, fish and vegetables, though these also owned land. There were also 16 people engaged in the fabric industry, everything from carding and weaving to sack-making. There is very little evidence of any production of luxury items or trades related to care of the body. As regards local government, because of the nature of the evidence one could easily get the impression of a highly bureaucratic system, but that would be to overdraw the picture since there is a striking absence of any imperial official. Nevertheless, the evidence suggests a well ordered community life, with the ubiquitous tax-collectors predominating. The *komarchs* had considerable powers, not just in terms of naming their own successors but also in distributing the various liturgies to be performed on behalf of the community, with almost half of the male population involved in some kind of public duty. There is also evidence of inter-village movement on several levels, not least through inter-marriage, and movement outside the district was not infrequent, mainly for official reasons when a visit to the nome capital was called for.[19]

While this picture is based on the specific conditions of fourth century CE Egypt and due allowance has to be made for the many changes that had occurred in imperial policy and government, nevertheless, many elements are recognizable in terms of what we know of first-century Palestinian village life, not least from the recently published Babatha archive.[20] If anything the picture of the village life from an earlier period shows a greater degree of prosperity and diversity of activity.[21] In the end, what may have distinguished village life (at least in the *'ayarot* as distinct from the *kefarim*) was the relationship to the land and with it the maintenance of traditional values. Insofar as we can judge, the Herodian land-policy did not favor the large estates on the basis of the evidence both from Batanea and Gaba (Josephus, *Antiquities,* 15:294; 17:24). This meant that side by side with the propagation of imperial ideology in the founding of Greek-style cities at carefully chosen sites other patterns of settlement and land distribution were also maintained, that did not disrupt earlier colonizing patterns established both by the

Hellenistic monarchies and the Hasmoneans. Sepphoris and Tiberias seem to have fallen somewhere between these two, because of the ambitions of Antipas, but also because of the limitations of his political position.

JUDAISATION OR URBANISATION?

This brings us back to Strange's urban overlay in Galilee and how we are to assess its symbolic significance. If the suggestion that the majority of the settlements of the Galilee are better understood by the Hebrew designation *'aryah* rather than the Greek *polis* or *kome*, then the question of the urbanisation of Galilee becomes the question of its judaisation, not, at least in the first instance that of its hellenisation! As is well known, this is a controversial issue with various views supported as much on the basis of the authority of modern scholarship as on that of the examination of hard evidence. Suggestions of the remnants of the old Israelite population,[22] the forced circumcision of the Itureans[23] or Hasmonean colonization, have all had their supporters. Originally, I supported Alt's position and may have consequently 'ruralised" Galilee more than was warranted, since my own experiences suggested that it was among such people living in a peasant ethos that folk memories, such as one might associate with an old Israelite presence continuing through the centuries, endured longer. The archaeological evidence, however, seems to point to the Hasmonean expansion/conquest as the most likely hypothesis. The Meiron Expedition Survey of a limited number of sites postulated a rapid expansion in the late Hellenistic period for Upper Galilee, within a hitherto sparsely populated area. However, preliminary indications of the Archaeological Survey of Israel, much more far reaching in scope, suggests a slightly different profile of a gradual upward curve in the number of settlements - from 93 in Hellenistic times to 138 in the Roman period to 162 in Byzantine times.[24] There are two further pertinent conclusions emerging from this survey: on the one hand, the abandonment of certain Hellenistic sites (e.g.. Har Mizpe Yamim, where clear signs of pagan worship were discovered),[25] and the emergence of new settlements, not previously inhabited, which on the basis of the coin finds, appear to be Hasmonean foundations. All students of Galilee in antiquity await with anticipation the detailed publication of this survey; however, current evidence points unmistakably to an aggressive Jewish colonization of the Galilee by the Hasmoneans in line with what we know from Josephus of their approach at Samaria and Scythopolis. Yet it would seem this development was able to build on a previously existing Hellenistic presence in the region.

How does such a profile fit with the urban overlay hypothesis? On the one hand, Strange is correct in seeing the grafting of a Jewish culture onto a previously existing Hellenistic one. However, the hellenisation of the Hasmoneans is sufficiently known from the literary sources to see how they could combine architectural, political and military aspects of Greek culture with a strongly religio-nationalistic ideology.[26] Strange's hypothesis raises the question of whether or not the remnants of that mix were sufficiently potent to resist the Roman overlay in its symbolic intentions of celebrating Roma Aeterna, while of course adopting certain aspects of that presence at the material, everyday level. In other words, my major difficulty is not with the Roman overlay of Galilean life, but with the understanding of what that was saying at a symbolic level to country Galileans, bearing in mind my own experience of how West of Ireland peasants resisted colonizing influences, and transformed those dimensions they did absorb. If one were to change the metaphor from the architectural to the anatomical, the question I want to ask is: was there an underbelly of resistance, and if so where was it located? How did it organise itself and what resources - religious and cultural - did it draw on? What memories inspired it and where did it find its symbolic and ritual expressions?

ARCHITECTURAL SYMBOLISM

This list of questions takes us well beyond the scope of this article. However, it does seem to me that, as stated, Strange's case needs to be nuanced. These stones do not speak; it is we who give them voice. But is our voice the same as those who originally spoke through them? The more pertinent question, perhaps, is how were these symbolic statements received? There were, and always are more than one 'local' voice. I agree fully that the building of Sepphoris and Tiberias were aggressive acts of Romanisation by Antipas. Even if we allow that the theatre at Sepphoris belongs to the earliest phase of Antipas' refurbishment of that site in order to be 'the ornament of all Galilee', there are still some notable absentees in terms of Greco-Roman architectural statements from those centers. Thus far at least, there are no pagan temples, no altar to Roma Aeterna, no large public statues as distinct from private figurines. Can archaeology tell us what images were visible in the agora at Sepphoris in the first century? Despite its different, more cosmopolitan character by contrast with nearby Jotapata or Gamla, I still remain to be convinced that it made the same bold statement that Caesarea Maritima, Caesarea Philippi/Banias, Scythopolis/Beth Shean, or Samaria achieved in terms of Roman power and presence. By those standards, it seems to my ear to be making a considerably more muted statement. Why, I wonder? Is it because the past history of the Herods in Galilee, including Sepphoris itself (Josephus, *Antiquities*, 17:289), meant that one had to tread cautiously, no matter how much one wished to celebrate Rome?

If therefore, reservation is called for in affirming a continuity of symbolic statement between Sepphoris and some of the other Greco-Roman cities of Palestine, what of the continuity between Sepphoris and its hinterland in Lower Galilee? I defer to the expertise of the archaeologists in terms of the actual evidence, but personal experience as well as social theory causes me to question any idea of a cultural continuum being established just because the peasants may find outlets for their produce at urban centres, or continue some, at least, of the urban architectural styles at lesser settlements (e.g. Chabulon, Josephus, *War*, 2:503f). My own experience has taught me that even in the case of language itself, the most basic of all cultural expressions, changes forced by commercial or administrative circumstances do not entail adoption of the cultural assumptions associated with the language in other contexts. Rather, native idioms give a new vitality to the alien tongue and can transform it, as anybody familiar with the poetry of W. B. Yeats or the plays of J. M. Synge can attest. Social anthropologists have pointed to the salient fact that not all aspects of culture are internalized by any individual, much less by any sub-group. Many features remain at the cliche level as far as the ideal culture is concerned. Motivational theory, as employed in cultural anthropology suggests that there is a far greater variety within any given cultural matrix than any of our generalized labels such as urbanization, inculturation or even urban overlay can capture.[27] All cultures are a complex network of factors coalescing to form certain general patterns of behavior, attitudes, life-styles, and values. The process of sifting, selecting or rejecting and internalizing is itself also highly complex. To infer the acceptance of all aspects of the dominant culture from the fact that building or decorative habits conform to an urban typology, or that certain styles of pottery, glass ware or other items of everyday requirement at rural sites are part of a cultural continuum between town and country, is to go well beyond the evidence. On reflection, it does not conform to our own experiences within the global culture of contemporary mass media communications.

BACK TO THE LITERARY EVIDENCE

This raises once again the importance of texts for historical reconstruction. It is fashionable today to point to the perspectives of all texts as tellings, not showings, from particular points of view. Yet the role of hermeneutic suspicion in uncovering such biases can be of interest to the social historian in terms of the factors that gave rise to those biases. The recognition that different literary genres are themselves based on social conventions is also highly significant as far as social historians are concerned, since literary works especially in antiquity are intended as oral communicative exercises that depend on their verisimilitude in order to achieve their desired effect.

As already mentioned, the application of the Redfield-Singer model to Josephus' *Vita* made it clear to me that both Sepphoris and Tiberias are presented as heterogenetic as far as Galileans 'from the land' are concerned. However, one might be suspicious of this depiction, in that it conforms to Josephus' own concern to vilify Justus and other Galilean leaders and to present himself as the agent of moderation in an otherwise volatile situation.[28] As part of his strategy, Josephus deliberately portrays the Galileans as his loyal supporters, ready to vent their anger on the two Herodian centres, for religious as well as social reasons, thereby aligning themselves with the Jerusalem perspective of the author.[29] Does this mean that we must dismiss this whole account as pure fabrication, or does it in any sense conform to reality, even if Josephus has highlighted certain aspects for his own purposes? Before jumping to the 'obvious' conclusion of a total fabrication, Josephus' self-characterization and his relations with various factions in Galilee have to be evaluated from the point of view of the encomiastic nature of the work as a whole.[30] Josephus seeks to uphold the pivotal value of honor, not just with regard to his own conduct of affairs, but also in relation to the stance of Sepphoris, in that it maintained its *pistis* or trust with Rome by refusing to join the revolt, unlike Justus' native place, Tiberias, which betrayed its trust to King Agrippa (Josephus, *Vita*, 30f., 103.346). This is something Josephus admires despite his own rejection by the city (Josephus, *Vita*, 104-110). At the same time he is critical of its refusal to support Jerusalem and tells of the Galileans' anger in attacking it, causing the chief citizens to flee to the acropolis, an action that corresponds to the complicity of some Galileans in the sack of Herod's palace in Tiberias (Josephus, *Vita*, 66.273-80.348f). It thus would appear that once the *Vita* is read in terms of the prevailing conventions, especially those to do with honor/shame, its statements and characterizations of the various personalities cannot be so lightly dismissed as Josephan fabrication.

Interesting confirmation of this conclusion might be gleaned from the Jesus tradition. Strange rightly points to the urban as well as the rural imagery in the earliest strata of that tradition. The really pertinent question, however, is how does the imagery function within that setting? It is true that such urban characters as the merchant, the judge and the wealthy landowner (usually an urban resident) can function as personalities in some parables, side by side with farmers, shepherds, and tenant farmers. But this does not amount to espousing the values of the urban elites. The consistent criticism of wealth, as well as the rejection of the Herodian court life-style, point unmistakably to a distancing from that world, both physically and emotionally.[31] Jesus is not in principle critical of the city, just as he does not romanticize rural life, but I do believe that the silence about a visit to Sepphoris or Tiberias is not accidental. His opposition is not to places as such, but to certain values that are associated with city dwellers, notably among the elites who shaped and dominated their ethos, especially as this was viewed from the distance of the peasant.

Thus in the Jesus tradition dating from the thirties to the fifties of the first century and in the *Vita* of Josephus, though written in the nineties, but purporting to describe the situation in the sixties, there appears to be a converging picture from the literary sources of on-going tensions between town and country in first century Galilee, not because such hostility was inevitable, but because the Herodian foundations of Galilee represented alien values as far as 'country' Jews were concerned. The Jewish population of the Galilee living in *'iroth* or *kefarim*, remained loyal to Jerusalem and the symbolic world represented by its cult-centre despite the social and physical distance that separated them from the center. The urban overlay, detectable in their environment did not represent any capitulation on that score. The very fact of the revolt, however disorganized the Galilean phase, must be seen as the failure of imperial propaganda, as far as at least some of the inhabitants were concerned. In short, the archaeological evidence does not disconfirm the literary evidence, and can itself be understood without recourse to the idea of an 'urbanized' Galilee, in the sense that some of the proponents of that idea have wished to maintain.

CONCLUSION

James Strange's article called for a genuine dialogue between spade and text, and in this brief response I have sought to address the challenge. For me the exercise has been more than worthwhile in forcing me to take a critical look at my own methodological assumptions and my choice and use of evidence. The conversation with the archaeological work that I have conducted has been for me a most fruitful encounter with another view of how the world of ancient Galilee looked, reminding me that all our worlds are constructions in constant need of revision. I hope that this contribution, offered in appreciation of James Strange and his work will lead to further fruitful dialogue between the proponents of spade and pen, archaeology and text.

NOTES

[1] J. Strange, D. Groh, and T. Longstaff, "Excavations at Sepphoris: The Location and Identification of Shikhin, Part I," *Israel Exploration Journal* 44 (1994) 216-227; 45 (1995) 171-87.

[2] M. Goodman, *State and Society in Roman Galilee. A.D. 132-212*, (Totowa, NJ; Rowman and Allenheld, 1983) 27-31.

[3] S. Freyne, *Galilee from Alexander the Great to Hadrian* (Wilmington, Del: Glazier, University of Notre Dame Press, 1980) 101-56.

[4] E. Meyers, J. Strange and D. Groh, "The Meiron Excavation Project: Archaeological Survey in Galilee and the Golan," *BASOR* 230 (1978) 1-24.

[5] M. Douglas, *Natural Symbols* (New York: Pantheon, 1982) 59-76.

[6] S. Freyne, "Urban-Rural Relations in First-Century Galilee: Some Suggestions from the Literary Sources," in *The Galilee in Late Antiquity*, ed. L. Levine (New York: Jewish Theological Seminary, 1992) 75-94.

[7] R. Redfield and M. Singer, "The Cultural Role of Cities," *Economic Change and Social Development* 3 (1954) 57-73.

[8] J. Strange, "Some Implications of Archaeology for New Testament Studies," in *What Has Archaeology to do With Faith*, ed. J. Charlesworth (Philadelphia: Trinity Press, 1992) 23-59.

[9] Ibid., 27 and 53, n. 40.

[10] J. Strange, "Six Campaigns at Sepphoris: The University of South Florida Excavations, 1983-1989," in *The Galilee in Late Antiquity*, 339-56 and E. Meyers, "Roman Sepphoris in Light of New Archaeological Evidence and Recent Research," in *The Galilee in Late Antiquity*, 321-38, 342.

[11] See for example, Neusner's response to P. Schäfer's work in this volume.

[12] C. Dauphin, "Les 'Komai' de Palestine," *Proche-Orient Chrètien* 37 (1987) 251-67.

[13] Meyers, Strange, and Groh, "The Meiron Excavation."

[14] Z. Yeivin, "Chorazin, A Mishnaic City," *Bulletin of the Anglo-Israel Archaeological Society* 2 (1983-4) 46-8.

[15] D. Adan-Bayewitz, "Kefar Hananya," *Israel Exploration Journal* 37 (1986) 178f. and *Israel Exploration Journal* 39 (1989) 87f.

[16] Z. Ma'oz, "The Golan: Hellenistic Period to the Middle Ages," in *The New Encyclopedia of Archaeology of the Holy Land*, ed. E. Stern (Jerusalem: The Israel Exploration Society, 1993) 2:534-46.

[17] C. Dauphin and J. Schonfield, "Settlements of the Roman and Byzantine Periods on the Golan Heights," *Israel Exploration Journal* 33 (1983) 189-206 and C. Dauphin and S. Gibson, "Ancient Settlements and their Landscapes: The Results of Ten Years of Survey on the Golan Heights (1978-1988)," *Bulletin of the Anglo-Israel Archaeological Society* 12 (1992-3) 7-31.

[18] F. Villeneuve, "L'economie Rurale et la Vie des Campagnes dans le Hauran Antique," in *Recherches Ar-*

chéologiques sur la Syrie du Sud à L'Époque Hellenistique et Romaine, ed. J.-M. Dentzer (Paris: Librairie Orientaliste Paul Geuthner, 1986) 63-129.

[19]R. Bagnall, *Egypt in Late Antiquity* (Princeton: Princeton University Press, 1993) 110-47.

[20]B. Isaac, "The Babatha Archive: A Review Article," *Israel Exploration Journal* 42 (1992) 62-75.

[21]G. McLean Harper Jr., "Village Administration in the Roman Province of Syria," *Yale Classical Studies* 1 (1928) 107-68.

[22]A. Alt, "Galiläische Problemen," in *Kleine Schriften zur Geschichte des Volkes Israels*, (Munich, 1953-64) 2:363-465.

[23]E. Schürer, *The History of the Jewish People in the Age of Jesus Christ* 4 vols. revised by G. Vermes, F. Millar, and M. Black (Edinburgh: T and T Clark, 1973-84).

[24]M. Aviam, "Galilee: the Hellenistic to the Byzantine Period," in *The New Encyclopedia of Archaeological Excavation of the Holy Land*, 2:452-58.

[25]R. Frankel, "Har Mispe Yamin - 1988/89," in *Excavations and Surveys in Israel 1989/90*, (Jerusalem: Jewish Antiquities Authority, 1989/90).

[26]D. Mendels, *The Rise and Fall of Jewish Nationalism* (New York: Doubleday, 1992).

[27]R. D'Andrade and C. Strauss, *Human Motives and Cultural Models*, (Cambridge: Cambridge University Press, 1992).

[28]S. Cohen, *Josephus in Galilee and Rome, His Vita and Development as a Historian* (Leiden: E.J. Brill, 1979).

[29]S. Freyne, "The Galileans in the Light of Josephus' *Vita*," *New Testament Studies* 26 (1980) 397-413 and "Galilean-Jerusalem Relations According to Josephus," *New Testament Studies* 33 (1987) 600-9.

[30]J. Neyrey, "Josephus' *Vita* and the Encomium: A Native Model of Personality," *Journal for the Study of Judaism* 25 (1994) 177-206.

[31]S. Freyne, "Jesus and the Urban Culture of Galilee," in *Texts and Contexts. Biblical Texts in Their Textual and Situational Contexts*, ed. T. Fornberg and D. Hellholm (Oslo: Scandinavian University Press, 1995) 597-622.

6

Jesus and His Galilean Context

Eric M. Meyers
Duke University

None of the members of this panel is more aware of their own limitations with respect to our three-year theme, "Jesus in Historical Context," than I.[1] Indeed, I am honored to sit between such distinguished scholars of the New Testament, scholars who each for different reasons is also deeply immersed in Judaic learning of the period of Jesus and the rise of early Christianity; and I am especially happy to say that we all share some common ideas on these times. However, I come before you today presumably with something different from the others, namely, a hands-on perspective gained after some thirty years of digging in the dirt, twenty-five of them in Galilee, the place where much of what we are concerned with began. I am in fact a latter-day Galilean, laboring in a field which in recent years has witnessed an explosion of interest and an emergence of a host of new excavations that are dramatically changing the data base for archaeological interpretation.

To name only a few of the new excavations that are being conducted in and around Galilee that will have a future impact on Galilean studies I would list the following: the four excavations now at Sepphoris; two at Beth Shean/Scythopolis; Tiberias; Jotapata; Capernaum; Banias; Bethsaida; Gaba; Hippos; Umm Qeis/Gadara; Kefar Hananiah; the three excavations at Caesarea Maritima; and I would add several other important cities of the Decapolis, Gerasa (Jerash), Capitolias (Bet Ras), Pella, and Abila (all in (trans) Jordan), and Gadara, which overlooks the Sea of Galilee. In Syria we should make special mention of Apamaea and work in and around Damascus. This short list leaves aside the dozens of rescue operations that are annually carried out by the Israel Antiquities Authority, the Department of Antiquities of Jordan, and the ongoing publications programs of many others. Computerized data banks listing survey sites and what is found at them as well as excavated sites are now in operation in Israel and Jordan and can easily be accessed and studied at the Albright Institute in Jerusalem (AIAR) or at the American Center in Amman (ACOR), each member schools of the American Schools of Oriental Research (ASOR).

EARLIER WORK ON GALILEAN REGIONALISM

I would like to think that my own work first in Upper Galilee and more recently in Lower Galilee has played some role in spawning so much activity and interest. At any rate by way of introduction and review I should like to revisit some of my earlier reflections on Galilean regionalism and place them clearly within the context of current research on Galilee, on Jesus, and inter-regional trade and movements in Galilee and elsewhere.[2]

When I first undertook my own survey and excavations at Khirbet Shema[c] in Upper Galilee I was very much intent on choosing a site that was small, off the beaten track, and hence typical of the region.[3] As much as our team was interested in ancient synagogues we were equally interested in establishing a ceramic typology for the later periods that would assist future excavators in investigating houses and other aspects of everyday life including local industries, and in establishing the social setting of early Judaism in Palestine based on new archaeological data recovered under controlled field conditions.[4] In order to cast our net even more widely we supplemented our regular excavation work with a systematic survey of the major sites in both Galilees and in the Golan.[5] The other sites excavated during this period (1968-1982) were Meiron, Gush Halav, and Nabratein.[6]

By the end of this period we had trained sufficient numbers of archaeologists that most of the senior members of that team went on to direct, co-direct, or assume major leadership roles in numerous other excavations including Sepphoris, Caesarea Maritima, and Nessana.

One of the main insights gained in that first decade of new work in the Upper Galilee was that the special geographical conditions of that region contributed significantly to aspects of the culture that flourished there in Roman and Byzantine times. It was also apparent early in our work that the first century of the common era was poorly preserved in most places and that in order to make a secure hypothesis about that period we would have to select alternative sites. In recognizing the enormous natural distinctions between Upper and Lower Galilee, and even within northeast Upper Galilee along the great Rift Valley and Jordan River, I formulated a theory regarding aspects of hellenization in certain areas of everyday life, many details of which have stood the test of time. Some aspects of these reflections, especially on the distribution and trade of common ceramic wares and types, however, have had to be revised in light of new excavations and scientific analysis of shards through neutron activation analysis, petrographic examination, and thin-section analysis.

The absence of cities in the Upper Galilee is one of the area's most noticeable features--even Josephus refers to the region as Tetracomia, with the implication being that there were at least four larger villages around which the regional economy and politics were focused. The Golan similarly was devoid of cities in the Roman era, and many aspects of the common material culture it shared with Upper Galilee derived from this lack of cities. In an age when Roman policies and propaganda were realized through its poleis, its major cities, such areas not yet touched by urbanization were significant exceptions. It is obvious therefore that some residents of Upper Galilee/Golan chose to trade via those gentile cities which encircled Upper Galilee and influenced the local trade and economy. Chief among the Palestinian cities were Tyre, whose influence is disproportionately well reflected in the coins found in both Galilees but especially in Upper Galilee, and Acco-

Ptolemais, both cities situated on the Phoenician coast. The autonomous city of Caesarea Phillipi at the northeast corner of the Upper Galilee is another important point of contact with an urban center. Lest I mislead you, however, let me say at the outset that the presence of cities in the eastern Empire, especially the cities of the Decapolis or the Phoenician cities, does not mean that they only exhibited or represented those forms of Greco-Roman culture that were antithetical to the indigenous Semitic culture of towns and villages. On the contrary, recent scholarship has indicated that such urban centers reflected indigenous cultures "with the cultural veneer of their masters."[7] That is to say even the new external forms of Greco-Roman civilization could not conceal the strong Semitic base in such aspects as religion and cult, architecture, and language. Needless to say also, many of these gentile cities such as Tyre or Beth Shean-Scythopolis had significant Jewish minorities.[8]

The absence or presence of cities in portions of Galilee or its periphery, therefore, need not reflect the degree to which indigenous culture became a vehicle for expressing aspects of Hellenistic culture, because Hellenism could and often did provide a vehicle for serving as a framework for preserving and promoting local Semitic culture. Upper Galilee's relative isolation from the great urban centers of the day, while perhaps sparing its populations from some of the more obvious trappings of the hellenistic lifestyle, e.g., theater and Greco-Roman statues, did not make it immune to the economic realities of the times. Imported ceramic fine-wares are regularly found in excavations, the local currency of the region certainly included Tyrian coinage, and luxury items such as jewelry and glass were doubtless imported from outside the region as well. The kitchen wares used were purchased from the Kefar Hananiah manufacturing center at the border of Upper and Lower Galilee, approximately 12 miles from the Meiron area, or from local itinerant peddlers showing those wares.[9]

In other words, the Upper Galilee was not as isolated as I first thought. Yet, the following characteristics of the region may still be observed: 1. the architectural decorations employed in public and large domestic buildings while clearly hellenistic are relatively devoid of ionographic excess, especially animal or human forms in the Middle and Late Roman era-the first century is very poorly preserved-and decorated mosaics are virtually unknown, the chief exception being the late synagogue site of Meroth;[10] 2. Greek epigraphic remains are virtually unknown in Jewish sites in the Roman period, pointing to Hebrew and Aramaic as the dominant languages; and 3. the more common features of urban life (aqueducts, baths, statues, nymphaea, frescoes, temples, and theaters) are virtually absent in Tetracomia. A strong case therefore remains for calling the Upper Galilee, and parts of the

Golan, conservative, Semitic and overwhelmingly Jewish, and rural. The degree to which it may be called "isolated" therefore, in view of the considerable presence of traded items brought in from the outside, is certainly worthy of further discussion. But here I would sound a cautionary note and take an example from modern society. The most conservative and right-wing of Jewish Orthodox groups today may very well disavow aspects of urban life and even reject the state of Israel, but they frequently use the best imported china and flat ware, have their clothes made of the finest imported textiles, and buy jewelry from all over the world.

While I would not for a moment suggest that Jesus' ministry had very much to do with Upper Galilee, his appearance in Tyre and Sidon (Q 10:13 and 10:14) and movement about in "all Galilee" and other places so close to the Upper Galilee makes it quite probable that he traversed broad sections of it at one time or another. It is even possible to imagine that references to Tyre or Sidon might connote portions of Upper Galilee, which we have noted had extensive trade with Tyre, and which is only 36 aerial miles from Sepphoris in Lower Galilee. In fact Mark says that Jesus visited only the borders of Tyre (7:24,31), the village of Caesarea Phillipi (8:27) and the territory of Gadara (5:1), perhaps purposefully avoiding the urban centers, which would have surely put him in Upper Galilee or its fringes.

LOWER GALILEE AND REGIONALISM

With good reason the Lower Galilee has been the primary object of recent attention with respect to establishing the background for Jesus in Galilee. Although its territory is closer to and encircled by Greek cities such as Beth Shean-Scythopolis and Acco-Ptolemais, where Jews had lived as a minority population for some time, the population of Lower Galilee prior to the Great War and up to the Second War with Rome, was also overwhelmingly Jewish. Undoubtedly the Jewish Herodian cities of Sepphoris and Tiberias were the major urban centers of Galilee, the former covering an area of at least 60 hectares with a population of ca. 18,000, and Tiberias an area of 80 hectares and population of 24,000.[11] Hoehner, following Josephus, points to Tarichaeae and Gaba as the two other major cities in the region, but they are clearly much smaller, below 20 hectares and with a population of ca. 3,000 each.[12] Taking the figures of 200 villages in all Galilee, at approximately 500 inhabitants per village, which seems reasonable, we estimate the population to be 150,000-175,000 with the vast majority of inhabitants occupying villages rather than cities, not far from the figure of 200,000 proposed by Hoehner.[13] As Jonathan Reed has recently cautioned in proposing a "modest" population estimate of 1700 for Capernaum, making accurate estimates based on limited excavation and exposure is problematical.[14]

To suggest, therefore, that recent excavation and work in Galilee demonstrates and supports the idea that there are significant urban influences on Jesus's early life and teaching is a gross oversimplification.[15] Taking the example of the work of Crossan that an urbanized Galilee was the appropriate setting for the transmission of popular Cynic ideas, a particular Mediterranean philosophy that enabled agrarian peoples to cope with the inequalities of life, we must say that this is not evident from the data of either of the Galilees we have explored.[16] On the contrary, despite some inroads of Roman urbanization in pre-70 Galilean society, reflected best in Sepphoris and Tiberias, such a setting can only be found in places like Scythopolis or Ptolemais, and the cities of the Decapolis. Such changes for Galilee did occur but mostly after 70 C.E. and in Lower Galilee only - and long after Jesus' ministry.

A rather prominent author/journalist recently quizzed me about the ultimate significance of the Sepphoris excavations for re-evaluating the life and teaching of Jesus. Before giving me a chance to reply fully he said: "Doesn't the work at Sepphoris at the very least demonstrate that Jesus was not a country bumpkin (sic) but rather was someone who had access to the highest forms of contemporary culture and learning?" I will answer this question before concluding this presentation; but first I should like to continue to make a case for establishing the character of Lower Galilee in the pre-70 period based on archaeology and some of the new material.

It cannot be maintained--let alone inferred from archaeology--that towns or villages were devoid of culture and learning. It cannot even be claimed that the Greek cities were entirely Greek in their cultural ambiance - "oriental" or Near Eastern might be a better way to describe it. As Sean Freyne has communicated to me: "In my opinion it is unrealistic to assume that close proximity to an urban culture means that the population as a whole was likely to be imbued with the attitudes and values, alleged or real, of these centers. One would have to ask to what ends certain strata of the population adopted those attitudes and values and why they might have abandoned older ones?"[17]

Upper Galilee, though certainly distinct from Lower Galilee, also had significant similarities. I have already pointed out the tendency to overemphasize the "urban" character of Lower Galilee because of the existence of Sepphoris and Tiberias. It was Herod Antipas who in 4 B.C.E. became Tetrarch of Galilee and Perea and governed to 39 C.E. During the first four decades of the first century Antipas ordered the rebuilding and refurbishing of Sepphoris, from whence he first administered Galilee beginning in 2 B.C.E., and the founding and establishment of the city of Tiberias ca. 17-23 C.E. Antipas, except for laying the foundations of Tiberias on a Jewish necropolis (*Antiquities* 18.38), marrying Herodias (*Antiquities* 18.109-36), and commissioning animal images from his palace in Tiberias (*Life* 65-66), largely respected the religious sensibilities of his Jewish subjects. Especially in regard to the second commandment concerning images or idolatry Antipas would seem to have allowed the Galilee to remain essentially aniconic during the first half of the first century C.E. No statues of Octavian or Tiberias have been recovered, there is no trace of an imperial cult, and no images of the Greco-Roman pantheon were displayed. Indeed the coins of Antipas were aniconic, lacking any figural devices. All in all one would have to conclude that the Tetrarch displayed marked sensitivity to Jewish religious concerns, or at the very least opportunistically honored Jewish laws in order to rule more effectively. On the other hand Antipas did not effectively administer justice in the Galilee (*Antiquities* 18. 106-108) and his order to kill John the Baptist was reckless. One might wonder how Jesus avoided getting into trouble with Antipas. The main point is that Antipas was careful not to offend the Jewish religious elements in Galilee by not placing images on his coins. He also did not promote a pagan ethos like his father had done in Caesarea and Samaria/Sebaste. The archaeological remains at Sepphoris that may date to the first half of the first century C.E., to date indicate no fragments of anything that could be identified as a pagan temple, altars or statues, relevant inscriptions, or large foundations. On the contrary, what has been found are ritual baths in houses, and other items of everyday life, all non-figural in character, and rather mundane by anyone's standards.

Certainly reflecting the sensitivity of the issue of iconography is the Markan pericope at 12:13-17 concerning tribute money and coins, in which Jesus carefully avoids getting pulled into a situation from which it is too difficult to extricate himself.[18] The very structure of the pericope and the use of a coin to redirect the argument and transform it shows both the negative potential of the situation to entrap Jesus into commenting on an image and the positive action that results when he refocuses attention in his clever rejoinder. Although he might have observed the images depicted on the coin, Jesus responds to a larger issue, namely, spheres of authority, God's and Caesar's. He requests his petitioners to produce a coin, which they do although they have to go and get it. Considering the fact that the coin described is a Tiberian silver denarius, depicting Caesar as son of god on the obverse, and a female figure facing right on the reverse, representing Pax, Pharisees and Jesus would have found either side equally offensive. Jesus's answer as preserved in the logion of Mark 12:17 enables him to offer a fitting and clever response: "Render to Caesar the things that are Caesar's, and to God the things that are God's." With this rejoinder the Jesus as

represented by the Markan editor avoids the embarrassment of having to comment on what is obviously a violation of the aniconic sensitivities of first century Jews. Such a depiction of Jesus in the second Gospel is consistent with the picture of life in Galilee in the reign of Antipas, whom we have noted, heeded Jewish laws pertaining to idolatry and iconography in Galilee during his reign.

If we may conclude that the Galilee was an area congenial to and supportive of Jewish halakhic norms in the time of Jesus, and that the archaeology of Sepphoris and other sites strongly supports this, we may disavow the contention of numerous scholars who still adhere to the view that the Galilee was mainly peasant and rural and the people "simple."[19] Because the Jesus movement took root in such a setting, the argument goes, there is no mention in the New Testament of any Jewish urban centers such as Sepphoris or Tiberias. When Jews would have met gentiles, the argument continues, their encounters, probably in cities, would be strained, their uneasiness would stem from tensions between town and city, with the city presumed to be the oppressor in terms of taxes and land acquisition.[20] Because urbanization of the Lower Galilee may be linked to Sepphoris and Tiberias, the silence of the New Testament regarding them should be explained, if we wish to utilize any of our data on Galilee to explain aspects of the Jesus movement.

While not devoid of geographic detail or information, the Gospels are surely deficient in providing the detailed information about Galilee that is available in Josephus, the rabbis, and the pagan writers (e.g. Strabo and Pliny). As we have already noted Jesus moved freely about in all Galilee en route to several of the urban territories, though not to their centers. If the New Testament references are accurate Jesus may well have visited the northern edges of the Upper Galilee, which borders on Acco-Ptolemais, Sidon, and Tyre. If Mark were written just before or after the Great War with Rome, it seems unlikely that Jesus could have moved so freely about since Jewish-Gentile relations would have been most strained at that time especially in the Greek cities (Jos. *War* 2.457-465). But why are the two Jewish cities of Sepphoris and Tiberias never mentioned? Having so central role in the cultural and economic life of Galilee such an omission can hardly be thought to be an oversight. Lack of success on the part of Jesus or being unwelcome in the Herodian cities would undoubtedly have resulted in some sort of condemnation, as we have in relation to Capernaum, Corazin, and Bethsaida.

Part of the reason for Jesus's visit to the gentile cities was to preach to the Jews resident in the gentile cities, i.e., to "the lost sheep of the house of Israel." Tyre, Gerasa, and Scythopolis all had significant Jewish populations, as did many other gentile cities. It seems reasonable therefore to conclude that Jesus's Galilean ministry could hardly have avoided the two Herodian cities, Sepphoris and Tiberias.

Insofar as both Herodian cities represent the changing ethos of Galilee at the end of the Second Temple period, i.e., moving from the village-centered and agrarian to the urban-centered whose population now included members of the retainer class, such an omission in the New Testament would seem to have significance. We would stress, however, that these Jewish centers were not like their gentile counterparts in the first century: Sepphoris struck its first coins only in 66 C.E. and Tiberias only in 100 C.E. It was at these later dates that both cities began to exert even greater economic influence since no coins of Herod Antipas are known to have been found in Judea. Apparently his economy exerted little influence outside a fairly confined area.[21] Relative independence and a change in character, hence, is more plausible later than earlier, when war refugees from the south moved north and when Roman soldiers followed to maintain order.

We now turn to the question of the degree to which Galilee, especially Lower Galilee, was frequented by outsiders. On the one hand, a case based mainly on literary sources can be made for Galilee being relatively accessible and open to outsiders in the lifetime of Jesus and we may also show that household ceramic wares from Kefar Hananiah were traded and sold in both Galilees and the Golan as well as in Acco-Ptolemais and Caesarea Philippi (Banias). At the same time no such wares appear to be traded or exported south of the Nazareth ridge, according to Adan-Bayewitz. Moreover, no synagogues have been found south of the Nazareth latitude in Galilee in the entire Roman period, according to Aviam.[22] What does the ceramic data indicate about the situation after 70 C.E. and how does such data inform us about the urban/rural divide that supposedly separated city and town? With regard to the latter the data surely indicate a continuum of positive interaction between city and town in the early Roman period. Theories that suggest that urban centers exploit the surrounding countryside are to be soundly rejected on the basis of archaeological evidence alone. Moreover, the data also show that rural Galilee in this period was not exclusively agricultural, as numerous scholars have maintained. In addition, since the same ceramic data pertaining to provenience obtain for the entire Roman period and into the beginning of the Byzantine period, we must not limit our conclusions merely to the early Roman period. Rural towns such as Kefar Hananiah continued to serve the needs of both cities and towns throughout the Roman period, even as the Galilee became more and more urbanized and as more and more gentiles came to settle there in the second and third centuries C.E.

In my opinion, therefore, and in partial agreement with others, the silence of the New Testament with regard to the Herodian Jewish cities is deliberate and artificial. It strains credulity to imagine any sort of ministry of Jesus in Galilee without coming into contact with the population of either Tiberias or Sepphoris. Whether or not it was their politics or their economic roles that Jesus questioned remains to be seen. A prior question must be asked, however: what does the archaeology of Galilee say about such an issue? Is such a picture consistent with the one depicted in or interpreted in the literary sources? To put it another way, is the picture that one draws of Galilee and the Galileans based on literary sources consistent with the one drawn using archaeology as a starting point? Do the archaeological realia of pots, coins, and structures "impinge on the symbolic universe of a culture and thus play a role in the culture's religion?"[23] Are these realia to be placed in dialogue with the sifted record of literary sources? Or are we to favor one over the other because archaeology "produces a less impressionistic picture of ancient reality..." and provides "the preeminent original sources for the history of illiterate and subordinate social strata?"[24]

In an essay published some years ago on the state of biblical archaeology I came out in favor of a dialogue between text and spade, between literary analysis and archaeological analysis.[25] Ideally this should be so. But because there are so few of us around who can remain critical or keep current in both fields one always runs the risk of running afoul of one group or the other, literary historians or archaeologists. I was more concerned with scholars of the Hebrew Bible and its context when I wrote that essay, and in that field I am happy to say that a true dialogue has begun. In regard to the so-called field of New Testament archaeology the situation is more complex because consideration of the social setting involves two additional fields: Jewish Studies and Classical Studies. For the time being then, for our consideration of the social world of Jesus, I intend to give archaeology priority of place in what is really a four-way discussion.

I now address the degree to which Lower Galilee was open or closed to outside influences. As noted earlier Upper Galilee was more isolated than Lower Galilee. Nonetheless, in the second century C.E. in Upper Galilee a Roman Temple was built there at Kedesh (Cadasa), the most impressive one found in all of Eretz Israel. Not very far to the northwest another temple of the same period, dedicated to Apollo and Diana, has been found inside southern Lebanon, surrounded by a string of rural pagan villages.[26] The "Jewish" line of northern Upper Galilee, and of all Galilee, thus runs just north of Sasa, Baram, and Qatzyon, north of which no Jewish remains have been found. The definitive urban influence in this region, especially in the north (near Meiron, Gush Halav, and Khirbet Shema') is Tyre. If we move slightly to the west, southwest, no synagogal remains have been found in Upper Galilee west of Peqi'in-Rama, or west of a line through

Rama, I'billin, and Tivon in Lower Galilee. The southern extent, according to both ceramic and architectural material, is the Nazareth ridge. The areas to the west of these lines fell into the cultural and economic orbit of Acco-Ptolemais.

The situation to the east is more complicated and less well published so far as Jewish remains are concerned, because many of them are located in Transjordan. As for Lower Galilee the city demarcating the westernmost limit of the Decapolis and the extent of Lower Galilee southeast is Beth Shean-Scythopolis, a city with a sizeable Jewish presence. While it is commonplace to assume that the cities of the Decapolis represented a band of gentile cities that contained the extent and spread of Jewish culture, such assumptions are quite misleading. The oriental cities of the Decapolis and other gentile cities should not be viewed solely as purveyors of Greco-Roman culture but rather as eastern cities with a hellenistic overlay that often facilitated the expression of aspects of Semitic religion and practice, including Judaism. Jewish remains from the Roman period are well known from Gerasa (Jerash), Gadara (Umm Qeis), Abila, and possibly Capitolias (Beit Ras) all in the Decapolis. Also, a significant Jewish population is known from Moab in early Roman times, as came to light in the recent publication of the Greek papyri from the Cave of Letters by N. Lewis.[27] These finds underscore the importance in the late Hellenistic period of the vast holdings of the important banking and trading firm of the Tobiad family at Araq el-Emir just south of Amman (Philadelphia).[28]

Eric Lapp, my former graduate student, is presently at work on a study of Roman and Byzantine lamps and their places of manufacture, and hence how they were traded. Using microscopic petrography, x-ray diffraction and neutron activation analyses, following some of the methods of Adan-Bayewitz and Peacock, his preliminary research already shows a far greater economic exchange system at work between Jewish areas and sites and the cities of the Decapolis than previously assumed. In the early Roman period, for example, the so called "Herodian" spatulated lamp nozzles commonly found in Judea, often thought to be *the* "Jewish" lamp of the first century, are found at all of the cities of the Decapolis just mentioned plus Pella. Similarly other lamp types of the first century, such as the "Darom" lamp, thought to be of Jewish manufacture, are also found in Transjordanian cities of the Decapolis.

What can be said is that the eastern gentile cities were far more open to contacts with Jewish merchants and traders than was heretofore thought, if indeed the so-called "Herodian" and "Darom" lamps are of Jewish and Judean manufacture. A logical inference to be drawn is that contacts between Lower Galilee-moreso than Upper Galilee-and some cities of the Decapolis were far greater than we had thought. Such contacts would help explain the journey and/or spread of the Jesus movement into the Decapolis region and need not reflect any Markan perspective, as Doug Edwards has recently pointed out basing his conclusion on the presence of Kefar Hananiah pottery in gentile cities and towns.[29] Moreover, with substantial Jewish communities there also, Jesus's visits to such territories are much more understandable.

Even so, I would also be cautious about inferring too much on the basis of archaeological research and remains. Adan-Bayewitz was fair in pointing out that some of the Kefar Hananiah wares, marketed primarily to Jews and produced by Jews, have also been found at sites whose ethnic population is non-Jewish, e.g., Tel Anafa (pagan), Tabgha (Christian), Capernaum (mixed), and the non-Jewish, gentile cities of Acco-Ptolemais and Susita.[30] Similarly, the presence of Herodian lamps at some sites that have a mixed population need not be indicative of Jewish presence. A better way of putting it is that Herodian lamps manufactured in Judea, or possibly elsewhere, are found more frequently in gentile cities where there is a Jewish population. Similarly, not all aspects of urban life have clear associations with gentile, Roman culture. Rather, they constitute an urban overlay that has been grafted on to Galilean society, which reflects indigenous building patterns. Aspects of urban life that might be clearly associated with Hellenism or urbanization would be theaters, temples, statues, hippodromes, etc., but agoras, markets, walls, streets, and domestic architecture could as well reflect indigenous culture. Jonathan Reed has preferred to test urbanization on the basis of population size and certain architectural features, both assessments that can be made on the basis of archeological data alone at well-excavated sites. Thus, urbanizing patterns in the Galilee, for the first century at least, occur at only two cities in the Lower Galilee, Sepphoris and Tiberias, and no where in Upper Galilee.[31]

The appearance in 4 B.C.E. and ca. 18 C.E. of these two Lower Galilean cities surely had an enormous impact on everyday life. Numerous villages, farms, and hamlets were now called upon to provide food for the growing populations of the cities, and the fertile lands nearby, which heretofore had sustained independent, self-subsistent farmers, now were transformed into places where products were grown on a much larger scale for cash. Some products such as wine, olive oil, grain, flour, were also transferred to the cities for production. The cities also became great centers of consumption, as is attested in pottery manufactured at Kefar Hananiah, some building materials, especially marble, and stone vessels that were made at Reina near Sepphoris, some 4 km. southeast of Nazareth.

There are no towns and villages in all of Galilee that are more than 25 km. in aerial distance from either Herodian center. Some smaller towns and villages in parts of Galilee kept their distance from some of the gentile cities both literally and figuratively. It seems less likely that they would have kept a similar isolation from Sepphoris and Tiberias, which called upon their populations for food, sundry goods and supplies, and labor to construct new buildings.

In summary Lower Galilee in light of recent archaeology was less isolated than Upper Galilee and presumably less conservative. It was more Greek-speaking--a judgment based on epigraphy--and more hellenized; i.e., it exhibited more aspects of Greco-Roman urbanization as judged from archaeological data, and was less rural, based on the obvious role and influence of Sepphoris and Tiberias on the local economies. Although neither city is mentioned in the New Testament, Reed's recent study of Q has demonstrated ample familiarity with aspects of Jewish urban existence in Galilee. Even the Gospel of Mark reflects a familiarity with the considerable trade and traffic between city and town and between Galilee and the gentile cities. To a degree the existence of Roman roads in Lower Galilee facilitated much of their movement. The physical setting of Lower Galilee, with its three trans-Galilean east-west natural crossings, was a natural point of contact. The main road was the Acco-Tiberias road, remains of which have been found along the Nahal Eblayim, with a branch off to Sepphoris and another continuing southwest to Acco, intersecting the Legio-Sepphoris road. A second major, east-west Roman road linked Banias with Tyre along the exterior northern edge of Upper Galilee on the Galilee panhandle, where virtually no Jewish remains have been found.[32]

The only imperial roads connecting the northern and southern portions of Galilee were 1) the coastal road linking Acco and Antioch, with milestones dating to Nero uncovered at Nahariya, 2) the inland road connecting Banias with Tiberias, and 3) the Legio-Sepphoris connection, which achieved its real importance only after the placement of the Sixth Legion (Ferrata) ca. 130 C.E.[33]

SEPPHORIS

Before concluding I will comment on recent excavations at Sepphoris. In responding to Professor Sanders' paper last year I noted that the archaeology of Sepphoris tended to support his notion that Antipas did very little either to aggravate Jewish religious sensibilities or to annoy Rome. Unfortunately, as is the case in most Roman-period excavations in Israel, the early Roman, first century C.E. material has not been well preserved, due to the continual rebuilding that occurred during the entire Roman period, a period of approximately 426 years, i.e., 63 B.C.E. (Pompey's conquest) to the great earthquake of 363 C.E. A major reconfiguration of the site, at least on the western summit occurred only in the Byzantine period

(i.e., after 363).

According to Josephus, Sepphoris was conquered by the Romans after Herod's death in the so called "War of Varus when many of the inhabitants were sold into slavery" (*War* 2.68; *Antiquities* 17.289). Though this report seems to be accurate and reliable no definite destruction level has been found to relate to this event. Josephus is quite clear (*Antiquities* 18.27) in pointing to a major recovery and rebuilding of the city under Antipas (4 B.C.E.-39 C.E.). Presumably, after renaming the city "Autocratoris", and possibly refortifying it in honor of Augustus (*War* 2.117f.), it became the "ornament of all Galilee," the phrase "ornament" apparently referring to the impregnable nature of the city, which is the meaning of the term *proschema*.[34] Surprisingly, Josephus provides no further details on what happened there during Antipas's reign, and we have to turn to archaeology for a reconstruction. During the Great War with Rome (the First Revolt), Josephus reports that the inhabitants of Sepphoris supported Vespasian and surrendered the city to him, minting coins in his honor in 67-68 C.E. as "peacemaker," and calling the city, "City of Peace," *Eirenopolis* (*War* 3.30-34). There are some indications in Josephus, however, that the adoption of such a pro-Roman policy did not come easily (War 2.574; 2.629; 2.636-45).

The priestly clan of Jedaiah settled in Sepphoris after the Great War and before the Second Revolt in 135 C.E. Stuart Miller, however, has shown quite clearly that a strong priestly component existed in the city before the first revolt.[35] There can be little doubt that until the time of Hadrian (117-138 C.E.) the overwhelming majority of residents in Sepphoris were Jews. Even in the reign of Trajan coins were minted by the Jewish government, and the words "the Emperor gave" were stamped on them.[36] During the reign of Hadrian the old government was absolved and a gentile government installed, and the city became known as "Diocaesarea," city of Zeus and of the emperor. A Capitoline temple was apparently built at this time, as coins with such a temple appear from the time of Antoninus Pius (138-161 C.E.). The coins dramatically change from ones decorated with the common Jewish motifs of laurel wreath, palm tree, caduceus, and ears of grain to ones of pagan themes and images; this change best expresses the cultural issue in the population of Sepphoris in the second century C.E. Contrasting Herod and his son Antipas's periods of indirect rule, the Romans after the First Revolt were determined to have much greater control over the local population, primarily through a system of expanding urbanization and colonization via local administrators and armies. Where there were already large clusters of gentile inhabitants, e.g. Caesarea Maritima, Scythopolis, Ptolemais, and Sebaste (Samaria), they placed more soldiers. But even after the Great Revolt of 70 C.E. there were only 10,000 Roman Soldiers in Judea, comprised of the Tenth Legion and six to twelve auxiliary units. The Sixth Legion arrived in Galilee around 120 C.E. and 1,000 soldiers were stationed at Legio (Kefar 'Otnai). By 135, after the Bar Kochba War, that number increased to approximately 15,000.[37] Sepphoris, thus, on the basis of historical sources, remained overwhelmingly Jewish in the first century, and probably still had a majority population throughout the late antique period.

From the archaeology conducted at the site the theater would seem to date to the period 50-120 C.E. Even if further excavation shows that Antipas built it, we cannot gainsay the evidence that there was no *gymnasion*, that there are dozens of ritual baths in both well-to-do homes and smaller living units, and that the linguistic data from epigraphs in the later synagogues and some earlier tombs indicates a disposition toward Aramaic or Hebrew, though the later the material the more likely it is bi-lingual, i.e., Aramaic or Hebrew and Greek, or even simply Greek. Many of the kitchen wares are imported from Kefar Hananiah but alongside them are some local-made pots and numerous vessels of foreign imported wares, i.e., from outside Eretz Israel, some from distant regions. Much of the glass seems to be of local or regional manufacture.

Hence, the archaeology and history of Sepphoris strongly supports a case for Sepphoris in the time of Jesus being overwhelmingly Jewish in population, traditional in orientation toward language and common religious practice, urban in character but still not a city of the magnitude of one of the gentile cities, connected to the other towns and villages of Galilee by trade and the new requirements of an expanding population base, somewhat aristocratic because of its priestly component, retainer class and pro-Roman posture during the Great War, and perhaps an uncongenial but not unfamiliar place for Jesus as he went about Galilee preaching and teaching the new gospel. Jesus's relative avoidance of Sepphoris, if we interpret the silence of the New Testament somewhat narrowly, could well have been to avoid a clash with Antipas, the authorities, or some of the upper class citizens who might have been uncomfortable with his message. The evolving urban Galilean ethos is negatively depicted in the story of Antipas's birthday in Mark 6:21 ff., which results in the arrest and decapitation of John the Baptist.

CONCLUSION

On the basis of Galilean regionalism, archaeology, the gospels, and Josephus, it is the inescapable and unavoidable conclusion that Jesus's Galilean context was first and foremost a Jewish one both in content and in its political, administrative form. Despite the first advances of a growing urbanism in Palestine its manifestation in first century Galilee is somewhat modest when compared to the urbanism of gentile cities like Beth Shean, where a Jewish mi-

nority flourished and where apparently a gentile administration tolerated the Herodian client king, Antipas.

Hellenization was not so much an invasive force thrust upon indigenous culture from the outside to snuff it out, as it was a cultural force that enabled indigenous cultures, both Jewish and gentile, to express themselves authentically. Therefore, the appearance of some forms of Greco-Roman culture need not signify compromise, accommodation, or traumatic change but simply a way of expressing local culture in new and often exciting ways. In Galilee the most dramatic manifestations of this seemed to have occurred in the second century C.E. and later, especially at Sepphoris where the contextual setting of Rabbi Judah the Patriarch's literary activities and achievements was adorned by colorful scenes of the Dionysos legend preserved in stone mosaic.

In such a Galilee as we have described I cannot yet imagine a Mediterranean (read hellenistic or Graeco-Roman) tradition in which Cynic philosophical teaching had replaced Jewish learning and piety. Crossan in my opinion has confused the ethos of Galilee with the ethos of the autonomous cities, or even with the culture of the hellenistic cities of the west. The character of those places despite important Jewish minorities was pagan and gentile, and the environment for the Jewish residents was alien and sometimes hostile. Antipas for all his problems did little to offend his Jewish populace. He was careful to avoid images on his coins and did not propagate pagan culture.

In truth, the Galilean context of Jesus was such that both its incipient urbanism and its predominantly rural village culture could live in harmony. City and town were economically interlinked as we have demonstrated from ceramics, and even the Jewish towns and the four large villages of Upper Galilee and the two Herodian cities of Lower Galilee were in regular contact with one another as ceramics and coins indicate. As Douglas Edwards has proposed elsewhere[38] such data suggest that Mark and Q reflect both the images of town and city as well as point to continuing Jewish-gentile contact as the early Jesus movement moved about in its quest for followers. In particular, the focus of Q as Jonathan Reed notes where images of rural agricultural and urban life seem quite in place, is surely Galilee. To use his words: "I am therefore certain that the Q community, like all Galileans, bought, sold, and visited in the cities of Sepphoris and Tiberias. In fact, one can not preclude the possibility, from the agricultural and urban imagery, that many members of the Q community lived in Sepphoris and Tiberias."[39]

Finally, when all is said and done the Galilean context of Jesus is overwhelmingly Jewish in every respect, and this should come as no great surprise. Why so many scholars have associated the rural landscape of Galilee with all its towns and villages as being devoid of Jewish learning as well as lacking in the everyday accountrements of a Greco-Roman lifestyle, is hard to understand, and I leave it for others in the discipline of New Testament to reflect on. From the point of view of archaeology we have known otherwise for a long time, even from the mute stones and silent pots. As the present generation gets more accustomed to reading archaeological reports, perhaps the simplest artifact, or any object that is left behind when one culture disappears, will speak to historical questions with the same authority and clarity as one of the acknowledged sayings of Jesus. Judging from what has occurred the last few years, that time is not too far distant.

NOTES

[1] This paper was presented in 1993 at a joint session affiliated with the Annual Meetings of the Society of Biblical Literature and the American Schools of Oriental Research and sponsored by the Endowment for Biblical Research. Other members of the panel that looked at "Jesus in Historical Context" were E.P. Sanders and Paula Fredrikson.

[2] My principal earlier articles on this subject are these: "Galilean Regionalism as a Factor in Historical Reconstruction, *BASOR* 221 (1976) 93-101; "The Cultural Setting of Galilee: The Case of Early Judaism," *ANRW* 2.19.1, (Berlin: Walter De Gruyter, 1979) 686-701; "Galilean Regionalism: A Reappraisal," in *Approaches to Ancient Judaism*, vol. V, ed. W. Green (Atlanta: Scholars Press, 1985) 115-31. See also my essay, "An Archaeological Response to a New Testament Scholar," *BASOR* 295 (1995) 17-26.

[3] The final report on this work was jointly authored with A. Kraabel and J. Strange, *Ancient Synagogue Excavations at Khirbet Shema^C*, AASOR 42 (Durham: Duke University Press, 1976).

[4] With C. Meyers, "Expanding the Frontiers of Biblical Archaeology," *Eretz Israel* 20 (1989) 140-147; we have called this general field "socio-archaeology."

[5] With J. Strange and D. Groh, "The Meiron Excavation Project: Archaeological Survey in Galilee and Golan, 1976," *BASOR* 230 (1976) 1-24.

[6] For Meiron see the final report co-authored by J. Strange and C. Meyers *Excavations at Ancient Meiron* (Cambridge: ASOR, 1981); for Gush Halav see E. Meyers and C. Meyers, *Excavations at the Ancient Synagogue of Gush Halav* (Winona Lake: Eisenbrauns, 1990); for Nabratein see *BASOR* 246 (1982) 35-54, and literature there.

[7] J. Bowsher, "Architecture and Religion in the Decapolis: A Numismatic Survey," *Palestine Exploration Quarterly* 119 (1987) 62; see also G. Bowersock, *Hellenism in Late Antiquity* (Ann Arbor: University of Michigan, 1990) and the author's discussion of the general problem of Hellenism in the East, "The Challenge of Hellenism for Early Judaism and Christianity," *BA* 55 (1992) 84-91.

[8] The story of John of Gischala's trade in olive oil with the Jewish community of Tyre is especially intriguing in this regard. On this see T. Longstaff in Meyers and Meyers, *Excavation at the Ancient Synagogue of Gush Halav*, 1992, pp. 16-21. The Jewish presence at Beth Shean is amply documented in the literature but see entry in *NEAEHL* (1993) 1: 214-235.

[9] D. Adan-Bayewitz, *Common Pottery in Roman Galilee: A Study of Local Trade* (Ramat Gan: Bar-Ilan University Press, 1993).

[10] See entry in *NEAEHL* 3: 1028-1031.

[11] J. Reed, "The Population of Capernaum," Occasional Papers of the Institute for Antiquity and Christianity 23 (1992), has collected and commented upon the recent literature on population estimates. He has expanded his discussion in his recent doctoral dissertation at Claremont University, 1993, "Places in Early Christianity: Galilee, Archaeology, Urbanization, and Q." For this discussion the remarks of M. Broshi are most relevant: "The Population of Western Palestine in the Roman-Byzantine Period," *BASOR* 236 (1980) 1-10.

[12] Ibid; and *Herod Antipas* (Cambridge: Cambridge University Press, 1972).

[13] Using the methodology outlined by Broshi and Reed (see footnote no. 10) I come up with such a figure. Reed avoids trying to come up with such a global figure but it seems useful for the purposes of our discussion.

[14] Reed, *Places in Early Christianity*, 68-70.

[15] As for example do J. Overman, "Who were the First Urban Christians? Urbanization in Galilee in the First Century," *SBL Papers* 1988, 160-168 and H. Kee, "New Finds Illuminate the World and Text of the Bible: The Greco-Roman Era," in the *The Bible in the Twenty-first Century*, ed. H. Kee (New York: American Bible Society, 1993) 89-108 and "Early Christianity in the Galilee: Reassessing the Evidence from the Gospels," in *The Galilee in Late Antiquity*, 3-22.

[16] J. Crossan, *The Historical Jesus: The Life of a Mediterranean Jewish Peasant* (San Francisco: Harper, 1991).

[17] Personal communication. In this connection however, see his searching remarks in *Galilee, Jesus and the Gospels: Literary Approaches and Historical Investigations* (Philadelphia: Fortress Press, 1988) and "Urban Rural Relations in First Century Galilee: Some Suggestions from the Literary Sources," in *The Galilee in Late Antiquity*, 1992, 75-94.

[18] I am grateful to Professor Paul Corbey Finney for insights into this pericope. He has allowed me to read his unpublished paper, "The Rabbi and the Coin Portrait (Mark 12.15b & 16): Rigorous manqué," originally pre-

sented to the Center for Theological Inquiry in February, 1992.

[19] As proposed by G. Vermes in *Jesus the Jew* (Philadelphia: Fortress Press, 1972) 48-49. Cf., however, the remarks of D. Edwards, "The Socio-Economic and Cultural Ethos of the Lower Galilee in the First Century: Implications for the Nascent Jesus Movement," in *The Galilee in Late Antiquity*, 53-54.

[20] So R. Horsley and J. Hanson, *Bandits, Prophets, and Messiahs: Popular Movements at the Time of Jesus*, (New York: Winston Press, 1985).

[21] Y. Meshorer, *Jewish Coins of the Second Temple Period* (Tel Aviv: Massada, 1967) 75.

[22] Adan-Bayewitz, *Common Pottery in Roman Galilee*, and Aviam, "Galilee," *NEAEHL* 2: 453-458.

[23] Reed, *Places in Early Christianity*, 41.

[24] G. Pucci, "Pottery and Trade in the Roman Period," in *Trade in the Ancient Economy*, ed. P. Garnsey, K. Hopkins, and C. Whittaker (Berkeley: University of California Press, 1983) 105-117; Reed, *Places in Early Christianity*, 42.

[25] "The Bible and Archaeology," *BA* 47 (1984) 36-40 and J. Strange, "Some Implications of Archaeology for New Testament Studies," in *What Has Archaeology to do With Faith*, ed. J. Charlesworth and W. Weaver (Philadelphia: Fortress Press, 1992) 23-59. See also E. Meyers, "Second Temple Studies in the Light of Recent Archaeology: Part I: The Persian and Hellenistic Periods," *Currents in Research* 2 (1994) 25-42, and "Part II: The Roman Period: A Bibliography," *Currents in Research* 3 (1995) 129-152, with A. Lynd-Porter, M. Aubin, and M. Chancy.

[26] See M. Aviam, "Galilee."

[27] *The Documents from the Bar-Kochba Period in the Cave of Letters* (Jerusalem: Israel Exploration Society, 1989).

[28] See "ᶜIraq el-Emir," *NEAEHL* 2: 646-649.

[29] D. Edwards, "The Socio-Economic and Cultural Ethos of the Lower Galilee in the First Century," 72.

[30] Adan-Bayewitz, *Common Pottery in Roman Galilee*, 220.

[31] *Places in Early Christianity, passim.*

[32] Aviam, "Galilee." For further discussion of the road systems in Galilee, see also articles by J. Strange and D. Edwards/T. McCollough in this volume.

[33] Aviam, "Galilee." See also E. Meyers, E. Netzer, and C.L. Meyers, *Sepphoris* (Winona Lake, Indiana: Eisenbrauns, 1992).

[34] E. Meyers, "Roman Sepphoris in the Light of Recent Archaeology," in *Early Christianity in Context: Monuments and Documents*, ed. F. Manns and E. Alliata, Testa Festschrift. Collectio Maior vol. 38. (Jerusalem, Franciscan Printing Press, 1993) 84-91. And S. Miller,

"Sepphoris: The Well Remembered City," *BA* 55 (1992) 74ff. See also, C. Meyers and E. Meyers, "Sepphoris," in *The Oxford Encyclopedia of Archaeology in the Near East* (New York, Oxford University Press, 1996).

[35] In *Studies in the History of Traditions of Sepphoris* (Leiden: E.J. Brill, 1984).

[36] Z. Weiss, "Sepphoris," *NEAEHL* 4: 1324-1328.

[37] Z. Safrai, "The Roman Army in Galilee," in *Galilee in Late Antiquity*, 103-114 and *The Economy of Roman Palestine* (London: Routledge, 1994).

[38] D. Edwards, "The Socio-Economic and Cultural Ethos of the Lower Galilee in the First Century," 88-90.

[39] *Early Places in Christianity*, 145.

7

Jesus of Galilee and the Historical Peasant

J. Andrew Overman
Macalester College

The so-called Quest for the historical Jesus has a long and obstinate history. It is one of the few questions in biblical studies and the study of early Christianity which persists within both popular and scholarly discourse. Many scholars as well as the general public have a stake in the issues surrounding the historicity of the life, sayings and actions of Jesus of Nazareth. For most of the history of this debate in North America and in Europe the method used for engaging in the Quest has been a close literary-critical analysis of the Gospels. This approach has been augmented over the last generation by studies which offer broad historical analyses of the social and political milieu of Palestine in the time of Jesus. Those who combine these approaches suggest that any continuity between the events, setting, or ethos of early Roman Palestine on the one hand and the words and actions of Jesus in the Gospels on the other sheds further light on the Jesus of history. Practitioners search for *verisimilitude* between the social world of the first century figure Jesus of Nazareth and the life and actions of Jesus as they come to us in the Gospels. Within the history of the Quest for the historical Jesus this synthetic approach is still rather recent and has not replaced the approach which has prevailed over the last two hundred years. A close literary analysis of sayings, literary forms, and redactional layers remains the dominant method employed in the perpetual Quest for the historical Jesus within biblical scholarship.

Only recently has the question about the nature of Galilee in the first century emerged as a viable and debatable question within the larger arena of the Quest for the historical Jesus. Galilee has become a fertile field for working out social, political and theological issues related to the on-going Quest for the historical Jesus. This is, in part, a result of the work of Jim Strange and Eric Meyers and the twenty-five years of excavations they have conducted in Upper and Lower Galilee. Their ground-breaking research in Galilee, and the unusual sacrifice made by both men to bring Galilean archaeology into the modern era, has resulted in Galilee becoming fodder and fuel for the Quest for the historical Jesus. This may be an unintended consequence of their twenty-five years of work. But the historical Galilee is quickly emerging--in certain circles--as epiphenominal to the Quest for the historical Jesus. That is, predictably, parts of Galilee, now excavated and interpreted by archaeologists like Jim Strange, have become the domain of, and a resource for, Quests for the historical Jesus. Within predominantly Christian culture work in Galilee will henceforth always be implicated in the history of Jesus and his subsequent impact. And archaeological data and various interpretations of the ethos and nature of early Roman Galilee will now be employed in the service of answering Quest questions. Because of the extraordinary work of Meyers and Strange, and the responsibility they have exhibited in getting their findings and reports out to others, the historical Galilee is now data and a debate which has been incorporated into the historical Jesus question by consumers and manufacturers of the Quest-business.

Though Galilean archaeology in the Roman period is a relatively recent endeavor, there are already numerous examples of interpretations of the historical Galilee which are utilized to substantiate and legitimate existing paradigms for the historical Jesus. For example, Richard Batey's interpretation and reconstruction of the life of Jesus and the influences which acted upon him in *Jesus and the Forgotten City: New Light on Sepphoris and the Urban world of Jesus*, stress the urban environment which must have so impressed Jesus.[1] This environment influenced Jesus' vocabulary, provided him an opportunity to react to broader Hellenistic influences in lower Galilee, and helped to fashion his message of personal and corporate renewal. In Batey's romantic reconstruction the urban milieu of Jesus' upbringing helped him fashion a vision of the kingdom of God. In the city of Sepphoris Jesus witnessed abuses by elite members of society who focused on law, money and power, and not the kingdom of God as it had been traditionally understood in the language and experience of Jesus. Jesus is not hostile to the city in the view of Batey. But salient urban images and experiences,-- high taxes, city government and officials, the theater-- these influences impacted Jesus profoundly. The archaeological material is utilized by Batey in such a way that the city is seen as the place where Jesus' mission and message was shaped. The pivotal Hellenistic convention and institution of the *polis* also became the stage where others could hear the message of commitment and renewal which Batey sees as the heart of the Jesus message. The archaeological material from Sepphoris, together with a selection of texts and stories from Josephus, form the basis of the portrait Batey constructs. In first-century lower Galilee, Greek language and Hellenistic cultural practices inform Jesus' outlook and convictions.[2]

Another example exists in portions of the "Q" seminar of the Society of Biblical Literature (SBL) and among those who pursue reconstructions of a Cynic-like Jesus. In the reconstructions emanating from this scholarly circle one can observe the utilization of material culture of Galilee in a manner not dissimilar to Batey. Here again the so-called Hellenistic milieu of Galilee is used to place Jesus squarely within a context informed by popular Hellenistic philosophies. Central in this regard is the popular Hellenistic street-wise philosophy of Cynicism. Jesus' way of speech and teaching mirrors the wise sayings and aphorisms of Cynic-like peripatetic philosophers from other parts of the Hellenistic world. Occasional archaeological material is drawn upon to confirm the presence of these Hellenistic influences in the time and setting of Jesus' life and that of his first followers. Scholars of Q, the source common to Matthew and Luke in the New Testament, tend to assume a Galilean origin for this early Gospel source. The Galilee of Q--and apparently also of Jesus--possessed the social, political and philosophical Greek influences that they see imbedded within the Gospels themselves. Occasionally scholars then extrapolate from the material and so-called social world of Galilee to find a Jesus and early followers imbued with the cultural conventions and worldviews typical of Cynic philosophers and Hellenistic wise men.[3]

From time to time the "historical Galilee" has been utilized and evaluated in a manner analogous to the Q group by another corner of the SBL, "The Historical Jesus" seminar. In that particular venue Galilee has been reconstructed and construed to illumine and reinforce portraits of Jesus presented by a range of contemporary scholars. Evidence from the material world of Galilee is usually strained to lay the foundation for a Galilee in revolt, or a Galilee awash in Greco-Roman influences and power as a result of trade, commerce, and development which threaten traditional life there. These influences constitute the context from which Jesus emerged and form the background against which his message should be interpreted and understood.[4]

In these examples we can see verisimilitude at work. In both instances--whether in the "Q" or the "Historical Jesus" seminars -archaeological material from Galilee is used selectively to pursue contemporary paradigms and claims about Jesus or his first followers. The Hellenistic influences and practices long elevated in the field of New Testament studies and most prominently associated with the work of Rudolf Bultmann, have received renewed impetus through certain archaeological discoveries in Galilee. The older dichotomy between so-called Hellenistic culture on the one hand and Palestinian on the other has been dissolved in part because archaeological discoveries in Galilee have demonstrated a larger degree of "hellenization" in Palestine than Bultmann or his disciples could have imagined. Proponents of the Cynic-Jesus paradigm find in the material evidence for greater hellenization in Galilee grist for their mill. Jesus becomes a popular Hellenistic philosopher who combined a cynic-like worldview with certain innovative interpretations of Jewish laws and traditions. It turns out that Galilee was ripe for such a development and virtuoso sometime in the early Roman period. Again, Sepphoris serves as the celebrated instance for these developments, but material from Capernaum and some other smaller Galilean sites is also utilized in this reconstruction.

For people working explicitly on the historical Jesus the very same Hellenistic influences are utilized to lay bare the socio-economic tensions which form Jesus' context and outlook. The cities of Galilee are prime symbols of these influences and tensions. These tensions provoked Jesus' ministry and were responsible for his death. Jesus is a traditional Galilean responding to the pressures and the changes brought about by Roman imperialism and local corruption. The material world of Galilee has been interpreted by Questers to further outline the plausibility of their particular reconstructions of Jesus.

I too wrote an article in 1988 and followed it up with several other pieces which also focused on the "urban" character of lower Galilee.[5] I did not pursue this line in order to place Jesus within or against any particular Hellenistic philosophies. And I certainly do not think that archaeological material can be used to determine historicity questions with regard to Jesus' sayings and actions. Archaeology can be used to determine some historical questions. For example, the presence or date of an earthquake, the cessation of a village, or the arrival of certain sorts of cultural conventions or influences into a city are all legitimate historical questions which archaeologists can reasonably address.[6]

My approach in these earlier pieces was an attempt to use select archaeological finds to draw attention to the broader political reality of imperial rule and client lordship during the time of Jesus in Galilee. So, while I was explicitly pursuing political or socio-political questions, I too looked for verisimilitude between parts of the Gospels and certain select archaeological finds. The archaeological material did not shed any light on whether Jesus actually did or said anything. But, I did use the archaeological material to frame much of the Gospel material within a set of political and cultural tensions. Also, like two prolific contemporary Questers, Richard Horsley and Dominic Crossan, and many others studying early Roman Galilee, I utilized narratives from Josephus to identify putative parallels between the social tensions he describes and the archaeological material as we could identify it.

In the examples mentioned above, including my own, archaeological material was used tangentially and selectively to construct a picture or paradigm of Jesus and his first followers. In most reconstructions, the paradigm or picture being offered, with occasional reference to archaeology, is actually a retrieval, or a recovery of an earlier paradigm based almost solely on textual and historical analysis. In the case of the Cynic Jesus we see Rudolf Bultmann's Paul re-emerge as Q's Jesus. Where the stress upon the urban life of first century Galilee and its effect on Jesus and his first followers is concerned, much of what S. J. Case and some of the other American Social Gospel proponents said earlier in this century has found its way back into the research and the archaeology of Galilee. Leroy Waterman's initial excavations at Sepphoris were inspired in part by the conjecture of the role and thought of the city in the ministry of Jesus in the 1920's and 1930's in American urban Divinity Schools. To the extent that archaeology is now part of the Quest business, its role is to reinforce existing paradigms and assumptions.

This is also true in the case of the recent and popular titles by R. Horsley and J.D. Crossan.[7] The works of these Questers attempt to use, however sparingly, cultural and archaeological remains to offer up a reconstruction of Jesus and his movements. Their primary sources are Josephus and the Gospels. But the archaeological material is utilized and is relevant when it seems to bear on the paradigm they offer concerning the life and aims of Jesus of Nazareth. I should, however, point out that Horsley has just written another book on Galilee which attempts to examine the archaeological material more thoroughly and systematically. This is an interesting development. But in this later work Horsley's paradigm and reconstruction of Jesus and his movement is virtually unchanged after his fuller analysis of the archaeological material from Galilee.[8]

When viewed within the broader and protracted context of the Quest for the historical Jesus, Crossan and Horsley offer basically the same paradigm and reconstruction. There are differences, but they are slight and without much consequence. Jesus came from a peasant-agrarian experience, forged in lower Galilee, and formed a social program to renew or reform Galilean (and perhaps) Judean society. Traditional ways of life and long standing social structures which provided for continuity and safety among traditional peasant villagers had been disrupted by Roman imperialism and the imposition of Judean politics and religio-political leaders upon Galilee. Jesus resisted these influences and believed they were destroying the way of life God had given traditional Galileans. This resistance and his teaching and actions directed against wicked colonial realities and local carriers of imperial power and influence finally got him killed as a social revolutionary.

One key feature of the approaches of Horsley and Crossan is the cross-cultural data they import into their paradigm. This can be an enriching and constructive exercise. But, the material must ultimately be analogous to be illuminating. Both Horsley and Crossan utilize evidence from early medieval Europe about peasant societies and revolts.[9]

Fundamental to both of these reconstructions is the image of Jesus as a peasant. Peasant represents a type of person--and more importantly--a type of social and economic existence and experience which can be traced and studied synchronically. That is, the peasant is a typos historically. And peasant movements and phenomena from other periods and places constitute important information for Horsley and Crossan. The metasocial analyses of Lenski, Sjoberg, Hobsbawm, Kautsky, Boissevain, and others provide important models and analogical information for both scholars.

But peasants and peasant revolts are not the same across time and peasants should not be spared the historical and interpretive rigor scholars apply to elite authors or ancient ideologues with an ax to grind. There are myths and legends about peasants that can mislead attempts at meaningfully applying medieval analogies to the history of Jesus. In my view both Horsley and Crossan have made this mistake. A most interesting case in point is Yves-Marie Brece's 1986 book, *Histoire des Croquants*, translated in 1990 as, *The History of Peasant Revolts*.[10] This book on the origins of rebellion in early modern France provides a serious warning to people who wish to draw inferences and information about peasant life and behavior generally for the purposes of conducting their Quests.

Brece, an archivist and historian, has provided an anatomy of peasant revolts in 16th and 17th century France. Perhaps more significantly, he has illumined the myths which frequently surround peasant revolts. Rebels involved in four revolts in this period in France left a total of thirty-five texts in the form of manifestos or codes of conduct. According to Brece, these texts are largely consistent with one another. Among peasant bandits and rebels they reveal a basic and consistent concern with food prices and taxes. These are the usual causes of peasant disturbance. In southwest France the burden of billeting troops also played a role in isolated disturbances.[11]

Of course, these concerns are echoed in the Gospels. There is talk of taxes, the issues surrounding resistance and perhaps, in Matthew's Sermon on the Mount, an allusion to billeting soldiers or at the very least, a reference to the burden of an imperial setting for the indigenous population (cf. Matt.5:38-41).[12] But these initial impressions and apparent parallels between so-called peasants of the first and sixteenth centuries can be misleading.

Contemporary Questers utilizing peasant models and histories have not been very critical when speaking about peasants. Of course, the overwhelming amount of evidence about first century peasantry in Palestine and peasant revolts in particular, comes from Josephus. The tendentious nature of Josephus' work has long been recognized, but a critical interpretation of him is not really very much in evidence when we read about first century peasants.

Through a careful study of the small amount of archival information available Brece has shown the importance and the role of myth making in the stories of peasants and peasant revolts in 16-17th century France. These are precisely the people and places that contribute so much to peasant studies and reconstructions and to the cross-cultural analyses which provide important information for the Peasant-Jesus. For example, small disturbances become, in peasant lore, full fledged revolts and victorious expressions by the oppressed masses. Brece has noted this is particularly the case with taxes. In seventeenth century France taxes were condemned in subversive speeches and manifestos. What Brece refers to as a "doctrine" about taxes among French peasants also includes a more or less

neutral, if not positive view of the King. The King, however, has been deceived and mislead by his ministers and clients. He has been provided deceptive data. Had he been given the right information he would understand and alleviate the situation of the peasantry. Some of these clients would actually rob from the King's coffers in extreme expressions of this mythology.

Most myths around taxes were optimistic. People spoke and dreamt of better times. But also, imaginary taxes were spoken of. Frequently in peasant tax mythology one can hear of some additional, and even more brutal tax approaching. This is the case with the famed *gabelle*, or legendary salt tax in southwest France. Leaflets, for example, were printed in Guyenne in 1638 warning that soon twenty four new edicts with respect to this tax would soon be introduced. The *gabelle* was presented as an "ever-present" menace. Throughout the century people were on the alert. And vigilance against the imminent *gabelle* helped to foster a self-image among peasant people.

One crucial point in Brece's work is this: there is a popular world of tax resistance that is at least as much mythology as it is fact among peasant communities. This mythology and these stories have been crucial for peasant self-understanding, for fostering local lore, and for developing a kind of peasant eschatology and cohesion. But to read these peasant accounts as if they were historical events is as uncritical as a similar reading of the Gospels. Horsley and Crossan do not do the latter, but freely engage in the former. The noble peasant has some urgent issues at had. These have tended to be planting, harvesting, and the engagements of daily life. Stories about resistance and rebellion, Brece has helped us to see, is more for the tavern than for the battlefield.

There are occasional rebellions. Rebellion among peasant communities is not a complete fabrication. Certain regions and towns became known for their inclination toward resistance. And there seems to be some demonstrable proof that this was indeed the fact.[13] There is always some historical thread out of which entire peasant myths and legends are spun. Somewhere somebody did revolt at sometime against marauding soldiers, rude tax collectors, or an escalation in the price of bread or salt. But these events, became the stuff out of which entire mythologies about peasants, their determined resistance, and their *dramatis personae* were created. As Brece says, "sometimes resistance took the form of a dozen people slamming their doors in the face of a bailiff."[14]

The myths about taxes, imperial and military behavior, and peasant uprisings constituted an important part of the social order and balance. These stories provided identity and heroic grist for the peasant mill and tavern. But these stories also, when developed and circulating around medieval France, served as a reminder and check to overly zealous soldiers and clients of the King or ruler. These stories formed a social and political check and balance in early modern Europe.

Let us reflect on first century Galilee informed by this rather different reconstruction of peasants, their lives, legends, and resistance. When one reads the legend of the siege of Jotapata in Josephus, we are confronted with a lengthy narrative about the resistance of the Galileans against the onslaught of Vespasian's troops (*War* 3.111ff.). With some brief asides, the narrative of the siege of Jotapata goes on for over two hundred lines in the Loeb Classical Library! What a dramatic and spectacular episode of resistance we find in the Galilean village of Jotapata!

Excavations have been on-going at Jotapata since about 1990. Roman presence and to some extent a conflict has been confirmed by the discovery of a plastered siege platform or staging area. To date there have been no bodies found, no first century destruction layer, and the number of ballistae and Roman projectiles do not seem commensurate with the size and vigor of Josephus' siege.

Something did occur at Jotapata. There is little or no domestication of the top of the site after the early Roman period. And it appears the buildings on top of the hill were stripped to bedrock. The cut stones from the houses and buildings of the village were taken down the hill and reused in the later Byzantine period structures. But does the material evidence from Jotapata correspond to the story from *War* 3? Of course not.

Like Brece's France, a core or kernel of resistance became a protracted and fanciful narrative which served the larger purpose of peasant (and Roman military) story-telling, myth-making, and, as noted above, a social check and balance.

The legends of the Fourth Philosophy, an upper Galilean tax resistance group, known to us, of course, only from Josephus (cf. *Antiquities* 18.4-9//*War* 2.117-118)), are also suggestive after having considered Brece's analysis. The stories from Josephus are freely and literally reproduced by Horsley and Crossan as a means of constructing a certain sort of verisimilitude which accords well with their paradigm of the historical Jesus and the Jesus movement.[15] The model operative in Horsley and Crossan could be called "Jesus-*Croquant*;" that is, Jesus the Rebel-Peasant.

Josephus, in the longer description in *Antiquities* 18, describes the Fourth Philosophy, lead by Judas from the Golan Heights, as a tax resistance movement. But Josephus accuses them of being motivated by private gain, and claims that, ultimately, they were responsible for corrupting the nation because they "planted the seeds of trouble which subsequently overtook it." While Josephus is here characteristically negative about those people who do not promote peace and stability, Horsley and Crossan are characteristically trusting in what this story tells them

about Jesus' Galilee. These movements, and these disruptions are demonstrative of the kind of system and context in which Galilean peasants lived and in which Jesus developed his message of social reform and the commonwealth of God.

With respect to analogies from medieval peasant movements, the story of the Fourth Philosophy is perhaps the most interesting. One of the largest peasant uprisings in France took place in Perigord, between 1637 and 1641. Taxes were at the root of this uprising. A specific tax had been added in 1637 toward support of the troops at Bayonne. This was ordered by the governor of Guyenne. Corn had gone up in price and this new "ration" seemed pretty hefty by February of 1637.[16] By March certain acts of violence were being manifest by the peasants, who came to be called *Croquants*, and around whom legends and lore developed. This in fact became the popular term for a rebel peasant.

With regard to tax *resentment*, it is usual for people to voice their displeasure, but historically, this very rarely develops into violence or outright resistance for that matter. This is worth noting. Tax resentment is responsible for much of the popular legends about taxes, tax exisemen, and even tax resistance. But the Croquant did evidence some violence. Two sergeants dispatched to collect the tax were lynched. Though this was one of the largest expressions of peasant revolt in medieval France, many of the citizens of the towns resisted the Croquant, and barred them from entry into their towns.[17] The Croquant did finally take the town of Bergerac, which was unfortified and had no garrison. But even this, the largest of tax resistance movements in France during this period, held this town for a mere twenty days.

The text from Josephus concerning the Fourth Philosophy, reads very much like a small expression of resistance, reflecting a larger, more pervasive feeling of tax resentment among the people. And the story of the Fourth Philosophy, especially in *Antiquities* 18, is greatly expanded and developed to serve other purposes. When compared against the larger history of peasant revolts and tax resistance, this was a small "event," which like other peasant narratives developed its own mythology, and was reiterated by Josephus. But this should not be utilized to punctuate the putative resistance that is part of the fabric of Galilee and very fiber of the Galilean peasant. A closer and more critical reading of peasant "histories" is called for.

With respect to general and sporadic peasant uprisings, Brece's comments are helpful for those looking for Galilean peasants in first century. Many accounts of peasant resistance were circulating in France of the late middle ages. And these accounts formed an important part of peasant mythology. "Uprisings which broke out in cities threw up a number of ringleaders. Previously unknown leaders rose to prominence in the course of the secret discussions which took place in shops, taverns, and the seditious meetings which were held in daylight in the open space afforded by the public square or churchyard. When the rising seemed about to collapse in the face of general apathy and fear of government reprisals, a core of diehards would also emerge from the ranks of the population to make an unexpected last-ditch stand...This desperation usually drove them to suicidal tactics...They clung to the legends which circulated in the world of tax resistance, and preferred to die rather than to lose a traditional (though an illusion) freedom, or submit to an (imaginary?) *gabelle*."[18]

This quotation from Brece is a caution against reading isolated, and often developed and largely fictionalized events, into any larger social history. He captures the isolated, fringe, and largely unpopular nature of sporadic peasant uprisings. But the stories and myths that developed around such famous leaders, or groups like the *Croquant, sound* very much like some of the stories of resistance and occasional rebellion reiterated by Josephus. Josephus had heard these legends grounded in a strain of fact, and he believed them, or retold them for his particular purposes.

Songs, stories and legends developed and were expanded over time in the seventeenth century as much for accompaniment with *paysant* brew and story telling in tavern or town square, as to advance a peasant cause or retell any sort of history. Small uprisings and feats of resistance become noble acts of defiance by famous peasants few had met in the notorious region of Crocq. The Perigord rebellion of 1637 fostered such legends. "Jack Flour," a ploughman named "Cornstore," or one "Captain Clog," were the legendary rebels who were the stuff of barroom historians and older story tellers who could entertain younger workers amid breaks or a fallow season.

And the Galilean peasantry had its own *dramatis personae*; John of Gischala, Judas, Theudas, (Jesus?). Josephus talks of peasant and brigand actions and attitudes with much the same flair as the popular stories of seventeenth century France. Why? At this point we can only surmise. Josephus would like his audience to think of the Jews as a noble and virtuous race. This will certainly facilitate their incorporation into the broader Roman world and empire. And, of course, Josephus was a Flavian author. Much of what he had to write was driven by a fairly well defined and pervasive, Flavian propaganda program. Josephus' themes of peace being restored to a widely disrupted region, and Flavian virtue and wisdom making its way around the world, are the very themes seen in other Flavian writers.[19] In fact, in *War* 2.375ff., Josephus explicitly connects his story of the Jewish war with the other Flavian accomplishments around the empire. He mentions the British and German victories, and tries to as-

sert that if Vespasian could handle them, he certainly could handle the Jewish rebels. In fact, very little happened at Batavia in Germany, and it is possible nothing happened in Britain.[20] Nevertheless, Josephus sings the same tune as another famous Flavian writer, Cornelius Tacitus, that Vespasian had purged the empire of instability and civil war (*Hist*.4.3). Naturally, popular unrest and uprisings were necessary for the Flavians to be the world restorers their propaganda claimed. These popular, and now predictable peasant stories and myths fit nicely into Josephus', and the Flavian's, scheme. Josephus has reiterated these legends for a reason, and we, too often and too easily, have believed him.

The material culture certainly does not support, or deny, the Peasant-Jesus paradigm. The archaeological evidence is extraneous to this argument. It rests instead, I would suggest, on too facile a reading of Josephus which supports some apprehendable, contemporary reconstruction of the Jesus of history.

Whether Jesus was a rebel-peasant, a reformer, a pacifist, or religious reactionary looking back toward a purer and simpler time, or an eastern popular version of a Greek philosopher depends on the interpreter or Quester. But from now on, evidence from the material culture of Galilee will be used, however selectively, by Questers to support the views and reconstructions of Jesus they promote. The archaeological evidence from Galilee is value neutral concerning these various interpretations. What transpires now is that data from the material culture of Galilee is marshaled and construed variously to conform to the *historical* picture or paradigm of Jesus which emerges in the work of contemporary Questers.

This can happen now because a handful of archaeologists, and Jim Strange is a huge figure among them, worked diligently to uncover whatever the ground would yield up from early and middle Roman Galilee. That Galilee is forever ensconced in the Quest business may be an unhappy and unintended consequence for Jim Strange and Eric Meyers. But to the extent that archaeology is even utilized by biblical scholars and Questers to conform first century Galilee to their paradigm, they owe a great debt to these two men who opened up the archaeology of the Galilee in this period.

NOTES

[1] Grand Rapids: Baker, 1991.

[2] See also Batey's earlier article, "Jesus and the Theater," *NTS* 30 (1984) 563-574. The inspiration and influence of an earlier quester who was part of the so-called American social Gospel movement out of the University of Chicago, Shirley Jackson Case, is in evidence in this article. Case himself, much earlier in this century, wrote

about the influence of the city on the historical Jesus in "Jesus and Sepphoris," *JBL* 45 (1926) 14-21.

[3]There is of late numerous examples of this approach to Jesus and Galilee through the study of Q. See recently L. Vaage, *Galilean Upstarts: Jesus' First Followers According to Q*, (Valley Forge: Trinity Press International, 1994), and B. Mack, *The Lost Gospel: The Book of Q and Christian Origins*, (San Francisco: HarperCollins, 1993).

[4]An example of this approach at work are the four papers on Galilee delivered at the Historical Jesus Seminar at the Annual meeting of the Society of Biblical Literature in 1988. See D. Lull (ed.), *Society of Biblical Literature 1988 Seminar Papers*, (Atlanta: Scholars Press, 1988) 160-209.

[5]J. Overman, "Who were the First Urban Christians: Urbanization in First Century Galilee," 160-168.

[6]This is developed further in my, "Recent Advances in the Archaeology of the Galilee in the Roman Period," *Currents in Research: Biblical Studies* 1 (1993) 35-58.

[7]In the case of Crossan see, *The Historical Jesus: The Life of a Mediterranean Jewish Peasant*, (San Francisco: HarperCollins, 1991). The front cover claims this book is, "the first comprehensive determination of who Jesus was, what he said, what he did." This was the first indication that HarperCollins was aiming to become the next big voice in the on-going quest for the historical Jesus. What is interesting here, however, is that in this instance, a business, with a primary focus on the market, was going to be the driving force, and not particular scholars. Harper-Collins has published numerous subsequent books on the historical Jesus with similar grand claims and dramatic breakthroughs. In the case of Horsley, see *Jesus and the Spiral of Violence: Popular Jewish Resistance in Roman Palestine*, (San Francisco: Harper & Row, 1987), and--with J. Hanson--*Bandits, Prophets, and Messiahs: Popular Movements at the Time of Jesus* (Minneapolis: Winston, 1985).

[8]*Archaeology, History, and Society in Galilee: The Social Context of Jesus and the Rabbis* (Valley Forge: Trinity Press International, 1996).

[9]For Crossan, the essential role of Jesus as peasant is built in the title. He is a "mediterranean Jewish *peasant*." He is both "peasant and protester," as the title of chapter seven claims. For Horsley, Israel's origins are found in the covenant "the peasantry" struck with God. See, *Bandits, Prophets, and Messiahs*, 5. See also *Galilee: History, Politics, People*, (Valley Forge: Trinity Press International, 1995) 189.

[10]Tr. A. Whitmore, (Ithaca: Cornell University, 1990).

[11]Some of his findings are developed in a more general way in his 1987 work, *Revolt and Revolution in Early Modern Europe: An Essay on the History of Political Violence*, tr. J. Bergin (New York: St. Martin's Press, 1987).

[12]The Roman imperial setting of the Sermon, and much of Matthew's larger narrative is detailed in, J. Overman, *Church and Community in Crisis: The Gospel According to Matthew*. The New Testament in Context, (Valley Forge: Trinity Press International, 1996).

[13]Brece, *History of Peasant Revolts*, 109 ff.

[14]Ibid., 197.

[15]See Horsley, *Jesus and the Spiral of Violence*, 77ff. and Crossan, *The Historical Jesus*, 112ff.

[16]Brece, History of Peasant Revolts, 109.

[17]Brece, *History of Peasant Revolts*, 113

[18]Brece, *History of Peasant Revolts*, 276.

[19]See P. Taylor, "Valerius' Flavian *Argonautica*," *CQ* 44 (1994) 212-235; D. Edwards, "Religion, Power and Politics: Jewish Defeats by the Romans in Iconography and Josephus," in J. Overman and R. MacLennan (eds.), *Diaspora Jews and Judaism*, (Atlanta: Scholars Press, 1992), 293-309; And Z. Yavetz, "Reflections on Titus and Josephus," *GRBS* 16 (1975) 411-432.

[20]See M. Smallwood, "Valerius Flaccus' Argonautica I.5-21," *Mnemosyne* 15 (1962) 170-172.

8

German Scholarship on Rabbinic Judaism: The Goldberg-Schäfer School

Jacob Neusner
University of South Florida and Bard College

The character and future of the study of a given religion within a particular cultural context provide insight into the issues of national intellectual life in general, as these are played out in specific distinctive problems. That is particularly the case when we take up a nation such as Germany, which gave birth to the science of the study of religion in general and to the academic study of Judaism (*Wissenschaft des Judenthums*) in particular. That is why on-going debates on the future of Judaic studies in Germany do well to survey not only the past, but also the present state of that field. It is the simple fact that, today, German is not an important language in scholarship on the study of Judaism; students have to learn the language only to read articles and books of historical, but not of contemporary, scholarly consequence. Little comes out that demands attention from scholars of Judaism in its classical and normative phases. That is not solely because of the events of the National Socialist period; it is also because, in the half century that followed, such scholarship on Judaism that did get underway in Germany remained essentially isolated and out of touch with the rest of the world. Declining to debate with others who hold different opinions from their own, the new generation paid a very heavy price for the *Todschweigen* that it chose to practice,

as we see in a specific case. No one burned obnoxious books; they just did not read and debate with them.

While acknowledging the definitive role of German scholars of Judaic learning (*Wissenschaft des Judenthums*) in founding the field within the framework of the academy, parties to the discussion do well to consider the concrete facts of scholarship in our own times. And, when they do, they will come to recognize the parlous and flimsy foundations for future scientific work. For, as we shall see with reference to the study, in Germany, of the classics of Judaism, the field proves not only small but idiosyncratic and asymetrical to world scholarship. The dominant German school of Rabbinic Judaism today, the Goldberg-Schäfer School, shows the price paid when a tiny, isolated group pursues a subject in an essentially subjective manner. In that fact we discern how a great academic tradition breaks down; the causes hardly require close examination in this context.

That school takes as its gravamen the importance of critical editions of the classics, which is surely a common truth, but then imagines that no one but that school appreciates the importance of diverse versions of a single document. The study of the Rabbinic classics--Mishnah, Talmud, Midrash- compilations--in contemporary Germany focuses upon the mechanical distribution of variant readings among the manuscript and earliest printed testimonies to those documents. That, of course, forms a familiar and unexceptionable field of learning. From the beginnings of the formation of the Rabbinic literature at the closure of the Mishnah, "our sages of blessed memory" and their heirs and continuators recognized the fluid state of the textual tradition, both mnemonic for the Mishnah, and in writing or in notes for other components of the canon, redacted as documents and redacted in documents alike. The pages of the Talmud present rich evidence of the variety of readings and versions that sages possessed, and some of the most adventurous--and successful--analytical-dialectical compositions propose to interpret textual variations by appeal to conflicting legal theories--a standard hermeneutic in the great tradition of Rabbinic exegesis of Rabbinic documents.

In modern times as well, a landmark study of the text of the Mishnah, which sits on the shelf of every active scholar of the field, came forth from Y.N. Epstein, *Mavo Lemusah Hamishnah.*[1] The diversity of the readings finds its match in the paucity of manuscript evidence. Finally, modern scholarship, under academic and theological auspices alike, has yet to produce critical texts for the various documents, or even reach a consensus on what we can mean by a critical text. It follows that admonitions to the scholarly world to take account of the parlous textual tradition for the Rabbinic documents repeat the obvious.

Two centers of the study of Judaism today take as their critical standpoint that obvious fact, Jerusalem and Germany. The two schools are scarcely comparable, the former comprised by many active scholars, the latter by scarcely a handful. The more important difference between them is that the former treats the fact as important but not determinative, while the latter finds itself fixated on the problem of manuscript variants. While the Jerusalem school distinguishes itself in its meticulous concern for variant readings, the entire scholarly community takes full cognizance of the problem. I cannot point to a single scholar who builds tall structures by ignoring the shifting sands of printed editions and variant readings. That fact has not prevented the German school, in the persons of the late Arnold Maria Goldberg of Frankfurt and Peter Schäfer of Berlin, from insisting that, by reason of the broad variation in readings of this or that manuscript or passage, no substantive historical work can be carried on in the study of Rabbinic Judaism. In the context of the profoundly historistic universe in which that judgment is set forth, such a position removes from the realm of active culture and contemporary discourse the entire presence of Judaism, embodied as it is in its classical, Rabbinic documents. It is, therefore, a nihilistic position, which reduces scholarship to computerization of manuscript variations and the consequent reproduction thereof--without judgment, indeed, without palpable purpose.

Having devoted forty years to research into the history of the formative age of Judaism, that is, the first six centuries C.E., I took an interest in the German school's position on this matter; but it was a special interest, since I have been the primary focus of that school's negative criticism. In the Goldberg-Schäfer school, no historical work, no history of ideas, no investigation of the context for the text, can take place, for--and let me state with emphasis--in that school's conception, to begin with we have no text. My own work was explicitly dismissed because, in Schäfer's view, I posit a text that can be studied historically; thus I found it necessary to take an interest in his criticism, to see what is to be learned from it.

The one thing no one had to learn from Schäfer was that the various documents come to us in diverse versions. Along with everybody else, I was taught to take account of variants, large and small. That is why, from the very beginning of the documentary method,[2] I took account of the problem of determining that on which I was working, taking full account of the uncertainty of the text tradition for any given passage or even for documents as a whole. Indeed, the uncertainty of readings in any one passage provoked the search for recurrent and large-scale formal uniformities. For the case of the Mishnah, for example, the method focused upon the characteristics that recur throughout a document, not on the details that appear only here or there. Not episodic but fixed traits of form therefore dictated the analytical procedures: recurrent patterns in rhetoric, definitive traits in the principles of logical coherence in holding together compositions in composites, composites in a whole and complete statement.

At no point does the description of a document rest upon a specific reading or unique traits that occur in some one place. On the contrary, the very essence of the documentary method is to describe the whole, and that means, traits that are uniform throughout. By definition, these traits of the document as a whole also will characterize the diverse manuscript evidence of the bits and pieces of the part, and no one who has examined the problem of the text of the Mishnah can fail to recognize that simple fact! That focus on the permanent, the recurrent, and the characteristic and definitive takes full account of variations of detail. It goes without saying that no thesis on the history or the religion set forth in a given document can rest securely on the foundations of one reading as against some other, any more than we can rely for facts on attributions of sayings to specific named sages, on the one side, or narratives of events involving them, on the other. Other data have to be identified, described, analyzed, and interpreted, for the study of history and the history of the religion, Judaism.

Now, when we ask which text tradition, or which version, of a document we subject to documentary description, analysis, and interpretation, we therefore take up a question that by definition simply does not apply. Every Rabbinic document we possess from the formative age exhibits throughout its textual testimonies precisely those uniformities of rhetorical, topical, and logical traits that come under description in the documentary method. I cannot point to a single judgment of a documentary character set forth in any of my accounts that relies upon one reading, rather than another. Where we have critical editions, it goes without saying I translate and analyze those versions, e.g., Theodor-Albeck for Genesis Rabbah, Finkelstein for Sifra and Sifre to Deuteronomy; where we do not, I work on the standard printed edition.

And this brings us back to the German school of Rabbinic Judaism. The only major players in that school, Goldberg and his student, Peter Schäfer, have found themselves so impressed by the obstacles put forth by a fluid and sparse text tradition as to claim we have no documents at all, only variant readings. That nihilistic position then defines the task of learning as the assembly of variant readings and the publication, with virtually no critical judgment, of a mass of this and that. Work of a historical and cultural character simply loses its bearings, if we have no documents at all.

That is the rather odd position of Arnold Maria Goldberg, "Once it has been written, every text is exclusively synchronic, all the textual units exist simultaneously, and the only diachronic relation consists in the reception of the text as a sequence of textual units whose 'first' and 'then' become 'beforehand' and 'afterwards' in the reception of the text...The synchronicity of a text is...the simultaneous juxtaposition of various units, independent of when the units originated."[3]

Schäfer proceeds, "This emphasis on a fundamental synchronicity of the texts of rabbinic literature is completely consistent with Goldberg's methodological approach. The text as it stands is exclusively synchronic and, since we cannot go back beyond this state, there remains only the classifying description of that which is there...A historical differentiation is deliberately excluded, because in effect the texts do not permit it. Whilst analysis of the forms and functions of a text makes its system of rules transparent, the comprehension of rabbinic texts through habituation and insight could be superseded by a comprehension of the rules of this discourse as competence...."[4]

Goldberg's dogmatic definition of matters notwithstanding, a sustained examination of the various documents leaves no doubt whatsoever that we can identify not only "beforehand" but "first," showing that the formation of composites out of fully-articulated compositions took place prior to the definition of a document's distinctive traits. Had Goldberg read my *The Formation of the Jewish Intellect. Making Connections and Drawing Conclusions in the Traditional System of Judaism*, he would have found ample grounds, based on the logics of coherent discourse alone, to reconsider his position.[5]

But now data that prove the exact opposite of Goldberg's premised position emerge fully and completely, for the Talmud, in my *The Talmud of Babylonia. An Academic Commentary* and in its companion, *The Talmud of Babylonia. A Complete Outline*.[6] Not only so, but I have devoted Initial Phases to just this problem.[7] Why Goldberg takes the position that he does I cannot say, since it contradicts the facts of the characteristics of the documents that he purportedly discusses. The facts that are set forth in Academic Commentary, Complete Outline, and Initial Phases, indicate that Goldberg certainly cannot have known through his own, first-hand analysis, a great deal about the literary traits of the Rabbinic literature as exemplified by the Bavli. For he seems to have confused a kind of abstract philosophizing with the concrete acts of detailed learning that scholarship requires. That explains why he left no imposing legacy of scholarship to sustain his opinion, which is at once doctrinaire, ignorant, and eccentric. Goldberg's nihilism has no continuators,[8] except for his student, Peter Schäfer, and I do not see much basis on which to contend with his obscure and solipsistic legacy. We shall deal with Schäfer's own, equally nihilistic, position in due course.

I do not share Goldberg's position, because I have shown, on the same basis of phenomenology on which he lays out his view, that the contrary is the fact. Having completed the work on the Talmud of Babylonia, I only now begin the equivalent academic commentary and complete outline for the Yerushalmi, and comparison of the outlines of the Bavli and the Yerushalmi,[9] with the plan of proceeding to the score of Midrash-compilations, so I cannot say what I shall find in continuing a uniform analysis. But the naked eye suggests that Goldberg's position will not find in the other documents any support at all. The documents as we know them certainly encompass not only materials that serve the clearly-manifest program of the framers or compilers of the documents, but also the self-evident interests of authors of compositions and framers of composites who had other plans than those realized in the documents as we have them. But the question is, how do we identify components of a composition, or of a composite, that took shape outside of the documentary framework and prior to the definition of the documentary traits of a given compilation? Unless we take at face value the attributions of sayings to specific, named authorities at determinate times and places, we must work by paying close attention to the material traits of the compositions and composites. That requires, as I said, moving from the end-product backward and inward--and in no other way. Two intellectually lazy ways have led nowhere, Goldberg's denial that it is a question, and the Israelis' insistence that attributions equal facts. Finding no promise in such labor-saving devices--settling questions by decree--I have resorted to sifting the facts, and that is what I have done and now do.

This brings us, finally, to the explicit statement of Peter Schäfer that we have no documents, just variant readings.[10] Schäfer's statement of matters proves murky and obscure, so exact citation of his language is required, lest I be thought to caricature or exaggerate the full confusion that envelopes his position. Let me cite his exact language, beginning with his critique of Goldberg and pronouncement of a still more extreme position; I number those paragraphs that I shall discuss below.

1. The question that arises here is obviously what is meant by 'texts.' What is the text 'once it has been written'--the Babylonian Talmud, the Midrash, a definite Midrash, all Midrashim, or even the whole of rabbinic literature as a synchronic textual continuum whose inherent system of rules it is necessary to describe? Indeed, in such a description, neither the concrete text concerned, nor the form a particular textual tradition takes, needs to be important. Every text is as good--or rather as bad--as every other, the 'best' being presumably the one representing the latest redactional stage.

2. But this is precisely where the problem begins. Goldberg himself must finally decide on one text, and, in doing so...must decide against several other texts. Whether he wants to or not, he inevitably faces historical questions. This problem can be elucidated by the second line of research within the 'literary' approach.

3. This second line of research...is that of the interpretation immanent in the work. Complete literary works are analyzed as a whole, as literary systems so to speak, and are examined for their characteristic arguments...Neusner has ...sent to press such analyses...The plane on which this research approach moves...is the final redaction of the respective work...Two closely related problems arise from this.

4. The approach inevitably disregards the manuscript traditions of the work in question. But especially in the case of rabbinic literature, this is essential. Thus, to give an example, both Vatican manuscripts of the Bereshit Rabba...represent texts which are quite different from that of the London manuscript...The variations are sometimes so great that the redactional identity of the work is debatable. Is it meaningful to speak of one work at all, or rather of various recensions of a work? But then how do these recensions relate to one another? Are they different versions of one and the same text...or are they autonomous to a certain extent, and is Bereshit Rabba merely an ideal or a fictitious entity? What then constitutes the identity of the work 'Bereshit Rabbah'? Any preserved manuscript or the modern 'critical' edition by Theodor-Albeck...

5. The problem becomes more acute when the question of the boundaries of works is taken into consideration. To remain with the example of Bereshit Rabba, the problem of what relation Bereshit Rabba and the Yerushalmi bear to one another has been discussed since the time of Frankel...How are Bereshit Rabba and Yerushalmi related to one another...? Does Bereshit Rabba quote Yerushalmi, i.e., can we regard Bereshit Rabba and Yerushalmi at the time of the redaction of Bereshit Rabba as two clearly distinguishable works, one of which being completed? Did the redactor of Bereshit Rabbah therefore 'know' with what he was dealing and from what he was 'quoting'? With regard to the Yerushalmi, this conclusion is obviously unreasonable, for we immediately have to ask how the Yerushalmi of the Bereshit Rabba is related to the Yerushalmi existent today. The Yerushalmi cannot have been 'complete' at the time of the redaction of Bereshit Rabba since it is not identical to the one we use today.[11]

6. A brief reference to Hekhalot literature will constitute a last example. This is without doubt the prototype of a literature where the boundaries between the works are fluid. Every 'work' in this literary genre that I have investigated more closely proves to be astonishingly unstable, falls into smaller and smaller editorial units, and cannot be precisely defined and delimited, either as it is or with reference to related literature. This finding is of course valid with regard to the works of Hekhalot literature to a varying degree, but can be generalized as a striking characteristic feature of the whole literary genre....[12]

7. The questioning of the redactional identity of the individual works of rabbinic literature inevitably also disavows the research approach to the work at the level of the final redaction. The terms with which we usually work--text, *Urtext*, recension, tradition, citation, redaction, final redaction, work-- prove to be fragile and hasty definitions that must be subsequently questioned. What is a "text" in rabbinic literature? Are there texts that can be defined and clearly delimited, or are there only basically "open" texts which elude temporal and redactional fixation? Have there ever been "Urtexte" of certain works with a development that could be traced and described? How do different recension of a "text" relate to one another with respect to the redactional identity of the text? How should the individual tradition, the smallest literary unit, be assessed in relation to the macroform of the "work" in which it appears? What is the meaning of the presence of parts of one "work" in another more or less delimitable "work"? Is this then a quotation in work X from work Y?

8. And finally what is redaction or final redaction? Are there several redactions of a "work"--in chronological order--but only one final redaction? What distinguishes redaction from final redaction? What lends authority to the redaction? Or is the final redaction merely the more or less incidental discontinuation of the manuscript tradition?[13]

Enough of Schäfer's presentation has now been quoted to permit a simple statement in response.

It is simply put forth: the "text" loses its quotation-marks when we describe, analyze, and interpret recurrent formal properties that occur in one document, but not in some other, or, in the particular congeries at hand, not in any other. To state matters as required in the present context, we simply reverse the predicate and the subject, thus: a writing that exhibits definitive traits of rhetoric, logic, and topic, that occur in no other writing constitutes a text.

That simple definition permits us to respond to the long list of questions and to sort out the confusion that characterizes Schäfer's conception of matters. Let me systematically respond to Schäfer's unsystematic formulation of his position, which, as we see at the end, rests heavily on his observations of an odd and unrepresentative writing, which may or may not originate in the Rabbinic canon at all.

[1] I shall stipulate that my "document" corresponds to Schäfer's "text." The rest of this paragraph is unintelligible to me. I do not grasp the distinctions that Schäfer thinks make a difference, e.g., between "a definite Midrash, all Midrashim, or even the whole of rabbinic literature...." Here Schäfer seems to me to shade over into sheer chaos. How the several following sentences relate to one another I cannot discern. I am baffled by the sense of his allegation, "Every text is as good--or rather as bad--as every other, the 'best' being presumably the one representing the latest redactional stage." It is not clear to me whether this is his view or one he imputes to someone else, and, as is clear, apart from Goldberg, I know no one to whom these words even pertain.

[2] Goldberg's comments leave no doubt on his meaning; he denies all possibility of historical or cultural research. This he says in so many words. As I said, in the context of German academic culture, such a result condemns the Rabbinic classics to the dustbin.

[3] Schäfer's characterization of my description ("for their characteristic arguments") proves uncomprehending. I define a document by appeal to the standard indicative traits of classic literary analysis: rhetoric, logic, topic. Rhetoric covers the forms of expression; logic the principles of coherent discourse; topic pertains to the prevailing program, hermeneutics, or even proposition of a given piece of writing. (Not all compilations can sustain such documentary analysis, Mekihilta--dubiously assigned to late antiquity to begin with--standing apart from all the other items in the Rabbinic canon, for instance.) Still, Schäfer is correct in his main point: I do focus on what in his terms is "the final redaction of the work," and, in my terms, the definitive congeries of traits distinctive to this complex of composites and no other.

[4] Here Schäfer spells out what he means by disregarding manuscript traditions, and he gives as his example the diverse versions of Genesis Rabbah. But he would do well to address more directly the question of the occurrence of a single pericope in two or more documents. When we find such a case, are we able to identify the document to the definitive traits of which the pericope conforms? If we are, then we can safely describe the pericope within the framework of one document and not the other(s) in which it appears.

When Schäfer made these statements, they formed a set of fair and pertinent questions. But they have been answered, and whether or not Schäfer has found the answers persuasive (or has even understood them) I cannot say, since so far as I know, he has not followed up on this point. Indeed, his astonishing silence on this matter since

his article suggests that Schäfer appears quite oblivious to work that raised and answered precisely the question he asks. I refer in particular to *From Tradition to Imitation. The Plan and Program of Pesiqta deRab Kahana and Pesiqta Rabbati*.[14] I raised that question when I reflected on Schäfer's problem and systematically addressed the challenge he set forth; that is why it is so disappointing to find no evidence of his serious response to the answer. There I show that pericope common to both compilations conform to the definitive traits that characterize Pesiqta deRab Kahana and do not conform to those that characterize those pericopes of Pesiqta Rabbati that do not occur, also, in Pesiqta deRab Kahana. It is not clear that Schäfer follows the scholarly literature on the very matters on which he passes his opinion.

[5] Here Schäfer wanders a bit, and his problem with "boundaries of works" suggests he cannot hold to a single subject. For the problem of the peripatetic pericope has nothing to do with that of the shared pericope. The entire range of questions he raises here reveals an underlying confusion, which can be overcome by detailed work, an examination of the specifics of matters; this Schäfer has never done for the matter at hand. But, at any rate, for reasons already stated, his questions have nothing to do with the documentary method.

[6] Schäfer here talks about that on which he is expert. His allegation about generalizing from the document he knows to those on which he has not worked therefore hardly demands serious consideration. He can be shown to be wrong in treating the one as in any way analogous, or even comparable, to the other. What he does not know and cannot show, he here simply assumes as fact.

[7] This is the most egregious break in the strain of coherent argument, for here Schäfer confuses the pre-history of documents with the documents as we now know them. What I have said about the phenomenological inquiry into the pre-history of documents suffices to answer the questions that he raises. His questions are probably meant, in his mind, to form arguments in behalf of his fundamental proposition. In fact they are susceptible to clear answers; his labor-saving device of sending up obscure clouds of rhetorical questions accomplishes no good purpose. But for his instruction, let me take up his questions and address those that pertain to the documentary method. To do so systematically, I proceed as follows:

[A] What is a "text" in rabbinic literature? A text in Rabbinic literature is a writing that conforms to a distinctive set of definitive traits of rhetoric, topic, and logic.

[B] Are there texts that can be defined and clearly delimited, or are there only basically "open" texts which elude temporal and redactional fixation? The Rabbinic canon (with only a few exceptions) contains texts that can be defined and clearly delimited (from one another) by reference to the distinctive congeries of rhetoric, topic, and logic, characteristic of one but not the other, or, as I said, characteristic solely of the one. We can establish sequence and order among these documents, determining what is primary to a given document because it conforms to the unique, definitive traits of that document. What Schäfer means by "open" texts I cannot say, so I do not know the answer to his "or"-question, but what I do grasp suggests he is reworking Goldberg's position.

[C] Have there ever been "Urtexte" of certain works with a development that could be traced and described? The answer to this question remains to be investigated, text by text (in my language: document by document).

I do not know the answer for most of the documents. I have stated the answer for some of them. The Mishnah, it is clear, proves uniform through all but two of its tractates, Eduyyot and Abot. The others conform to the single program of formulary traits, logical characteristics, modes of exposition and argument. That does not suggest that Mishnah does not contain already-completed compositions, utilized without much change; the contrary can be demonstrated on formal grounds alone. Compositions are formed by appeal to the name of a single authority, as in Mishnah-tractate Kelim, or by utilization of a single formulary pattern, as in Mishnah-tractate Arakhin and Megillah, or by illustration through diverse topics of a single abstract principle,--all these other-than-standard modes of composition and composite-making occur. But these ready-made items take up a tiny proportion of the whole and do not suggest the characteristics of an Urtext that would have held together numerous compositions and even composites of such an order. We may then posit (and many have posited) the existence of documents like the Mishnah but in competition with it, formed on other rhetorical, logical, and even topical bases than the Mishnah. But these do not stand in historical relationship with the Mishnah, e.g., forming a continuous, incremental tradition from some remote starting point onward to the Mishnah as we know it.

[D] How do different recensions of a "text" relate to one another with respect to the redactional identity of the text? This repeats Schäfer's earlier question, e.g., concerning Yerushalmi and Genesis Rabbah. By text he seems to mean a given saying or story that circulates from one document to another. Part of Schäfer's problem is imprecision in the use of terms, e.g., employing the same word when he means different things.

[E] How should the individual tradition, the smallest literary unit, be assessed in relation to the macroform of the "work" in which it appears? The answer to this question is both clear and not yet fully investigated. It is obvious that we move from the whole to the parts, so the individual composition (Schäfer's "tradition," whatever he means by that word) finds its place within the framework of the document's definitive characteristics. But the inves-

tigation of the traits of compositions and composites that stand autonomous of the documents in which they occur has only just begun, and only with the continuation and completion of my Academic Commentary will the data have been collected that permit us to deal with this question document by document. For the Bavli we have a set of viable answers; for no other document do I claim to know the answer. For the Mishnah, as I said, I do not think that this is an urgent question, though it is a marginally relevant one.

[F] What is the meaning of the presence of parts of one "work" in another more or less delimitable "work"? Is this then a quotation in work X from work Y? The question of the composition or even composite that moves hither and yon is a variation of the question just now considered. This is a question I explored previously, but Schäfer does not appear to know that work, which appeared long before the article under discussion here.[15] Here again, he sets obstacles in the path of scholarly progress when he ignores work already in print at the time of his presentation.

[G] And finally what is redaction or final redaction? Are there several redactions of a "work"--in chronological order--but only one final redaction? What distinguishes redaction from final redaction? What lends authority to the redaction? Or is the final redaction merely the more or less incidental discontinuation of the manuscript tradition? These questions suggest only more confusion in Schäfer's mind, and since I cannot fathom what he wants to know, or why he frames matters as he does, I also cannot presume to respond. If Schäfer spelled out with patience and care precisely what he wishes to know, others could follow his line of thought, e.g., what he means by "authority...redaction?" Schäfer makes such remarkable statements as the following: And finally what is redaction or final redaction? What distinguishes redaction from final redaction? What can he possibly mean by this set of questions? When we look at such unintelligible sentences as this, we wonder, indeed, whether Schäfer is not simply saying the same thing over and over again.

This specific address to his concrete questions yields a single generalization: a great deal of verbiage has served only to confuse issues. My best sense is that Schäfer has not reflected very deeply on the premises and arguments of the work he wishes to criticize; if he had, he would have grasped the monumental irrelevance of his critique. The formulation of his thought suggests to me not so much confusion as disengagement; the wordiness conceals imprecision, for we naturally assumed that each sentence bears its own thought and are not disposed to conclude that he is repeating himself. But one judgment surely pertains: in the end, Schäfer has not understood that in taking account of precisely the considerations that he raises, I formulated the form-analytical problem that addresses the issue of the definition of a text. As I reflect on questions and slowly examine each in turn, I find not so much a close engagement with issues as utter disengagement, an offhand contentiousness rather than a considered critique. But Schäfer's inattention to how others have responded to precisely the problems he highlights finds its match in the case that comes next, which draws our attention to a failure even to grasp the data that yield the results of form-analysis. This is not to suggest that the study of Rabbinic Judaism on the contemporary German academic scene promises no important results, only to state that, to date, the results prove at best mechanical.

NOTES

[1] Y. Epstein, *Mavo Lemusah Hamishnah*, 2nd ed., 2 vols. (Jerusalem and Tel Aviv, 1964).

[2] Spelled out in *Introduction to Rabbinic Literature*. (New York: Doubleday, 1994) and see also *The Documentary Foundation of Rabbinic Culture. Mopping Up after Debates with Gerald L. Bruns, S. J. D. Cohen, Arnold Maria Goldberg, Susan Handelman, Christine Hayes, James Kugel, Peter Schäfer, Eliezer Segal, E. P. Sanders, and Lawrence H. Schiffman* (Atlanta: Scholars Press for South Florida Studies in the History of Judaism, 1995).

[3] "Der Diskurs im babylonischen Talmud. Angerungen für eine Diskursanalyse," *Frankfurter Jüdaistsche Beitrage* 11 (1983) 1-45. Cited in P. Schäfer, "Research into Rabbinic Literature," *Journal of Jewish Studies* 37 (1986) 145.

[4] Schäfer, "Research," 145.

[5] *The Formation of the Jewish Intellect. Making Connections and Drawing Conclusions in the Traditional System of Judaism* (Atlanta: Scholars Press for Brown Judaic Studies, 1988).

[6] *The Talmud of Babylonia. An Academic Commentary* (Atlanta: Scholars Press for USF Academic Commentary Series, 1994-95); *The Talmud of Babylonia. A Complete Outline* (Atlanta: Scholars Press for USF Academic Commentary Series, 1994-95).

[7] *The Initial Phases of the Talmud's Judaism.* (Atlanta: Scholars Press for South Florida Studies in the History of Judaism, 1995) I. *Exegesis of Scripture. The Initial Phases of the Talmud's Judaism.* (Atlanta: Scholars Press for South Florida Studies in the History of Judaism, 1995) II. *Exemplary Virtue. The Initial Phases of the Talmud's Judaism* (Atlanta: Scholars Press for South Florida Studies in the History of Judaism, 1995) III. *Social Ethics. The Initial Phases of the Talmud's Judaism* (Atlanta: Scholars Press for South Florida Studies in the History of Judaism, 1995) IV. *Theology.*

[8] When in late April, 1991, on the very day on which Goldberg died, I came to Goldberg's University, the University of Frankfurt, as Martin Buber Visiting Professor of Judaic Studies, for the Summer Semester, I was saddened to find that he had left as his legacy strict instructions to his students, not only not to study with me but not even to meet me. That fact does not represent the standards of German scholarship, which maintains a high standard of intellectual professionalism. In no other country have I ever encountered such a "boycott."

[9] *The Two Talmuds Compared.* (Atlanta: Scholars Press for South Florida Studies in the History of Judaism, 1995-97) I.A *Tractate Berakhot and the Division of Appointed Times in the Talmud of the Land of Israel and the Talmud of Babylonia. Tractates Berakhot and Shabbat.* I.B *Tractate Berakhot and the Division of Appointed Times in the Talmud of the Land of Israel and the Talmud of Babylonia. Tractates Erubin and Yoma.* I.C *Tractate Berakhot and the Division of Appointed times in the Talmud of the Land of Israel and the Talmud of Babylonia. Tractates Pesahim, Sukkah, and Besa.* I.D *Tractate Berakhot and the Division of Appointed Times in the Talmud of the Land of Israel and the Talmud of Babylonia. Tractates Taanite, Megillah, Rosh Hashanah, Hagigah, and Moed Qatan.* II.A *The Division of Women in the Talmud of the Land of Israel and the Talmud of Babylonia. Tractates Yebamot and Ketubot.* II.B *The Division of Women in the Talmud of the Land of Israel and the Talmud of Babylonia. Tractates Nedarim, Nazir, and Sotah.* II.C *The Division of Women in the Talmud of the Land of Israel and the Talmud of Babylonia. Tractates Qiddushin and Gittin.* III.A *The Division of Damages and Tractate Niddah in the Talmud of the Land of Israel and the Talmud of Babylonia. Tractates Baba Qamma, Baba Mesia, and Baba Batra.* III.B *The Division of Damages and Tractate Niddah in the Talmud of the Land of Israel and the Talmud of Babylonia. Tractates Sanhedrin and Makkot.* III.C *The Division of Damages and Tractate Niddah in the Talmud of the Land of Israel and the Talmud of Babylonia. Tractates Shebuot, Abodah Zarah, Horayot, and Niddah.*

[10] Schäfer, "Research ," 145ff.

[11] Ibid., 146-147.

[12] Ibid., 149.

[13] Ibid., 149-150.

[14] *From Tradition to Imitation. The Plan and Program of Pesiqta deRab Khana and Pesiqta Rabbati* (Atlanta: Scholars Press for Brown Judaic Studies, 1987).

[15] See my preliminary probe into the question in *The Peripatetic Saying: The Problem of the Thrice-Told Tale in Talmudic Literature.* (Chico: Scholars Press for Brown Judaic Studies, 1985) which is a reprise and a reworking of the material in *Rabbinic Traditions about the Pharisees before 70*, vols. 1-3 (Leiden: E. J. Brill, 1971).

9

The Zodiac in Synagogue Decoration

Lucille A. Roussin
New York, New York

In tractate Shabbat (156b) of the *Babylonian Talmud* there is a debate about the validity of astrology for Jews. Rabbi Hanina, a Babylonian who came to Palestine to study with Rabbi Judah-ha-Nasi (d. before 230 C.E.), says: "The planetary influence gives wisdom, the planetary influence gives wealth and Israel stands under planetary influence." In contrast to this, Rabbi Johanan, who lived in Tiberias in ca. 250, declares: "There are no constellations for Israel." The rest of this section of the Talmud is devoted to the arguments put forth in support of Rabbi Johanan's position against planetary influence.

The synagogue pavements of the late Roman and early Byzantine period in Palestine offer evidence that some Jews did, indeed, believe that Israel stood under planetary influence. The prominence in ancient synagogue decoration of the representation of the twelve signs of the zodiac in a radial arrangement around Helios in the chariot of the sun with the personifications of the seasons surrounding it has long posed a problem for scholars of late antique art and religion. The zodiac composition appears in Palestinian pavement decoration in the fourth century synagogue of Hammath Tiberias, near the Sea of Galilee (fig. 1) and thereafter becomes a regular feature of mosaic pavement decoration in Palestinian synagogues from the fourth through the sixth centuries. To date there is no evidence of the use of the signs of the zodiac in the decoration of Christian buildings in Palestine.

As the principal motif of a mosaic pavement the signs of the zodiac surrounding Helios driving the quadriga are unusual. Outside Palestine only two pavements with the Helios-in-zodiac composition, both from villas, have been found: a fragmentary zodiac pavement dated to ca. 250 C.E. was found at Avenches, Switzerland, and a mid-third century C.E. pavement at Bingen, near Mainz.[1] In the Avenches mosaic Atlantes rather than the four seasons appear in the corners, and in the Bingen pavement the spandrels are filled with cantharoi flanked by fish. A zodiac mosaic from Sparta, dated to the fourth century, has the signs of the zodiac in a radial arrangement with personifications of the sun and the moon in the center.[2] Illustrated astronomical treatises may have played a role in the dissemination of zodiac compositions. The miniature in the Vatican Ptolemy, (Vat. gr. 1291 fol. 9r), depicts Helios in the center circle driving the chariot of the Sun drawn by four white horses through the blue sky. In the outer circle are the representations of the twelve signs of the zodiac (fig. 2).[3]

Seven zodiac pavements are preserved in Palestinian synagogues, and all repeat the same basic composition, with the circle of the zodiac inscribed in a square with the four seasons represented in the spandrels.[4] The placement of the zodiac panel is the same in three of the synagogues; Hammath Tiberias, Beth Alfa, and Na'aran (figures 1, 3, 4). In the lowest panel is an inscription or a figural scene, in the center is the zodiac panel, and on the top is the representation of the Torah Shrine with menorahs and other

Figure 1. Hammath Tiberias, view. Photo: Roussin

objects used in the Jewish liturgy.

At Khirbet Susiya, a synagogue of the broad house type with the entrance in the short wall at the east and the bema along the north wall facing Jerusalem, the plan necessitated a somewhat different format. Although the arrangement was different, the components were the same (fig. 5). The zodiac, of which only fragments remain, was placed in front of a bema. The pavement to the westwas divided into three panels, one of which was decorated with a scene of Daniel in the lion's den; to the east was a geometric carpet which probably had depictions of animals. The Torah Shrine panel is along the north wall in front of a second bema.

At Husifa the zodiac panel was placed at the east end, the side oriented toward Jerusalem (fig. 6). Of the zodiac panel only fragments of Sagittarius, Capricorn, Aquarius, Pisces, and Aries and one of the personifications of the seasons remain. Below the zodiac was a vine scroll composition and a narrow inscription panel. At the entrance to the prayer hall two panels decorated with menorahs and liturgical objects flank a wreath enclosing an inscription that reads "Peace upon Israel."

A fragmentary pavement from the synagogue at Yafia, near Nazareth, has a slightly different composition of two concentric circles; in the outer circle were twelve interlocking circular medallions, of which only two at the west are preserved (fig. 7). The two fragmentary figures in these medallions represent the bull of Taurus and the ram of Aries.[5] The placement of these figures in the western quarter of the circle corresponds to the placement of the same signs in the Hammath Tiberias zodiac (cf. figs. 1 and 7).

The origins of the radial zodiac composition are probably to be sought in ceiling decoration. Suetonius described the ceiling of Nero's Domus Aurea as "circular and constantly revolving day and night, like the heavens," and

Figure 2. Vatican Ptolemy (Vat. Gr. 1291), fol. 9r.
Photo: Biblioteca Apostolica Vaticana

recent investigations indicate that the ceiling of the octagonal dining room in the Domus Aurea could have been mechanically operated, creating in effect a planetarium.[6] The domed ceiling of the Temple of Bel in Palmyra, dated to the first century C.E., was decorated with the busts of the seven planetary deities in hexagonal relief compartments framed by the circle of the zodiac, which was supported by diagonally placed sirens.[7] In pavement decoration the late second century C.E. mosaic from Bir Chana, Tunisia, displays a similar composition--busts of the planets in hexagonal frames occupy the center of the composition, followed by the emblematic animals of the planets in rectangular frames and then the signs of the zodiac in the outer ring.[8] The earliest radial scheme seems to be the second century C.E. calendar mosaic from Antioch.[9] Like

the zodiac pavements, the composition consists of a smaller inner circle with a representation of a celestial deity and a larger outer circle inscribed in a square and divided into twelve segments. The months of the year are represented in the segments of the large circle and the four seasons occupy the spandrels.

The representations of the signs of the zodiac exhibit an increasing tendency toward stylization, but the iconography remains faithful to the classical prototypes: a ram for Aries; a bull for Taurus; the twins of Gemini; the crab for Cancer; a lion for Leo; a draped female for Virgo; scales for Libra; a scorpion for Scorpio; an archer for Sagittarius; a goat for Capricorn; a water bearer for Aquarius; fish for Pisces.

Figure 3. Beth Alfa. Photo: Israel Antiquities Authority

Figure 4. Na'aran
Photo: after *New Encyclopedia of Archaeological
Excavations in the Holy Land*,
Vol. 3, p. 1076

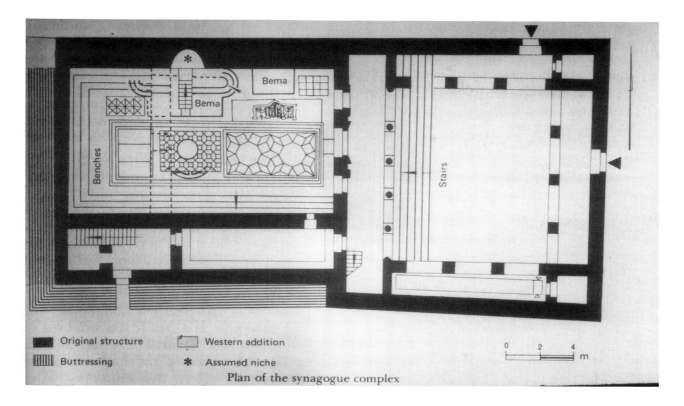

Figure 5a. Khirbet Susiya, view
Photo: after *New Encyclopedia of Archaeological Excavations in the Holy Land,*
Vol. 4, p. 1419

It is the variations from the established types that appear in the synagogues that provide some insight into the adaptation of the imagery to a Jewish context.[10] Virgo at Hammath Tiberias is unique in the zodiacal series by the fact that she carries a torch (fig. 8); the only other instance of a female personification carrying a torch occurs in the calendar at Antioch, where Levi has interpreted it as a symbol of the Antiochene feast of the Maioumas.[11] The addition is deliberate, and meaningful in a Jewish context. In the Calendar of 354 C.E., June holds a flaming torch as he points to a sundial. The accompanying verses refer to the ripening of the corn, ready for harvest; the torch is a symbol of the rites of the sacrifice to Ceres that signals the beginning of the harvest.[12] Virgo's flaming torch in the Hammath Tiberias zodiac is a symbol of Succoth, the Festival of Torches, the Jewish autumnal harvest festival. The Mishnah describes the ceremony of Simchat Beth HaShoevah, celebrated on the first day of Succoth, during which "pious men and men of good deeds used to dance before them with burning torches in their hands."[13] Virgo's torch was borrowed from a late Roman calendar illustration, but in this new context it acquired a specifically Jewish significance as a reference to Succoth.

Virgo in the Beth Alfa mosaic, an enthroned female wearing a long yellow tunic and red shoes that indicate her official or royal status, represents another variation from the classical draped female figure (fig. 3). The back of her throne is indicated by the black and orange frame that encircles the figure; the cushion of the throne is represented frontally as small circles at each side of the figure. Imperial iconography provided the model for this figure. A copper coin dated to the reign of Justin II shows the Empress Sophia enthroned frontally beside her husband.[14]

Aquarius in the Beth Alfa pavement offers a local variant of the water bearer: a figure who draws a bucket of water from a well (fig. 3). The image is a practical one, as the literal translation of the Hebrew name of Aquarius is bucket. At Husifa the anthropomorphic Aquarius is replaced by an amphora flanked by a bare branch. This substitution cannot be explained as a rejection of the human form on religious grounds, since the fragmentary remains of Sagittarius depict the usual image of the archer (fig. 6). As at Beth Alfa, the image is probably the result of the literal translation of the Hebrew "bucket" or "water carrier."

Like the signs of the zodiac and the personifications of the seasons, the figure of Helios in the center of the zodia-

Figure 5b. Khirbet Susiya, detail, remains of zodiac. Photo: Roussin

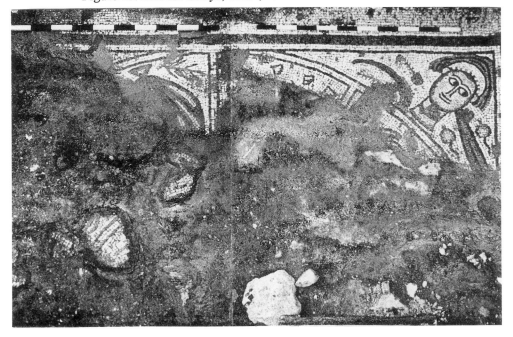

Figure 6. Husifa. Photo: Israel Antiquities Authority

cal circle is based on earlier prototypes. Helios stands in the chariot of the Sun in the center of the composition, a visual translation of Aratus' description: "In them, twelve in all, has the sun his course as he leads the whole year, and as he fares around this belt all the fruitful Seasons have their growth."[15] L'Orange has identified among the standard types of Sol Invictus representations those that are depicted on the Hammath Tiberias mosaic and in the miniature of the Vatican Ptolemy. "The Sol of the third century stands erect in the chariot, ignoring the horses, sometimes clad in chlamys, sometimes in chlamys and chiton, on his head a radiant halo, in his left hand the globe or whip (or globe and whip), the magic conquering right hand raised, the reins of the raging horses on the chariot post or attached to Sol's girdle."[16] The magic conquering right hand raised with palm turned outward and fingers extended as a symbol of power is a gesture long associated with representations of Sol in the East, and as such is found on Eastern coins. This image is also frequent on magical amulets; a bloodstone in the Ruthven Collection shows the Sun god standing in his chariot with his right hand raised, palm out, a whip in his left hand.[17] The gesture of the raised right hand is particularly marked on the Hammath Tiberias mosaic and in the Vatican Ptolemy miniature, where Helios turns his head and raises his eyes to his right hand (cf. figs. 2, 9).

The Hammath Tiberias pavement depicts the divine Basileus Helios. The later synagogue mosaics depict a more abstract Sol Invictus, still in the quadriga and with radiant halo, but without the globe crossed by the planispheres and, most noticeably, without the gesture of power inherent in the raised right hand. At Na'aran Helios holds a whip in his left hand, which emerges from under a starry mantle (fig. 4). The starry mantle is symbolic of the starry heavens, but it is perhaps also a reference to the robes of the high priest, and may ultimately be derived from the iconography of Jupiter Capitolinus; in Imperial iconography the starry mantle is also a symbol of the *triumphator*.[18] At Beth Alfa, Sol Invictus is reduced to a large frontal bust, with his head framed in a radiant halo above a striped chariot drawn through the starry evening sky by four highly patterned horses (fig. 3).

The frequency and longevity of the Helios-in-zodiac composition in Palestinian synagogue decoration indicates that it cannot have been an unconscious copying of a pagan model, but is rather a deliberate adoption of the composition. The zodiac in itself is not new to synagogue decoration: the signs of the zodiac decorated some of the ceiling tiles of the synagogue of Dura Europos, and were carved in relief on the lintel of the synagogue at Er-Rafid.[19] A long and unusual inscription in the pavement of the synagogue at En-Gedi lists the signs of the zodiac followed by the names of the Hebrew months.[20] The figure of Helios is frequently found on Jewish magical

amulets, often with inscriptions naming the deity and the names of the angels.[21] Avi Yonah sought to explain the presence of the zodiac in the synagogue mosaics as a kind of liturgical calendar.[22] He based his argument on the relationship of the twenty four priestly courses of I Chronicles XXIV: 1-9, which lists the priestly families and their order of service in the Temple, to Hebrew liturgical poetry. Two stone fragments found in Caesarea and dated to the late third or early fourth century contain an inscription of a list of the twenty four priestly families, the weeks of their service in the Temple, and the names of the villages to which they were exiled after the destruction of the Temple. The priestly courses are also mentioned in the *piyyutim*, liturgical poems read in the synagogue. In one of the early *piyyutim* the name of each of the priestly courses is associated with a sign of the zodiac and a Hebrew month.[23] This relationship of the priestly courses with the Hebrew months and the signs of the zodiac in the liturgical poetry led Avi Yonah to connect the synagogue inscriptions of the priestly courses to the representations of the zodiac in the synagogue pavements. He argued that since each sign of the zodiac represents one of the twelve months of the year and the list of priestly courses divides the year into weeks, together they formed a complete set of chronological indications, a visual representation of the liturgical calendar.

A number of factors militate against acceptance of this theory. The Jewish festival calendar is a lunar calendar, and the priestly courses were related to that calendar and not the solar zodiacal calendar. Unfortunately, none of the synagogues in which we have evidence of interest in the priestly courses has preserved mosaic floors, and none of the synagogues in which we have mosaic floors with the representation of the zodiac has preserved evidence of inscriptions of the priestly courses. Consequently, there is no clear archaeological evidence of the relation of the two themes at this time.

The fact that in most of the preserved zodiac pavements most of the seasons and months do not correspond also makes calendrical interpretation unlikely. Only in the Hammath Tiberias mosaic do the months and the seasons correspond. In the Beth Alfa mosaic the seasons should be rotated counterclockwise to match the appropriate months.[24] At Na'aran the signs of the zodiac are clockwise and the seasons are counterclockwise, with the result that Spring governs the Autumn months and Autumn the Spring months. At Husifa the remaining season, be it Summer or Autumn, is placed above the Winter and Spring months, Pisces and Aries.

There is also no evidence to support the theory that the direction of the signs of the zodiac has a symbolic meaning. To date, the only instance in which the direction of the signs of the zodiac can perhaps be interpreted symbolically is on the relief from Khirbet Tannur, where they

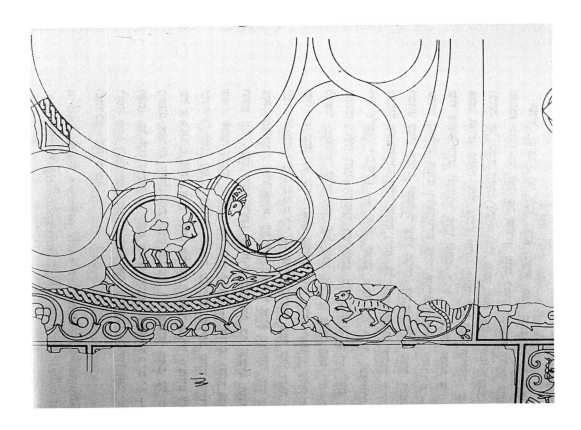

Figure 7. Yafia. Photo: after *Rabinowitz Bulletin II*, p. 19, fig. 5

are divided into two clockwise and counterclockwise halves starting from the top of the circle and descending down both sides.[25] The archetype of the zodiac composition was created to correspond with the Age of Aries, and this is the form that survives, despite the fact that it is no longer astrologically accurate. The placement of the sign of Aries in the Palestinian zodiac compositions, despite clockwise or counterclockwise movement, is consistent: Aries is placed in the segment of the zodiacal circle closest to Helios' right or left hand. It is neither the calendrical nor the scientific significance that accounts for the presence of the Helios-in-zodiac composition in synagogue decoration.

In seeking to understand the symbolism of the zodiac composition in the late antique synagogue, we turn again to the statement of Rabbi Johanan: "there are no constellations for Israel."[26] Contrary to this statement, there seems to be abundant evidence for the practice of magic, astrology and angel worship among the Jews.[27] Jewish worship of angels is further attested to by many early Christian writers. According to the *Preachings of Peter*, referred to by Clement of Alexandria, the Jews "thinking that they only know God, do not know him, adoring as they do angels and archangels, the months and the moon."[28] Origen writes in *Contra Celsius* that "the Jews adore the angels and are given to the practice of magic," and further, "what is astonishing about the Jews is that they adore the sky and the angels which inhabit it."[29] That

Figure 8. Hammath Tiberias, Virgo, Photo: Roussin

the Christians saw a connection between astrology and angel worship in the method by which the Jewish holidays were set is made evident in the *Epistle to Diognetus*: "As to surveying the course of the planets and the moon in order to fix the observance of the months and the days, as to dividing, to suit their own wishes, the divine dispensations and the changes of the seasons, some into feast days and others into days of penance, is this proof of piety?

No! It is stupidity!"[30] The Christian attitude toward the relationship of Judaism and angel worship may provide an explanation of why the zodiac is not used in church decoration. Canon 35 of the Council of Laodicia, held in the middle of the fourth century, contains an interdiction to all priests and clergy against the practice of magic, incantations and astrology, all of which were considered Jewish practices.[31]

Figure 9. Hammath Tiberias, Helios. Photo: Roussin

Jewish texts are even more eloquent in shedding light on the worship of angels and provide an insight into the symbolism of the zodiac pavements in the synagogues. Josephus writes of the high priest's robe that the "sun and the moon are indicated by the two sardonyxes wherewith he pinned the high priest's robe. As for the twelve stones, whether one would prefer to read in them the months or the constellations of like number, which the Greeks call the circle of the zodiac, he will not mistake the lawgiver's intention."[32] In a 12th century Midrash on Numbers 14:18, which may reflect earlier sources, Rabbi Pinhas ben Yair says that all of the objects and animals used in the dedication of the altar of the Temple, all of which were twelve in number, "corresponded to the twelve constellations, the twelve solar months, the twelve lunar months..."[33]

The *Sefer HaRazim (Book of Secrets)*, a text of the late third or early fourth century, discovered among the texts in the Cairo Geniza, is particularly important because it was widely influential even among rabbinic Jews and shows that the worship of angels was accepted as compatible with worship of Yahweh as the sole, supreme God.[34] The *Sefer HaRazim* begins with a Preface describing the presentation of the book to Noah before the flood by the angel Raziel; after the flood it was passed down through the Biblical generations to Solomon. It then describes the seven firmaments, the names and functions of the angels in each firmament and the magical praxis which can be fulfilled by calling upon those angels. The fourth firmament is the "lovely bridal chamber of the sun, filled with light and all aflame," and is divided between thirty one angels who lead the sun during the day and thirty one angels who lead the sun during the night.[35] Among the prayers in this section is one to Helios; in Greek, but written in Hebrew letters, it reads "Holy Helios who rises in the east, good mariner, trustworthy leader of the sun's rays...who of old didst establish the mighty wheel of the heavens..."[36] A late antique magical amulet with the image of Helios driving the chariot of the sun, now in the Ruthven Collection, is interesting in this connection: on the amulet are Greek inscriptions of the names of angels.[37]

In the fifth firmament are "twelve princes of glory seated on magnificent thrones...They quarter the heavens at the middle by facing the four directions of the world, three by three toward each direction...They are in charge of the twelve months of the year and understand what will be in each and every month...Each is stationed over his month since they make known month by month that which will be in each and every year." This is followed by a list of the names of the twelve angels and the text continues, "these are they who are in charge of the twelve months of the year, from the month of Nisan to the month of Adar, as they are written."[38]

Although the four seasons and the seven planets are not specifically mentioned in the *Sefer HaRazim* they are mentioned in other texts. The "angels of winter and of spring and of autumn and of summer...which He hath prepared in the knowledge of His heart," are included in a long list of angels in the apocryphal Book of Jubilees.[39] An Aramaic inscription on a clay vessel records the oath "I swear by the holy angels and in the names of Metatron...Hadriel and Nuriel and Uriel and (Sasgabiel?) and Haphakiel and Metaphiel...these are the seven angels which make the heavens and the earth and the planets and the moon and the sea go around and change."[40]

In the seventh and highest firmament is Yahweh, "the one who sits upon the throne of glory. For He alone sits in the Heaven of His holiness...His appearance is hidden from all...By His strength He upholds the heavens, And in all the heavens He is feared, and by all the angels He is revered."[41]

This kind of stratigraphic approach in describing the cosmos is evidenced as early as Philo, who writes of Moses' ascent on Mt. Sinai in *Questions and Answers on Exodus*: "What is the meaning of the words, 'Come up to Me to the mountain and be there?' This signifies that a holy soul is divinized by ascending, not to the air, to the ether, or to heaven (which is higher than all), but to a region above the heavens, and beyond the world where there is no place but God."[42]

The liturgical poems read during the service in the synagogue, the *piyyutim* of the late antique and early Byzantine period, do, as Avi Yonah thought, provide numerous references to the zodiac, but independent of any connection to the priestly courses. Thus in an acrostic poem to Exodus 12:2 found in the Cairo Geniza we read "There arose a dispute among the months, when the August One sent to the land of Egypt. Come let us cast lots on the zodiac, that we might know in which of us Israel is to be redeemed."[43] In a lamentation of the Ninth of Av--still recited on the eve of that day in the Ashkenazic ritual--the

first eight signs of the zodiac bewail the fate of Jerusalem, while the last four are practically accused of betrayal.[44] A parallel poem found in some Geniza manuscripts, which are thought to preserve remnants of ancient eastern prayerbooks, describes the joyous reaction of the constellations on the successful return of the High Priest from the Holy of Holies on the Day of Atonement. To these we may add the better known poems of Eliezer ben Kallir, the outstanding representative of the classical *piyyut*, who lived in Palestine in the late sixth century. In two of his most famous compositions, *On Rain*, read in the synagogue on Sukkoth, and *On Dew*, read at Passover, every other stanza contains a prayer for rain or dew in one of the Hebrew months and the following stanza mentions one of the signs of the zodiac.[45]

Literary evidence thus confirms the importance of the constellations in Jewish worship of late antiquity. If we turn once again to the *Sefer HaRazim,* all the elements described therein have their counterparts in the Helios-in-zodiac compositions depicted in the synagogue pavements: Helios driving the chariot of the sun surrounded by the twelve months of the year with the "angels" of the four seasons in the corners. From the evidence of the prayer to Holy Helios in the *Sefer HaRazim* and the numerous magical amulets with depictions of Helios, it is possible to suggest that Helios on the synagogue floors represents a minor deity to whom some members of the congregation might have addressed prayers -- not to the image itself, but to the deity it represents.[46]

When the overall compositions of the synagogue pavements are analyzed in terms of the structure of the *Sefer HaRazim* the symbolism becomes clear. The lowest level represents the earthly realm, the Helios-in-zodiac panel in the center represents the celestial sphere, and in the highest sphere is the Torah Shrine panel, symbolic of the seventh firmament where, according to the *Sefer HaRazim,* Yahweh resides, "the King of Kings, ruling over all the kings of the earth and exalted kings of the earth and exalted among the angels of heaven."[47]

It is the underlying theological basis that accounts for the frequency of the zodiac theme in synagogue decoration, and, at the same time, explains why this decoration was never used by Christians. The iconography of the synagogue pavements--the zodiac, the Torah Shrine, and the liturgical objects--is a coherent decorative scheme that expresses Jewish political and eschatological hopes.

NOTES

[1]G. Gundel and P. Böker, *RE* 10A:649, nos. 129-130, s.v. "Zodiacus," is the most complete list of zodiac representations in all media. For the Bingen pavement see K. Parlasca, *Die römischen Mosaiken in Deutschland* (Berlin, Römisch-germanisches Museum, 1959) 86ff., no.

127. For the Avenches pavement see V. von Gonzenbach, *Die römischen Mosaiken der Schweiz* (Basel Komission, 1961) 43ff.

[2]*Archaeological Reports for 1983-84* 30 (1984) 27; illustrated on the cover. For a discussion of the concept of time in the ancient world see the essays in *Aion. Le Temps chez les Romains*, ed. R. Chevallier, Institut d'Études Latines de l'Univ. Centre de Recherches A. Piganiol, Tours, vol. 10 (Paris, 1976). The more common zodiac composition is that in which a youth, usually Aion, holds the ring of the zodiac, often with the four seasons standing to the side. This type of composition is especially popular in North African pavement decoration; see K. Dunbabin, *The Mosaics of Roman North Africa. Studies in Iconography and Patronage* (Oxford: Clarendon Press, 1978) 158-160, and L. Foucher, "Annus and Aion," *Le Temps chez les Romaines*, 197-203; Idem, "La représentation du génie de l'année sur les mosaiques," *La Mosaique romaine tardive. L'Iconographie du Temps*, ed. Y. Duval (Paris, 1981). This imagery is also found on Imperial coins, on the Parabiago Patera from Northern Italy, and on one of the Antioch mosaics; G. Hanfmann, *The Season Sarcophagus in Dumbarton Oaks*. 2 vols. (Cambridge: Harvard University Press, 1951) 1:227, 2:437ff; for the Parabiago patera *Age of Spirituality. Late Antique and Early Christian Art, Third to Seventh Century*. Catalogue of the exhibition at the Metropolitan Museum of Art, Nov. 19, 1977 through Feb. 12, 1978, ed. Kurt Weitzmann (New York: The Metropolitan Museum of Art, 1979) 185, no. 164; D. Levi, *Antioch Mosaic Pavements*. 2 vols. (Princeton: Princeton University Press, 1947) 1:147, 2:43d.

[3]The manuscript dates to the ninth century, but the Helios miniature probably reflects a Hellenistic model; I. Spatharakis, "Some Observations on the Ptolemy Ms. Vat. Gr. 1291: Its Date and the Two Initial Miniatures," *Byzantinische Zeitschrift* 71 (1978) 41-49. F. Boll, "Zur überlieferungsgeschichte der grieschischen Astrologie u. Astronomie," *Sitzungsberichte der kgl. beyerischen Akademie der Wissenschaften*. Philos.-Philol.Kl. 1 (1899) 110f., 126. Boll postulated a date of 250 C.E. for the original of the Helios miniature, but Spatharakis points out that he used modern astrological tables in calculating this date.

[4]The zodiac pavements are found in the synagogues of Hammath Tiberias, Khirbet Susiya, Na'aran, Husifa, Yafia, Beth Alfa, and in the newly discovered synagogue at Sepphoris. For the Sepphoris mosaic see Netzer and Weiss in this book. The zodiac may have been represented in the pavement of the Samaritan synagogue at Beth Shean; according to the excavator's reconstruction drawing the center section of the nave pavement had a design of large and small concentric circles inscribed in a square.

See N. Zori, "An Ancient Synagogue at Beth Shean," *Eretz Israel* 8 (1967) 149-167, esp. 153-155 (Hebrew). The geographical pattern of these synagogues with the zodiac composition is interesting: Khirbet Susiya and Na'aran are in southern Judea; Husifa, Yafia, and Sepphoris are all relatively near each other in southern Galilee; Beth Alfa lies near to Beth Shean, just a short distance south of Hammath Tiberias. In all these places the Jewish population was well established and obviously took a liberal view of the Second Commandment, perhaps influenced by their Christian neighbors.

[5]E.L. Sukenik, "The Ancient Synagogue at Yafia," *Rabinowitz Bull.* 2 (1951) 6-24; D. Barag, *Encyclopedia of Archaeological Excavations in the Holy Land*, 2:541ff., s.v. "Japhia"; E.R. Goodenough, *Jewish Symbols In the Greco-Roman Period* 13 vols. (New York, 1953-68) 1:216ff. A rectangular panel in the southwest corner of the border is decorated with a golden eagle that stands upon a double volute which grows from a Medusa head. Both the eagle and the head of Medusa can be interpreted as solar symbols (Goodenough, *Jewish Symbols*, 1:217, 7:224-29, 8:215, n. 253).

[6]Suetonius, *Nero* xxxi, 2; H. Pruckner and S. Storz, "Beobachtungen im Oktagon der Domus Aurea," *Römische Mitteilungen* 81 (1974) 324-339, esp. 330f. Lehmann's thesis, "The Dome of Heaven," *Art Bulletin* 27 (1945) 1-27, of a continuous tradition of celestial symbolism in vault decoration, which was then transferred to floor decoration, has been shown to have been based on inaccurate drawings of the ceilings of Hadrian's villa (H. Joyce, "Hadrian's Villa and the Dome of Heaven." Paper read at the Fourth Colloquium of the North American Branch of the Association pour l'Étude da la Mosaique Antique, 7-9 November, 1986, Université Laval, Quebec City, Canada). Lehmann's broad analysis and conclusions, especially with regard to Early Christian and Byzantine art, have also been challenged by T. Mathews, "Cracks in Lehmann's 'Dome of Heaven'," *Source* 1 (Spring, 1982) 12-16. According to Lehmann's interpretation of the eighteenth century drawing, the ceiling from Hadrian's Villa was decorated with an image of Jupiter or Sol on a quadriga with the signs of the zodiac in groups of three, separatedby the personifications of the seasons.

[7]Lehmann, "Dome of Heaven," 3, fig. 8.

[8]Lehmann, "Dome of Heaven," 8f.; Dunbabin, *Mosaics*, 161, fig. 162.

[9]Lehmann, "Dome of Heaven," 8f.; Levi, *Antioch*, 1:36, 2:5b.

[10]Local interpretations of the signs of the zodiac are not unusual; the zodiac pavement from Bingen has several unusual signs. The scales usually held by Libra have been transferred to Virgo, foreshadowing the Carolingian per-

sonification of Justice (H. Stern, *Le Calendrier de 354* [Paris, 1953] 191). Libra holds the amphora that belongs to Aquarius, and a stalk of wheat which is the attribute of Summer. Aquarius is crowned by antlers, symbolic of the custom of putting on antlers during the Calends of January; he holds bare branches, usually associated with the personification of Winter, in his left hand. The globe held by Capricorn has been associated with the standard of the XXII Primigenia Legion stationed in the Rhineland. The most recent study of the pavement is by I. Krueger, "Zum Tierkreis im Sonnengott-Mosaik aus Munster-Sarmsheim," *Das Rheinische Landesmuseum Bonn* 3 (1973) 33-36.

[11]D. Levi, "The Allegories of the Months in Classical Art," *Art Bulletin* 23 (1941) 251-291.

[12]Ibid., 262; M. Salzmann, *On Roman Time* (Berkeley and Los Angeles: University of California Press, 1990) 92; Stern, *Calendrier*, 227.

[13]Mishnah Succah 5, 3-4; H. Schauss, *The Jewish Festivals* (New York, 1938) 183; J. Gaster, *Festivals of the Jewish Year* (New York, 1952) 82f.; see further *Babylonian Talmud*, Seder Mo'ed III, Sukka 53a.

[14]P. Whitting, *Byzantine Coins* (New York: G. P. Putnam's Sons, 1973) no. 157, p. 100. If Byzantine Imperial coins furnished the model for the Beth Alfa Virgo we have additional evidence that the mosaic should be dated to the reign of Justin II; Sophia was the first empress to share the honor of appearing on Imperial coins with her husband (A. Cameron, "The Artistic Patronage of Justin II," *Byzantion* 50 (1980) 62-84; reprinted in *Continuity and Change in Sixth Century Byzantium* (London, 1981).

[15]Aratus, *Phaenomena*, 550, 2nd ed., trans. G.R. Mair (Cambridge: Harvard University Press, 1955) 251.

[16]H. L'Orange, "Sol Invictus Imperator. Ein Beitrag zur Apotheose," in *Likeness and Icon* (Odensee: Odensee University Press, 1973) 329f, n. 17.

[17]C. Bonner, *Studies in Magical Amulets Chiefly Graeco-Egyptian* (Ann Arbor and London, 1950) 148f., 291, no. 227, pl. XI. The Bingen pavement presents another aspect of the iconography of Sol Invictus, one associated with the Imperial cult. That the Bingen Helios is derived from the Sol Invictus Imperator can be inferred from the transposition and transformation of the whip in the left hand to a scepter in his raised right hand. L'Orange traces the origin of the conflation of the Eastern Sol Invictus with the Imperial cult to the Severans. In this context Sol Invictus is divorced from the belt of the zodiac. The iconography of Sol Invictus also influenced circus representations, see A. Frazer, "The Cologne Circus Bowl," *Marsyas*, suppl. I, *Essays in Honor of Karl Lehmann* (1964) 105ff.

[18]R. Eisler, *Weltenmantel und Himmelzelt*, 2 vols. Munich (1910) 1:25, 39-45, 71. Suetonius, *Nero*, xxv,1,

describes Nero's cloak in his triumphal entry from Greece as "vestes purpurea distinctaque stellis aureis chlamyde." On the equestrian statue in the Hippodrome, Justinian wore a starry mantle with images of the Sun and the Moon; *Anthologia graeca*, xvi, 63.

[19]C. Kraeling, *The Excavation at Dura Europos. Final Report VIII. Part I. The Synagogue* (New Haven: Yale Univ. Press, 1956) 42, pl. 9:1-3; Goodenough, *Symbols*, 1:211, 3:541.

[20]D. Barag et al., "The Synagogue at En-Gedi," *Ancient Synagogues Revealed*, 118; L. Levine, "The Inscription at En-Gedi," *Ancient Synagogues*, 140-42.

[21]Goodenough, *Symbols*, 2:258f., 3:1116-7; Bonner, *Magical Amulets*, 148f., 291, no. 227.

[22]M. Avi Yonah, "The Caesarea Inscription of the Twenty Four Priestly Courses," *The Teachers Yoke Studies in Memory of Henry Trantham* (Dallas: Baylor University Press, 1968) 46-57. Most scholars have accepted this theory; see R. Hachlili, "The Zodiac in Ancient Jewish Art: Representation and Significance," *BASOR* 228 (1977) 61-77; M. Dothan, *Hammath Tiberias* (Jerusalem, 1983) 48f.

[23]Similar inscriptions have been found in Ascalon, Kissufim and Beit el-Khader in Yemen, see J. Naveh, "Ancient Synagogue Inscriptions," *Ancient Synagogues*, 136; I. Davidson, *Osar ha Shirah ve ha Piyyut*, New York (1929) 2:210f., no. 11; M. Zulay, "On the History of the Piyyut in the Land of Israel," *Studies of the Research Institute for Hebrew Poetry* 5 (1939) 116, 121 (Hebrew).

[24]This has been the subject of much scholarship, much of it with very forced solutions. I. Renov, "Some Problems of Synagogal Archaeology," (Ph.D. dissertation, Hebrew Union College-Jewish Institute of Religion, New York, 1952), 99ff.; I. Stone, "The Zodiac Theme in Ancient Synagogues and in Hebrew Printed Books," *Studies in Bibliography and Booklore* 1 (1953) 11; R. Wischnitzer, "The Beth Alfa Mosaic, A New Interpretation," *Jewish Social Studies* 17 (1955) 143ff.

[25]N. Glueck, "The Zodiac of Khirbet et Tannur," *BASOR* 126 (1952) 5-10. Glueck believes that the division is symbolic of the two New Year divisions, one in spring and one in autumn.

[26]*BT*, Shabbat 156b.

[27]P. Schäfer, "Jewish Magic Literature in Late Antiquity and Early Middle Ages," *Journal of Jewish Studies* 41 (1990) 75-91; P. Alexander in E. Schürer, *The History of the Jewish People in the Age of Jesus Christ (175 B.C.-A.D. 135)* 3 vols. rev. and ed. G. Vermes, F. Millar, and M. Goodman (Edinburgh: T & T Clark, 1986) 3:342-379.

[28]Clement of Alexandria, *Stromata*, VI, v, 41; *The Ante-Nicene Christian Library*, vol. 12, ed. A. Roberts and J. Donaldson, Clement of Alexandria, vol. 2, 327; M. Simon, "Remarques sur l'angélolatrie Juive au début de l'ère

Chrétienne," *Comptes Rendus de'Academie des Inscriptions* (1971) 120-134; M. Smith, "Helios in Palestine," *Eretz Israel* 22 (1982) 207ff.

[29]*Contra Celsius* I:26, V:6; T. Reinach, *Textes d'Auteurs Grecs et Romaines Relatifs au Judaisme* (Paris, 1895) 165-67; Simon, *Verus Israel*, 403.

[30]*A Diognète*, trans. H.I. Marrou, *Sources Chrétiennes* (Paris: Le Éditions du Cerf, 1951) IV, 5. Cf. the description of determining the holidays by the rising of the new moon in *Mishnah Rosh Hashanah* 2:8: "Rabban Gamaliel had diagrams of the shapes of the moon on a tablet and on the wall in his upper chamber. These he used to show the ordinary people, asking, `Didst thou see it like this, or like that?'" I owe this reference to Professor Burton Vissotsky of Jewish Theological Seminary.

[31]J. Hefele, *Histoire des Conciles* (Paris, 1907), I, ii, 1017; Simon, *Verus Israel*, 422. There is, however, evidence for Christian worship of angels and the sun, identified with Christ, as late as the fifth century; F.J. Dölger, *Sol Salutis*, 2nd ed. (Münster, 1945).

[32]*Antiquities*, III, 185-6, Loeb Classical Library, 405-7; cf. a similar passage in Philo, *Quaest. in Exod* II, 109, trans. R. Marcus, Loeb Classical Library, suppl. 2 (Cambridge: Harvard Univ. Press, 1970) 158.

[33]*Midrash Rabbah*, Numbers XIV:18, 3:629.

[34]Smith, "Helios in Palestine," 209; *Sefer HaRazim*, ed. M. Margalioth (Jerusalem, 1966). The text has been translated by M. Morgan as *Sepher Ha-Razim. The Book of the Mysteries,* Society of Biblical Literature. Texts and Pseudepigraphia Series 11 (Chico, Ca.: Scholars Press, 1983). See also Goodenough, *Jewish Symbols*, 2:145f., 161, 174-89, 199f.

[35]Morgan, *Sepher Ha-Razim*, 6, 67.

[36]Ibid., 71.

[37]Bonner, *Magical Amulets*, 148f., 291.

[38]Morgan, *Sepher Ha-Razim*, 73f.; "as they are written" means that the preceding list gives them in the order of their months from Nisan to Adar.

[39]*Jubilees*, 2:2.

[40]J. Barbel, *Christos Angelos* (Bonn, 1941) 219. For the names of other angels and the charms or amulets in which they are used see Goodenough, *Jewish Symbols* 2:180-208.

[41]Morgan, *Sepher Ha-Razim*, 81ff.

[42]Philo, *Questions and Answers on Exodus*, 39-42, as translated in A. Segal, *Rebecca's Children. Judaism and Christianity in the Roman World* (Cambridge: Harvard University Press, 1986) 138.

[43]M. Klein, *Genizah Manuscripts of Palestinian Targum to the Pentateuch*, 2 vols. (Cincinnati: Hebrew Union College-Jewish Institute of Religion, 1986) 1: 192.

[44]J. Yoholam, "Piyyut as Poetry," *The Synagogue in Late Antiquity*, ed. L. Levine (Philadelphia: The American Schools of Oriental Research, 1987) 119f.

[45]D. Feuchtwang, "Der Tierkreis in der Tradition und im Synagogenritus," *Monatsschrift für Geschichte und Wissenschaft des Judentums* 59 (1915) 257ff.

[46]M. Smith, "Goodenough's Jewish Symbols in Retrospect," *Journal of Biblical Literature* 86 (1967) 61.

[47]Morgan, *Sepher Ha-Razim*, 83. It is interesting to compare the text of the En Gedi inscription with that of some of the passages of the *Sefer HaRazim*. (For the inscription see L. Levine, "The Inscription in the En Gedi Synagogue," *Ancient Synagogues*, 140 ff.) The En Gedi inscription has been cited as proof that the zodiac mosaics constitute a calendar, because in the inscription the names of the Hebrew months are mentioned immediately following the names of the signs of the zodiac and are therefore cited as an attempt to correlate the lunar and solar calendars (see Dothan, *Hammath Tiberias*, 82, n. 285 with further bibliography). The list of the generations that opens the inscription has its parallels in the Preface of the *Sefer HaRazim* (see Morgan, 17-19). The generations are followed by the signs of the zodiac and the names of the Hebrew months. One of the purposes of the *Sefer HaRazim* mentioned in the Preface is "to observe all the astrological signs" (Morgan, 17). As Levine notes, the names of the Patriarchs and Hananiah, Mishael and Azariah of lines 7 and 8 of the inscription are mentioned as the pillars of the world in whose names people take oaths; the names of the Patriarchs are also mentioned in the Preface of the *Sefer HaRazim*. The second part of the inscription puts a curse on anyone who "reveals the secret of the town to the Gentiles."

10

A Second-First Century B.C.E. Fortress And Siege Complex In Eastern Upper Galilee

Mordechai Aviam
Israel Antiquities Authority &
University of Rochester

Impressive remains of a fortress, circumvallation wall and army camps were lately investigated at Qeren-Naftali (Khirbet Hurrawi) a high peak in eastern Upper Galilee (r.p. 2029 2774). The summit, 410 meters above sea level, rises steeply, about 400 meters above the Hula Valley (photo 1).[1] From its top is an outstanding overlook: north to the Baqa and the Hermon mountains, east to the Golan, south to the Hula Valley and Mt. Knaan and west to the valley of Qedesh, the mountains of Upper Galilee and Lebanon. At its foothill, flows the largest spring in the Hula Valley, the Einan spring. The site was first surveyed by Guerin who describes the remains of the fortress "...about 112 paces in length from north to south, twenty eight paces broad towards the north, fifty towards the center, forty towards the south. It was flanked by several square towers constructed, like the wall itself, of great blocks rudely squared and lying one upon the other without cement."[2] He also describes some remains of a settlement on the eastern slope of the hill, with remains of a large (public?) building with a lintel and large, simply decorated jamb-stones, 2.7 meters long and 0.7 meters wide. The survey of Western Palestine does not add more details about the fortress but mentions a couple of rock-cut tombs with loculi.[3]

In the beginning of this century, two Greek inscriptions had been found at the site by Masterman. One of them, longer than the other, and curved on a lintel, was dedicated to Athena. The other, in *Tabula Ansata* was dedicated to Zeus Heliopolitanus.[4] The inscriptions might have once belonged to the same building mentioned by Guerin, which was probably a temple. Based on Masterman's description the building with the inscription of Athena lay in the center of the small platform, covered with the remains of an ancient village, below the summit on which the fortress stood.

In 1981, limited salvage excavations on behalf of the Israel Department of Antiquities took place at the southern edge of the small village which revealed wall segments dated to the Roman period.[5] During the beginning of this century, a couple of houses that were built on the eastern platform and on the top of the hill, damaged the ancient remains. The smaller inscription mentioned above, was found in one of these houses and probably belonged to the public building whose walls are still visible (photo 2). The fortress (photo 3), was built according to the topography of the summit (see plan 1). Its length is 110 meters, its width is 29 meters in the north, 40 meters in the center and 50 meters in the south.[6] Two corner-towers, 9x9 meters in

Photo 1. Summit of Khirbet Hurrawi in Eastern Upper Galilee

the north are the same size as the Hellenistic tower in area C at Tel Dor.[7] Along the western wall, three rectangular towers were built, projecting 5 meters out of the wall line. An opposite tower was located in the eastern wall. The most southern one, in the west wall, is 11 meters long, the same size as the Hellenistic tower in area A at Tel Dor and as the Hellenistic tower at Yodefat.[8] The south-eastern side is covered by large heaps of stones that collapsed from the Arabic building and make it impossible to follow the fortress' wall line. The southern and western walls are preserved to a maximum height of 2 meters (photo 4). The only place it is possible to measure the width of the wall is near one of the western towers where it is 2.8 meters wide. In the north, west and south, the walls and towers were thickened by an addition of a wall that was built 2.8-3.0 meters from the fortress wall. The space between the walls was filled up with field stones. One substantial wall divides the fortress from west to east. Seven large rolling-stones, 0.5 meters in diameter, were located in the south-west corner of the fortress (photo 5), and two more were found at the bottom of the summit near the village. They are all nearly the same size, with a rough cut and rounded shape. One of them weighed 156.5 kg. Their size and weight support the identification as rolling-stones rather than ballista-stones. Very large ballista-stones, were found in Pergamon, but much lighter than the

ones from Qeren-Naftali.[9] According to Vitruvius, the heaviest ballista-stones weighed up to 117.9 kg. (Book XI, 3). According to Shatzman there were no machines that could shoot such heavy stones as those found at the site.[10] During the survey we also identified two cisterns inside the fortress, in the south-eastern side, which were reused in later periods and two or three other cisterns in the northern side, outside the wall.

The pottery collected at the site belongs to different periods; the largest quantities were shards dating to the Hellenistic period and included a large quantity of "G.C.W." (Galilean Coarse Ware).[11] Many E.T.S. (Eastern Terra Sigillata) shards from the late Hellenistic and the Early Roman periods were found as well. The rest date to the Middle Roman and Late Arabic periods. Two coins were found, both minted at Tyre in the Late Hellenistic period.[12] Relying on the ceramic evidence, it seems that the fortress was built in the second century B.C.E. at the southern borders of the territory of Tyre. The settlement closest to the fortress is Qedesh--"Kadasa of Tyre" (Jos., *War* 4.2.3).[13]

Proof for the importance and size of Qedesh at the Hellenistic period became evident during an intensive survey at the site.[14] In the Early Hasmonaean period, a heavy battle between Jonathan and Demetrius took place at the "Hazor plain", below the summit of Qeren Naftali and

Photo 2. Remains of Public Building

Photo 3. The Fortress

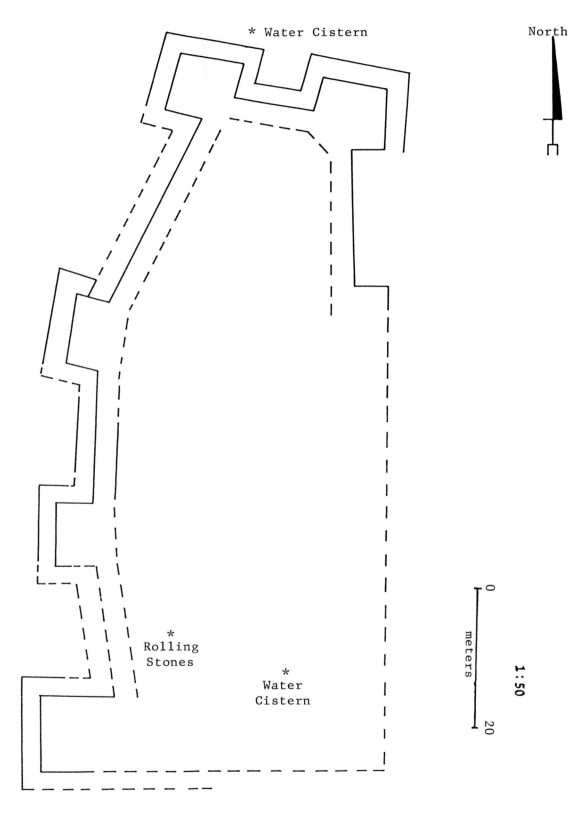

Plan 1

Photo 4. Southern and Western Walls

Photo 5. Group of Large Rolling Stones

southwards. When the Syrian troops were defeated, according to Josephus they retreated back "as far as Kadasa where the enemy had their camp" (*Antiquities* 13.7). If the site, as suggested above, properly dates to the second century B.C.E., then the fortress existed during this battle and thus would have protected the ascent from the valley to Qedesh. When the Hasmonaeans took control over the Galilee at the time of John Hyrcanus, the fortress was captured during the conquest of the northern Galilee and became part of the defense system of this area.[15] Additional evidence that Hasmonaean garrisons were stationed in Galilean fortresses comes from Josephus: "He (Herod) set out to reduce the remaining strongholds of Galilee and to expel the garrisons of Antigonus" (*War* 1.16.11).

When Herod took over the Galilee he led some campaigns in this area. The first one was against Marion, the master of Tyre that was directed by Ptolemy son of Menaos. Marion conquered three strongholds in the Galilee (probably from the Hellenistic and Hasmonaean period) and was expelled from them by Herod (*War* 1.12.2). I suggest that the fortress at Qeren Naftali was one, and maybe the most important, of the fortresses mentioned by Josephus. It is still difficult to identify the two others. One of them could be in South-Lebanon, but this area has not been properly surveyed. The third one might be in Tzfat (Safed) where Hellenistic G.C.W. pot-shards were found under heavy debris during a survey of the Crusader castle. Another suggestion for the location of the third fortress, could be the large and impressive fortified site of Beer-Sheba (of the Galilee), where large quantities of G.C.W. and other Hellenistic and Early Roman pot-shards and coins were collected.[16]

The next Herodian campaign was against the Jewish zealots who supported Antigonus (*War* 116.2-6). Herod arrived in Galilee, operated at Zippori (Sepphoris) and then fought against the zealots at the caves located in the Arbel Cliffs. He left Ptolemy, one of his best commanders, in the area and went to Samaria. At this point the tumult started again in the Galilee. Herod immediately moved back and according to Josephus he "killed a large number of the rebels, *besieged* and destroyed all their fortresses" (*War* 1.16.5). According to Josephus's description of the main battle in Arbel, it seems likely that the center of the rebellion was in eastern Galilee. In two cases, Josephus emphasizes that the rebels retreated to the Jordan River and to the marshes. If so, I suggest that the fortress at Qeren Naftali took on an important role in those incidents, mainly because of its location close to the Jordan River and above the largest marsh in the country in the Hula Valley. An important clue that supports this suggestion is the remains of a siege complex around the mountain (see Photo 6). The fortress was transferred from one hand to another in a short time. In the beginning it was in Herodian hands. It was conquered by Marion's troops only to be recaptured by Herod. Then the fortress fell to the

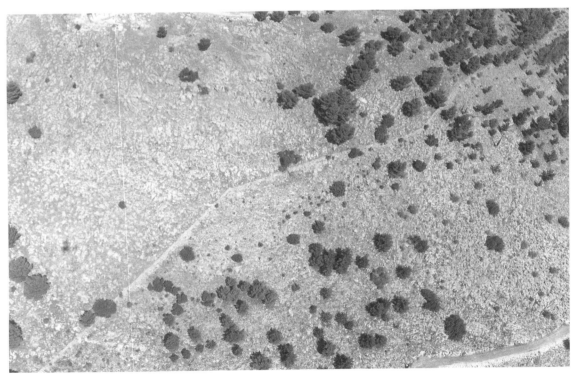

Photo 6. Siege Complex

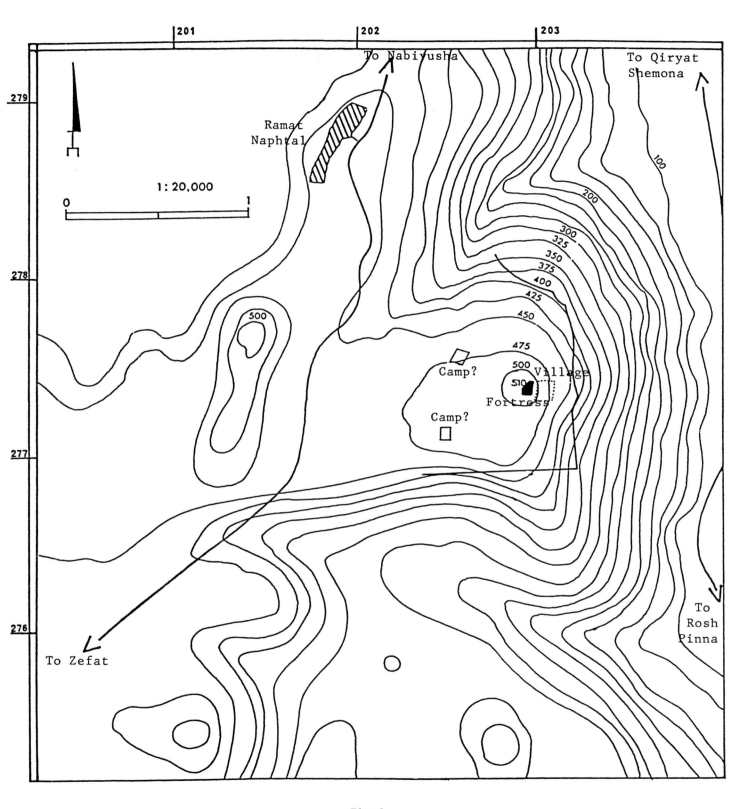

Plan 2

hands of the Galilean Zealots, was besieged, and then re-conquered by Herod. Yet another campaign might have taken place at this site in the time of Herod. It all started when Herod was at Daphne near Antioch and the message about the death of his brother, Joseph, reached him. He strengthened his forces with 800 mountaineers and some units from a Roman Legion, and invaded the Galilee. The main battle was against a Jewish fortress that was later evacuated by its defenders (*War* 1.17.3).

When we took aerial photos, we discovered two long, perpendicular walls, built on the eastern and southern slopes of the mountain, which were later surveyed by foot (plan 2). Both are built in similar fashion using two rows of medium-size field stones, with fill of un-cemented small field stones. The width of the wall is 0.8-1.1 meters. They are preserved to a maximum height of 1.6 meters. The length of the southern wall is about 800 meters. It runs from the east, at the point where the walls create a corner, to the west in a straight line. It climbs onto a small range, cuts a shallow wadi and abruptly stops. The eastern wall is about 1400 meters long in a broken line. It climbs steeply on the eastern slope and reaches to a distance of 200 meters from the fortress's east wall. Then the wall runs downhill towards a steep wadi but stops before getting to its bottom.

The walls are not for agricultural use nor do they serve as borders of fields. The area circumscribed by the walls is very rocky, with no remains of terraces or any other agricultural elements. In addition lines of the wall are almost completely straight and long. The best explanation for the existence of these walls is to view them as siege-walls built around the fortress.[17] There are similarities between this complex and other Hasmonaean siege complexes at Horqania, Doq and Alexandrion.[18] On the steep and rocky slope in the east, the wall reaches to a distance of about 200 meters from the fortress wall a distance similar to the siege-wall at Horqania. At both sites the far most point of the walls is about 700 meters from the fortresses.

It seems that the forces besieging the fortress at Qeren Naftali, started to build the complex in the less accessible areas, the eastern slope and the wadis at the south and the north. They probably were afraid that reinforcements could secretly climb to the fortress from those sides. The western side, where the difference in the levels between the plateau and the peak is only 40 meters is the natural place for army camps and the most suitable direction from which to start the attack. The intense cultivation of this area during the last 40 years explains why no archaeological remains were found in our survey. In an aerial photo taken by the R.A.F. in 1945, two square enclosures can be seen on both sides of the plateau more than 300 meters west of the fortress, a suitable distance to avoid ballista shooting. The northern enclosure is about 70x80 meters

and the southern one is about 70x90 meters. I propose that they are army camps (see plan 2).

The suggestion to identify the archaeological remains as siege complexes does present some problems. The walls, for example, are narrower than similar walls in fortresses found in the Judean Desert. These complexes are not built on the mountain, which would have allowed the besiegers to control the approaches to the site. The two walls end suddenly and there are no towers or camps along them. One answer might be that the complex was never finished and the defenders surrendered before the project was finished. I suggest that the remains of the siege belong to the operations of Herod against the Jewish Zealots, the supporters of Antigonus, in the Galilee. If this is the case, this is the first archaeological evidence for vigorous Galilean resistance to Herod. The Galilean support for the Hasmonaean dynasty was well established in the traditions that emphasized the conquest and the resettling of the Galilee by the Hasmonaean monarchs. Nevertheless, it is possible that the siege complex was part of the battle between Herod and Marion. This is the first, and up till now, the only siege complex in the Galilee and one of the earliest known in the country. The first appearance of a circumvalation wall is in the Hellenistic-Hasmonaean period. One of our earliest historic references concerns this type of siege practice, a triple wall built by Alexander Janneus around Gerasa at the time he besieged the town (Jos., *War* 1.4.8).[19]

The pottery from the small settlement below the fortress includes shards dated to the Hellenistic, Early Roman and Middle Roman periods. The inscription dedicated to Athena should not be dated earlier than the mid-first century C.E. and not later than mid-second century C.E. The other inscription is probably from the third century C.E.[20] Based on these dates, one can conclude that the temple and the small village around it were built after the destruction and abandonment of the fortress. The evidence from the fortress and the village support the thesis of a demographic change that took place in the Galilee from the mid-first century C.E[21]

According to our previous analysis, I propose the following historical reconstruction: the fortress was built by the Seleucid government on the boundaries of Tyre to maintain control of the settlements in the Hula Valley that lay above the main spring and on the main road in the north.[22] At the time of the Hasmonaean conquest of the Galilee, the fortress was part of the Jewish territories in the north and shifted from hand to hand in the battles between the Galileans and Herod. After Herod Antipas was exiled by the Romans, the Jewish territories started to shrink to the borders described by Josephus. In this stage, the fortress shifted into Gentile hands, and it was at this time that the temple was erected. More work must be done at the site, including excavations that will shed additional light upon the significance of the fortress and the village.

NOTES

[1] The site was visited by the author as part of the "sites survey in Upper Galilee" that will be published at the end of 1996. R. Getzov and B. Inbal took part in the survey of this site. The site was revisited for the writing of this article with D. Shalem and I. Shaqed. The aerial survey was done with the help of the pilot Y. Tor and the aerial photos were shot by H. Smithline.

[2] M. V. Guerin, *Description de la Palestine III* (1880).

[3] C. Konder and H. Kitchener, *The Survey of Western Palestine I* (1897).

[4] E. Masterman, "The Greek Inscription from Khurbet Harrawi," *Palestine Exploration Quarterly* (1908) 41-2.

[5] The site was excavated by D. Bahat and the information is from the Israel Antiquities Authority.

[6] According to Guerin's documentation, the fortress gets narrow towards the south. He probably saw the site in a better condition of preservation but we could not identify the lines of the walls in the south because of the ruins of a Arab building. We estimated the width to about 50 meters as it is in the schematic plan.

[7] E. Stern, "The Wall of Tel Dor," *Israel Exploration Journal 38* (1988) 6-14.

[8] M. Aviam and D. Adan-Bayewitz, "Yodefat," *Hadashot Archeologiot 104* (1995) [Hebrew].

[9] A. Von-Szalay and F. Bohringer, "Die Artillery von Pergamon," *Altertumer von Pergamon X* (1937) 48-54.

[10] I. Shatzman, "Stone-Balls from Tel Dor and the Artillery of the Hellenistic World," *SCI 16* (1995) 52-72.

[11] M. Aviam, "The Hasmonaean Dynasty Activity in the Galilee," *Idan* (1995) [Hebrew, in print].

[12] The coins were identified by R. Getzov. From oral information, I heard of Hasmonaean coins found at the site.

[13] The excavations in the Roman temple at Qedesh, uncovered inscriptions, dated to the third century B.C.E. by the Tyrian era, which establishes that Qedesh was on the southern border of Tyre.

[14] A survey-excavation at Tel Qedesh by Y. Portugali together with the Roman temple expediton revealed a layer dated to the third-second century B.C.E. that covered most of the Tel.

[15] Aviam, "The Hasmonaean Dynasty."

[16] Ibid.

[17] The suggestion to identify the wall as siege walls was brought up during a visit with I. Shaqed.

[18] See Z. Meshel, "Siege Complexes for the End of the Hasmonaean Reign," *Eretz Israel* 17 (1984) 251-56 [Hebrew] and "Siege Complexes in the Days of the Hasmonaeans," *Z.Vilnay Book* I (1984) 254-58 [Hebrew].

[19] In the past, it was suggested that the wall with half-round towers on top of Mt. Nitai, is a siege wall associated with the Herodian attack on the Jewish caves of Arbel. Elsewhere, I argue instead that the wall is part of Josephus' fortifications in the Galilee ("On the Fortifications of Josephus in the Galilee," *Qatedra* 28 (1983) 33-46). The Roman campaigns at Yodefat and Gamela did not leave any remains of siege walls.

[20] The inscriptions were dated by L. Di-Segni, according to their style.

[21] Aviam, "The Hasmonaean Dynasty."

[22] I. Shaqed surveyed a larger number of Hellenistic sites in the Hula valley on behalf of the Israel Antiquities authority. One of the most important sites is Tel Anafa.

11

Long-Distance Trade In
The Lower Galilee:
New Evidence From Sepphoris

Arlene Fradkin
Florida Museum of Natural History

INTRODUCTION

Sepphoris, the largest city and the capital of the Lower Galilee in late antiquity[1] was a major center of culture and of trade and commerce. Archaeological excavations conducted over the past 14 years have revealed a sophisticated urban metropolis complete with colonnaded streets, a theater, an aqueduct system, villas, synagogues, and a large public building.[2] Like most urban centers, Sepphoris was linked to other regions by means of roads and extensive trade routes.[3] Such evidence for trade is reflected in some of the animal remains recovered at Sepphoris, particularly those of fish and aquatic mollusks, whose origins were as distant as the Mediterranean Sea, the Nile River, the Sea of Galilee, and the Jordan River (figure 1).

This paper examines the kinds of fish and aquatic mollusks that were recovered from Roman and Byzantine period contexts at Sepphoris during the 1993, 1994, and 1995 excavations of the University of South Florida, Tampa. The animals are grouped and discussed here according to their source, or place of origin. Other archae-ological sites in neighboring regions with similar faunal remains are also mentioned. Finally, suggestions for the possible uses of these nonlocal animals by the inhabitants of Sepphoris are presented.

METHODS

Analysis of the fish and aquatic mollusk remains recovered from Sepphoris followed standard zooarchae-ological procedures.[4] Specimens were identified using the private comparative fish collection of Dr. Omri Lernau and the comparative mollusk collection housed at Hebrew University of Jerusalem. Identifications were carried out to the lowest taxon possible following standard zoological classification and nomenclature. For each specimen iden-tified, a record was made of the element represented, por-tion of element recovered, its symmetry (right or left), and any evidence of modification (burnt, perforated, and/or polished).

Quantification of the animal remains included a count of the total number of identified specimens of each taxon (NISP) and calculated estimates of the minimum number of individual animals represented (MNI). The MNI figures were determined separately for each locus. Because this study was limited to Roman and Byzantine contexts, the materials examined represented a subsample of the total aquatic animal remains recovered from the site.

RESULTS AND DISCUSSION

The fish and aquatic mollusk remains analyzed clearly indicate a system of trade between Sepphoris and more distant regions in late antiquity.

All taxa identified are listed in Table 1. A total of 33 taxa were represented, of which 7 were fish and 26 were mollusks. Quantification of the remains is presented in tabulated form in Table 2. A discussion of the animal remains follows.

The Mediterranean Sea

The majority of the fish and molluscan species represented at Sepphoris came from the Mediterranean Sea.

The Mediterranean fish remains included bones of grouper and of mullet (photo 1). Both are considered edible today and, in fact, are regarded as excellent food.

Groupers (*Epinephelus* spp.) are large marine fish that occur in the warm waters of the eastern Mediterranean [5] and are common along the coast of Israel.[6] Typically carnivorous, they feed on other fishes as well as crustaceans and mollusks.[7]

At least two species of grouper were represented at Sepphoris. The white grouper (*Epinephelus aeneus*) averages 50 centimeters (20 inches) in length, though it may attain a maximum size of 100 centimeters (40 inches). It inhabits sandy and muddy bottoms of the continental shelf down to depths of 150 meters (492 feet). The dusky grouper (*Epinephelus guaza*) is somewhat larger, averaging 60 centimeters (24 inches) long, and has a maximum size of 140 centimeters (55 inches). Typically a solitary species, this fish lives amongst rocks and in caves in depths ranging from 10 to 120 meters (33 to 394 feet).[8]

Gray mullets (Mugilidae) are smaller than groupers, ranging from approximately 20 to 50 centimeters (8 to 20 inches) in length, and are very common in warm shallow inshore waters, lagoons, and estuaries along Israel's Mediterranean coast.[9] Moving in dense schools, these fish feed primarily on plant material.[10]

Six species of gray mullet inhabit Israel's Mediterranean waters. Although all six species are marine, five of them also enter brackish and even fresh waters. These mullets, particularly the young, often concentrate near freshwater outflows, or estuaries, and regularly ascend coastal rivers. Spawning, however, occurs exclusively in the sea to which the adults return prior to the appropriate season.[11] The gray mullets represented at Sepphoris were

fairly small, possibly juveniles, and therefore were most likely caught in the estuaries and lower reaches of coastal rivers.

Mullets were well known to ancient Egyptians, who observed and described their migrations up the Nile River, which signalled the approach of the flood season. Fisherfolk today catch the young fish on winter nights in the estuaries of coastal rivers and then raise them in freshwater fish ponds.[12]

Fish caught in the Mediterranean Sea had to be processed by salting, drying, or some other means in order to preserve them during their transport to market. According to one 19th-century source, fish from the Mediterranean were packed onto donkey or mule trains and transported inland to the central Lower Galilee, which was a distance of approximately 30 kilometers (18 miles), or a half-day's journey. Donkey pack trains leaving the Mediterranean coast early in the morning would arrive at Sepphoris at noon, and the traders would spend the rest of the day selling their fish and other goods at the market.[13] This trading pattern could have occurred in previous centuries as well.

Both grouper and mullet remains were recovered at other archaeological sites. Several examples include the Late Roman-Byzantine castella sites of En Boqeq and Tamara, located on the western shore of the Dead Sea and in the northeastern Negev, respectively.[14] Moreover, at the City of David excavations, archaeological bone remains of these fish were found in Bronze and Iron Age contexts, thus providing evidence for an extensive trade network already in place in Jerusalem in even earlier time periods.[15]

Marine mollusks of Mediterranean origin at Sepphoris included both bivalves and gastropods (photo 2). Of the Mediterranean bivalves, the most abundant species was the violet bittersweet clam (*Glycymeris violacescens*). This mollusk typically occurs in shallow waters and is the most common bivalve found today on the shores of the Mediterranean Sea, particularly along the coast of Israel.[16] Specimens of this clam have been found at a number of archaeological sites throughout Israel, including 'Ain Mallaha (Hula Basin), Abu Gosh, Pisgat Ze'ev, the City of David (Jerusalem) and Sde Boqer (central Negev), which range in time from the Neolithic through Early Arab periods.[17]

Like those recovered at other sites, several of the violet bittersweet clam shells at Sepphoris exhibited a hole near the umbo, or top, of the shell. The top section is the oldest (as it is where shell growth begins) and therefore the weakest part of the shell. It has been suggested that this hole may have been formed naturally either through erosion caused by wave action or as a result of boring activity by another organism.[18] An alternative suggestion is that

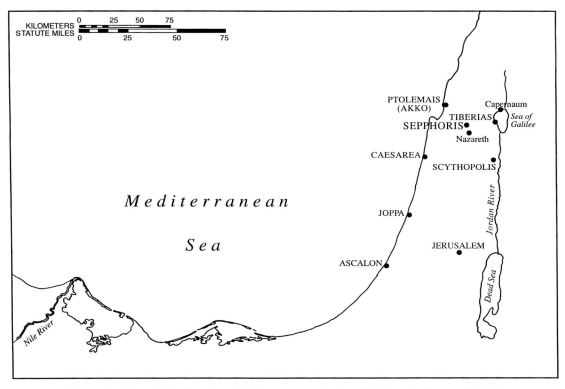

Figure 1: Map of the Southern Mediterranean Region During the Roman Period.

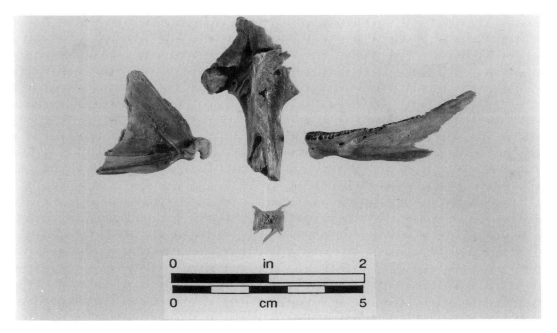

Photo 1: Fish Remains from the Mediterranean Sea.
top row, left to right: *Epinephelus aeneus*, left quadrate;
Epinephelus sp., right hyomandibular;
Epinephelus guaza, left dentary.
bottom row: Mugilidae, caudal vertebra.

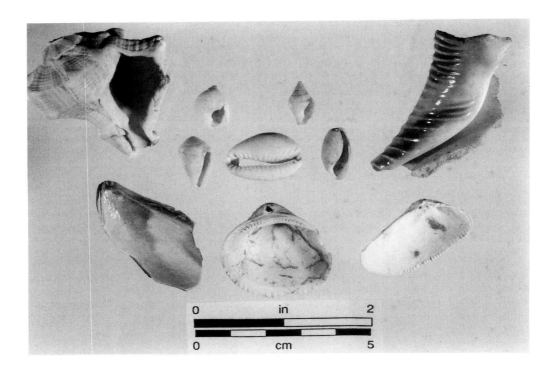

Photo 2: Mollusk Remains from the Mediterranean Sea.
top left: *Bolinus brandaris.*
top right: *Charonia tritonis variegata,* columella.
top center, clockwise: *Columbella rustica,*
Bulla striata, Cypraea spurca, Conus mediterraneus,
Nassarius gibbosulus.
bottom row, left to right:
Mytilus galloprovincialis, left valve;
Glycymeris violacescens, left valve;
Donax trunculus, left valve.

the hole was humanmade and the shell was used for ornamental purposes, such as pendants.[19]

Other Mediterranean bivalves recovered at Sepphoris included truncate donax (*Donax trunculus*), tuberculate cockle (*Acanthocardia tuberculata*), common Mediterranean cockle (*Cerastoderma glaucum*), Mediterranean blue mussel (*Mytilus galloprovincialis*), as well as several oyster shells (*Ostrea stentina*) and an ark shell (*Anadara diluvii*).

Mediterranean gastropods were more common than were Mediterranean bivalves at Sepphoris in number of taxa represented, number of specimens identified, and estimated number of individual animals.

The purple-dye murex (*Bolinus brandaris*) typically occurs in shallow waters along the Mediterranean coast and, in the past, was widely exploited to produce the so-called Tyrian purple dye.[20] This shell has been recovered

from such archaeological sites as Abu Gosh, Pisgat Ze'ev, and the City of David.[21]

The yellow cowrie (*Cypraea spurca*) is another common Mediterranean shore species and is usually found in shallow waters on seaweed and sandy bottoms.[22] In one of the specimens recovered at Sepphoris, the dorsum section, or back, of the shell had been completely removed. Cowrie shells similarly altered have been found at a number of other archaeological sites as well (e.g., Abu Gosh [Jerusalem] and Abu Salem [central Negev]).[23] Such a condition may have been the result of natural erosion or of deliberate modification by humans. Cowries, including this species, have been and still continue to be used as ornamental objects such as necklaces, brooches, and beads, or as amulets in various cultures throughout the world.[24]

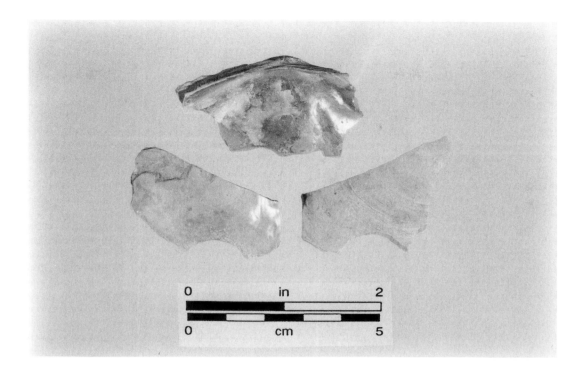

Photo 3: Mollusk Remains from the Nile River
top row: *Aspatharia rubens*, left partial valve with hinge.
bottom row: *Aspatharia rubens*, 2 valve fragments

The trumpet triton (*Charonia tritonis variegata*) is a very large gastropod, approximately 25 to 33 centimeters (10 to 13 inches) in length, that inhabits shallow eastern Mediterranean waters near coral reefs.[25] This mollusk is often used as a shell-trumpet: A small hole is drilled in the spire section of the shell, and, when blown, the shell produces a sound resembling a modern cornet.[26]

Several species of very small shallow-water Mediterranean gastropods were recovered, including rustic doveshell (*Columbella rustica*), Mediterranean cone (*Conus mediterraneus*), decollated nassa (*Nassarius circumcinctus*), and swollen nassa (*Nassarius gibbosulus*).[27] At other archaeological sites, such as 'Ain Mallaha, these shells exhibited holes, evidence of their possible use as beads.[28]

The occurrence of these very small shells at Sepphoris, however, may be incidental. They were not used for food as they contain an infinitesimal amount of meat, and, moreover, they were not modified into beads or other objects of adornment. More likely, they may have been present in the seaweed or salt water used in packing Mediterranean fish for transport inland. In fact, the small dove shells typically feed on soft algae and often cling to seaweeds.[29]

The Nile River

One molluscan species identified at Sepphoris came from the Nile River in Egypt, which is a distance of approximately 830 kilometers (500 miles) away. The large Nilotic freshwater mussel *Aspatharia rubens* (photo 3) has been found at many archaeological sites throughout Israel, ranging from 'Ain Mallaha in the north to Timna in the south, and in contexts dating from as early as the Neolithic, Chalcolithic, Bronze Age, and Iron Age, through the later Hellenistic, Roman, Byzantine, and Early Arab periods.[30]

Aspatharia rubens served multiple uses. Its meat may have been used as food, and its shell was modified into utensils such as combs, spoons, scoops, make-up plates, and small containers, and, occasionally, into ornaments such as beads and pendants. These uses are suggested by a number of *Aspatharia* shells at several archaeological sites which show evidence of modification. Some of the larger shells exhibited wear on their edge, whereas other shells had drilled holes. These modified specimens may indicate that this mollusk was valued more for its shell than for its meat.[31] The *Aspatharia* shell remains at Sepphoris, however, were too fragmented to detect any evidence of modification.

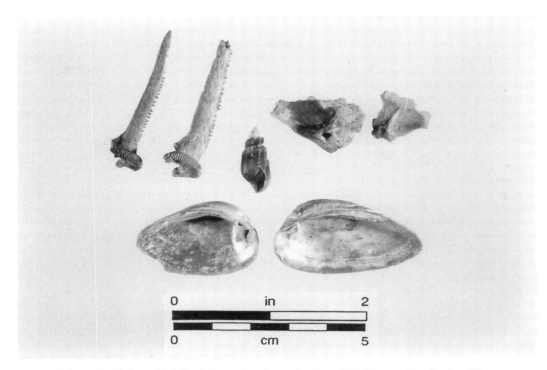

Photo 4: Fish and Mollusk Remains from the Sea of Galilee and/or Jordan River.
top row, left to right: *Clairas gariepinus*, 2 left pectoral spines;
Melanopsis praemorsa jordanica;
Tilapiini, left and right opercula.
bottom row, left to right: *Unio terminalis terminalis*, left and right valves.

The Sea Of Galilee, The Jordan River, And Coastal Rivers

Several kinds of freshwater fish and mollusks recovered at Sepphoris were from the Sea of Galilee, the Jordan River, and/or coastal rivers (photo 4).

The Nile catfish (*Clarias gariepinus*) is the largest freshwater fish in Israel and is the only catfish species in Israel today. This fish can attain a maximum length of 100 centimeters (40 inches) and a maximum weight of 20 kilograms (44 pounds). An inhabitant of lakes, large sluggish rivers, and slow water streams, the Nile catfish naturally occurs in the Sea of Galilee and other waters of the Jordan River system and in coastal rivers in Israel, in the Nile River in Egypt (hence the name Nile catfish) as well as throughout Africa.[32] Like other members of the family Clariidae, this species has evolved an accessory air-breathing organ above the gills which allows it to survive in such harsh conditions as poor oxygenation or desiccation. An omnivorous fish, the Nile catfish feeds on any available organic food source, including fish, frogs, reptiles, birds, small mammals, snails, crustaceans, and plant seeds and fruit. It is considered edible and is an important food fish species today.[33]

Tilapias (Tilapiini) are small freshwater fish, up to 33 centimeters (13 inches) in length, and are very common in many of Israel's lakes, ponds, and streams. Several genera and species of tilapia naturally occur in the Sea of Galilee, the Jordan River, and/or Israel's coastal rivers.[34] A popular table fish today, tilapias have been introduced into various parts of the world where they are raised on fish farms and are important in commercial and subsistence fisheries.[35]

Remains of the Nile catfish and of tilapias have also been recovered at the City of David (Bronze and Iron Age deposits) and at the Late Roman-Byzantine sites of En Boqeq and Tamara.[36] Several sources have mentioned the thriving fishing industry around the Sea of Galilee. Some of these fish were sold in local markets; the rest were probably exported in salted form to other regions.[37]

Two molluscan species recovered at Sepphoris came from the Sea of Galilee and the Jordan River. The freshwater clam *Unio terminalis terminalis* and the freshwater snail *Melanopsis praemorsa jordanica* are both edible species.

CONCLUSIONS

The Lower Galilee was one of the most fertile and productive and, consequently, one of the most densely populated regions in late antiquity. Its gentle topography allowed for the development of roads and various trade routes, thereby connecting settlements within the Galilee area proper as well as linking the Galilee area with other major regions.[38]

According to several sources, Galilean products, particularly olive oil, were in great demand and were exported to other parts of the ancient world. In exchange, the Galilee imported such items as Egyptian smoked fish and lentils, Spanish mackerel, and wines.[39]

Sepphoris, a major city lying in the heart of the Lower Galilee, must have played a significant role in the economy of this region. Indeed, Sepphoris probably served as the center for the sale and distribution of both locally produced goods as well as imported commodities from more distant regions. The fish and mollusks from the Mediterranean Sea, the Nile River, and the Sea of Galilee/Jordan River identified in this study provide substantive evidence for the importance of Sepphoris as a major center of trade and commerce in the Lower Galilee.

ACKNOWLEDGMENTS

I would like to express my appreciation to Dr. Omri Lernau for the use of his comparative fish collection and to Dr. Henk Mienis for his assistance in the identification of the mollusk remains. I especially thank Dr. James F. Strange for having invited me to join the staff team of the University of South Florida Excavations at Sepphoris, which has proven to be a truly enjoyable research and learning experience.

NOTES

[1]See W. Whiston, *The Works of Josephus* (U.S.: Hendrickson, 1987).

[2]See E. Meyers, "Roman Sepphoris in Light of New Archaeological Evidence and Recent Research," in *The Galilee in Late Antiquity* ed., L. Levine (New York: The Jewish Theological Seminary, 1992) 321-38; E. Meyers, E. Netzer and C. Meyers, *Sepphoris* (Winona Lake: Eisenbrauns, 1992); J. Strange, "Six Campaigns at Sepphoris: The University of South Florida Excavations, 1983-89," in *The Galilee in Late Antiquity*, 339-55; T. Tsuk, *Sepphoris and Its Site* (Tel Aviv: Society for the Preservation of Nature in Israel, 1987) [in Hebrew]; "The Aqueducts of Sepphoris," in *The Aqueducts of Ancient Palestine* eds., D. Amit, Y. Hirschfeld, and J. Patrich (Jerusalem: Yad Izhak Ben-Zvi, 1989) 101-8 [in Hebrew].

[3]See M. Goodman, *State and Society in Roman Galilee, A.D. 132-212* (Totowa, NJ: Rowman and Allanheld, 1983) and E. Meyers, "Galilean Regionalism as a Factor in Historical Reconstruction," in *BASOR* 221 (1976) 93-102.

[4]See E. Wing and A. Brown, *Paleonutrition. Method and Theory in Prehistoric Foodways* (New York: Academic Press, 1979).

[5]See *FAO Species Identification Sheets for Fishery Purposes. Mediterranean and Black Sea (fishing area 37).* Volume 1 (Rome: Food and Agriculture Organization of the United Nations, 1973).

[6]See A. Ben-Tuvia, "Mediterranean Fishes of Israel," *Bulletin of the Sea Fisheries Research Station* 8 (1953) 1-40 and "Revised List of the Mediterranean Fishes of Israel," *Israel Journal of Zoology* 20:1 (1971) 1-39.

[7]See *FAO Species* and J. Lythgoe and G. Lythgoe, *Fishes of the Sea. The Coastal Waters of the British Isles, Northern Europe and the Mediterranean* (Garden City, NY: Anchor Press, 1975).

[8]See Ben-Tuvia, "Mediterranean Fishes," and *FAO Species.*

[9]See Ben-Tuvia, "Mediterranean Fishes," and "Revised List," and *FAO Species.*

[10]See *FAO Species* and Lythgoe and Lythgoe, *Fishes of the Sea.*

[11]See M. Abraham, N. Blanc, and A. Yashouv, "Oogenesis in Five Species of Grey Mullets (Teleostei, Mugilidae) from Natural and Landlocked Habitats," *Israel Journal of Zoology* 15:3-4 (1966) 155-72 and *FAO Species.*

[12]See, M. Abraham, et al. "Oogenesis," 156 and H. Lernau and O. Lernau, "Fish Remains," in *Excavations at the City of David, 1978-85,* Volume 3, ed. A. DeGroot and D. Ariel (Jerusalem: Hebrew University, 1992) 131-48.

[13]Reference provided by J. Strange.

[14]See H. Lernau, "Fishbones Excavated in Two Late Roman-Byzantine Castella in the Southern Desert of Israel," in *Fish and Archaeology. Studies in Osteometry, Taphonomy, Seasonality and Fishing Methods,* British Archaeological Reports International Series, No. 294, eds., D. Brinkhuizen and A. Clason (Oxford: British Archaeological Reports, 1986) 85-102.

[15]See Lernau and Lernau, "Fish Remains."

[16]See R. Abbott and S. Dance, *Compendium of Seashells* (New York: E.P. Dutton, 1982) 296 and A. Barash and Z. Danin, "Mediterranean Mollusca of Israel and Sinai: Composition and Distribution," *Israel Journal of Zoology* 31:3-4 (1982) 86-118.

[17]See H. Mienis, "Molluscs from the Prehistoric Sites of Abu Gosh and Beisamoun, Israel," *Memoires et Travaux Centre Recherche Prehistorique Francais, Jeru-*

salem 2 (1978) 269-72; "Notes on the Shells from the Bronze Age Strata from Tel Mevorakh," in *Excavations at Tel Mevorakh (1973-76). Part Two: The Bronze Age,* ed., E. Stern (Jerusalem: Hebrew University, 1984) 106-8; "The Molluscs of the Excavation of the Early Arabic Site of Sde Boqer: Some Further Remarks," *Levantina* 60 (1986) 657-62; "Molluscs from the Excavation of Mallaha (Eynan)," *Memoires et Travaux Centre Recherche Prehistorique Francais, Jerusalem* 4 (1987) 157-78; "A Second Collection of Shells from Neolithic Abu Gosh," *Levantina* 66 (1987) 695-702; "Nahal Hemar Cave: The Marine Molluscs," *'Atiquot* (English Series) 18 (1988) 47-9; "Molluscs," in *Excavations at the City of David,* "Molluscs from the Excavation of a Byzantine Church at Pisgat Ze'ev, Jerusalem, Israel," *Soosiana* 20 (1992) 21-4; "The Archaeomalacological Material Recovered During the Second Season of the Excavation of Tel Harisim," in *The Third Season of Excavation at "Tel Harasim" 1992 Preliminary Report 3,* ed. S. Givon (Tel Aviv: Tel Aviv University, 1993) 28-38.

[18] See the studies of Mienis.

[19] Ibid.

[20] See Mienis "Notes on the Shells," and "Molluscs," in *Excavations.*

[21] See the studies of Mienis.

[22] See C. Burgess, *The Living Cowries* (New York: A.S. Barnes, 1970) 157.

[23] See the studies of Mienis.

[24] See J. Walls, *Cowries* 2nd ed. (Neptune, NJ: T.F.H., 1979).

[25] See Abbott and Dance, *Compendium of Seashells,* 119.

[26] See R. Abbott, *A Guide to Field Identification. Seashells of North America.* (New York: Golden Press, 1968) 118 and Mienis, "Molluscs," in *Excavations,* 123.

[27] See Abbott and Dance, *Compendium.*

[28] See the studies of Mienis.

[29] See Abbott, *A Guide,* 130.

[30] See D. Reese, H. Mienis, and F. Woodward, "On the Trade of Shells and Fish from the Nile River," *BASOR* 264 (1986) 79-84.

[31] See Mienis, "Notes on the Shells," "Molluscs from the excavation of a Byzantine Church," "Shells from the Excavation of a Byzantine-Early Arabic Site in the Southern Negev, Israel" *Die Kreukel* 28e:1 (1992) 6 and Reese, Mienis, and Woodward.

[32] See M. Goren, "The Freshwater Fishes of Israel," *Israel Journal of Zoology* 23:2 (1974) 67-118 and P. Skelton, *A Complete Guide to the Freshwater Fishes of Southern Africa* (Halfway House, South Africa: Southern Book Publishers, 1993) 229-30.

[33] See Skelton, *A Complete Guide,* 229-30.

[34] See Goren, "The Freshwater," and E. Trewavas, "The Cichlid Fishes of Syria and Palestine," *Annals and Magazine of Natural History* 9 (1942) 526-36 and "*Tilapia aurea* (Steindachner) and the Status of *Tilapia nilotica exul, T. monodi* and *T. lemassoni* (Pisces, Cichlidae)," in *Israel Journal of Zoology* 14:1-4 (1964) 258-76.

[35] See *The Biology and Culture of Tilapias,* eds., R. Pullin and R. Lowe-McConnell, Proceeding of the International Conference on the Biology and Culture of Tilapias (Manila: International Center for Living Aquatic Resources Management, 1982) and Skelton, *A Complete Guide,* 319.

[36] See Lernau and Lernau, "Fish Remains," and Lernau, "Fishbones."

[37] See Goodman, *State and Society,* 24.

[38] See Goodman, *State and Society.*

[39] See M. Avi-Yonah, "The Herodian Period," in *The World History of the Jewish People,* Volume 7, ed. M. Avi-Yonah (Jerusalem: The Magnes Press, 1975).

Table 1. Taxonomic List of Fish and Aquatic Mollusks Recovered in
Roman and Byzantine Period Contexts at Sepphoris.

Scientific Name	Common Name	Origin
OSTEICHTHYES	BONY FISH	
Clarias gariepinus	Nile catfish	Sea of Galilee/Jordan River
Epinephelus aeneus	white grouper	Mediterranean
Epinephelus guaza	dusky grouper	Mediterranean
Epinephelus spp.	grouper	Mediterranean
Serranidae	grouper	Mediterranean
Tilapiini	tilapia	Sea of Galilee/Jordan River
Mugilidae	gray mullet	Mediterranean
MOLLUSCA	MOLLUSKS	
Anadara diluvii		Mediterranean
Glycymeris violacescens	violet bittersweet	Mediterranean
Mytilus galloprovincialis	Mediterranean blue mussel	Mediterranean
Ostrea stentina		Mediterranean
Unio terminalis terminalis		Sea of Galilee/Jordan River
Aspatharia rubens		Nile River
Loripes lacteus		Mediterranean
Acanthocardia tuberculata	tuberculate cockle	Mediterranean
Cerastoderma glaucum	common Mediterranean cockle	Mediterranean
Donax trunculus	truncate donax	Mediterranean
Donax sp.	donax	Mediterranean
Gibbula adansonii		Mediterranean
Clanculus cruciatus		Mediterranean
Melanopsis praemorsa jordanica		Sea of Galilee/Jordan River
Cypraea spurca	yellow cowrie	Mediterranean
Charonia tritonis variegata	trumpet triton	Mediterranean
Bolinus brandaris	purple-dye murex	Mediterranean
Buccinulum corneum		Mediterranean
Pisania striata buccinidae	striate pisania	Mediterranean
Columbella rustica	rustic dove-shell	Mediterranean
Pyrene scripta		Mediterranean
Nassarius circumcinctus	decollated nassa	Mediterranean
Nassarius gibbosulus	swollen nassa	Mediterranean
Nassarius mutabilis	mutable nassa	Mediterranean
Conus mediterraneus	Mediterranean cone	Mediterranean
Bulla striata	striate bubble	Mediterranean

Table 2. Quantification of Fish and Aquatic Mollusk Remains Recovered in
Roman and Byzantine Period Contexts at Sepphoris.

Taxon	NISP	Percent	MNI	Percent
Clarias gariepinus	2	18.18	2	20.00
Epinephelus aeneus	1	9.09	1	10.00
Epinephelus guaza	1	9.09	1	10.00
Epinephelus spp.	2	18.18	2	20.00
Serranidae	1	9.09	1	10.00
Tilapiini	2	18.18	2	20.00
Mugilidae	2	18.18	1	10.00
TOTAL OSTEICHTHYES	11	100.00	10	100.00
Anadara diluvii	1	1.41	1	1.54
Glycymeris violacescens	4	5.63	4	6.15
Mytilus galloprovincialis	1	1.41	1	1.54
Ostrea stentina	2	2.82	2	3.08
Unio terminalis terminalis	2	2.82	2	3.08
Aspatharia rubens	10	14.08	5	7.69
Loripes lacteus	1	1.41	1	1.54
Acanthocardia tuberculata	1	1.41	1	1.54
Cerastoderma glaucum	1	1.41	1	1.54
Donax trunculus	3	4.23	3	4.62
Donax sp.	1	1.41	1	1.54
Gibbula adansonii	1	1.41	1	1.54
Clanculus cruciatus	1	1.41	1	1.54
Melanopsis praemorsa jordanica	2	2.82	2	3.08
Cypraea spurca	3	4.23	3	4.62
Charonia tritonis variegata	1	1.41	1	1.54
Bolinus brandaris	3	4.23	3	4.62
Buccinulum corneum	1	1.41	1	1.54
Pisania striata buccinidae	1	1.41	1	1.54
Columbella rustica	17	23.94	16	24.62
Pyrene scripta	1	1.41	1	1.54
Nassarius circumcinctus	1	1.41	1	1.54
Nassarius gibbosulus	1	1.41	1	1.54
Nassarius mutabilis	1	1.41	1	1.54
Conus mediterraneus	8	11.27	8	12.31
Bulla striata	2	2.82	2	3.08
TOTAL MOLLUSCA	**71**	**100.00**	**65**	**100.00**

12

Architectural Development of Sepphoris During the Roman and Byzantine Periods

Zeev Weiss and Ehud Netzer
Hebrew University, Jerusalem

Early in the fourth century C.E., the Church father Eusebius, living in Caesarea, described Diocaesarea, i.e. Sepphoris, as a big city populated by Jews.[1] This statement is undoubtedly an exaggeration since both the Talmudic sources and the archaeological and numismatic finds bear witness to the presence of pagans, and at a certain stage even Christians, at Sepphoris. In any event, even subsequent to the increase in number of its Christian inhabitants during the Byzantine period, the Jewish community in this city retained its relative majority.

Numerous historical sources, mainly Jewish, from the Roman period enable one to gain an idea of the city's appearance, its cultural and spiritual life, its economy and its varied population.[2] There are fewer records from the Byzantine period, but in this case the gaps in our knowledge are partially filled by the archaeological finds.

During the first years of renewed archaeological study at Sepphoris, when attention was focused on the summit of the hill, or the acropolis, the Byzantine city appeared to be on the decline (as a result of the damage caused by the earthquake in 363 C.E.). Following the extension of the excavations in recent years, mainly on the shoulder to the east of the hill, a completely different picture has emerged. It is evident that in the Byzantine period Sepphoris actually expanded and flourished. Moreover, it seems that its center shifted mainly to the lower city.[3]

Below we sketch the character of the city and the stages of its development from the first century B.C.E. up to the end of the Byzantine period. The latest research provides information about the public buildings and private homes that existed throughout the city, and it sheds new light on historical events relating to Sepphoris (notably, that the city was not destroyed during the suppression of the Gallus Revolt, but a few years later during the earthquake of 363 C.E.).

Sepphoris in the first century B.C.E. had not yet attained a notable size. During these years at least part of the acropolis (its western side) served as a quarry for building materials. Quarrying activity was gradually halted and domiciles were built in this area. (Apparently, the quarries were operational prior to the first century B.C.E., but we currently lack unambiguous evidence.) The character of the houses and their planning is reminiscent of the private architecture in Jewish Galilee during the first century B.C.E. and the following centuries.[4] The rooms of the houses were built around an open courtyard. Open courtyards, storerooms, silos and stepped pools that undoubtedly served as ritual baths were revealed in the lower levels of the houses. The excavations on the west of

Photo 1: A General View of the Acropolis, Facing Southeast. Photo: Gabi Laron.

the hill indicate that most of these houses continued to be used from the Hellenistic period up to the end of the Roman period, but many changes and additions were obviously made during this relatively long time interval. Especially noteworthy is the large number of ritual baths and cisterns in this area in particular and all over the acropolis in general.

It can be assumed that in the first century B.C.E. and the following century the city expanded onto the slopes of the hill on all sides, covering a sizable area of ca. 10 hectares. We are as yet unable to assess the exact character of the city on the hill itself nor can we determine whether its development was gradual, without meticulous planning, or whether parts of it were built as the result of organized planning. In the western part of the hill we can sense some sort of order in the layout of the houses and their relationship to the alley revealed here, but it is doubtful whether this was the outcome of real planning.

From the writings of Josephus one learns of the presence of a royal domicile in Sepphoris in the days of Herod the Great (*Antiquities* 17:271-72) the location of which should without doubt be sought on the acropolis. This building has not yet been discovered and the only remains that can perhaps be associated with this palace are fragments of colored plaster (frescoes) that were found (not *in situ*) in the fill below the floors of the Dionysiac building, on the eastern side of the acropolis (see below). The colors and the design on these pieces follow the pattern known from other Herodian sites. It was customary to think that the theater (discovered by Leroy Waterman in 1930) on the hill's northern slope should also be assigned to the Second Temple period--the first years of the reign of Herod Antipas,[5] but, as will be explained below, it seems that this is not the case. One should therefore question the theory of R. Batey that regards the term hypocrites (meaning an actor), appearing several times in the New Testament, as proof of Jesus' visits to the theater at Sepphoris.[6]

The first half of the second century C.E. witnessed a dramatic change in the urban layout. As a result of the initiative of the local inhabitants, it was decided to extend the city eastward in accordance with planning. This

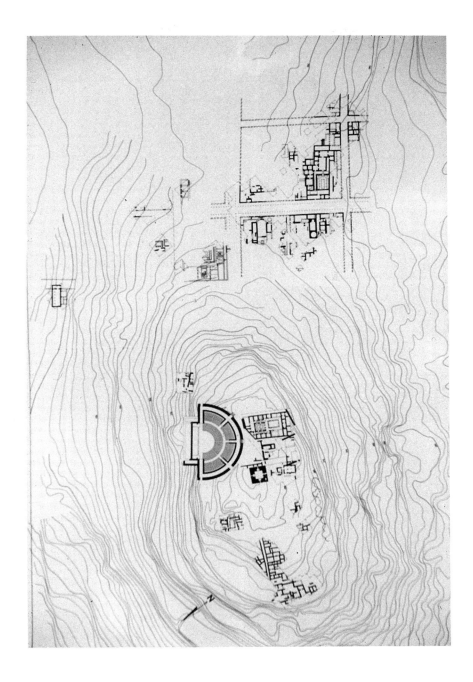

Plan 1: General Plan of Sepphoris, Facing Southeast. Courtesy of Zeev Weiss.

expansion took place in a fairly level area located to the east of the hill (see plan 1). An orderly street grid was marked out here, and public buildings and domiciles were erected in the *insulae* demarcated by the streets. This area was undoubtedly intended not only to expand the city's limits but also to serve from then on as the commercial and perhaps even social center of Sepphoris, the population of which had increased over the years. The size of the newly developed area is not yet clear but according to our present knowledge it occupied an area of at least five hectares. Further excavations in the coming years will make possible an accurate determination of its area.

Two of the streets revealed to the east of the hill were flanked by stoas; one of them extends in a north-south direction, and the other runs east-west. These two intersecting streets can be regarded as the *cardo* and *decumanus* of "New Sepphoris" (see photo 2). The streets themselves, some 6 meters wide, were paved with rectangular slabs of very hard limestone. The paving was so excellently executed that these streets remained in use for ca. 500 years without the need for repairs. This long period of continuous use finds expression in the ruts left by the wheels of

the wagons that traveled along them. The stoas were probably paved with mosaics from the outset, but this is not certain. Behind the stoas (evidently along their entire length) were shops in which an important part of the city's trade and commerce took place as early as the second century C.E. (The width of the two colonnaded streets, including the sidewalks on either side, is close to 14 meters.)

Some of the other streets were paved with stone slabs while others had a pavement of lime plaster. It seems that the paved streets were those that extended beyond the city limits, thus providing a linkup with the inter-urban roads and/or access to the fields that surrounded Sepphoris. Along these roads travelled wagons mainly bearing agricultural produce to the city's markets or workshops. In recent years an archaeological team from the U.S.A. led by Jim Strange has been exposing a large building that might have served as the forum or agora of Sepphoris. This building is located at the inter-section of the *cardo* and the *decumanus* (on the northwestern corner), one of the city's focal points and within the area of the shoulder to the east of the hill closest to its summit.

Photo 2. The Intersection Between the *Cardo* and the *Decumanus*, facing south. Photo: Gabi Laron.

Photo 3. A Dwelling Building from the Late Roman and Early Byzantine Periods.
Exposed at a Corner of Two Streets, facing southeast. Photo: Gabi Laron.

Only parts of a few private domiciles from the Roman period have been revealed to date in "Lower Sepphoris." It is therefore difficult to speak of their character. The discovery of two or three *mikva'ot* (ritual baths) in the area under discussion indicates that at least part, if not all, of the population of the newly developed area was Jewish. On a corner of two streets, in the southern sector of this area, part of a domicile featuring mosaic floors laid in two stages was exposed (photo 3). It is still difficult to determine the plan of this building as well as the date of the earlier of the two series of mosaic floors. In any event, from the style of the mosaics we learn that the building was erected after the construction of the Lower City. In some of the houses adjacent to the last-mentioned domicile, there is evidence of agricultural installations, including underground cellars for storage, but they are not necessarily from the early days of this area. Some of these installations were possibly built during the Roman period and continued in use during the Byzantine period.

Among the city's public buildings we shall mention two bathhouses revealed on either side of the *cardo*. The one on the east was probably the earlier of the two. At a first glance one is able to discern a great similarity between its remains and those of the bathhouses known to us from the Herodian period. A detail of interest is the fact that the eastern bathhouse, which had an elongated, fairly large *caldarium*, probably contained a ritual bath. The western, later and larger bathhouse (ca. 27 X 26 meters in size), included three *caldaria*, one of which was octagonal. It apparently had two *frigidaria* with small pools. Many of its rooms had mosaic floors with geometric patterns. Other public buildings, mainly close to the intersection of the *cardo* and the *decumanus*, will also evidently be revealed during the course of further excavations.

The theater itself has a diameter of 74 meters and contains 4,500 seats. It was entered via two *paradoi* and three *vomitoria*. It is of interest to mention that whereas the latter three entrances were from the summit of the hill, the *paradoi* were entered from the base of the hill, from an east-west street adjacent to the rear side of the stage. This street is a continuation of the one bounding the tentative forum building on the north. The *scaena frons* itself has been almost completely destroyed but remains of its architectural decoration found among the ruins of the theater indicate its splendor.

When was the theater at Sepphoris built? An assemblage of ceramic vessels from the second half of the first century C.E. was found in a cistern predating the construction of the theater, which is located below its semicircular outer wall. (This wall was based on an arch spanning the cistern.) Finds revealed in several other soundings within the area of the theater point to the same date. We are therefore of the opinion that the theater was built at the end of the first century or the beginning of the second century C.E. Its construction was possibly related to the above--described extensive building activity which found expression mainly in the erection of the planned area to the east of the hill. The architectural elements found in the debris on both sides of the stage are similar in character and style to those known from other theaters that have been dated to the second century C.E., thus corroborating the suggested date of construction of the building in Sepphoris.

It should be noted that, in addition to the above-mentioned cistern, remains of ancient buildings and cisterns were found beneath some parts of the theater on the hill's steep northern slope. We also exposed fairly well-preserved buildings from the Roman period (including a number of *mikav'ot*) on the slope to the northeast of the theater; this occupation is in contrast to the Arab village that existed in Sepphoris during the last few centuries (up to 1948), which extended only over the area of the western, southern and eastern slopes, leaving the summit of the hill and its northern slope free of buildings.

At the end of the second century or beginning of the third century C.E., a magnificent Roman mansion, was built at the eastern end of the acropolis[7] (see plan 1). This mansion is located adjacent to the theater on the south and actually extends across the entire width of the summit (acropolis). Between this building and the theater passes a street, the continuation of the *decumanus*, which ascends along the hill's eastern slope. The Roman house is 23 meters wide and 45 meters long. It had two stories and on its south side we found the remains of a basement that was utilized for storage (in the inner rooms) and for shops and workshops (e.g., a press for the production of olive oil) that faced the street that ran along the building's southern side.

At the center of the building is a large *triclinium* (9 x 7 meters) whose mosaic floor depicts the Dionysiac cult. Next to it is a peristyle courtyard surrounded by colonnades on three or four sides. The poor state of preservation prevents us from making a clear determination, but it seems that only three sides of this courtyard were flanked by stoas which apparently attained a height of two stories. The plan of the building, which has many parallels throughout the Roman world, e.g., in Antioch in northern Syria or at various sites in North Africa, typifies private architecture in the second to third centuries C.E.[8]

At the center of the floor of the *triclinium* (the house's dining and reception room) are 15 panels depicting various aspects of the Dionysiac myth, e.g., the bathing of the god as an infant, his education by the nymphs of Nyssa, his marriage to Ariadne, and his journey to India, or of his cult, e.g., the treading of grapes by satyrs in a winepress. The frame surrounding the 15 panels is made up of acanthus medallions containing hunting scenes. Also incorporated within it are the portraits of two women. One of them has been damaged beyond recognition, but the other certainly ranks among the most beautiful mosaic portrayals of a woman's face that has ever been discovered throughout the Hellenistic-Roman world. The Dionysiac cult, as it was actually practised in the Roman period, is depicted in the floor's outer U-shaped strip flanking the central carpet on the south. Here is located a procession of people bearing gifts, baskets of grapes, animals to be sacrificed, etc. The procession starts at the two ends of the strip and progresses toward the center which was destroyed in antiquity. On the basis of known parallels,[9] one can assume that at the focus of the procession stood a statue of Dionysos and/or an altar in his honor. The destroyed section was replaced by a Nilotic scene, the first but not the last one to be revealed at Sepphoris.

This floor is of importance not only to those interested in the history of art or scholars dealing with the Dionysiac cult, but also to researchers studying Jewish society and culture in the Galilee in general and at Sepphoris in particular. The existence of this floor in Sepphoris during a period when, according to the sources, its population was mainly Jewish raises several questions. Who built this villa and lived in it? Does the floor directly reflect the faith of its owner? To what extent did this floor, or others like it that will evidently be revealed in the future, influence the Jewish community in the city, or alternatively what can be concluded from this with regard to the character of this community?

A detailed study of the floor's components indicates that the mosaicist was well-versed in the mysteries of the Dionysiac cult. This does not signify that from the outset the owner of the building was familiar with all the details of the floor, but it can be assumed that the choice of subject met with his approval. One's first impression is that this person was one of the pagan inhabitants of Sepphoris; but one cannot rule out the possibility that he was a Jew, belonging to the city's aristocracy. It is easier to entertain such a thought if one takes into account that a fairly short time later (the mid-third century C.E.) a synagogue was built in Tiberias with the pagan god Helios in the center of its floor.[10] In any event, there is no doubt that this floor, like the nearby theater, was an expression of the Hellenistic spirit current in Sepphoris during the second and third centuries C.E.--the Mishnaic period in the life of the Jewish community which at the end of the second century had absorbed Rabbi Judah ha-Nasi (the Patriarch) who left Beth Shearim and took up residence in Sepphoris. His move to Sepphoris was not due solely to health reasons, as related by the Talmud (BT Ketubot, 103b-104a), but also expresses the strengthening of the Patriarchate's relationship to the urban aristocracy in Sepphoris, and his closer contacts with the Roman world.[11] This rabbi's positive tendencies toward Greek culture are reflected in a series of acts attributed to him, which find expression in the following statement made by him: "Why use the Syriac language in Eretz-Israel [where] either the Holy Tongue (Hebrew) or the Greek language (could be employed)" (BT, Bava Qamma, 82b-c).

The Dionysiac building, like many of the domiciles revealed on the acropolis, was destroyed by the earthquake in 363 C.E. This earthquake, which occurred a short while after the attempt to rebuild the Temple in Jerusalem, is described in a letter attributed to Cyril, a Church father in Jerusalem at that time. He lists the cities damaged by the earthquake and mentions Sepphoris as one of them.[12] The villa collapsed and the abundant debris preserved the floors in its northern part.

Significant changes apparently took place in Sepphoris after the earthquake of 363. In certain parts of the city the damaged buildings were restored and in other parts new buildings were erected, some on top of the ruins (as in the area of the villa to the east of the acropolis) and others after the clearing of the debris. At least one section of the city, to the north of the above-mentioned putative forum building, the built-up area was extended. This expansion was carried out in accordance with planning and incorporated the network of streets established here more than 200 years earlier. The extension of the built-up area started in an area with a fairly steep slope and the construction of the buildings was preceded by large-scale dumping of earth fill. The study of this area is still in its early stages and it is not yet clear whether it contained only domiciles or perhaps also public buildings.

The largest and most striking building from the Byzantine period that has been discovered to date was revealed to the east of the *cardo*. This building, probably constructed at the beginning of the period in question (end of the fourth century or beginning of the fifth century) and featuring spectacular mosaic floors, was termed by us the Nile Festival House. In order to erect this building, which occupied the corner of an *insula*, an area measuring ca. 50 x 30 meters was leveled at the expense of earlier buildings that had stood here. At the center of the Nile Festival House was a basilican hall surrounded on all sides by corridors. To the east of the hall was probably an inner courtyard around which were built rooms, all of them decorated with colored mosaic floors, mostly with geometric designs.

The main entrance to the building was from the *cardo* through a stone-paved courtyard. On the floor of the colonnade fronting the building, which was redesigned when it was erected, is a Greek inscription which mentions the names of the artists who participated in designing the building's floors. The figurative patterns appearing in the rooms with mosaic floors include hunters, a centaur, and two scenes featuring Amazons. The largest and most impressive figurative mosaic in this building was found in one of its northern rooms.[13] It measures ca. 7 x 7 meters and combines depictions of the Nile landscape with various hunting scenes. The main elements in this room are the Nilometer (see photo 4), a procession progressing toward Alexandria to celebrate the Nile Festival, and a statue marking the same event. In the upper two corners of the mosaic carpet appear two reclining figures--a man serving as the deity of the Nile, the source of water and plentitude, and a woman who is the personification of Egypt. The Nile itself, issuing from the nostrils of a Nile animal, divides the room in two. In the lower part of the floor there are hunting scenes.

The largest room was probably the hall (ca. 15 x 10 meters in size), the basilican form of which can be reconstructed. Only a few parts of its floor have survived *in situ*, including scenes of hunting Amazons, but there is no doubt that other scenes were once depicted here. The building was divided into wings and has many corridors. Noteworthy among the rooms that have survived is one that served as a lavatory, which was originally flanked by benches on all four sides.

During the exposure of this building we found evidence of activities that had taken place in certain of its rooms and were in some way connected with water, including a system of channels intended for the drainage of water from the large room containing the Nile Festival mosaic and from the basilican hall. We also revealed in a room adjacent to these two halls an installation from which water could be drawn almost at all times. In our view, this system is connected with water festivals held in the building. An allusion to such water festivals is to be found in the midrash of Genesis Rabba that deals with the question of how it came about that Joseph remained alone in the house with the wife of Potiphar. Rabbi Judah comments: "On that day there was a festival in honour of the Nile, everyone went to see it, but he went into the house to cast up his master's accounts" (Genesis Rabba, 87,7). Festivals of a pagan character continued to be held during the Byzantine period, notwithstanding the objections of Christianity. An inscription dated to 535 C.E., which was discovered close to a pool to the north of Gerasa, tells of water festivals that took place there.[14] The "Maiuma," as this festival is called in the Gerasa inscription, is also known to us from Jewish sources and is connected with celebrations in honor of the harvest and water, the symbols of fertility.[15] Festivals of this kind were possibly held at Sepphoris even during the Byzantine period. The existence of drainage systems, particularly in the Nile Festival Room where the main theme of the mosaic is the abundance of water that brings in its wake a plenteous harvest, suggests that water was poured on the celebrants or on the floors of both halls during the festivities.

Photo 4. A Detail from the Nile Festival Floor. Photo: Gabi Laron.

The building's location within the urban layout, its artistic wealth, size and many rooms, as well as the fact that no elements characteristic of residential use were found in it, led us to conclude that it was a public building, perhaps a municipal basilica. The basilica is mentioned in Byzantine sources as the place where public meetings, discussions, lectures, etc. were held.[16] "A basilica for the public benefit," in the words of Choricius, was erected in Gaza in the sixth century C.E.[17] Such an institution is also known to have existed in other cities in Palestine,[18] and is prob-

ably mentioned in one of the stone inscriptions found in Sepphoris.[19]

During the construction of the Nile Festival House and the above-mentioned domicile with mosaic floors (located next to the intersection of the two streets at the southern sector), the same mosaicists were employed. At a later stage, still during the Byzantine period, significant changes were introduced close to the intersection of the *cardo* and the *decumanus*, the most important crossroads

Photo 5. Foundation-Walls of a Church. Exposed to the west of the *Cardo*, facing east. Photo: Gabi Laron

in Sepphoris at that time. It seems that at one and the same time a church was built here (to the west of the *cardo* and to the south of the forum building) and the adjacent colonnades were repaved with mosaics featuring geometric designs (see photo 5). Traces of another church larger than the first one were found to the east of the main thoroughfare. Three dedicatory inscriptions, all of them in a round frame, mention the *Episcopus* Eutropius during whose period of office the stoas were renovated. From the wording of the inscription one gathers that Eutropius played an important role in initiating this project, hence his honorable mention (see photo 6). The urban activities of the *Episcopus* sometimes extended far beyond the religious sphere.[20]

This name is not recorded in other sources, and we are thus unable to date accurately the years of his activity. In any event, Eutropius may be added to the names of two other Episcopi who were active in Sepphoris and are known to us from the literary sources.[21] Architecturally and stratigraphically, the two churches mentioned above

relate to the improvements carried out in the streets nearby, a fact that enables us to attribute the construction of both churches to Eutropius.

We now return to the hill on which Sepphoris started its development beginning with its steep northern slope. Fairly intensive construction on this side of the city had already been indicated by finds to the northeast of the theater. Here we found evidence of the existence of domiciles from the Byzantine period above the ruins of the aforementioned buildings from the Roman period. Worthy of mention is the Byzantine mosaic floor decorated with geometric designs, birds and pomegranates, that was found in one of these houses.

Byzantine remains were meager on the west side of the acropolis, at least in the area exposed by the Joint Expedition, probably due to damage in later periods owing to their proximity to the surface. We discovered a variety of remains from this period in the eastern part of the acropolis, both above and within the ruins of the Roman luxurious mansion and also to the south of the small Crusader

Photo 6. Medallion with an Inscription Revealed in one of the Sidewalks Flanking the *Cardo*. Photo: Gabi Laron.

citadel. This splendid mansion was replaced by a rather wretched building. One or two ritual baths were exposed here. The shops and workshops in the basement of the Roman mansion were probably renovated and remained in use. Notable among them are an oil press and a stable that probably had existed in the original building, as well as a shop that sold metalware according to the various artifacts found here.

In contrast to the domiciles above the ruins of the Roman mansion, the structures from the Byzantine period in front of the citadel have a public and/or commercial character. Here is located a fairly large underground cistern-- the main one. A broad flight of stairs descending to the bottom of this cistern suggests that at least for a certain period of time it might have served as a *mikveh*. An underground conduit was connected to the cistern by means of a lead pipe and made possible a regular supply of water to the southern part of the hill. The cistern and the underground conduit were probably built in the Roman period. A building probably used for storage was exposed above

the cistern. Its central hall contained pithoi of a type known as "dolia." This storehouse, like the adjacent buildings (mainly the above-mentioned shops and workshops and the various buildings in the Lower City), was burnt at the end of the Byzantine period. It is not yet clear whether this conflagration marks the Persian conquest in 618 C.E. or the Arab conquest a few decades later.

Presently we know little about the many synagogues that once existed in Sepphoris. During the course of time there were undoubtedly several dozen synagogues in this city. It should be mentioned that on the death of Rabbi Juda ha-Nasi, according to historical sources, his funeral cortege passed through 18 synagogues (PT *Kela'im* 9:32a-b). In any event, this important institution was an integral part of the Jewish community that existed here apparently from the end of the Second Temple period up to the beginning of the Arab period.

At the beginning of the present century the Franciscans exposed the remains of a synagogue with a mosaic floor to the west of the hill, close to the remains of a

Photo 7. *Menorah* and Other Jewish Symbols, part of the Mosaic Floor.
Recently Exposed at the Northern Side of the Site. Photo: Gabi Laron.

Crusader church which Christian tradition links with the site of the house of Joachim and Anne, the parents of Mary, mother of Jesus. A stone inscription related to this synagogue was also found nearby.[22] The Joint Expedition also revealed fragments of a mosaic floor, which were not found *in situ*, on the west of the acropolis.[23] During the 1993 season we exposed, for the first time in Sepphoris, a complete synagogue. It is dated to the Byzantine period and is located in an area with a fairly steep slope, on the northern side of the city, close to a road leading out of Sepphoris.[24] (This road possibly linked Sepphoris with the Acre-Tiberias highway.) The building is situated ca. 175 meters to the north of the intersection of the *cardo* and the *decumanus* and the above-mentioned church. The synagogue was built on top of earlier domiciles which were demolished in order to prepare the site for its construction. Its plan differs from that of all the other synagogues known to us from this period in two features: only one aisle extends along the main hall, in contrast to the two or three customary ones; and its elongated shape--a length: width ratio of 2.5:1.[25] The synagogue is not orientated toward Jerusalem, but toward the northwest, but it is not the sole exception to this general rule. The building was entered directly from the above-mentioned road. From the entrance room the worshippers turned at a right angle into the main hall or the aisle next to it. The synagogue has a magnificent mosaic floor decorated with geometric designs and numerous scenes as well as many Hebrew, Aramaic and Greek inscriptions (see photo 7). Extending along the full length of the main hall is a single carpet divided into several strips, some of which are further subdivided into two or three panels. The scenes include the story of Abraham and the three angels, the binding of Isaac, a zodiac similar to the one found at Hamat-Tiberias, many items connected with the Tabernacle ritual, the Holy Ark with two seven-branched lampstands (*menarot*) beside it, and two lions, each of them gripping the head of a cow or an ox with one paw. Although only traces of the *bema* that stood at the end of the hall have been found, its size can be estimated. Likewise, it can be assumed that the wall behind the *bema* was straight without any niche or apse. The aisle also featured a single, long and narrow carpet in which were incorporated several dedicatory inscriptions in Aramaic. Almost all of the other dedicatory inscriptions are in Greek and were inserted between the numerous scenes of the large carpet in the main hall.

It is too early to determine whether the location of the synagogue indicates the extensive spreading of the Jewish community in Sepphoris in Byzantine times or alternatively expresses its displacement to the margins of the city by the non-Jewish population. The location of the above-mentioned synagogue discovered to the west of the hill can be linked with either of these two explanations. Significantly, the discovery of the synagogue on the north of the city indicates the presence of a deep-rooted Jewish community at a time when written sources offer little information about Jewish life in Sepphoris.

The city apparently retained this general layout up to the end of the Byzantine period. Data are insufficient to establish how Sepphoris was finally destroyed. On the other hand, it is clear that the city deteriorated markedly during the Arab period, as indicated by the looting of masonry and the erection of structures on earlier remains. It is also difficult to envisage the features of the city after the Arab conquest and what fate befell its Jewish inhabitants at that time.

The picture of Sepphoris emerging from the new excavations raises several questions in regard to the city's cultural character and the makeup of its population. Jewish remains have come to light here, including the Byzantine synagogue revealed in 1993. But the dominant finds in many areas give expression to Hellenism at its best and serve as testimony of the city's pagan character. This stands in contrast to the information provided by literary sources, that during most of the periods under discussion here, Sepphoris was a Jewish city that served as the administrative, religious, social and cultural center for the Jews of Palestine and the Diaspora.

The colonnades, streets, theater, bathhouses and splendid mansions represent the best of Roman architecture and are even mentioned repeatedly in the rabbinic literature.[26] Although we have not yet found any inscription testifying that the initiative for the planning and execution of these structures was Jewish, one cannot refrain from thinking that in the end they served the Jewish community which was the dominant element in the city's population. The theater in particular symbolized the essential difference between Graeco-Roman and Jewish culture, as is vividly expressed in one of the Sage's statements: "The nations of the world, when Thou givest them holidays, eat and drink and go into their theaters and circuses, and they anger Thee, but it is the way of Israel [the Jewish people], when Thou givest them holidays, to eat and drink and be merry, and they go to synagogues and academies (*batei midrash*) and pray...." (Pesikta Rabbati, Supplement 1,4). The presence of a theater in Sepphoris, as well as the other finds revealed there, reflect the danger which the Sages saw in Hellenistic culture, an everyday reality with which they were obliged to deal. Many scholars have discussed the extent of Hellenistic penetration and its influence on Jewish society in general and on the rabbinic circles in particular, as expressed in their literature.[27] The excavations at Beth She'arim opened a door to this multi-faceted world. The finds at Sepphoris afford us an ever clearer picture of the character of Hellenistic culture in Palestine during these periods and the extent of its penetration into Sepphoris, one of the centers of rabbinic creativity.

NOTES

[1]Eusebius, *History of the Martyrs in Palestine*, ed. W. Cureton (London: William and Norgat, 1861) 29.

[2]S. Safrai, "The Jewish Community in the Galilee and Golan in the Third and Fourth Centuries," *Eretz Israel from the Destruction of the Second Temple to the Muslim Conquest* eds. Z. Baras et al. (Jerusalem: Yad Izhak Ben Zvi, 1982) 145-158 (in Hebrew); S. Miller, *Studies in the History and Tradition of Sepphoris* (Leiden: E.J. Brill, 1984); Y. Neeman, *Sepphoris in the Period of the Second Temple, the Mishna and Talmud* (Jerusalem: Shem, 1993 (in Hebrew).

[3]The Joint Expedition of the Hebrew University and Duke University, U.S.A. (1985-89) under the direction of E. Meyers, E. Netzer and C. Meyers, *Sepphoris* (Winona Lakes, Indiana: Eisenbrauns, 1992). The excavations since

1990 were carried out by a team from the Hebrew University led by E. Netzer and Z. Weiss; see E. Netzer and Z. Weiss, "Sepphoris," *Israel Exploration Journal* 43 (1993) 190-196; idem, *Sepphoris* (Jerusalem: Israel Exploration Society, 1994); idem, "New Evidence for Late-Roman and Byzantine Sepphoris," in *The Roman and Byzantine Near East: Some Recent Archaeological Research*, ed. J. Humphrey (Ann Arbor: Journal of Roman Archaeology, 1995) 162-176.

[4]E. Meyers, *Ancient Synagogue Excavations at Khirbet Shema, Upper Galilee, Israel 1970-1972* (Durham, North Carolina: The American School of Oriental Research and Duke University Press, 1976) 103-118; idem, *Excavations at Ancient Meiron, Upper Galilee, Israel 1971-1972* (Cambridge: The American School of Oriental Research, 1981) 23-78; see also Y. Hirschfeld, *The Palestinian Dwelling in the Roman-Byzantine Period* (Jerusalem: Franciscan Printing Press, 1995) 15-19.

[5]S. Yeivin, "Historical and Archaeological Notes," *Preliminary Report of the University of Michigan Excavations at Sepphoris*, ed. L Watermann (Ann Arbor: University of Michigan Press, 1937) 29-30. See also, A. Segal, "Theatres in Eretz-Israel in the Roman Period," *Greece and Rome in Eretz-Israel*, ed. A Kasher, et al., (Jerusalem: Yad Izhak Ben Zvi, 1989) 532 (in Hebrew).

[6]R. Batey, "Jesus and the Theatre," *New Testament Studies* 30 (1984) 563-574. In connection with this see also: S. Miller, "Sepphoris the Well Remembered City," *Biblical Archaeologist* 55 (1992) 74-83; E. Meyers, "The Challenge of Hellenism for Early Judaism and Christianity," *Biblical Archaeologist* 55 (1992) 84- 91.

[7]E. Meyers, E. Netzer and C. Meyers, "A Mansion in the Sepphoris Acropolis and Its Splendid Mosaic," *Qadmoniot* 21 (1988) 87-92; R. Talgam and Z. Weiss, "The Life of Dionysos in the Mosaic Floor of Sepphoris," *Qadmoniot* 21 (1988) 93-99 (both in Hebrew).

[8]See, R. Stillwell, "Houses of Antioch," *DOP* 15 (1967) 47-57; Y. Thebert, "Private Life and Domestic Architecture in Roman Africa," in *A History of Private Life, from Pagan Rome to Byzantine*, ed. P. Veyne (Cambridge, Mass: Harvard Univesity Press, 1987) 353-409.

[9]See for example the procession and the preparation for the feast of Dionysos on the glass vessel from the Morgan collection: D. Harden, *Glass of the Caesars* (Milan: Olivetti, 1987) 80-82.

[10]See article by L. Roussin in this book.

[11]L. Levine, *The Rabbinic Class in Palestine during the Talmudic Period* (Jerusalem: Yad Izhak Ben Zvi, 1985) 61-91; A. Oppenheimer, *Galilee in the Mishnaic Period* (Jerusalem: Merkaz Zalman Shazar, 1991) 39-99 (in Hebrew).

[12]S. Brock, "A Letter Attributed to Cyril of Jerusalem on the Rebuilding of the Temple," *BSOAS* 40 (1977)

267-286. See also J. Geiger, "The Gallus Revolt and the Proposal to Rebuild the Temple in the Time of Julianus," in *Eretz Israel from the Destruction of the Second Temple to the Muslim Conquest,* ed. Z. Baras, et al., (Jerusalem: Yad Ishak Ben-Zvi, 1982) 202-217 (in Hebrew).

[13]E. Netzer and Z. Weiss, "Byzantine Mosaics at Sepphoris: New Finds," *Israel Museum Journal* 10 (1992) 75-80.

[14]C. Welles, "The Inscriptions," *Gerasa, City of the Decapolis*, ed. C. H. Kraeling (New Haven: Yale University Press, 1938) no. 279.

[15]See, A. Kohut, *Aruch Completum* (Jerusalem: Makor, 1970) vol. 3, "Maiumas" and the references cited there.

[16]I. Malalas, *Chronographia*, ed. L. Dindorf (Bonn: Impensis W. Webri, 1831) 338-339, 360.

[17]*Choricii Gazaei*, ed. R. Foerster and E. Richtsteig, (Leipzig: Aedibus B. G. Teubneri, 1929) 3, 55.

[18]B. Lifshitz, "Inscriptions grecques de Casarae en Palestine," *Revue Biblique* 68 (1961) 122-123.

[19]This conclusion is based on Leah Di Segni's new reading of the Sepphoris inscription. We are indebted to her for bringing this item to our attention. On the inscription, see M. Avi-Yonah, "A Sixth Century Inscription from Sepphoris," *Israel Exploration Journal* 11 (1961) 184-187.

[20]See, Y. Dan, *Urban Life in the Land of Israel at the End of Ancient Times* (Jerusalem: Yad Izhak Ben Zvi, 1984) 93-102 (in Hebrew) and C. Rouché, *Aphrodisias in Late Antiquity* Journal of Roman Studies Monographs, no. 5 (London: Society for the Promotion of Roman Studies, 1989) 75-79.

[21]M.le Quien, *Oriens Christianus* III (Graz: Akademische Druck-u, Verlagsanstalt, 1958) 714.

[22]For the Aramaic inscription, see Y. Naveh, *On Mosaic and Stone* (Jerusalem: Israel Exploration Society, 1978) 51-52 (in Hebrew). For the Greek inscription see, L. Gerson, *The Greek Inscriptions from Synagogues in the Land of Israel* (Jerusalem: Yad Izhak Ben Zvi, 1987) 105-110 (in Hebrew).

[23]E. Netzer and Z. Weiss, *Zippori* (Jerusalem: Israel Exploration Society, 1994) 55.

[24]Z. Weiss and E. Netzer, *Promise and Redemption: A Synagogue Mosaic from Sepphoris* (Jerusalem: The Israel Museum, 1996).

[25]On the synagogues of Palestine see G. Foerster, "The Ancient Synagogues of Galilee," *The Galilee in Late Antiquity*, ed. L. Levine (New York: The Jewish Theological Seminary of America, 1992) 289-319; R. Hachlili, *Ancient Jewish Art and Archaeology in the Land of Israel* (Leiden: E.J. Brill, 1988) 141-160.

[26]See Z. Weiss, "Roman Leisure Culture and Its Influence upon the Jewish Population in the Land of Israel," *Qadmoniot* 109 (1995) 2-19 (in Hebrew).

[27]See S. Lieberman, *Hellenism in Jewish Palestine* (New York: Jewish Theological Seminary, 1962).

13

A Note on "Miqvaot" at Sepphoris

Hanan Eshel
Bar Ilan University

In this short note I discuss whether the baths which were found at Sepphoris are really "*miqvaot*" (purification baths).[1] During the past few years there has been much speculation about the "*miqvaot*" found in Sepphoris. There has yet to emerge a detailed research of these facilities, but the claim regarding these complexes as *miqvaot* has been put forward orally in a variety of popular settings.[2] In order to present my reservations regarding these claims, I must first give some background to the history of the archaeological research of *miqvaot*, for it is important to remember that these Galilean facilities were identified as *miqvaot* only after Second Temple period *miqvaot* were discovered in Judea.

The first to identify a *miqveh* was Y. Yadin, while digging on Masada in the Judean Desert. Yadin discovered two *miqvaot* at Masada.[3] Both of these miqvaot contained two pools. One had stairs and was designated for immersion, and the other was designated for collecting rain water. The second pool was connected by a pipe to the immersion pool: the pipe connecting the two pools was opened from time to time, allowing rain water to come into contact with the immersion pool, a necessary condition for adding water to the immersion pool for ritual purposes. This principle was articulated in *Mishna miqvaot* 6: 7-11. It was thus possible to ascertain that any pool with stairs, which had an adjacent reservoir with a pipe connecting them, was in fact a *miqveh*. After this discovery at Masada similar structures were discovered at Herodion, the Hasmonean palace which was built by John Hyrcanus in Jericho, and in the lower city of Jerusalem.[4]

R. Reich pointed to another criterion by which one could ascertain a *miqveh*.[5] This criterion was a double entrance and/or a low partition cut out of the rock or built on the stairs as a separating line. In some *miqvaot* we found a wall instead of a line. Those features were used to distinguish between those who went down into the *miqveh* and those who ascended from it. S. Lieberman showed that this line of separation is mentioned in The Letter of Aristeas 106, in *Mishnah Sheqalim* 8:2, and also in a Greek Apocryphal Gospel which was discovered in Egypt.[6] This separating wall exists in *miqvaot* of the Second Temple period which were discovered in Qumran, Jerusalem, Gezer, and at Mt. Hebron.[7] *Miqvaot* without the adjacent reservoir are significantly larger than the *miqvaot* with the reservoir.

Since neither the reservoir nor the separation wall are essential for ritual immersion, other pools with stairs, similar in structure and size to the pools with the separation line but lacking this line, were declared *miqvaot* as well.[8] E.P. Sanders pointed out that the *miqvaot* that had the accompanying reservoirs were always discovered in areas known to have been populated by Pharisees, such as in the lower city of Jerusalem, in the palace built in Jericho by John Hyrcannus I (who was a Pharisee for most of his life), and in structures built by the Zealots at Masada and Herodion.[9] In contrast, these reservoirs are not in evidence in the upper city of Jerusalem or in Qumran. It should be stressed that adjacent to the *miqvaot* discovered in Judea were found other bathing facilities, resembling a modern bathtub, which without a doubt were used for bathing and not for ritual purification.

Now let us return to the *"Miqvaot"* of Sepphoris, noting the following:

A. they are significantly smaller than the *miqvaot* of Judea,

B. they never contain a separating line or a double door,

C. they do not have an adjacent reservoir,[10]

D. in the houses where they were found there were no other bathing facilities.[11]

Therefore if we do indeed regard these facilities as *miqvaot*, we must assume that these houses had no other private bathing facilities. Recently, at Sepphoris a public bath house was discovered.[12] However, it would seem implausible that the entire population of the town would have used a public bath-house for bathing purposes, while at the same time owning private *miqvaot* in every house for ritual immersion. In addition, most of these facilities were discovered in the upper quarter of the city, which is located at a higher level than the aqueduct. As we have stated, none of these *miqvaot* contained an adjacent reservoir, and if we are to assume that the people of Sepphoris were observants of Jewish Law as stated in the *Mishnah*, it was virtually impossible for the owner of these *miqvaot* to assure the necessary amount of water in their pools.

Therefore it seems that the pools which were discovered at Sepphoris were used as baths for washing, and should not be considered *miqvaot*.[13] Perhaps a large public *miqveh* with a reservoir will be discovered at Sepphoris in the future.[14]

NOTES

[1]I would like to thank D. Amit and Professor Stuart S. Miller for their important notes. *Miqveh* is a Hebrew technical term for ritual purification bath. *Miqveh* is singular and *Miqvaot* is plural.

[2]E. Meyers, E. Netzer and C. Meyers, "Sepphoris - 'Ornament of All Galilee'" *Biblical Archaeologist* 49 (1986) 17; E. Meyers, "The Challenge of Hellenism for Early Judaism and Christianity," *Biblical Archaeologist* 55 (1992) 90; Z. Weiss and E. Netzer, "Archaeological Finds from the Byzantine Period at Sepphoris," *Michmanim* 8 (1995), 76-77 (in Hebrew). Similar facilities were found at Jotapata and identified as *miqvaot* as well: D. Adan-Bayewitz, M. Aviam and D. Edwards, "Yodefat 1992" *Israel Exploration Journal* 45 (1995) 195.

[3]Y. Yadin, "The Excavation of Masada - 1963/64: Preliminary Report," *Israel Exploration Journal* 15 (1965) 91; Y. Yadin, *Masada: Herod's Fortress and the Zealots' Last Stand* (Weidenfeld and Nicolson, London, 1966) 164-167. E. Netzer, *Masada III, The Yigael Yadin Excavations 1963-1965, Final Report: The Buildings Stratigraphy and Architecture.* (Jerusalem: Israel Exploration Society, 1991) 13-17, 507-10.

[4]V. Corbo, 'L'Herodion gli Giabal Fureidais' *Liber Annus* 17 (1967) figs 7, 18, Pianta No II, Nos 24-25; E. Netzer, "Ancient Ritual Baths (Miqvaot) in Jericho," *Jerusalem Cathedra* 2 (1982) 106-119; M. Ben-Dov, *The Dig at the Temple Mount* (Jerusalem: Keter, 1982) 150-153, (in Hebrew). W. LaSor, "Discovering what Jewish Miqvaot can tell us about Christian Baptism," *BAR* 13/1 (1987) 52-59. On *miqvaot* with an adjacent reservoir at Gamla and Chorazin see note 14.

[5]R. Reich, "Mishnah, Sheqalim 8:2 and the Archaeological Evidence," in *Jerusalem in the Second Temple Period: Abraham Schalit Memorial Volume*, ed. A. Oppenheimer, U. Rappaport and M. Stern (Jerusalem: Yad Yzhak Ben Zvi, 1980) 225-256 (in Hebrew); R. Reich, "A Miqweh at 'Isawiya near Jerusalem," *Israel Exploration Journal* 34 (1984), 220-223.

[6]S. Lieberman, "Notes." *P'raqim* 1 (1967-68) 97-98 (in Hebrew); B. Pixner, "An Essene Quarter on Mount Zion," *Studia Hierosolymitana, part I, Archaeological Studies* (Jerusalem, 1976) 270-271.

[7]For such *miqvaot* at Qumran see B. Wood, "To Dip or Sprinkle? The Qumran Cistern in Perspective." *BASOR* 256 (1984) 45-60; at Jerusalem see Reich above note 5; at Gezer see: R. Reich, "Archaeological Evidence of the Jewish Population at Hasmonean Gezer," *Israel Exploration Journal* 31 (1981) 48-52; and for Mount Hebron see D. Amit, "Ritual Baths (Miqva'ot) from the Second Temple period in the Hebron Mountains." in *Judea and Samaria Research Studies: Proceedings of the 3rd Annual Meeting - 1993* (Jerusalem: Kedumim and Ariel, 1994) 157-189 (in Hebrew).

[8]R. Reich, "*Miqvaot* (Jewish Ritual Immersion Baths) in Eretz-Israel in the Second Temple and the Mishnah and Talmudic Periods," (Ph.D. Dissertation) Hebrew University, Jerusalem, 1990; R. Reich, "The Great Mikveh Debate," *BAR* 19/2 (1993), 52-59.

[9]E. Sanders, *Jewish Law from Jesus to the Mishnah* (London and Philadelphia: SCM Press and Trinity Press International) 214-27. At Masada other *miqvaot* were identified by R. Reich which did not have reservoirs adjacent to them. Those *miqvaot* were built by Herod.

[10]While more than a dozen "miqvaot" were found at Sepphoris, only one might have had an adjacent pool.

[11]Although in front of some of the installations found in Sepphoris there is a small pool which might have been used for washing the feet before entering the installation. Those small pools are different from the stone "footbath" which were found in the upper city of Jerusalem. See N. Avigad, *Discovering Jerusalem* (Jerusalem: Shikmona, 1983) 84-86.

[12]E. Netzer and Z. Weiss, "Sepphoris (sippori) 1991-1992," *Israel Exploration Journal* 43 (1993) 191. See also their discussion in this book.

[13]Step pools for bathing were found not only in Jewish settlements but in pagan ones as well; for example in the lower city of Marisa in an Edomite house that was destroyed by John Hyracanus in 112/111 BCE such a bath was found. See A. Kloner, "Maresha." *Qadmoniot* 24 (1991) 81 (in Hebrew). Similar structures were found in different cities at the northern part of the coastal area as well (e.g., Tyre).

[14]A few *miqvaot* have been found in and near the Galilee. In Gamla near the synagogue (area A) a large public *miqveh* (4.5x4 meters) with an adjacent reservoir was discovered. In area B a *miqveh* (2.5x2.3 meters) was found. Near it there is a bathing facility which resembles a modern bathtub. Near the oil press in area S another pool which Gutman identified as a *Miqveh* was found. See S. Gutman, *Gamla* (Tel-Aviv: Hakibbutz Hameuchad, 1984) 59 (in Hebrew); Ibid, *Gamla - A City in Rebellion* (Tel-Aviv: Ministry of Defense, 1994) 103-106, 118-120, 132. (in Hebrew). D. Syon, "Gamla, Portrait of a Rebellion," *BAR* 18/1 (1992) 30 and from the late Roman period at Khirbet Shema' a large *miqveh* was found: E. Meyers, A. T. Kraabel and J. Strange, "Archaeology and Rabbinic Tradition at Khirbet Shema' 1970 and 1971 Campaigns," *BA* 35 (1972) 21-25; E. Meyers et al., *Ancient Synagogue Excavations at Khirbet Shema, Upper Galilee Israel 1970-1972* (Durham, NC: Duke University Press, 1976) 113-117, figs. 4.8, 4.9 pls. 4.8-4.12. In Ceresin north of the sea of Galilee a public *miqveh* with an adjacent reservoir was found, see Z. Yeivin, "Ritual Bath (Miqveh) at Ceresin." *Qadmoniot* 17 (1984) 79-81 (in Hebrew). On other *miqvaot* at Sasa and Beit She'arim see R. Reich, "Synagogue and Ritual Bath during the Second Temple and the Period of the Mishna and Talmud," in *Synagogues in Antiquity,* ed. A. Oppenheimer, A. Kasher, and U. Rappaport (Jerusalem: Yad Ishak Ben Zvi, 1987) 208-209 (in Hebrew). The similarity between the *miqvaot* in Gamla to those found in Judea proves that the difference between the so-called 'miqvaot' of Jotapata and Sepphoris to those of Judea are not because of regional reasons.

14

Transformations of Space: The Roman Road at Sepphoris

C. Thomas McCollough
Centre College, Danville, KY
and
Douglas R. Edwards
University of Puget Sound

Archaeologists interpret data obtained through excavations using a variety of frameworks of meaning. At Sepphoris, this has meant, among other things, an effort to link urban structures with patterns of social and historical development in lower Galilee, Roman Palestine, the province of *Syria Palestina*, and the Roman empire itself. This article uses an artifact, a paved Roman road found at Sepphoris, to elucidate a larger set of social, historical, and regional issues. During the 1993 excavations of the ancient city of Sepphoris in lower Galilee, a portion of a paved Roman road or street was exposed by the University of South Florida expedition. This road connects with a section recovered by the Hebrew University excavations.[1] In addition to excavating strata associated with the use of the road, pavers were lifted at two different points along the road and the underlying bedding was sectioned. Further excavations below the bedding exposed an earlier road surface. The following report addresses the history of the use of the paved road, the period and method of its original construction, and its transformation of an earlier road that lay directly below it. Our study locates the road in the larger network of roads in Galilee as well as relevant regions of the Roman *provincia* of Syria. It pays particular attention to the social, political and economic im-plications of the site as the road transforms the landscape at Sepphoris.

ROMAN ROADS

Roman road systems have been studied, surveyed and mapped since the time of Julius Caesar and Mark Anthony who sponsored a survey of Italy in 44 B.C.E. Agrippa added a survey of Gaul which was used to create a sculptured chart set up near the Pantheon. This chart may have served as the basis for itineraries, the earliest being the Antonine Itinerary (*Itinerarium Provinciarum Antonini Augusti*) compiled in the third century C.E. Nicolas Bergier's *Histoire des Grandes Chemins de l'Empire Romain* written in 1622 utilized predominantly literary and epigraphic records in the first serious effort at a systematic description of the entire Roman road system. The twentieth century has brought to light a wealth of archaeological data relating to roads and more recent studies have combined allusions to roads by classical writers with epigraphic and archaeological finds to provide extensive information about construction methods (*viam munire*), the impressive network of roads throughout the empire (estimated now at fifty-three thousand miles of road) and the relationship between the stone-paved imperial roads (e.g., *Via Triana Nova*) and rural dirt roads (*via terrena*), secondary roads (*via rustica*), and gravel roads (*via glareae*).

While there are road systems that clearly pre-date the Roman achievement (e.g., the Persian royal road from Susa to Sardis), the Romans' engineering of road construction with its deep-laid road-bed and cambered paved road was without precedent in the ancient world. Vitruvius' description of building roads in *De Architectura* is typically cited as the paradigm for ancient road construction. As Von Hagen has pointed out, however, Vitruvius' construction with "polygonally shaped, thick selce-lava stones...in a deep-set road-bed was not always necessary."[2]

Oversight of road construction, especially in the provinces, fell typically to the army. The army provided expertise, materials and the labor. As Watson has observed, "the Roman armies, as torch bearers of civilization possessed skills and technical expertise uncommon in the surrounding population."[3] While the army had no separate specialist engineering corps, it did privilege those with particular skills by giving them *immunes* from heavy fatigue. Among those enjoying such privileges were those who held the appointment of *praefectus fabrum*. These men were charged with the direction of the *fabri* who were described as workers in wood, stone or metal; they were the 'engineers in the army.' The *fabri* and their officers provided the engineering expertise for road construction. Sasel's description of Trajan's construction of the Canal at Iron Gate proves instructive on this point:

All these constructions, the road in the cliff face, the canal, flood gates, watchtower, and fort were carried out by technical units from the Moesian garrisons...The question of the identity of their commander can also be answered. He was C. Manlius Felix...whose service as *praefectus fabrum* on the emperor's staff falls in the years 100 to 101 C.E.[4]

Labor for the demanding job of digging the foundation for the roads as well as setting the bed and fitting the stones was most often supplied by the Roman legions. As MacMullen observes, "Soldiers' labors were considered healthy from the point of view of discipline, desirable from the point of view of the treasury, and essential in problems requiring enormous numbers of men."[5] Inscriptions note the role of the legions (e.g., "the III Legion Augusta built this road"); periodically some legionnaires who grew weary of work revolted.[6] Supplementing the labor of the army were slaves and, on occasion, freedmen. As Chevallier observed, "To carry out the work there must have been a work force of some size, provided by the army and helped, of course by conscripted civilians, as Cicero's *Pro Fonteio* tells us (7.17). All were obliged to share in the work...Nobody was exempt."[7] Indeed the tax system could serve as a source of labor as services as well as currency could be demanded for the sake of public works, *opera publicae*.

The question of how road building was financed has proven a difficult one to answer. The funds seemed to have come from any number of sources. Prior to Augustus, the roads of Italy seem to fall under the responsibility of censors who assigned paving contracts, designated the responsibility for costs and arranged for the building of bridges. Consuls are also mentioned as taking responsibility for roads especially outside of the immediate vicinity of Rome and often in conjunction with or after a military campaign. In the early part of the first century B.C.E. we find reference to the office *curator viarum* typically held in conjunction with the tribunate, aedileship, praetorship, or consulship. Julius Caesar, for example, was *curator* of the Via Appia while *aedile*.

The founding of the Empire and the rule of Augustus brought on massive reorganization, including a change in the administration of the roads. Initially, senators were asked to finance building and repair of roads but this was short-lived and the Emperor himself took over much of the responsibility. The Emperor Augustus financed a repaving of the Via Flaminia, and Hadrian is reported to have paid for a repair of the Via Appia. Trajan is known to have spent large sums of his personal wealth as well as income from the royal estates to finance the extensive road building projects he undertook throughout the Empire.[8] There are references to road costs being borne by leaders of the legions and costs coming from the booty taken. Individual citizens were expected to contribute to the financing of the road as it ran through their estate. In the first century C.E. certain regions had highway commissioners (*curatores viarum*) who collected taxes for road repair and construction. They also insured that no encroachment occurred from private individuals building on the roads or damaging it with intrusions such as drains. These *curatores* are replaced in the fourth century by *praefect pratorio*. Municipalities sometimes contracted to have a road paved. They apparently raised the funds through taxes, tolls levied at city gates and bridges, and contributions from the *curialis*. A city's decision to fund its own road project at times reflected an effort to identify itself as a legitimate candidate for prominence within the Roman administrative network.[9] With such prominence could come certain rights (e.g., the right to mint coins) and honors that provided the city and its leaders honor and prestige as well as economic and political benefits. This may explain the paving of the road in Sepphoris in the second century C.E. just prior to or in conjunction with the city's new designation as Diocaesarea during the Hadrian period.

Some hint of the cost of road construction comes from literary sources, although the conversion of Roman monetary units is difficult. Von Hagan, drawing on literary sources estimates the cost of road building varied from 43 sestertii per Roman foot (50 sestertii equalling approximately $1.00) for the paving of a city street to 13.3 sestertii per foot for repairing a road.[10]

In time, one of the most characteristic features of Roman roads was the milestone (*miliaria*). In part the decision to mark the Roman mile (1000 Roman paces, or 1480 meters) seems to have been the outgrowth of the public works concept of Gaius Gracchus (and perhaps his brother Tiberias) in the early part of the second century B.C.E. According to Plutarch, Gaius established work projects for the masses to include "the construction of roads and erection of milestones...he had them measured off, that is every road by miles and had stone-pillars (*miliaria*) placed in the ground to mark the distances. He caused all the road to be divided into miles and marked with stone-pillars, that is milestones, signifying the distance from one place to another."[11] These massive stone pillars also transformed the landscape on which they resided. Not only did inscriptions record distances from the city of origin (in effect putting the stamp of the particular city on the region) but they often included adulations for those benefactors responsible for the construction; sometimes this included the legion that had contributed the labor. While many of these milestones have been moved and serve now a new landscape, as museum artifacts, those that remain *in situ* have proven to be critical in locating road paths and chronology of construction; in Roman Palestine, the milestones have typically been the primary evidential guide.

One of the main reasons the Empire committed resources for road construction was its persistent effort to establish an effective means of administrative and military control over its far flung Empire. The imperial roads and the regional, local and rural roads that connected with these main routes provided a network that could quickly move officials in times of peace and the legions in times of revolt and war. Rome could transfer troops with remarkable speed from a major urban center like Alexandria to the *limes* along the border in Provincia Arabia by way of the Via Maris and the connecting roads from near Gaza to Jerusalem then on to Heshbon.[12]

Such an extensive road network, which linked cities with each other and with towns and rural areas invariably had an economic and demographic impact and generally reflected the work of autonomous governing authorities. In second century Palestine such authorities included the rabbis who sought to promote inter-regional trade and "to aid in the incorporation of Jewish rural settlements within the economic framework of the Empire."[13] In later periods it contributed to the cultural grid of the Mediterranean as Christian pilgrims moved along the roads and brought in their wake structures that denoted sacred sites and provided shelter.

ROMAN ROADS IN PALESTINE

Milestones have been the primary evidence for studies of the Roman roads of Palestine.[14] This evidence has revealed major Roman roads that utilized long established routes through Palestine, notably the Via Maris or the coastal road.[15] The coastal road had two branches that crossed Palestine.[16] One running from Antioch in Syria to Alexandria was paved as a Roman road as early as 56 C.E. The coastal road also had a branch running north and east beginning at ancient Meggido. As described by Aharoni, this branch actually followed two routes, one across the Plain of Jezreel passing between Mt. Tabor and Littel Hermon (the Hill of Moreh) and headed toward the northwest shore of the Sea of Galilee. There is no evidence that this branch was developed during the Roman period. The other branch descended first to Beth Shean and then crossed the Jordan linking with the King's Highway (what was to become Trajan's *Via Nova Triana*). To quote Aharoni:

> The various branches of the Via Maris converge, therefore, like the spines of a fan at Meggido and unite to form one chief route. Thus we can understand the great value of the Palestinian coast for controlling this important international route, as well as the decisive position of Megiddo at the main junction."[17]

As Roll and Isaac have discussed, this branch of the Via Maris continued to be of great importance in the Roman and Byzantine periods. The earliest milestone indicates that it was paved in 69 C.E. no doubt in association with Vespasian's campaigns in the lower Galilee.[18] Vespasian installed the tenth legion at Scythopolis and the fifteenth legion at Caesarea and the road provided the linkage between the camps as well as facilitating the movement of the legions to the east for the operations against Perea in Trans-Jordan.

The area in the immediate vicinity of Sepphoris is linked also to the campaigns of Vespasian but there is no milestone evidence to suggest a paved Roman road until the third decade of the second century, the earliest milestone dates to 130 C.E. It was found on the road that was built to connect Legio or Caparoconta with Sepphoris. This date places the building of the road at the same time Hadrian responded to the unrest in the province.[19] Hadrian had moved the sixth legion to Legio-Caparoconta and as a result Legio-Caparoconta became a hub for roads running north to the Galilee, south to Jerusalem, east to Scythopolis and the Decapolis and west to the coast. The road connecting Legio and Sepphoris was part of this administrative/military network. A group of later milestones dating to 162, 193, and 333 C.E. indicate the continued importance of the northern connection to the Galilee by way of Sepphoris.

A second Roman road associated with Sepphoris linked Ptolemais on the coast and Tiberias on the Sea of Galilee. The earliest milestone associated with this road dates to 135 C.E. The inscription is difficult to read and it is uncertain whether it indicates a repair of an existing road or a first paving. In either case this road is also associated with Hadrian and his military response to the Second Jewish Revolt.

One aspect of the recovery of these roads is the corresponding recovery of the settlements in close proximity to the path of the road. In Roll and Isaac's study of the Legio-Scythopolis (Beth Shean) road they located and examined 21 sites along the road. Of these, 8 had remains that predated the Roman paving while 4 show signs of being newly established at the time of the Hadrianic paving of the road.[20] This implies that roadways preexisting the paving by Hadrian did not primarily serve the military but rather provided connections for village and city trade and travel. Unfortunately, no systematic survey of the roads that link Sepphoris with Ptolemais and Legio, nor the adjacent sites has been undertaken. Our own initial work on the regional road system southwest of Sepphoris on the Legio-Sepphoris road identified at least one village with early Roman through Byzantine shards located on a hill overlooking the road. At the bottom of the hill we found milestone 14 of the Legio-Sepphoris road. This section of the road is approximately 1 km south and west of the Sepphoris acropolis. The existence of other pre-Roman and early Roman sites near road systems have important implications for our Sepphoris road as we discuss below.[21]

THE USF EXCAVATION OF THE ROMAN ROAD AT SEPPHORIS

I. Strata of Deposition and Phases of Habitation

The deposition of material over the paved road at Sepphoris was typically 1 meter in depth. The elevation of the surface soil was usually 262.5 meters above sea level while the road surface was 261.2 meters. Modern fill associated with the Arab village of Tsippori and the later Jewish moshav accounted for approximately 15% of the deposited material. The Arab village apparently used the area for grain threshing while the moshav had filled and scraped the area for a variety of agricultural and livestock purposes. The modern fill gave way to deposits related to various phases of occupation directly on and to the side of the road (photo 1).

The excavated section of the road consistently revealed that the road served as either a limestone or paved road from the late Hellenistic to the Byzantine period. In later periods, the late Byzantine through Arab II (14th century C.E.), the occupational pattern suggests that the stone pavers were covered with a significant layer of silt. At the northeast end of the excavated section of road a Byzantine bath complex was uncovered against which the road stops unexpectedly. Some robbing of road pavers is also associated with this period. In the Arab period, buildings extend over the paved road. Courtyards and industrial installations from the Arab periods overlap the paved road indicating that although a roadway was still in use, the paving itself was no longer a functional feature.

Fully exposed, the paved road is 4 meters wide, with limestone pavers, bordered by drains, columns and sidewalks covered with mosaics. The relation of this paved section with major roads connecting Legio, Sepphoris, Ptolemais, and Tiberias is not yet known. We suspect this is a branch off the main road that approaches the city from the southwest. If this were a branch then it served to introduce a grid to the eastern flank of the city, and to facilitate commercial traffic by steering around the difficult climb to the acropolis.[22] This would also have brought the commercial traffic immediately to the east of a large peristyle

Photo 1: Road, looking north.
USF Sepphoris Excavations, 1993

building which the USF excavations have tentatively identified as a market building with early Roman foundations and second century monumental renovations.[23]

II. Sectioning the material below the pavers

Having exposed the paved road surface, a probe was made beneath the pavers in two areas. Two pavers from area 77 and four pavers from area 59 were lifted. The pavers, cut from local limestone, varied in size, the larger averaging 1.25m by 40 cm and the smaller 50 cm x 40 cm. The thickness of the stones averaged 25-30 cm with some as large as 50 cm.

In square 77 two pavers were removed on the east side of the street. The make-up beneath the pavers was composed of soil and small stones mixed with a layer of flat cobble stones used to level the pavers. The make-up for the paved road contained only early Roman shards and earlier. The make-up rested on three separate layers of hard-packed lime surfaces that appear to be a series of earlier roads or one road repaired several times. Each lime surface was separated by thin lenses of dirt. The uppermost lime surface was pock marked perhaps caused by stones used as part of the bedding for the paved road. Under one of the pavers and under the make-up for the road was found a small drain running perpendicular to the road. The drain (about 8-10 cm wide) had no capstones and was clearly out of use after the paved road was built. It was surely associated with the uppermost of the earlier lime-packed roads. Roman body shards found in hard packed material at the bottom of the drain suggest that it went out of use in the early Roman period at the same time as the last phase of the lime-packed road. We conclude that it functioned to drain the lime-packed road.

The second hard packed surface had a higher clay content interspersed with the lime. In the top 5 cm of this locus was found a coin of Herod Archelaus (4 B.C.E. - 6 C.E.). All pottery associated with the coin and at lower levels were Hellenistic II with a few possible early Roman shards mixed in. This suggests that the earliest phase of the road is associated with a Herodian period of construction. The lowest and earliest lime surface (a road?) was founded on bedrock. An ashy layer containing some bone found on this hard packed surface (1-2 cm thick) suggests that someone built a campfire or that destruction took place in the immediate area. In either case, the layer suggests that the road in this earliest phase went out of use for a time before the second hard packed road was built over it. Nearby squares had early first century finds on bedrock suggesting an early first century C.E. date for the earliest phase of the road. Soil and flat cobblestones were used to level out the bedrock and perhaps to help absorb any ex-

cess moisture that might undercut the road. Large amounts of clay, very dense and hardpacked were used to level the bedrock. No earlier structures appear underneath indicating that this space was transformed from an open area (pasture?) in its earliest use to create this road. The monumental road followed the earlier first-century road(s).

In square 59, four more pavers were removed (see photo 2). The pavers were constructed to be higher in the middle of the road so that water drained off to either side. The make-up under the pavers was like that found in square 77. In the construction of the pavers, a row of cobblestones was laid in a wet soil and lime mix creating a mortar that held the pavers in place. Most importantly, a coin was found in the makeup under a paver where no contamination could occur. The coin was a Tiberias city coin minted in 119-120 C.E. during the reign of Hadrian. This clearly dates the monumental paved road to at least the second decade of the second century C.E.

The large quantity of Early Roman pottery found with not a single Middle Roman shard suggests that the founding of the monumental road took place in the early part of the second century, perhaps at the beginning of Hadrian's reign, on a hard packed limestone surface like that found in square 77. Based on the date when work on the Legio-Sepphoris road occurred, a corresponding building operation in the 130s seems likely. In square 59 the uppermost hard-packed lime surface appears to be 40-50 cm lower than the uppermost surface in square 77. Dark soil appears under this surface in the same manner as in square 77 and additional hard packed lime surfaces appear further down. One difference is that a succession of four such layers (each 1-2 cm. thick) is separated by a .5 cm lens of dirt. This suggests a series of road surfaces or repairs laid within a short period of time. These layers are approximately 65 cm lower than corresponding layers in 77. This suggests that the earlier roads followed more closely the corresponding drop in the bedrock (roughly 75 cm lower in 59). When the monumental road was built the area was leveled somewhat so that the change in elevation was roughly 40-50 cm.

In summary, there exists at least two major phases of the road system in this part of Sepphoris. The first road or series of roads occurred during the early Roman period probably during the reign of Herod Antipas. The area, which does not seem to have major building activity or occupation prior to this appears to have been significantly transformed in this period as the city expanded to the east. A few very early shards were found but almost everything under the road was Hellenistic or early Roman. The coin of Herod Archelaus in square 77 combined with the

Photo 2: Square 59
USF Sepphoris Excavations, 1993

Hellenistic and early Roman pottery found associated with the hard packed lime surfaces indicate that this road was founded in the early Roman period, again most likely during the period of Herod Antipas when the city was experiencing significant reconstruction. The hard packed lime road appears to correspond to a similar surface found running northwest-southeast directly north of this road and probably intersected with it in antiquity. That surface which also has several layers dates to the early Roman period.[24] It appears that in its earliest phase the hard-packed lime road formed part of a grid that divided the space according to a systematic pattern. This suggests that this area was part of a planned systematic expansion of the city to the east on previously unoccupied territory, probably during the reign of Herod Antipas.

CONCLUSION

The monumental road altered this landscape.[25] No evidence exists at present to suggest that the paved road intersects with another paved road to the north (in other words the hard-packed lime road bounding the north side of the monumental building does not appear to have had a paved road over it). Thus the paved road seems part of a grand entrance bringing people into a prominent and prestigious area of the city. The founding of the large public building, possibly an agora currently under excava-

tion by the University of South Florida team, to the west of the road may correspond to this same time period. The period for this transformation may well coincide with the refurbishing of the theater that took place during the second century, as well as second century renovations of a villa uncovered by Leroy Waterman in 1931 and again by the University of South Florida excavations. The renovations probably occurred during the reign of Hadrian when the city was seeking greater prestige. The coin evidence suggests that this occurred with the change in polity and name of the city to Diocaesarea, a change that happened during the reign of Hadrian. While it is possible that the paved road could have been built as late as the latter part of the second century, it seems unlikely. All pottery is early Roman or earlier and the coin evidence comes from the reign of Hadrian, making a Hadrianic founding likely. As Eric Meyers notes this is a period of change in Sepphoris and the Galilee as a whole.[26]

At the same time, the recovery of the earlier lime-packed road suggests elements of continuity between the second century and the period when Sepphoris was undergoing transformation under the hand of Herod Antipas. Antipas, educated and trained in Rome, acquired Galilee at the death of his father Herod the Great in 4 B.C.E. Upon doing so, he undertook building programs reminiscent of those carried out by Octavian and by his father. The building programs were an explicit attempt on Antipas' part to integrate the region under his control with imperial power. Sepphoris and then Tiberias reflect the kind of urbanization that took place across much of the Greek East during this period. Slightly before this period and during it, we also see the establishment of a number of nucleated settlements, many of them in close proximity to Sepphoris.[27] The connection between the urban centers and the surrounding areas was significant. The centers provided a place to market one's goods and produce and in turn it offered opportunities for jobs and even culture.[28] What is clear is that the urban centers were within easy reach of almost every town and village in Galilee. Moreover, the ceramic evidence from the lower Galilee villages of Kefar Hananiah and Shikin make clear considerable interchange between village and city.[29] In addition, coins found at almost every site, village and town, indicate that members of these communities were actively involved in the market economy of the region. The road is one further indicator of this web of economic and political connections.

The monumental road constructed during the Hadrianic period continues earlier travel routes, primarily trade routes that linked the emerging urban centers with the surrounding villages. The roads were not only to facilitate the movement of imperial troops during and following the Jewish revolt, but were already serving as one element in the linkage between town and village. The road is symbolic of the changes taking place across Galilee. The earlier road at Sepphoris occurs when Sepphoris and Galilee come under the rule of the Herodians, especially the early days of Herod Antipas. It reflects the transformation of space brought about in this new political and cultural order. The early part of the second century, and especially during the reign of Hadrian begins a second significant political and cultural change in the city and Galilee. The road as artifact has become an important piece of data in understanding Galilee and the evolution of the city and relations between city and village.

NOTES

[1] Ehud Netzer and Ze'ev Weiss, "Zippori - 1990/1991" *Excavations and Surveys in Israel* 12 (1993) 14. See also their discussion and photos of the road in this book.

[2] V. Von Hagen, *The Roads That Led to Rome.* (New York: World Publishing Company, 1967) 35.

[3] G. Watson, *The Roman Soldier* (Bath: 1969) 144. Cited in C. O'Connor, *Roman Bridges* (New York: Cambridge University Press, 1993) 42.

[4] J. Sasel, "Trajan's canal at the Iron Gate," *Journal of Roman Studies* 63 (1973) 80-5. Cited in O'Connor, *Roman Bridges*, 41.

[5] R. MacMullen, *Soldier and Civilian in the Later Roman Empire* (Cambridge, MA: Harvard University Press, 1963) 31. Cited in O'Connor, *Roman Bridges*, 42.

[6] V. Von Hagen, *The Roads That Led to Rome*, 68.

[7] R. Chevallier, *Roman Roads*, tr. N. Field. London: 1976, 84. Cited in O'Connor, *Roman Bridges*, 43.

[8] See the discussion of imperial patronage in Greece by S. Alcock, *Graecia Capta: The Landscapes of Roman Greece* (Cambridge: Cambridge University Press, 1993) 121-123.

[9] For the concern of local elites across the empire to acquire power and prestige in conversation with Roman authority see D. Edwards, *Religion and Power: Pagans, Jews, and Christians in the Greek East* (New York: Oxford University Press, 1996). See also the discussion by M. Sawicki in this volume.

[10] Von Hagen, *The Roads That Led to Rome*, 69-70.

[11] Plutarch, *Lives, Caius Gracchus*, VII. 2, cited in Von Hagen, *The Roads That Led to Rome*, 50.

[12] See S. Alcock's excellent discussion for the role roads played in consolidating Roman power in Achaia. In *Graecia Capta*, 121-122.

[13] Z. Safrai, *The Economy of Roman Palestine* (London and New York: Routledge, 1994) 57.

[14] The initial and still foundational publication of the milestones for Palestine is that of P. Thomsen, "Die romischen Meilensteine der Provinzen Syria, Arabia und Palestine," *Zeitschrift des Deutschen Palestine-Vereins* 40 (1997) 1-103.

[15] See also Ze'ev Safrai, *The Economy of Roman Palestine* (London: Routledge, 1994) 274-276.

[16] See the excellent discussions on road systems in Palestine by Z. Safrai, *The Economy of Roman Palestine*, 274-290 and D. Graf, B. Isaac and I. Roll, "Roads and Highways (Roman)," (with bibliography) *Anchor Bible Dictionary* 5 (1992), 782-787.

[17] Aharoni, *The Land of the Bible, A Historical Geography*, 49.

[18] B. Isaac and I. Roll, *Roman Roads in Judea I: The Legio-Scythopolis Road.* (London: BAR International Series 141) 1982.

[19] The milestone evidence for the roads related to Sepphoris is cited and discussed in J. Iliffe, "Latin and Greek Inscriptions in the Museum," *Quarterly of the Department of Antiquities in Palestine* 2 (1933) 120; M. Avi-Yonah, "Greek and Latin Inscriptions in the Museum," *QDAP* 12 (1946) 96-102; M. Hecker, "The Roman Road Legio-Sepphoris," *BJPES* 25 (1962) 175-86 (in Hebrew); B. Isaac, "Milestones in Judaea, From Vespasian to Constantine," *Palestine Exploration Quarterly* 110 (1978) 47-59; and B. Isaac and I. Roll, *Roman Roads of Judea*.

[20] B. Isaac and I. Roll, *Roman Roads of Judea*, 38-40.

[21]See discussion of road systems by J. Strange and Z. Weiss/E. Netzer in this volume. See also Z. Safrai, *The Economy of Roman Palestine*, 276-291.

[22]This pattern of installing roads to direct and facilitate commercial traffic around the acropolis is noted at other sites and discussed at some length in I. Roll and E. Ayalon, "The Market Street at Apollonia-Arsuf," *Bulletin of the American Schools of Oriental Research*, 267 (1982) 61-76.

[23]J. Strange, "Six Campaigns at Sepphoris: The University of South Florida Excavations, 1983-1989," in *The Galilee in Late Antiquity*, ed. L. Levine, 349-351.

[24]J. Strange, "Six Campaigns at Sepphoris," 349.

[25]Who built this road is uncertain. It took significant engineering skills. Troops from Legio are the most logical choice. No doubt Roman troops had a hand in the building of the road connecting Legion Sepphoris as well.

[26]E. Meyers, "Roman Sepphoris in Light of New Archeological Evidence and Recent Research," in *The Galilee in Late Antiquity*, ed. L. Levine, 328-330.

[27]Compare the illuminating models of development proposed by Z. Safrai, *The Economy of Roman Palestine*, 27-30.

[28]D. Edwards, "The Socio-Economic and Cultural Ethos of the Lower Galilee in the First Century: Implications for the Nascent Jesus Movement," in *The Galilee in the Late Antiquity*, 53-73.

[29]D. Adan Bayewitz, *Common Pottery in Roman Galilee: A Study of Local Trade* Ramat-Gan: Bar-Ilan Press, 1993). See also articles by J. Strange and E. Meyers in this volume.

15

Magic and Medicine in Byzantine Galilee: A Bronze Amulet From Sepphoris

C. Thomas McCollough and Beth Glazier-McDonald
Centre College

The ongoing excavations of the ancient city of Sepphoris have exposed a city graced with structures of large proportions and exquisite decoration. The well publicized mosaic floors and the monumental buildings of Roman and Byzantine Sepphoris speak of affluence and the persistence of Hellenistic influence.[1] The excavations of the domestic area combined with the literary evidence tell of a Jewish population that was pious and at the same time readily coexisting with a Hellenized culture. In fact, the evidence that has so far come to light has insured the defeat of any sort of simple or reductionistic portrait of urban life in Byzantine Galilee.

In excavating a city of this magnitude and complexity archaeology has the advantage if not the responsibility, of producing images not only of life lived at the macro and elite level but also something of the life of the non-elite and the ordinary. The ceramics and small finds, such as the hardware of cosmetics and jewelry help create a sense of the concerns of life in the household and the values and the convictions of those not ordinarily represented in the literary traditions. As Dennis Groh has put it so eloquently, "Through archaeology we are learning to bend closer to the ground for our evidence, nearer to our own humanity, to hear the voices of people who speak so softly because of the passage of time and their own low station."[2]

During the summer of 1992, the University of South Florida excavations at Sepphoris found a small piece of this life of the non-elite in the form of a magical amulet.[3] This study focuses on this amulet and what it might reveal about the values and convictions of the people of Sepphoris.

The amulet was found in the course of the excavation of Field V. This Field is on the eastern flank of the city and the focus of the excavations in this field is a large (approximately 60 meters x 40 meters) basilical building. The building was founded on bedrock in the early Roman period and at least two major periods of renovation have come to light. The first occurred in the late 2nd and 3rd century C.E. when ornate mosaic floors were laid, columns with stylobates set, and painted plaster installed. At this point the building may have functioned as a market with shops lining the perimeter around a central courtyard. In the mid-fourth century the city suffered two major destructive events: the Gallus revolt of 351 C.E. and the earthquake of 363 C.E. These events, along with a transition in occupation, affected the building to the extent that at least a portion of its western half was transformed into a place for storage and industry while the eastern half remained opened to commercial traffic.

The amulet was recovered near the north-western corner of the building. The amulet was in soil 55 centimeters below the surface and 43 centimeters above the mosaic floor. The floor was part of a large (3 meters x 7 meters) rectangular polychrome mosaic decorated with animals, flowers and geometrical patterns that appears to define an entryway. Coin and ceramic evidence date the stratum in which the amulet was found to the late fourth/early fifth century C.E.

The depositional history of the amulet and related materials is difficult to decipher. There is erosion fill in this part of the building from a hill to the west. At the same time, occupational debris from the building itself, even at this height above the mosaic, resulted from churning and robbing at later points in the history of the building. We would venture that this is the relevant depositional history and that the amulet was originally dropped at or near where it was found in the building.

When discovered, the amulet was tightly rolled and not in a case. It was, nevertheless, remarkably well preserved. Unlike most amulets that have been recovered, this one has its original edges still intact. The difficult task of unrolling and preserving the amulet was the work of the Joseph 'Dodo' Shenhav, head of the restoration laboratories and national center for restoration of the Israel Museum in Jerusalem.

Unrolled, the amulet which was made from bronze, measures 8.2 cm in length and 3.5 cm in width. The words and symbols which are uncommonly clear, were likely incised by a stylus, also made from bronze. The amulet is partially broken at the bottom, although it is unlikely that the inscription continued much beyond the row of *sins* partially exposed. The language of the inscription is Palestinian Jewish Aramaic.

Who is responsible for making this amulet? Is it the work of a magician, a professional amulet maker or the individual who sought protection from disease? While we have no direct evidence from Sepphoris, the literary and epigraphical evidence suggest, in general, that it was common to secure this protective device from a practicing amulet maker who had some professional skills as a scribe. The realities of market forces seemed to have contributed to such a division of labor as the demand for and use of amulets persisted and in fact expanded through the late antique period. The Greek magical papyri give directions for making amulets and recipes for inscriptions according to needs.[4] The formulaic nature of many of the inscriptions suggest that the amulet maker had available lists of prescriptions which could be reproduced upon demand and personalized if requested.[5]

In terms of clients, we know more about them from the literary references as well as from the amulets themselves. The inscriptions and the comments in the ancient literature make it clear that the clientele was a diverse group in terms of needs, religious convictions and economic means. Typically, amulets were sought as phylacteries to provide protection from evil power (especially its incarnation in the 'evil eye') that might cause illness or ill fortune.[6] But amulets might also be sought to manipulate the fate or condition of another person other than the client. This sort of social magic is expressed by way of inscriptions that are intended to accomplish such deeds as provoking amorous attention, destroying a competitor's business or negating athletic prowess.

As to the religious convictions of the clients, there has been much discussion about the relationship of religion and the sort of magical practice we see expressed by amulet use. Most recent discussions of magic have argued that rigid distinctions between the two spheres cannot be sustained in the ancient Mediterranean world. As A.D. Nock commented, "There is not, then, as with us, a sphere of magic in contrast to the sphere of religion."[7] In response, some scholars have proposed seeing religion and magic on a spectrum with magic on the end that is more coercive and manipulative, while religion is more supplicatory.[8] But this too has proven problematic as too often elements of each attitude are found crossing the border. As K. Thomas has shown the coercive/manipulative distinction is a legacy of the 16th century Protestant attack on Roman Catholic ritual.[9] For our purposes, we have chosen to follow the lead of the sociological approach to magic and religion which tends to see magical practice as "alternate to those normally sanctioned by the dominant religious institution."[10] This serves to correlate effectively with the evidence that incantations on amulets make use of a wide spectrum of religious language and invoke divine powers through formulae that are at times manipulative and at other points more supplicatory. Moreover, it resonates with the texts of the "religious authorities" who, faced with the reality of burgeoning trade in the magical arts, either condemn outright the practice or attempt to pull it within their control by designating appropriate symbols or language to be used. For example, as Henry Maguire has observed for the church fathers, it was the ambiguity and obscurity of the imagery used in magic that was so insidious. John Chrysostom, for example, "repeatedly stresses that only the cross is acceptable as an explicitly Christian protection...The woman who ties an amulet inscribed with the name of a river does not make a simple incantation, but is falling for a device of Satan; for the Christian's only weapon should be the cross."[11]

The leaders of the Jewish community in late antiquity also felt the need to control the use of magic. Judaism had long been associated with magical practice.[12] As an ancient religion, Judaism was widely acknowledged to have revealed a language and vocabulary that could influence divine power. Phrases, deity names, language drawn from the Hebrew Bible found their way into Greek and Coptic magical texts and onto the surface of *defixiones*, amulets, and magical bowls. Christian authors frequently berated their followers for "going to the Jews," for healing and magical charms. Isaac of Antioch, for example, writing in the fifth century composed a series of homilies against the Jews and also uses the opportunity to attack Christians who use amulets bearing Jewish symbols or who use mezuzahs and phylacteries for protection against evil spirits. In a homily entitled *De Mages* Isaac exclaims:

Whoever with the blood of his body write a yod and marks it in a book, stand with Jannes and Mambres, magicians of renown.[13]

Early rabbinic texts, many of which are associated with the tradition of Judah's residence at Sepphoris, comment on Jewish use of magic and at points specifically on the use of amulets. In terms of the use of amulets, the texts interest is in general in control rather than outright condemnation. For example, at M. Sabbath 61a there is a discussion of what qualifies an 'expert' amulet. The answer is given that an expert amulet is one that has cured on three occasions or one that was issued by an expert. In the M. Shavuoth 15b a distinction is made between curative and prophylactic amulets. The argument is over whether Torah may be used to cure disease. The answer is that Torah may be used on a amulet if the purpose is to protect against disease but it is forbidden to cure with the work of Torah.

In the case of Aramaic amulets of Palestinian provenance assembled and translated by Naveh and Shaked none carry the name of a pagan deity, although this rather striking fact may be simply a consequence of the very limited number found as much as the convictions of the clientele.[14] The Aramaic incantations do include numerous references to well known magical figures (e.g., Abraxas), and a host of angels (e.g., Azriel, Ishmael, Rabia). The God of Israel is referred to directly and by way of common epithets (e.g., El, Yahu, I-am-who-I-am). In addition the amulets incorporate other *topoi* of magical incantations such as magical signs, and holy letters. Naveh and Shaked, commenting on the mingling of powers and symbols, note, "The syncretistic mixture which they [Aramaic incantations on amulets] display,...was...part of the everyday piety of the age..."[15]

With this background, we turn to the amulet recovered at Sepphoris. We offer a transcription based on the drawing of Ada Yardeni, together with translation and commentary (see figure 1).

Commentary

Lines 1-3:

1. This amulet would probably have been carried originally in a case and worn around the neck. The noun קמיע, "amulet" (from a root meaning "to tie, bind") sug-

gests both the ideas of "tying" or "binding up," that is, incapacitating the threatening person, object or disease mentioned in the amulet, and the physical protection gained by "tying" the encased amulet around the neck.[16] The incantation is obviously for the purpose of warding off a serious and persistent fever. The fact that, unlike other Aramaic amulets, this one is in no way personalized (note Naveh and Shaked, amulet 2:1, "a proper amulet to heal Ya'itha;" amulet 13:2 "a proper amulet for Esther")[17] suggests that generic fever amulets were incised to be sold either to those who could not afford the more detailed, personalized ones or to clients who needed the "magic" quickly, and thus could not wait to engage a scribe. Actually, the availability of such generic fever incantations should not be surprising since fevers are by far, the health problem most frequently addressed by amulets. The Aramaic word used for "fever," אשה , is represented in several examples of the amulets published by Naveh and Shaked and, as the authors note, the term "is well known in all Aramaic dialects as 'the fire' or 'the fever.'"[18]

2 - 3. An attempt to discriminate among fevers is uncommon but not unknown in Aramaic and Hebrew sources. The addition of רבה to modify or distinguish the type or severity of the fever appears, so far, on only one other Aramaic amulet. In Naveh and Shaked's recently published collection of amulets, amulet 19 includes the same phrase (אשה רבה) along with references to tertiary (טרטיה), chronic (אש עדניה), and semi-tertiary fevers (חמיטרטין).[19] In contrast to the limitations of the Aramaic and Hebrew sources, Greek medical terminology's response to the variation in symptoms related to fever was long established and richer in vocabulary. Greek amulets readily picked up this vocabulary. For example, several of the fever amulets inscribed on papyrus and collected in the *Supplementum Magicum* include phrases or words which differentiate in terms of duration of fevers (e.g. τριτᾶιος, τέταρτος).[20] Likewise, the Greek magical papyri prescribe formulas for fever amulets that discriminate among fevers that occur daily (καθημέριος), nightly (νῦτερος) and at least in one case, perpetually (ἀειπῦρετος).[21] Greek medical terminology also commonly employs μέγας to designate a particularly harsh fever as in an amulet found near Evron in the Western Galilee and dated to the fourth/fifth century. The incantation, which is incised in both Hebrew and Greek, refers to a great (μέγας) and a slight (λεπτός) fever.[22] Another interesting occurrence of megas puretos is in the New Testament where the writer of the Gospel of Luke alters the description of the fever suffered by Simon's mother-in-law (Lk 4.38) from simply a fever (ὁ πυρετός, Mk 1.31, Matt 8.15) to a great or heavy fever (πυρετῷ μεγάλῳ). We would contend that this fixed Greek medical terminology provides the basis

Figure 1

Text

1. קמיע לאשתה
2. רבתה דאזיה
3. ולא שבקה
4. (THREE MAGIC SIGNS)
5. ננן והיהאן (ONE MAGIC SIGN)

6. אאאששש
7. קמיע לאשתה
8. רבתה דאזיה
9. (One Magic Sign) ולא שבקה
10. (THREE MAGIC SIGNS)
11. (ONE MAGIC SIGN) ננן והיה
12. אואא
13. [ש] שש

Translation

1. An amulet against fever
2. PROTRACTED THAT BURNS
3. AND DOES NOT CEASE.
4. (THREE MAGIC SIGNS)
5. (ONE MAGIC SIGN) Nun Nun (FINAL) Nun
   Waw He Yodh He Aleph Waw
6. Aleph Aleph Aleph Sin Sin Sin
7. An amulet against fever
8. PROTRACTED THAT BURNS
9. AND DOES NOT CEASE (MAGIC SIGN)
10. (THREE MAGIC SIGNS)
11. Nun Nun (FINAL) Nun Waw He Yodh He
12. Aleph Waw Aleph Aleph Aleph
13. Shin Shin [Shin]

for the terms used on this amulet. Thus the phrase רבה אשה would be an instance of a borrowing or translation of the Greek μέγας πυρετός.[23] It may be speculated that the borrowing of medical terminology resulted in attempts to clarify the unfamiliar construct. Note that an אשה רבה, a protracted fever, is clearly identified in this amulet as one that burns (דאזיה) and does not cease (ולא שבקה).

Another interpretive option is suggested by the possible connection between this amulet and the reference to fever in the *Testament of Solomon* 18. אשה רבה expresses the "fever" (πυρετός) of *TSol* 18 while דאזיה ולא שבקה clarifies its "incurable" (ἀνιάτος) nature. In the discussion below, we will note other points of convergence between the amulet inscription and the *Testament of Solomon*.

Is there a disease with the symptoms described that is the ultimate object of the incantation? Although malaria seems the most apparent possible referent, it is wise to be cautious on this point. Indeed, Poole and Holladay have argued that disease names are merely, " ...code words to help communication between medical practitioners" and that it is misleading and at worst meaningless to discuss "the same disease" when talking about medical conditions separated by centuries.[24]

Line 4: The figures (magical signs) drawn onto the amulet are not uncommon. They occur after the second century C.E. with remarkable regularity on Greek, Hebrew and Aramaic amulets, magic bowls, lamps, *defixiones*, and in texts. In the Greek magical papyri, they are identified as *charaktêres*. They are often woven into incantation formulas, but at times they stand alone and become the only power evoked. As Gager noted in a recent volume on curses and binding spells, "they [*charaktêres*] had taken on a life of their own and were seen as personifying, representing, and embodying great power."[25]

Despite the frequency and importance of *charaktêres*, the question of what precisely they represent remains a mystery, as is perhaps appropriate for symbols appearing in a magical context. A number of intriguing theories have been put forward. For example, Gaster argued that they were formed from letters of the ancient Samaritan alphabet. Over time, the letters took on a mystical quality and were used as charms, "sometimes distorted out of recognition and distinguished by the corners rounded off in small ringlets."[26] Bonner rejected Gaster's theories, arguing that the signs had become so ubiquitous that they had ultimately become meaningless exercises in "ignorant imitation" and "hocus-pocus."[27] A more recent theory holds that the *charaktêres* are related to astrology, "that they represent various planetary powers, powers that were in turn commonly identified with angels and archangels by late Roman astrologers." [28] In the case of this amulet, we tend to follow the third thesis. As others who have studied

magic have argued, it is dangerous and foolhardy to employ magical elements indiscriminately. Even the generic quality of this amulet does not warrant a presumption of "ignorant imitation." We suspect that these *charaktêres* have some relation to the cause and/or the eradication of fever. In this regard, the *Testament of Solomon* may provide a clue. The origins and date of the *Testament* are uncertain, but the most recent editor has suggested a late third century date and a possible provenance of Galilee.[29] *TSol* 18 contains a lengthy discussion of the "thirty six heavenly bodies" and their activities. Each of these bodies, identified as "decans of the zodiac," ruled over 10 degrees of the 360 degree zodiac. The sixteenth decan, Katrax, is responsible for "inflicting incurable fevers on men" (ἐπιφέρω τοῖς ἀνθρώποις πυρετοὺς ἀνιάτους). The remedy for Katrax is to pulverize coriander and rub it on the lips and then say, "I adjure you by Zeus (ὁρκίζω σε κατὰ τοῦ Δᾶν), retreat from the image of God..." (*TSol* 18.20). While the signs on the amulet cannot be linked conclusively with certain decans or zodiac signs, the interrelationship of *charaktêres*, the zodiac, and the *Testament's* reference to the decan's control of fever, suggests a framework of interpretation. Indeed, if an astrological connection may be posited, the *charaktêres* could function both to identify the cause of the fever (the decan, Katrax) and its remedy.

Lines 5 - 6: The series of letters that follows the magical signs is also not an uncommon feature of amulets. In some cases the series alludes to divine names or powers, and in other cases the letters have no apparent referential value in terms of known words or phrases. In the latter case, and to an extent one could argue even in the former case, this veiled intelligibility may either be a signal of the perceived power of the letters as such or a manifestation of the related idea of *voces mysticae*. As recent work on the *voces mysticae* has pointed out, the unintelligible speech forms are not mere gibberish. These speech forms are utilized because the conversation is with a higher realm which demands the different construct.[30] Clement of Alexandria commented in the second century, "Plato assigns a special discourse to the gods and he reaches this conclusion from the experience of dreams and oracles but most of all from those possessed by *daimones*, for they do not speak their own language or discourse but rather the language of the daimones who possess them."[31]

The first series of letters incised on this amulet, NNN, has no known meaning nor is this a common set for Aramaic amulets. The next series, WHYH, (Wah Yah), may represent the divine name. Such a rendering occurs on other Aramaic amulets[32] and in the Cairo Geniza.[33] The next series of letters is difficult to decipher. A possible reading is AW, AAA, SSS. If AW is some sort of contraction of the divine name, the series of alephs and sins could then be an elaboration on the root of fever (AS). This would give us a reading which, in part, invokes the divine name and fire or fever. A related but slightly different interpretation for these letters is suggested by later kabbalistic writings in which the initial letters of biblical verses were used as shemoth. In a list developed by Schrire based on the *Sefer Shoreshey Hashemoth, Shimmush Tehillim,* and *Sefer Gematriaot,* the letters yodh, aleph, sin (although in different order) serve as pointers to Deut 6:4-9. It is also possible that we have an allusion to Numbers 11:2, where invoking Yahweh (אז) results in a dying down of fire/fever (אש). Taken together, the letters suggesting the divine name, the illness and efficacious biblical verses become powerful tools to bind the power of the divine onto the amulet and thus into the sphere of the amulet owner to effect a cure, the diminution of the fever. However, as suggested above, the imposition of intelligibility on this set of letters may be entirely inappropriate. The letters may be intended for vocalization as a chant against the fever or as *voces mysterica.*

NOTES

[1] See for example, E. Meyers, E. Netzer and C. Meyers, "Artistry in Stone: The Mosaics of Ancient Sepphoris," *Biblical Archaeologist* 50 (1987) 4-19; E. Netzer and Z. Weiss, "Byzantine Mosaics at Sepphoris: New Finds," *Israel Museum Journal* 10 (1992) 75-80.

[2] D. Groh, "Jews and Christians in Late Roman Palestine: Towards a New Chronology," *Biblical Archaeologist* 51 (1988) 91.

[3] The University of South Florida Excavations at Sepphoris are directed by James F. Strange. Tom Longstaff and Dennis Groh serve as associate directors and Tom McCollough is the assistant director.

[4] *The Greek Magical Papyri in Translation,* ed. H. Betz (Chicago: University of Chicago Press, 1986).

[5] For an insightful discussion of the role of formulas in the construction of the incantation see, L. Schiffman and M. Swartz, *Hebrew and Aramaic Incantation Texts from the Cairo Genizah* (Sheffield: Sheffield Academic Press, 1992) 52-62.

[6] For a useful discussion of the evil eye as it was perceived, see M. Dickie, "The Fathers of the Church and the Evil Eye," in *Byzantine Magic,* ed. H. Maguire (Washington: Dumbarton Oaks Research Library and Collection, 1995) 9-34.

[7] A. Nock, "Paul and the Magus," in *Essays on Religion and the Ancient World,* ed. Z. Stewart (Cambridge, Mass.:Harvard University Press, 1972) I:314.

[8] See for example, J. De Vries, "Magic and Religion," *History of Religions* 1 (1962) 214-21.

[9] K. Thomas, *Religion and the Decline of Magic* (New York: Scribner) 1971.

[10] D. Aune, "Magic in Early Christianity," in *Aufstieg und Niedergang der römischen Welt* II.23.2, ed. H. Temporini and W. Haase (Berlin and New York: Walter de Gruyter, 1980) 1515.

[11] H. Maguire, "Magic and the Christian Image," in *Byzantine Magic,* 61.

[12] For ancient Jewish magic see the classic study of L. Blau, *Das altjüdische Zauberwesen* (Budapest: Jahresbericht der Landes-Rabbinerschule in Budapest für das Schuljahr, 1897-98) and more recently, J. Neusner, *A History of the Jews in Babylon* (Leiden: E.J. Brill, 1965-70) II: 147-50; III: 110-26; IV: 330-62; V: 174-96, 217-43.

[13] S. Kazan, "Isaac of Antioch's Homily Against the Jews," *Oriens Christianus* 49 (1965) 59.

[14] J. Naveh and S. Shaked, *Amulets and Magic Bowls: Aramaic Incantations of Late Antiquity* (Jerusalem: The Magnes Press, 1987) 37.

[15] Ibid, 38.

[16] R. Kotansky, J. Naveh, and S. Shaked make similar observations in a study of a Greek-Aramaic silver amulet from Egypt, "A Greek-Aramaic silver Amulet from Egypt in the Ashmolean Museum," *Le Muséon* 105 (1992) 5-26.

[17] J. Nahveh and S. Shaked, *Amulets and Magic Bowls,* 45, 99.

[18] Ibid, 47.

[19] J. Naveh and S. Shaked, *Magic Spells and Formulae: Aramaic Incantations from Late Antiquity* (Jerusalem: The Magnes Press, 1993) 60.

[20] *Supplementum Magicum,* ed. R. Daniel and F. Maltomini, 2 vols. Papyrologica Coloniensia, vol. 16 (Opladen: Westdeutscher Verlag, 1990-92) I.27,47-48.

[21] PGM XVIIIb.5-7, XLVII. 14.

[22] See the study of R. Kotansky, "An Incised Copper Amulet from `Evron," *Atiqot* (ES) 20 (1991) 81-7.

[23] We are aware of three instances in which the Babylonian Talmud inserts an adjective (e.g., יומא ילא ב יומא שימשא ב) to distinguish the nature of the fever under discussion (BT Shabbat 66b, 67a, and Gittin 67b). In the case of Aramaic incantations, Naveh and Shaked (*Magic Spells and Formulae,* 36) point out the appearance of the word "shivering" (עריה) in combination with fever in several Aramaic amulets.

[24] J. Poole and A. Holladay, "Thucydides and the Plague of Athens," *Classical Quarterly* 29 (ns) (1979) 228-300.

[25] J. Gager, *Curse Tablets and Binding Spells from the Ancient World* (New York: Oxford University Press, 1992) 11.

[26] M. Gaster, *Studies and Texts,* I (New York: KTAV Publishing House, 1971) 607.

[27]C. Bonner, *Studies in Magical Amulets: Chiefly Graeco-Roman.* (Ann Arbor: University of Michigan Press, 1950) 13.

[28]Gager, *Curse Tablets*, 11.

[29]D. Duling, *The Testament of Solomon*, in *The Old Testament Pseudepigrapha*, ed. J. Charlesworth (Garden City, NY: Doubleday, Inc., 1983) I. 935-87.

[30]S. Tambiah, "The Magical Power of Words," *Man* 3 (1968) 177-206.

[31]*Stromata* 1.143.1. Cited in Gager, *Curse Tablets*, 10.

[32]Naveh and Shaked, *Amulets and Magic Bowls*, 40.

[33]See for example, Schiffman and Swartz, *Hebrew and Aramaic Incantation Texts*, 69-73.

16

Palynology and Cultural Process:
An Exercise in the New Archaeology

Thomas R. W. Longstaff
Colby College
and
Tristram C. Hussey
Duke University

Although the theories and methods often referred to as the "new archaeology" have dominated new world archaeology for the last twenty-five years, the influence of these developments (including the debates about the several variations of "processual" and "post-processual" archaeology) has only recently become a significant factor in Near Eastern Archaeology. In this essay, after a brief consideration of what the new archaeology entails, we present the results of an analysis of pollen extracted from several archaeological strata at Sepphoris to illustrate one way in which new methods in archaeology can contribute to an understanding of ancient Galilee.

A BRIEF DESCRIPTION OF THE NEW ARCHAEOLOGY

A precise definition of the new archaeology is not possible. Although the label seems first to have been used by Joseph Caldwell in 1959, for simplicity's sake, the new archaeology can be seen as a development which began as a reform movement in the 1960's,[1] rose to almost faddish popularity in the 1970's, and today takes its place in the mainstream of archaeological theory and practice. It is an oversimplification, but essentially accurate, to state that

there are several developments in theory and method that define what is often called the new archaeology, and that together these distinguish it from "traditional" or "classical" archaeology. Although these developments are closely related, for the purpose of this brief introduction they may be considered sequentially.

Theory: The theoretical perspective of the new archaeology is usually associated with the work of Lewis Binford and his contemporaries, although there were earlier proponents of these methodological innovations. Central to the new archaeology is an emphasis on explanation rather than description. Envisioning human activity as dynamic, in constant evolution, proponents of the new archaeology focus their attention on cultural processes and attempt to *explain why*, rather than simply to *describe the ways that*, human activity has taken particular forms. Understanding human activity to be a complex system, composed of multiple, interrelated processes (*i.e.*, social, environmental, economic, technologic, symbolic, aesthetic, religious, etc.), the new archaeology attempts to build testable models to explain the dynamics of human society. Although, as we will see below, the term is somewhat too limited, "processual archaeology" may more accurately describe what is more widely called the "new archaeology."

In recent years processual archaeology has matured, in large part due to the challenges presented by post-processual archaeology (with its emphasis on structuralism, Critical Theory, and neo-Marxist theory), into what has been called cognitive-processual archaeology. In cognitive-processual archaeology more attention is given, in explaining human activity, to the role of ideology, internal conflict, and the formative influence of material culture. Self-conscious about archaeological theory, the new archaeology (as we would define it today) continually assesses the relationship between fact and theory, data and interpretation, attempting to be clear both about the explanation offered and about what it is that one is attempting to explain.[2]

Method: In practice, the methods of the new archaeology are consciously more those of the natural scientist and statistician and less those of the historian and sociologist. Adopting a model, rooted in the philosophy of science, where conclusions are to be based upon inferences, logically drawn from a body of empirical evidence, and subject to validation by tests which can be replicated by others, the new archaeology embraces the methods of geography, geology, chemistry, physics, biology, and mathematics in ways that increasingly make archaeology more quantitative and less qualitative in nature. This development has also greatly expanded the amount of archaeological evidence to be analyzed. A much wider range of materials, including soils and minerals, flora and fauna, is now understood to provide valuable information about past human activity. Three stages have occurred in the changing relationship of archaeology to the natural sciences; the last of these stages describes the methods of the new archaeology:

1.*The scientist as archaeologist.* This early stage is characterized by developments in the sciences (*e.g.,* radiometric dating and dendrochronology) which were seen to be useful for archaeology. Often these developments were the result of research quite unrelated to archaeology and the value for archaeology was an unexpected additional benefit of the work.

2.*The scientist and archaeologist as colleagues.* This stage is characterized by a greater interest among archaeologists in scientific analyses. Many archaeological projects now include biologists (experts both in flora and fauna), geologists, chemists, and other scientists either on the staff of the excavation itself or as consultants working in laboratories off-site.

3.*The archaeologist as scientist.* In the late twentieth century, the cutting edge of research in the sciences has moved into areas not immediately relevant or useful to archaeology. Furthermore, archaeologists have found that a

solid foundation in archaeology is necessary if scientific analyses are to produce results useful to archaeological research. Only a person with training and experience in archaeology is equipped to approach scientific analyses knowing what questions to ask and understanding what information will be useful. For these reasons many archaeologists find it necessary to acquire analytic skills in such disciplines as biology or chemistry, geology or mathematics and to bring those skills to the work of a particular archaeological project. Needless to say, no individual can become an expert in all of the analyses that must be conducted. Accordingly, the new archaeology is also characterized by the concept of an archaeological team, each of whose members bring different and complementary skills to the enterprise, rather than, as with "traditional" or "classical" archaeology, the concept of an excavation managed by a principle investigator whose authority and experience guide all aspects of the project.

Fortunately, the contrasts between traditional or classical archaeology on the one hand and the new archaeology on the other are no longer drawn as sharply or polemically as they were in the 1960's. Most contemporary archaeologists recognize that descriptive archaeology has considerable value. At the same time, the developments described as the new archaeology have changed the nature of archaeological research in ways that no critical archaeologist today can ignore. The new archaeology is no longer new nor novel.

James F. Strange, Director of the University of South Florida's Excavations at Sepphoris, is among those archaeologists working in the Levant who have been, from the outset, enthusiastic about the potential of the new archaeology. Building a team with broad and diverse skills, he has encouraged members of his staff to develop and employ a wide range of scientific and technological analyses while not sacrificing the traditional skills required of an active field archaeologist. With Professor Strange's encouragement, Thomas R. W. Longstaff (Associate Director of the Excavations), who had recently completed a year's work at the Center for Materials Research in Archaeology and Ethnology at the Massachusetts Institute of Technology, decided to investigate whether the highly alkaline soils of the Galilee contained sufficient pollen to provide significant information about this region in antiquity. In several archaeological seasons prior to 1990, soil samples from which pollen could be extracted were carefully collected by Longstaff. These were preserved in three layers of sealed plastic and stored in a secure metal cabinet until the analyses were undertaken. During the academic year 1990-1991, Tristram Hussey, then a senior at Colby College, enrolled in a Senior Scholars Program of research under the direction of Professor Longstaff, Professor Robert E. Nelson (Geology), and Professor David L. Nugent (Anthropology). His major work entailed the extraction and analysis of pollen from the Sepphoris samples. This essay is a revision by Longstaff and Hussey of the results of that work.

AN INTRODUCTION TO THE PALYNOLOGICAL ANALYSIS

Information about the environment is of great importance for archaeologists attempting to explain the dynamics of human activity in the past. Knowledge of the paleoenvironment assists archaeologists in understanding how human activity both responded to and modified the environment in which that activity took place. Pollen analysis has become a standard technique, perhaps the most important technique, for the reconstruction of a paleoenvironment. For the most part, however, palynologists have limited their analyses to lacustrine cores,[3] because of the high pollen concentrations and uncomplicated processing characteristic of such samples. This sampling technique yields excellent results but is seldom useful for archaeological inquiry. Few archaeological sites contain, or are located within, lacustrine basins and thus an analysis of pollen from a lake or bog core must be correlated with an archaeological site through ^{14}C dating. Correlations between ^{14}C dates from cores and ^{14}C dates (or dates determined by ceramic typology or other means) from an archaeological site introduce a potential error large enough to prevent a confident use of the results for anything this young.

The solution to this dilemma is to take sediment samples for pollen analysis directly from the archaeological site itself. If the samples are collected carefully (with techniques that avoid contamination) and if the sediments are suitably organic, then the analysis can yield results as reliable as those obtained from lacustrine cores. These results will, of course, be directly applicable to the site. More importantly, this procedure ensures that even if the chronological information is inaccurate, the paleoenvironmental information will still be firmly connected to the site and directly related to the cultural horizons where the samples were collected.

This study is the first step in a series of studies which will attempt to establish an environmental history for a region where pollen analysis is especially difficult. The soil samples from which the pollen was extracted were taken at the University of South Florida's excavations at Sepphoris in the Beit Natofa Valley of the Lower Galilee. Our goal was to examine evidence for climatic or other environmental change in this region from the Middle Roman to the Late Byzantine periods, the 2nd through the 7th centuries of the Common Era.

MODERN VEGETATION AND CLIMATE

Since one must always be concerned about the possibility of contamination from elements in the current environment and aware of environmental factors that would affect the preservation of the pollen recovered for analysis, some comments on the modern vegetation and climate are appropriate at this juncture.

The climate and vegetation of the lower Galilee are typical of the eastern Mediterranean, with short, wet winters and long dry summers.[4] The annual rainfall in the region of Sepphoris is 500-700 mm. Nearly all of this precipitation falls during the winter rainy season. Native plants are thus well-adapted to periods of plentiful water and periods of drought.

Vegetation zones fall into evergreen forests and maquis,[5] bathas, and garigues.[6] The bathas and garigues, which border the forest, are often grouped together and are areas of open shrub-grassland with aromatic and thorny taxa. Each zone is made up of taxa with similar ecological requirements. The differences between vegetation zones result from differences in human use of the land as well as from differences in the stages of vegetational development.[7]

The evergreen forests and maquis are areas dominated by sclerophyllous evergreen trees and shrubs up to about 4 meters in height. The leaves are generally thick and highly resistant to transpiration.[8] The species vary, each tree filling a particular niche in the ecology. The evergreen and deciduous trees commonly found in these forests/maquis include: *Pinus halepensis, Pistacia pinea, Pistacia lentescus, Pistacia Saportae, Larus nobilis, Ceratonia siliqua, Pistacia Palaestina, Phillyrea, Olea europea, Viburnum tinus, Myrtus communis, Rhamnus alaternus, Juniperus oxycedrus, Juniperus Phoenicia, Quercus calliprinos, Quercus infectoria, Quercus ithaburensis, Quercus aegilops, Quercus libani, Arbutus andrachne, Abies cilicica, Cupressus sempervirens, Crataegus azarolus, Cercis siliquas,* and *Styrax officinalis.*[9]

Bathas and garigues are shrubby landscapes containing mostly low sclerophyllous shrubs between 0.5-1 meters in height.[10] Occasionally bathas and garigues are not differentiated although bathas are usually considered to precede garigues in landscape evolution.[11] In general, both bathas and garigues are considered to be stages in a process leading toward climax vegetational stands (*i.e.,* maquis). At the edges of the Mediterranean zone, however, bathas and garigues often represent the climax vegetation.[12] Typical shrubs of the bathas and garigues are low, aromatic herbs that are drought resistant and include: *Poterium spinosum, Thymus capitatus, Fumma arabica, Fumma thymifolia, Teucrium polium, Teucrium divaricatum, Hyparrhenia hirta, Salvia graveolens,* and *Ballota undulata.*[13]

In recent years the State of Israel has supplemented the shrubbery and thorny taxa indigenous to the region by actively reforesting large areas with various species of *Pinus*. This has had predictable effects on the ecology (*e.g.*, it has raised the acidity of the soil).

BACKGROUND FOR THIS STUDY IN PREVIOUS PALYNOLOGICAL RESEARCH

Palynology in Israel is a difficult undertaking. The majority of the soils and sediments in Israel are derived from the limestone bedrock native to this region. Soil derived from limestone is highly alkaline and does not preserve pollen or other plant residue very well.[14] But, as we shall see, it is possible to get useful results from the analysis of pollen contained in these soils.

Pollen is one of the most resistant organic remains used for paleoenvironmental reconstruction. The pollen exine is made of sporopollenin, a complex, resistant, natural organic polymer, akin to modern plastic.[15] Sporopollenin resists attack by many chemical agents and is well-preserved in wet, acidic environments. Although pollen degrades readily in alkaline or oxidizing conditions, such as those characteristic of the Lower Galilee, this degradation takes place much more slowly in arid environments.[16] In Israel, however, even the lacustrine sediments do not preserve pollen well. The amount of pollen preserved in these environments is less than what most palynologists use, and the possibility of differential preservation, as we will see, becomes a complicating factor in the analysis.

The first study of Quaternary pollen from Israel was completed by Martine Rossignol in 1969.[17] Rossignol used marine sediment cores for her pioneering work. She found that pollen counts were generally low and that often individual samples did not contain sufficient quantities for statistically valid analysis.[18] In spite of this, her work was an excellent foundation for further Israeli palynology and her photographic plates were extremely useful as one means of identifying the taxa represented in the samples for this project.

Since 1969, substantial work has been done in Israel by several accomplished Israeli palynologists who have added significantly to the knowledge of the paleoenvironmental history of the country.[19] Nevertheless, the Quaternary climate and vegetational history of Israel remains a subject of considerable debate.[20] Many palynologists argue that work done on terrestrial sediments is untrustworthy since it must be corrected for differential preservation and no reliable techniques for this correction have been developed.[21]

Much of the recent work in Israel has been done at archaeological sites considerably older than Sepphoris, or has concentrated on periods much earlier than those represented by the samples collected for this study.[22] Indeed, the majority of the palynological research in Israel has been done at prehistoric archaeological sites where there can be no correlation of the results of the palynology with information from historical documents.[23]

Our analyses are important in at least three ways. First, this study is important because of the historical significance of Sepphoris and the region in which it was a leading city. Sepphoris has a long history, stretching from the Late Bronze Age into the modern period. In the period with which we are concerned (the 2nd to the 7th centuries, C.E.), Sepphoris was a center of political and economic activity for a much wider area. Furthermore, Sepphoris is an important city in both Jewish and Christian history. Second, the fact that our samples come from a period of Galilean history which is particularly well documented in literary texts as well as by rich archaeological remains, means that there is ample opportunity to correlate the results of palynological analysis with other evidence used for understanding human activity at this time. Finally, since the samples used for this study are from terrestrial sediments in an alkaline and modestly arid environment, we knew that only small quantities of pollen could be recovered. Nevertheless, our work has shown that useful quantities of pollen can be recovered through laboratory techniques that are somewhat more cautious than those generally employed and thus we hope that our efforts will lay a foundation for future analyses of pollen taken from archaeological sites.

THE SAMPLES SELECTED FOR THIS STUDY

Since the soils of the Galilee are derived from limestone, they are calcareous with a relatively high pH. This environment is not conducive to excellent pollen preservation; however we have demonstrated that if sufficent care is exercised in the laboratory (using the methods described below), pollen sufficient for useful analyses can be extracted. The soil samples collected for this study were taken from Middle Roman to Late Byzantine loci in two different areas of excavation. The samples from each area were processed separately and ordered chronologically.

Samples were taken in Field I (which may be called the acropolis) adjacent the fortress or citadel. Here the strata could be clearly and precisely separated. Occupation levels extending back to the Early Roman period were identified. Samples were also taken in Field II, an amphitheater located to the east of the citadel. The *cavea* of the theater was filled with rubble in the early Byzantine period when the area became a staging ground used in connection with the citadel. The samples taken for this study did not come from this fill, but were taken from stratified loci at the founding levels of the north corner of the stage (see Figure 1).

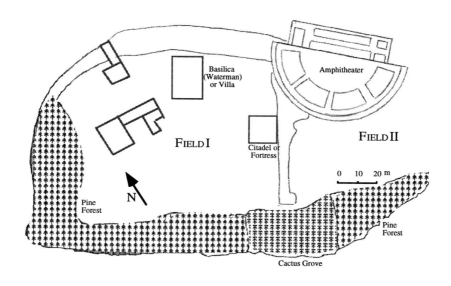

Figure 1. A Schematic Plan of Fields I and II

THE METHODS EMPLOYED FOR POLLEN EXTRACTION

In this study the method used for extracting the fossil pollen is based on standard techniques, modified to take into account the high pH and assumed low pollen content of the soils. The samples were processed six at a time over a period of approximately one month.

Initially 20 gram weights (samples SPA and SPB) were processed, but the sample size was soon reduced to 5 grams to allow for more rapid processing. After each sample was weighed, it was wet with 10% HCl until a portion of the carbonates had been dissolved and rapid chemical reaction had ceased. Then small amounts of concentrated HCl were added to dissolve the remaining carbonates in the sample. Once all of the carbonates had been dissolved in an excess of HCl, the samples were screened through 250µm wire mesh. The portion smaller than 250µm was then transferred into 15 millileter graduated Nalgene® test tubes. These test tubes were spun for 2 minutes at 2,000 rpm in a centrifuge, after which the supernatant was decanted and discarded. The residue was retained for pollen extraction. The portion larger than 250µm was rinsed into beakers, passed through paper filters, and dried. It was thereafter examined under low level magnification to identify any plant or animal macrofossils present.

Colloidal organics were dissolved by adding 1-2 times the samples' volume of 5% KOH. The test tubes were placed in a hot water bath for 5 minutes, after which the samples were immediately topped off with cold, distilled water (dH_2O) and centrifuged for another 2 minutes. The supernatant was decanted and discarded. Extreme care was necessary at this stage in the process since the supernatant was very viscous and difficult to decant. The samples were again washed with dH_2O, centrifuged and decanted once more.

To dissolve any dolomitic limestone in the samples, the second water wash was followed by the addition of fresh 10% HCl to the samples which were then heated in a hot water bath for 10 minutes. At the end of this period, the samples were topped with cold 10% HCl, centrifuged and decanted. The samples were left in an acidic state for the next stage of the procedure.

The silicates were dissolved using 48% HF. 2ml of HF was added to each sample which was then placed in a hot water bath for at least 1 hour. The samples were stirred every 10 minutes. At the end of 1 hour, the samples were topped with cold 10% HCl, centrifuged and decanted. This was followed by 2 further washes in 10% HCl and a wash in glacial acetic acid to prepare the samples for acetolysis.

The acetolysis solution used was the standard 9:1 acetic anhydride to concentrated sulfuric acid mixture.[24] The amount of acetolysis solution prepared allowed for 1.5-2 ml of solution per sample. The samples were then put into a hot bath for 4 minutes for acetolysis. They were stirred at 1 minute intervals during that period. Once the samples were removed, they were topped with glacial acetic acid, stirred thoroughly, centrifuged, and decanted. This was followed by one more wash with glacial acetic acid and two washes with dH_2O. After each wash, the samples were centrifuged and decanted.

Because the samples were expected to contain low concentrations of pollen, the residues were then screened over a 10μm mesh with dH_2O to remove fine mineral matter and other debris that could hamper identification. Material smaller than 10μm was discarded; the fraction larger than 10μm was carefully washed into beakers and transferred back to the centrifuge tubes for dewatering.

For dewatering, the samples were washed with 5 ml of 95% ethanol, centrifuged, and decanted. This procedure was followed by a wash with 5 ml of TBA (tertBuytl alcohol), centrifuged and decanted. The resulting residue was then mounted on glass slides in silicon oil (2000 c.s. viscosity) with 22mm x 22mm coverslips. Four slides were made from each sample. Each slide was checked visually to ensure that there was pollen on the slide.

PALYNOLOGY

As expected, the samples used for this study did not contain large amounts of pollen. Our goal was to identify at least 200 grains in each sample. This goal was achieved for more than half of the samples; however, a small number of samples produced fewer than 100 grains. In all of the samples the Asteraceae: (Liguliflorae [composites] and Poaceae [grasses]) made up the majority of the pollen identified. Smaller quantities of *Olea* and Asteraceae (Tubuliflorae) were frequently present. There were traces of *Pinus* and *Ostyra* in most samples, although not in

quantities large enough to support any conclusions about these taxa. In addition, most slides showed traces of fine charcoal.

The absence of spores from our analysis is intentional. Although the number of spores represented in each sample was often two or three times as great as the number of pollen grains, inaperturate spore taxa are extremely difficult to identify with precision. It was decided therefore that, despite possible loss to the project, greater accuracy would be obtained by ignoring these elements. The analysis of spores from archaeological sites may be a productive field for future work.[25] Appendix A records the number of pollen grains of each taxon counted in each sample. Appendix B shows the percentage that each taxon comprises of the total number of grains in the sample.

PALEOENVIRONMENTAL INFERENCES

The small quantity of pollen identified in the samples and the limited number of taxa found made analysis difficult, but not impossible. The conclusions that we offer are tentative and meant to encourage further analyses. The amount of Asteraceae (composites) in the samples is likely to be the result of the preferential preservation of those taxa in the sediments. Composites have very thick exines and thus resist degradation. In spite of the thick exine, often only the thin ektexine and pore structures remained. This suggests that other taxa might have been better represented had the soils been less alkaline.

In spite of the preservation problem, the data are useful. If one looks at the Poaceae, a pattern can be seen. As the following table shows, there is a significant decrease in the amount of Poaceae in both Field I and Field II from the Roman to the Byzantine period.

Poaceae	Middle Roman	Byzantine 1	Percent of Decrease
Field I	15.8%	14.2%	1.5%
Field II	29.0%	23.4%	5.6%
Combined	22.4%	18.8%	3.6%

Table 1. Total Percent of Poaceae in Analyzed Samples, combined data

This decrease in Poaceae could indicate a transition from a warm and humid period to a warm and drier period. Horowitz, who drew cores from the Hula basin in northern Israel, showed changes similar to those observed

in this study.[26] These cores yielded data from the Late Pleistocene to the Latest Holocene. He found in the Holocene several series of vegetational changes. The latest one, starting at 5,000 years BP (BP = 1950) or 3050

B.C.E., is relevant to this study. Horowitz determined that medium amounts of Poaceae (grasses)[27] and Cyperaceae (sedges)[28] represented warm and dry conditions. His pollen diagrams show that there was a significant decrease in both Poaceae and Cyperaceae. In three other cores, two from the Hula basin and the other from the region of Lake Kinneret, the resolution was better for the Holocene period, giving a radiocarbon date at the top of the core of about 2,500 years BP (or 550 B.C.E.). Horowitz observed an increase in Poaceae and Cyperaceae during the late Holocene. He interpreted this as representative of a warm and somewhat more humid climate with minor fluctuations.[29] The consistent decrease in Poaceae noted in this study might well reflect a short-term, localized fluctuation of this trend toward increasing humidity.

Unfortunately, Cyperaceae are not well represented in our samples since this pollen type has a thin exine and degrades rapidly in an alkaline environment. Indeed, Cyperaceae represent only 3.8% of all the pollen examined in this study, whereas Poaceae represent 18.0% of the pollen studied. Although the samples taken from Field I show a decrease in Cyperaceae, we noted a large increase in the samples from Field II. We consider these data inconclusive for this study.

Cyperaceae	Middle Roman	Byzantine 1	Percent of Decrease
Field 1	2.7%	1.2%	1.2%
Field II	4.5%	12.8%	-8.3%
Combined	3.6%	7.0%	-3.4%

Table 2. Total Percent Cyperaceae of in Analyzed Samples, combined data

There was less pollen and less variety in the pollen extracted from the soil samples taken in Field I than in the samples taken in Field II. The composites, which comprise about half of the pollen studied, show no significant change in quantity from the Middle Roman to the Byzantine period. The high quantity of *Pinus* in one sample, SPY, differs dramatically from the low, stable representation of this taxon in all of the other samples. It is entirely possible that this represents modern contamination since *Pinus* is a major element in the reforestation of the region (See Table 3). As just noted, the samples from Field II exhibited both greater numbers and greater variety of pollen than those from Field I. The decrease in Poaceae which we have described above was the most evident change observed in these samples. (See Tables 3 and 4.)

As one would expect, the samples do not present a neatly uniform picture. For the most part the differences are within the range which might be expected, especially given the poor conditions for preservation in these samples. The significantly higher quantity of Poaceae in samples SPD (34.8%) and SPS (29.0%), as compared to the 6.3% present in sample SPU (Table 6), is probably due to the presence of decaying plaster in these samples. It was common practice to use straw as a binder in the lime plaster of the period. Pollen might well have remained within the straw binder and been released when, during processing, the plaster was dissolved. As in Field I, Cyperaceae is generally steady, except for one sample, SPU, which is an anomaly, containing a much larger quantity of Cyperaceae than any other sample (Cf. tables 3-6).

CONCLUSION

On the basis of the analyses presented above, certain tentative conclusions may be drawn and suggestions for further study offered. The decrease in Poaceae in both Fields I and II suggests that the region was becoming somewhat drier and moving toward an environment of low shrubs and weedy taxa (*i.e.,* batha-garigue). The few samples in which unusually high levels of Poaceae were observed occur either as the result of contamination from the modern environment or, more likely, from extraneous Poaceae contained within the decaying building materials in these samples.

Short-term environmental fluctuations (such as the level of aridity) have had, and still have, great effects on the ecology of this region. If arable land remains fallow, even for a season, because of increased aridity or drought, weedy taxa begin to take over and subsequently other shrubs that require less moisture begin to appear. Gradually (or not so gradually) large areas of once arable land are transformed into batha or garigue. This process is well attested for land once used for agriculture and then abandoned.[30] It is interesting to note that, in this study,

Sample ID	SPE	SPG	SPV	SPW	SPP	SPM	SPA	SPX	SPH	SPY	SPK
Field	I	I	I	I	I	I	I	I	I	I	I
Period	MR	MR	MR	MR	MR	MR	LR	LR	BYZ1	BYZ1	BYZ1
Artemisia			12	3	39			1			
Tubuliforae	5	19	19	9	14	11		8	27	5	14
Liguliflorae	33	147	75	152	61	22	7	127	105	14	94
Poaceae	18	26	31	24	23	19	24	19	25	35	23
Quercus			4		5	1			3	13	
Salix			1		4			27			
Chenopods		2	6	3	10	2	4		8		1
Caryophylls					4						
Olea	1		17	2		4		5	29	14	3
Ostrya			1	2	1	10	3				5
Pinus	5		14			5			1	54	
Corylus											
Apiaceae		15				2			1	8	
Pistacia											1
Punica											
Cereals	1	1	1			6			1		
Ephedra			2	1	1			1	1		
Terminalia					2				2		
Cedrus											
Cyperaceae	1	11	2		8	5	7		4	1	
Brassicaceae	1		21	10		1	2	15	1	15	1
Ericales					1	1					1
Cupressaceae							1			1	
Asphodelus			2							2	
Tamarix	1	4	8		2				9		2
Boraginaceae										2	
Colchicum					1						
Lythrum			2								
Unknown	1	6	9	6	12	10	1	9	10	48	6
Total counted	67	231	227	212	188	99	49	212	227	212	151

Table 3. The Pollen from Sepphoris Numerical Counts of Pollen Grains by Taxon: Field I

while the amount of Poaceae steadily decreases (once the anomalies are removed), the composites (which represent the weedy plants) remain high in both fields throughout the periods under examination.

A key question for future study is: are changes in economic activity also reflected in the palynological evidence? The environmental and economic factors may well be related. The archaeological evidence from Sepphoris, reported elsewhere, indicates that this region remained populous throughout the period. Given the palynological evidence that increasing aridity has led to a decrease in agriculture, it would be useful to examine the archaeological evidence to determine whether there are other indications of economic change or evidence of a general decline in the level of affluence as one moves from the Roman into the Byzantine period. In short, one might ask how human activity was affected by the environmental changes that we have described.

Beyond the paleoenvironmental implications of this study, we have demonstrated the value of palynology for Galilean studies. These analyses show that, although the sample quality may be poor, solid data can be obtained from historical period archaeological sediments in Israel. There are a many sites in Israel with well-established chronologies based on a combination of archaeological and literary evidence. Careful palynological analyses could relate changes in the culture and economy of the region to broader environmental changes and provide archaeologists and historians alike with a richer and more complete understanding of Galilee in antiquity.[31]

Sample ID	SPO	SPN	SPJ	SPT	SPF	SPQ	SPC	SPI	SPL	SPR	SPD	SPU	SPS
Field	II	II	II	II	II	II	II	II	II	II	II	II	II
Period	MR	MR	MR	LR	LR	LR	LR/ B1	LR/ B1	LR/ B1	LR/ B1	BYZ1	BYZ1	BYZ1
Artemisia	1					6	2			13			6
Tubuliforae	9	6	14	41	8	35	19	28	19	18	13	9	16
Liguliflorae	42	26	120	105	53	102	76	86	90	9	32	54	51
Poaceae	59	30	44	19	30	40	45	40	19	70	48	13	53
Quercus	1	3		2	2			6	5	5	3		
Salix									2			1	
Chenopods	1	1		3	2		10	2		7	2	5	9
Caryophylls													
Olea	9	4	1	2	6		22	24	37	35	2	5	13
Ostrya	9	5	5	19			19		4		7	9	2
Pinus	1	2		1			3	2		1			1
Corylus							1				1		
Apiaceae		3							1				3
Pistacia		1			3								
Punica							2	2					
Cereals	3						1	3	1	9	1		2
Ephedra	1		1	2	1		2	3	1	4		2	
Terminalia			1					1					
Cedrus	2												
Cyperaceae	6	4	12	2	6	7	10	4	2	2	14	56	2
Brassicaceae	2	3			5		16	4	3	12	2	10	7
Ericales			2		1				1				
Cupressaceae													
Asphodelus	5	1		6		2	1			3	1	1	
Tamarix		1	3		10	2	7	11	18		3	4	
Boraginaceae							3				1		
Colchicum		2								3			
Lythrum													
Unknown	18	7	1	10	6	15	7	3	9	14	7	37	18
Total counted	169	99	203	210	134	211	246	215	216	204	138	206	183

Table 4. The Pollen from Sepphoris
Numerical Counts of Pollen Grains by Taxon
Field II

Note: Samples SPC, SPI, SPL, and SPR were taken from loci with two cisterns. Because the conditions affecting deposition and preservation are substantially different from those present in surface loci, these samples were not included in our analyses. The information is presented here for information only.

Sample ID	SPE	SPG	SPV	SPW	SPP	SPM	SPA	SPX	SPH	SPY	SPK
Field	I	I	I	I	I	I	I	I	I	I	I
Period	MR	MR	MR	MR	MR	MR	LR	LR	BYZ1	BYZ1	BYZ1
Artemisia			5.3	1.4	20.7			0.5			
Tubuliforae	7.5	8.2	8.4	4.2	7.4	11.1		3.8	11.9	2.4	9.3
Liguliflorae	49.3	63.6	33.0	71.7	32.4	22.2	14.3	59.9	45.3	6.6	62.3
Poaceae	26.9	11.3	13.7	11.3	12.2	19.2	49.0	9.0	11.0	16.5	15.2
Quercus			1.8		2.7	1.0			1.3	6.1	
Salix			0.4		2.1			12.7			
Chenopods		0.9	2.6	1.4	5.3	2.0	8.2		3.5		0.7
Caryophylls					2.1						
Olea	1.5		7.5	0.9		4.0		2.4	12.8	6.6	2.0
Ostrya			0.4	0.9	0.5	10.1	6.1				3.3
Pinus	7.5		6.2		5.1				0.4	25.5	
Corylus											
Apiaceae		6.5			2.0				0.4	3.8	
Pistacia											0.7
Punica											
Cereals	1.5	0.4	0.4			6.1			0.4		
Ephedra			0.9	0.5	0.5			0.5	0.4		
Terminalia					1.1				0.9		
Cedrus											
Cyperaceae	1.5	4.8	0.9		4.3	5.1	14.3		1.8	0.5	
Brassicaceae	1.5		9.3	4.7		1.0	4.1	7.1	0.4	7.1	0.7
Ericales					0.5	1.0					0.7
Cupressaceae							2.0			0.5	
Asphodelus			0.9							0.9	
Tamarix	1.5	1.7	3.5		1.1				4.0		1.3
Boraginaceae										0.9	
Colchicum					0.5						
Lythrum			0.9								
Unknown	1.5	2.6	4.0	2.8	6.4	10.1	2.0	4.2	4.4	22.6	4.0

Table 5. The Pollen from Sepphoris
Pollen Grains by Taxon as a Percentage of Each Sample
Field I

Sample ID	SPO	SPN	SPJ	SPT	SPF	SPQ	SPC	SPI	SPL	SPR	SPD	SPU	SPS
Field	II	II	II	II	II	II	II	II	II	II	II	II	II
Period	MR	MR	MR	LR	LR	LR	LR/B1	LR/B1	LR/B1	LR/B1	BYZ1	BYZ1	BYZ1
Artemisia	0.6					2.8	0.8			6.4			3.3
Tubuliforae	5.3	6.1	6.9	19.5	6.0	16.6	7.7	13.0	8.8	8.8	9.4	4.4	8.7
Liguliflorae	24.9	26.3	59.1	5	39.6	48.3	30.9	4	41.7	4.4	23.2	26.2	27.9
Poaceae	34.9	30.3	21.7	9.0	22.4	19.0	18.3	18.6	8.8	34.3	34.8	6.3	29.0
Quercus	0.6	3.0		1.0	1.5			2.8	2.3	2.5	2.2		
Salix									0.9			0.5	
Chenopods	0.6	1.0		1.4	1.5		4.1	0.9		3.4	1.4	2.4	4.9
Caryophylls													
Olea	5.3	4.0	0.5	1.0	4.5		8.9	11.2	17.1	17.2	1.4	2.4	7.1
Ostrya	5.3	5.1	2.5	9.0			7.7		1.9		5.1	4.4	1.1
Pinus	0.6	2.0			0.7		1.2		0.9		0.7		0.5
Corylus							0.4				0.7		
Apiaceae		3.0							0.5				1.6
Pistacia		1.0			2.2								
Punica							0.8		0.9				
Cereals	1.8						0.4	1.4	0.5	4.4	0.7		1.1
Ephedra	0.6		0.5	1.5	0.5		0.8	1.4	0.5	2.0		1.0	
Terminalia			0.5					0.5					
Cedrus	1.2												
Cyperaceae	3.6	4.0	5.9	1.0	4.5	3.3	4.1	1.9	0.9	1.0	10.1	27.2	1.1
Brassicaceae	1.2	3.0			3.7		6.5	1.9	1.4	5.9	1.4	4.9	3.8
Ericales			1.0			0.5			0.5				
Cupressaceae													
Asphodelus	3.0	1.0		2.9		0.9	0.4			1.5	0.7	0.5	
Tamarix		1.0	1.5		7.5	0.9	2.8	5.1	8.3		2.2	1.9	
Boraginaceae							1.2				0.7		
Colchicum		2.0								1.5			
Lythrum													
Unknown	10.7	7.1	0.5	4.8	4.5	7.1	2.8	1.4	4.2	6.9	5.1	18.0	9.8

Table 6. The Pollen from Sepphoris
Pollen Grains by Taxon as a Percentage of Each Sample: Field II

NOTES

[1]Heralded by Lewis Binford and his associates (including William Longacre, James Hill, Kent Flannery, and others), this movement has important roots in the work of Walter W. Taylor, Gordon Willey, Phillip Phillips and others who argued for a greater emphasis on what would later come to be known as "processual archaeology."

[2]The reader who wishes to learn more about the new archaeology might well begin by reading Chapters 1 and 12 of *Archaeology: Theory, Methods, and Practice* by C. Renfrew and P. Bahn (New York: Thames and Hudson, Ltd., 1991).

[3]Lacustrine cores are cores taken from lake sediments.

[4]A. Horowitz, *Quaternary of Israel* (New York: Academic Press, 1979) and M. Zohary, *Plant Life of Palestine* (New York: Ronald Press Co., 1962).

[5]Mediterranean scrubland vegetation composed primarily of leathery, broad-leaved evergreen shrubs or small trees. This is similar to chaparral.

[6]Bathas and garigues are poorer verions of maquis, found in areas with a thin, rocky soil.

[7]Zohary, *Plant Life*.

[8]Ibid.

[9]Horowitz, *Quarternary*.

[10]Ibid., and Zohary, *Plant Life*.

[11]Zohary, *Plant Life*.

[12]Ibid.

[13]Ibid., and Horowitz, Quaternary.

[14]Horowitz, *Quaternary*.

[15]G. McDonald, "Palynology," in *Methods in Quaternary Ecology: Geoscience of Canada*, ed. B. Warner, Reprint Series No. 5 (St. Johns, Newfoundland: Geological Association of Canada Publication, 1990) 37-52.

[16]Horowitz, *Quaternary*.

[17]M. Rossignol, "Sedimentation palynologique dan le domain marin quaternaire de Palestine: Étude de Paleoenvironment." in *Notes et memoires sur le Moyen-Orient* (Paris: Museum National D'Historie Naturelle, 1969) 270 and Horowitz, *Quaternary*.

[18]Horowitz, Quaternary.

[19]Ibid.

[20]Ibid.

[21]M. Weinstein-Evron, "Pollen Spectra from the Achulean Site of Mitzpeh Yrion, Israel: A Cautionary Tale," *Pollen et Spores* 28 (1986) 157-66.

[22]Horowitz, Quaternary.

[23]Hotowitz, *Quaternary,* Weinstein-Evron, "Pollen," and E. Galili and M. Weinstein-Evron, "Prehistory and Paleoenvironments of Submerged Sites along the Carmel Coast of Israel," *Paleorient* 11 (1985) 37-51.

[24]K. Faegri and J. Iverson, *Textbook of Pollen Analysis*, 3rd ed. (New York: Hafner Press, 1975).

[25]In a relatively dry climate, such as the Galilee, most spores would likely be fungal rather than those from mosses or ferns. These would not have produced useful data for this study.

[26]A. Horowitz, "Climatic and Vegetational Developments in Northeastern Israel During the Upper Pleistocene-Holocene Times," *Pollen et Spores* 13 (1971) 255-78.

[27]Poaceae include between 500-650 genera and 8000-10,000 species.

[28]There are some 5000 species of these grasslike herbs which grow in relatively wet regions throughout the world. It is one of the 10 largest families of flowering plants.

[29]Ibid.

[30]Zohary, *Plant Life*.

[31]The authors would like to acknowledge the helpful collaboration of several individuals. Dr. Robert E. Nelson and Dr. David L. Nugent provided valuable, collegial oversight during the original analyses and interpretation. Dr. Mina Weinstein-Evron of the University of Haifa graciously provided us with reference slides and reprints unavailable in the United States but essential for the success of this project.

Bibliography

Abraham, M., N. Blanc, and A. Yashouv. "Oogenesis in Five Species of Grey Mullets (Teleostei, Mugilidae) from Natural and Landlocked Habitats." *Israel Journal of Zoology* 15(3-4) (1966): 155-172.

Adan-Bayewitz, D. *Common Pottery in Roman Galilee. A Study of Local Trade, Bar-Ilan Studies in Near Eastern Languages and Literature.* Ramat-Gan, Israel: Bar-Ilan University, 1993.

Adan-Bayewitz, D. "A Lamp Mould from Sepphoris and the Location of Workshops for Lamp and Common Pottery Manufacture in Northern Palestine." In *The Roman and Byzantine Near East: Some Recent Archaeological Research*, ed. J. H. Humphrey. Supplemental Series Number 14, 177-182. Ann Arbor, MI: Journal of Roman Archaeology, 1995.

Adan-Bayewitz, D., M. Aviam and D. Edwards. "Yodefat 1992." *Israel Exploration Journal* 45 (1995): 191-197.

Aharoni, Y. *The Land of the Bible, A Historical Geography.* London: Burns & Oates, 1967.

Alcock, S. *Graecia Capta: The Landscapes of Roman Greece.* Cambridge: Cambridge University Press, 1993.

Alon, G. *The Jews in Their Land in the Talmudic Age (70-640 CE)* tr. and ed. G. Levi. Cambridge, MA and London: Cambridge University Press, 1989.

Alt, A. "Galiläische Problemen." In *Kleine Schriften zur Geschichte des Volkes Israels*, 3 vols., 2:363-465. Munich, 1953-64.

Amiran, D., E. Arieh, T. Turcotte. "Earthquakes in Israel and Adjacent Areas: Macroseismic Observations since 100 B.C.E." *Israel Exploration Journal* 44 (1994): 260-305.

Amit, D. "Ritual Baths (Miqva'ot) from the Second Temple Period in the Hebron Mountains." In *Judea and Samaria Research Studies: Proceedings of the 3rd Annual Meeting - 1993*, 157-189. Jerusalem: Kedumim and Ariel, 1994.

Applebaum, S. "Hellenistic Cities of Judaea and Its Vicinity--Some New Aspect." In *The Ancient Historian and His Materials: Essays in Honor of C.E. Stevens on His Seventieth Birthday*, 59-73. Westmead, Eng.: Gregg International and D. C. Heath, 1975.

Applebaum, S. "Economic Life in Palestine. The Jewish People in the First Century." *The Jewish People in the First Century: Historical, Geography, Political History, Social, Cultural, and Religious Life and Institutions*, ed. S. Safrai and M. Stern, 631-700. Philadelphia: Fortress Press, 1976.

Aviam, M. "On the Fortifications of Josephus in the Galilee." *Qatedra* 28 (1983): 33-46.

Aviam, M. "Galilee: the Hellenistic to the Byzantine Period." In *The New Encyclopedia of Archaeological Excavation of the Holy Land*, 2:452-58. New York: Simon & Schuster, 1993.

Avigad, N. *Archaeological Discoveries in the Jewish Quarter of Jerusalem. Second Temple Period.* Jerusalem: The Israel Exploration Society and The Israel Museum, 1976.

Avigad, N. *Discovering Jerusalem*. Nashville/Camden/New York: Thomas Nelson, 1980.

Avigad, N. "Jerusalem. Herodian Period." In *The New Encyclopedia of Archaeological Excavations in the Holy Land*, ed. E. Stern, 2:729-36. Jerusalem: The Israel Exploration Society & Carta; New York: Simon & Schuster, 1993.

Avi-Yonah, M. "Map of Roman Palestine." *Quarterly of the Department of Antiquities in Palestine* 5 (1936): 139-193 .

Avi-Yonah, M. *Map of Roman Palestine*. 2nd ed. rev. London: Oxford University Press, 1936.

Avi-Yonah, M. "Greek and Latin Inscriptions in the Museum." *Quarterly of the Department of Antiquities in Palestine* 12 (1946): 96-102.

Avi-Yonah, M. "A Sixth Century Inscription from Sepphoris." *Israel Exploration Journal* 11 (1961): 184-187.

Avi-Yonah, M. "The Caesarea Inscription of the Twenty Four Priestly Courses." In *The Teachers Yoke. Studies in Memory of Henry Trantham*, 46-57. Dallas: Baylor University Press, 1968.

Avi-Yonah, M. *The Holy Land From the Persian to the Arab Conquest (536 B.C.-A.D. 640). A Historical Geography*, rev. ed.. Grand Rapids, MI: Baker Book House, 1977.

Avi-Yonah, M. *The Jews Under Roman and Byzantine Rule: A Political History of Palestine From the Bar Kokhbah War to the Arab Conquest*. Jerusalem: Magnes Press, Hebrew University, 1984.

Bagnall, R. *Egypt in Late Antiquity*. Princeton: Princeton University Press, 1993.

Barag, D. et al. "The Synagogue at En-Gedi." In *Ancient Synagogues Revealed*, 116-19. Jerusalem: Israel Exploration Society, 1981.

Barash, A., and Z. Danin. "Mediterranean mollusca of Israel and Sinai: Composition and Distribution." *Israel Journal of Zoology* 31(3-4) (1982): 86-118.

Batey, R. "Jesus and the Theatre." *New Testament Studies* 30 (1984): 563-574.

Batey, R. *Jesus and the Forgotten City: New Light on Sepphoris and the Urban World of Jesus*. Grand Rapids, MI: Baker Book House, 1991.

Ben-Dov, M. *The Dig at the Temple Mount*. Jerusalem: Keter, 1982.

Ben-Tuvia, A. "Mediterranean Fishes of Israel." *Bulletin of the Sea Fisheries Research Station* 8 (1953) :1-40.

Ben-Tuvia, A. "Revised List of the Mediterranean Fishes of Israel." *Israel Journal of Zoology* 20(1) (1971) :1-39.

Biddick, K. "People and Things: Power in Early English Development." *Comparative Studies in Society and History* 32 (1990): 3-23.

Biran, A. and J. Naveh. "An Aramaic Stele From Tel Dan." *Israel Exploration Journal* 43 (1993): 81-98.

Bonner, C. *Studies in Magical Amulets Chiefly Graeco-Egyptian.* Ann Arbor and London, 1950.

Borowski, O. *Agriculture in Iron Age Israel.* Winona Lake: Eisenbrauns, 1987.

Bowersock, G. *Hellenism in Late Antiquity.* Ann Arbor: University of Michigan, 1990.

Bowersock, G. "The Challenge of Hellenism for Early Judaism and Christianity." *Biblical Archaeologist* 55 (1992): 84-91.

Brisson, J. *Autonisme et Christianisme dans l'Afrique romaine de Septime Severe a l'invasion vandale.* Paris: E. de Bochard, 1958.

Brock, S. "A Letter Attributed to Cyril of Jerusalem on the Rebuilding of the Temple." *BSOAS* 40 (1977): 267-286.

Broshi, M. "The Population of Western Palestine in the Roman-Byzantine Period." *Bulletin of the American Schools of Oriental Research* 236 (1980): 1-10.

Brown, P. "The Holy Man in Late Antiquity." In *Society and the Holy in Late Antiquity.* Berkeley: University of California Press, 1982.

Cameron, A. "The Artistic Patronage of Justin II." *Byzantion* 50 (1980): 62-84.

Casson, L. *Travel in the Ancient World.* Baltimore: Johns Hopkins University Press, 1994.

Charlesworth, J.H. "Archaeology, Jesus and Christian Faith." In *What Has Archaeology to Do with Faith?*, Faith & Scholarship Colloquies, ed. J. Charlesworth and W. Weaver, 1-22. Philadelphia: Trinity Press International, 1992.

Chevallier, R. ed. *Aion. Le Temps chez les Romains.* Institut d'Études Latines de l'Univ. Centre de Recherches a Piganiol, Tours, vol. 10. Paris, 1976.

Choricii Gazaei, ed. R. Foerster and E. Richtsteig. Leipzig: Aedibus B. G. Teubneri, 1929.

Cohen, S. *Josephus in Galilee and Rome, His Vita and Development as a Historian.* Leiden: E.J. Brill, 1979.

Cohen, S. "The Matrilineal Principle in Historical Perspective." *Judaism* 34 (1985): 5-13.

Cohen, S. "The Origins of the Matrilineal Principle in Rabbinic Law." *AJS Review* 10 (1985): 19-53.

Cohen, S. "Crossing the Boundary and Becoming a Jew." *Harvard Theological Review* 82 (1989): 13-33.

Cohen, S. "The Place of the Rabbi in Jewish Society of the Second Century." In *Galilee in Late Antiquity*, ed. L. Levine, 157-73. New York: The Jewish Theological Seminary of America, 1992.

Corbo, V. C. *Cafarnao I. Gli Edifici della Citta.* Jerusalem: Franciscan Press, 1975.

Crossan, J. *The Historical Jesus: The Life of a Mediterranean Jewish Peasant.* San Francisco: Harper, 1992.

Crouch, D. *Water Management in Ancient Greek Cities*. New York: Oxford University Press, 1993.

Dan, Y. *Urban Life in the Land of Israel at the End of Ancient Times*. Jerusalem: Yad Izhak Ben Zvi, 1984.

D'Andrade, R. and C. Strauss. *Human Motives and Cultural Models*. Cambridge: Cambridge University Press, 1992.

Daniel, R. and F. Maltomini. *Supplementum Magicum*. I. Oplanden: Westdeutscher Verlag, 1990-92.

Dauphin, C. "Les 'Komai' de Palestine." *Proche-Orient Chrètien* 37 (1987): 251-67.

Dauphin C. and S. Gibson. "Ancient Settlements and their Landscapes: The Results of Ten Years of Survey on the Golan Heights (1978-1988)." *Bulletin of the Anglo-Israel Archaeological Society* 12 (1992-3): 7-31.

Dauphin, C. and J. Schonfield. "Settlements of the Roman and Byzantine Periods on the Golan Heights." *Israel Exploration Journal* 33 (1983): 189-206.

Deines, R. "Jüdische Steingefässe und pharisäische Frömmigkeit: Ein archäologisch-historischer Beitrag zum Verständis von Joh 2,6 und der jüdischen Reinsheitshalacha zur Zeit Jesu." *WUNT* 2/52. Tübingen: Mohr-Siebeck, 1993.

Dölger, F. *Sol Salutis*, 2nd. ed. Münster: Aschendorff, 1925.

Dorsey, D. *The Roads and Highways of Ancient Israel*. Baltimore: Johns Hopkins University Press, 1991.

Dothan, M. *Hammath Tiberias: Early Synagogues and the Hellenistic and Roman Remains*. Jerusalem: Israel Exploration Society, 1983.

Douglas, M. *Natural Symbols*. New York: Pantheon, 1982.

Duling, D. "The Testament of Solomon." In *The Old Testament Pseudepigrapha*, ed. J. Charlesworth, 935-87, vol. I. Doubleday: Garden City, NY. 1983.

Dunbabin, K. *The Mosaics of Roman North Africa. Studies in Iconography and Patronage*. Oxford: Clarendon Press, 1978.

Dyson, S. "From New to New Age Archaeology: Archaeological Theory and Classical Archaeology--A 1990's Perspective." *American Journal of Archaeology* 97 (1993): 195-206.

Eakins, J. "The Future of 'Biblical Archaeology'." In *Benchmarks In Time And Culture*, ed. J. Drinkard, Jr., G. Mattingly, and J. Miller, 441-54. Atlanta, GA: Scholars Press, 1988.

Edwards, D. "The Socio-Economic and Cultural Ethos of the Lower Galilee in the First Century: Implications for the Nascent Jesus Movement." In *The Galilee in Late Antiquity*, ed. L. Levine, 53-73. New York: The Jewish Theological Seminary of America, 1992.

Edwards, D. *Religion and Power: Pagans, Jews, and Christians in the Greek East*. New York: Oxford University Press, 1996.

Edwards, D. "Jotapata." In *The Oxford Encyclopedia of Archaeology in the Near East*, ed. E. Meyers, 3:251-252. New York and Oxford: Oxford University Press, 1997.

Epstein, Y.N. *Mavo Lemusah Hamishnah*. 2nd ed., 2 vols. Jerusalem and Tel Aviv, 1964.

Eusebius. *History of the Martyrs in Palestine*, ed. W. Cureton, 29. London: William and Norgat, 1861.

Faegri, K. and J. Iversen. *Textbook of Pollen Analysis*, 3rd ed. New York: Hafner Press, 1975.

Fagan, G. "Three Studies in Roman Public Bathing: Origins, Growth, and Social Aspects." Ph.D. diss., McMaster University, 1992.

Fiensy, D. *The Social History of Palestine in the Herodian Period: The Land is Mine. Studies in the Bible and Early Christianity 20.* Lewiston: The Edwin Mellen Press, 1991.

Flesher, P. *Oxen, Women, or Citizens: Slaves in the System of the Mishnah.* Atlanta: Scholars Press, 1988.

Foerster, G. "The Ancient Synagogues of Galilee." *The Galilee in Late Antiquity*, ed. L. Levine, 289-319. New York: The Jewish Theological Seminary of America, 1992.

Foss, C. "The Near Eastern Countryside in Late Antiquity: A Review Article." In *The Roman and Byzantine Near East: Some Recent Archaeological Research*, ed. J. H. Humphrey. Supplemental Series Number 14, 213-234. Ann Arbor, MI: Journal of Roman Archaeology, 1995.

Foucher, L. "La représentation du génie de l'année sur les mosaiques." In *La Mosaique romaine tardive. L'Iconographie du Temps*, ed. Y. Duval. Paris, 1981.

Frend, W. *The Donatist Church*. Oxford: The Clarendon Press, 1954.

Freyne, S. "The Galileans in the Light of Josephus' *Vita*." *New Testament Studies* 26 (1980): 397-413.

Freyne, S. *Galilee From Alexander the Great to Hadrian 323 B.C.E. to 135 C.E.: A Study of Second Temple Judaism.* Wilmington: Michael Glazier, 1980.

Freyne, S. "Galilean-Jerusalem Relations According to Josephus." *New Testament Studies* 33 (1987): 600-9.

Freyne, S. *Galilee, Jesus, and the Gospels. Literary Approaches and Historical Investigations.* Philadelphia: Fortress Press, 1988.

Freyne, S. "Urban Rural Relations in First Century Galilee: Some Suggestions from the Literary Sources." In *The Galilee in Late Antiquity*, ed. L. Levine, 75-94. New York: Jewish Theological Seminary: 1992.

Freyne, S. "Jesus and the Urban Culture of Galilee." In *Texts and Contexts. Biblical Texts in Their Textual and Situational Contexts*, ed. T. Fornberg and D. Hellholm, 597-622. Oslo: Scandinavian University Press, 1995.

Frova, A. *Scavi di Caesarea Maritima*. Milano: Istituto Lombardo--Accademia di Scienze e Lettere, 1965.

Gager, J. *Curse Tablets and Binding Spells from the Ancient World.* New York: Oxford University Press, 1992.

Galili, E. and M. Weinstein-Evron. "Prehistory and Paleoenvironments of Submerged Sites along the Carmel Coast of Israel." *Paléorient* 11 (1985): 37-51.

Gaster, T. *Festivals of the Jewish Year.* New York: William Morrow, 1953.

Geiger, J. "The Gallus Revolt and the Proposal to Rebuild the Temple in the Time of Julianus." In *Eretz Israel from the Destruction of the Second Temple to the Muslim Conquest,* ed. Z. Baras, et al., 202-217. Jerusalem: Yad Ishak Ben-Zvi, 1982.

Gerson, L. *The Greek Inscriptions from Synagogues in the Land of Israel.* Jerusalem: Yad Izhak Ben Zvi, 1987.

Gesellschaft, F. *Die Wasserversorgung antiker Städte: Mensch und Wasser, Mitteleuropa, Thermen, Bau/Materialien, Hygiene.* Geschichte der Wasserversorgung. vol. 3. Mainz: Philipp von Zabern, 1987 and 1988.

Gesellschaft, F. *Die Wasserversorgung antiker Städte: Pegamon, Recht/Verwaltung, Brunnen/Nymphäen, Bauelemente.* Geschichte der Wasserversorgung, vol. 2. Mainz: Philipp von Zabern, 1991.

Gibbon, G. *Explanation in Archaeology.* Oxford: Oxford University Press, 1989.

Glueck, N. "The Zodiac of Khirbet et Tannur." *Bulletin of the American Schools of Oriental Research* 126 (1952): 5-10.

Golomb, B. and Kedar, Y. "Ancient Agriculture in the Galilee Mountains." *Israel Exploration Journal* 21 (1971): 136-140.

Goodenough, E. R. *Jewish Symbols In the Greco-Roman Period.* 13 vols. New York: Pantheon Books, 1953-68.

Goodman, M. *State and Society in Roman Galilee A.D. 132-212.* Totowa, NJ: Rowman & Allanheld, 1983.

Goodman, M. *The Ruling Class of Judaea: The Origins of the Jewish Revolt Against Rome, A.D. 66-70.* Cambridge: Cambridge University Press, 1987.

Goren, M. "The Freshwater Fishes of Israel." *Israel Journal of Zoology* 23(2) (1974): 67-118.

Graf, D., B. Isaac and I. Roll. "Roads and Highways (Roman)" (with bibliography). *Anchor Bible Dictionary* 5 (1992): 782-787.

Groh, D. "Jews and Christians in Late Roman Palestine: Towards a New Chronology." *Biblical Archaeologist* 51 (1988): 80-95.

Groh, D. "Judaism in Upper Galilee at the End of Antiquity: Excavations at Gush Halav and en-Nabratein." In *Studia Patristica XIX, Papers Presented to the Tenth International Conference of Patristics Studies Held in Oxford 1987,* vol. 1, 62-71, *Historica, Theologica, Gnostica, Biblica et Apocrypha,* ed. E. A. Livingston (Leuven: Peeters Press), 1989.

Groh, D. "Recent Indications of Hellenization at Ancient Sepphoris (Lower Galilee), Israel." In *The Ancient Eastern Mediterranean,* ed. E. Guralnik, 39-41, Figs. 17-22. Chicago: The Chicago Society of the Archaeological Institute of America, 1990.

Groh, D. "The Religion of the Empire: Christianity From Constantine to the Arab Conquest." In *Christianity and Rabbinic Judaism,* ed. by H. Shanks, 267-304. Washington, D.C.: Biblical Archaeology Society, 1992.

Groh, D. "The Stratigraphic Chronology of the Galilean Synagogue From the Early Roman Period Through the Early Byzantine Period (Ca. 420 C.E.)," In *Ancient Synagogues: Historical Analysis and Archaeological Discovery,* ed. D. Urman & P. Flesher. Leiden and New York: E.J. Brill, 1995.

Gutman, S. "The Synagogue at Gamla." In *Ancient Synagogues Revealed,* ed. L. Levine, 30-34. Jerusalem: Israel Exploration Society, 1981.

Gutman, S. *Gamla - A City in Rebellion.* Tel-Aviv: Ministry of Defense, 1994.

Gutman, S. and H. Shanks. "Gamla, The Masada of the North." *Biblical Archaeology Review* 5 (1) (1979): 12-19.

Hachlili, R. "The Zodiac in Ancient Jewish Art: Representation and Significance." *Bulletin of the American Schools of Oriental Research* 228 (1977): 61-77.

Hachlili, R. *Ancient Jewish Art and Archaeology in the Land of Israel*. Leiden: E.J. Brill, 1988.

Hanfmann, G. *The Season Sarcophagus in Dumbarton Oaks*. 2 vols. Cambridge: Harvard University Press, 1951.

Hanson, R. *Tyrian Influence in the Upper Galilee*, Meiron Excavation Project 2. Cambridge, MA: American Schools of Oriental Research, 1980.

Harden, D. *Glass of the Caesars*. Milan: Olivetti, 1987.

Hecker, M. "The Roman Road Legio-Sepphoris." *BJPES* 25 (1962): 175-86.

Hengel, M. "Das Gleichnis von den Weingärtnern Mc 12:1-12 im Licht der Zenonpapyri und der rabbinischen Gleichnisse." *ZNW* 59 (1968): 1-39.

Hirschfeld Y. and R. Birger-Calderon. "Early Roman and Byzantine Estates Near Caesarea." *Israel Exploration Journal* 41 (1991): 81-111.

Hirschfeld, Y. *The Palestinian Dwelling in the Roman-Byzantine Period*. Jerusalem: Franciscan Printing Press, 1995.

Hoehner, H. *Herod Antipas*. Cambridge: Cambridge University Press, 1972.

Horowitz, A. "Climatic and Vegetational Developments in Northeastern Israel During the Upper Pleistocene-Holocene Times." *Pollen et Spores* 13 (1971): 255-278.

Horowitz, A. *Quaternary of Israel*. New York: Academic Press, 1979.

Horsley, R. "Bandits, Messiahs, and Longshoremen: Popular Unrest in Galilee Around the Time of Jesus." In *Society of Biblical Literature Seminar Papers*, 183-99. Atlanta, GA: Scholars Press, 1988.

Horsley, R. *Galilee: History, Politics, People*. Valley Forge, PA: Trinity Press International, 1995.

Horsley, R. *Archaeology, History, and Society in Galilee: The Social Context of Jesus and the Rabbis*. Valley Forge, PA: Trinity Press International, 1996.

Horsley, R. and J. Hanson. *Bandits, Prophets, and Messiahs. Popular Movements at the Time of Jesus*. San Francisco: Harper & Row, 1988.

Hurlbut, J. and J. Vincent. *Bible Atlas: A Manual of Biblical Geography and History. Revised Edition*. Chicago: Rand, McNally & Co., 1910.

Isaac, B. "Milestones in Judaea, From Vespasian to Constantine." *Palestine Exploration Quarterly* 110 (1978): 47-59.

Isaac, B. "The Babatha Archive: A Review Article." *Israel Exploration Journal* 42 (1992): 62-75.

Isaac, B. and I. Roll. *Roman Roads in Judea I: The Legio-Scythopolis Road*. London: Biblical Archaeology Review International Series 141, 1982.

Jameson, M. "Domestic Space in the Greek City-State." In *Domestic Architecture*, 92-113. ed. S. Kent. New York: Cambridge University Press, 1990.

Jeremias, J. *Jerusalem in the Time of Jesus: An Investigation into Economic and Social Conditions During the New Testament Period*, tr. F. and C. Cave. Philadelphia: Fortress Press, 1969.

Kasher, A. "The *Isopoliteia* Question in Caesarea Maritima." *Jewish Quarterly Review* 68 (1977): 16-27.

Kee, H. "Early Christianity in the Galilee: Reassessing the Evidence from the Gospels." In *The Galilee in Late Antiquity,* ed. L. Levine, 3-22. New York: The Jewish Theological Seminary of America, 1992.

Kee, H. "New Finds Illuminate the World and Text of the Bible: The Greco-Roman Era." In *The Bible in the Twenty-first Century*, ed. H.C. Kee, 89-108. New York: American Bible Society, 1993.

Kent, S. "Activity Areas and Architecture: An Interdisciplinary View of the Relationship Between Use of Space and Domestic Built Environments." In *Domestic Architecture and the Use of Space: An Interdisciplinary Cross-Cultural Approach*, ed. S. Kent, 1-8. New York: Cambridge University Press, 1990.

Killebrew A. and S. Fine. "Qatzrin: Reconstructing Village Life in Talmudic Times." *Biblical Archaeology Review* 17 (1991): 44-56.

Klein, M. *Genizah Manuscripts of Palestinian Targum to the Pentateuch*. 2 vols. Cincinnati: Hebrew Union College-Jewish Institute of Religion, 1986.

Kotansky, R. "An Incised Copper Amulet from 'Evron." *Atiqot* 20 (1991): 81-7.

Kraeling, C. *The Excavation at Dura Europos. Final Report VIII. Part I. The Synagogue.* New Haven: Yale University Press, 1956.

Kraemer, R. "On the Meaning of the Term "Jew" in Greco-Roman Inscriptions." *Harvard Theological Review* 82 (1989): 35-53.

Kraemer, R. "Jewish Mothers and Daughters in the Greco-Roman World." In *The Jewish Family in Antiquity*, ed. S. Cohen. Atlanta, GA: Scholars Press, 1993.

Krueger, I. "Zum Tierkreis im Sonnengott-Mosaik aus Munster-Sarmsheim." *Das Rheinische Landesmuseum Bonn* 3 (1973): 33-36.

Lampe, P. *Die stadtroemischen Christen in den ersten beiden Jahrhunderten. Untersuchungen zur Sozialgeschichte*, Wissenschaftliche Untersuchungen zum Neuen Testament, Reihe 2. Tuebingen: J.C.B. Mohr [Paul Siebeck], 1987.

Landau, W. "A Greek Inscription Found Near Hefzibah." *Israel Exploration Journal* 11 (1961): 54-70.

LaSor, W. "Discovering what Jewish Miqvaot can tell us about Christian Baptism." *Biblical Archaeology Review* 13/1 (1987): 52-59.

Lehmann, K. "The Dome of Heaven." *Art Bulletin* 27 (1945): 1-27.

Leone, M. and B. Little. "Artifacts as Expressions of Society and Culture: Subversive Genealogy and the Value of History." In *History From Things: Essays in Material Culture*, ed. S. Lubar and W. Kingery, 160-81. Washington: Smithsonian Institution Press, 1993.

Lernau, H. "Fishbones Excavated in Two Late Roman-Byzantine Castella in the Southern Desert of Israel." In *Fish and Archaeology. Studies in Osteometry, Taphonomy, Seasonality and Fishing Methods*, ed. D. C. Brinkhuizen and A. T. Clason, British Archaeological Reports International Series, No. 294, 85-102. Oxford, England: Biblical Archaeology Review, 1986.

Lernau, H. and O. Lernau. "Fish Remains." In *Excavations at the City of David 1978-1985*, Vol. 3, ed. A. DeGroot and D. T. Ariel. Qedem, Monographs of the Institute of Archaeology, No. 33, 131-148. Jerusalem: The Hebrew University of Jerusalem, 1992.

Levi, D. "The Allegories of the Months in Classical Art." *Art Bulletin* 23 (1941): 251-291.

Levi, D. *Antioch Mosaic Pavements*. 2 vols. Princeton: Princeton University Press, 1947.

Levine, L. *Caesarea Under Roman Rule*. Leiden: Brill, 1975.

Levine, L., ed. *Ancient Synagogues Revealed*. Detroit: Wayne University Press, 1982.

Levine, L. *The Rabbinic Class in Palestine during the Talmudic Period*. Jerusalem: Yad Izhak Ben Zvi, 1985.

Levine, L. "The Sages and the Synagogue in Late Antiquity: The Evidence of the Galilee." In *Galilee in Late Antiquity*, 201-22, ed. L. Levine. New York and Jerusalem: The Jewish Theological Seminary of America, 1992.

Levine, L., ed. *Galilee in Late Antiquity*. New York and Jerusalem: The Jewish Theological Seminary of America, 1992.

Levine, L. "The Nature and Origin of the Palestinian Synagogue Reconsidered." *Journal of Biblical Literature* 115/3 (1996): 425-448.

Levy, J. and C. Claassen, ed. "Engendering the Contact Period." In *Exploring Gender Through Archaeology*, ed. C. Claassen, 111-26. Madison: Prehistory Press, 1992.

Lewis, B. *In Pursuit of the Past*. New York: Thames and Hudson, 1983.

Lewis, N. *The Documents from the Bar-Kochba Period in the Cave of Letters*. Jerusalem: Israel Exploration Society, 1989.

Lewis, P. "Common Landscapes as Historic Documents." In *History From Things: Essays in Material Culture*, ed. S. Lubar and W. Kingery, 115-39. Washington: Smithsonian Institution Press, 1993.

Lieberman, S. *Hellenism in Jewish Palestine*. New York: Jewish Theological Seminary, 1962.

Lieberman, S. *Greek and Hellenism in Jewish Palestine*. Jerusalem: Mosad Byalik, Yad Ben Tsevi, 1984.

Longstaff, T.R.W. "Nazareth and Sepphoris: Insights into Christian Origins." In *Christ and His Communities. Essays in Honor of Reginald Fuller*, ed. A. J. Hultgren and B. Hall, 8-18. Cincinnati: Forward Movement Publications, 1990.

Lythgoe, J. and G. Lythgoe. *Fishes of the Sea. The Coastal Waters of the British Isles, Northern Europe and the Mediterranean*. Garden City, New York: Anchor Press, 1975.

MacMullen, R. *Soldier and Civilian in the Later Roman Empire*. Cambridge, Mass.: Harvard University Press, 1963.

Magen, Y. "Samaritan Synagogues." In *Early Christianity in Context: Monuments and Documents*, ed. F. Manns and E. Alliata, 193-227. Jerusalem: Studium Biblicum Fanciscanum, Collectio Major 38, 1993.

Magen, Y. *'Purity Broke out in Israel': Stone Vessels in the Late Second Temple Period*. Haifa: University of Haifa, 1994.

Malinowski, F. "Galilean Judaism in the Writings of Flavius Josephus." Ph.D. diss., Duke University, 1973.

Manns, F. "Un centre judeo-chretien important: Sepphoris." In *Essais sur le Judeo-Christianisme*, Studium Biblicum Franciscanum Analecta 12, 165-90. Jerusalem: Franciscan Printing Press, 1977.

Maoz, Z. "The Typology of Second-Temple Synagogues." In *Ancient Synagogues Revealed,* 35-41. Jerusalem: Israel Exploration Society, 1981.

Maoz, Z. "The Golan: Hellenistic Period to the Middle Ages." In *The New Encyclopedia of Archaeology of the Holy Land* 2:534-46. Jerusalem: The Israel Exploration Society, 1993.

Mathews, T. "Cracks in Lehmann's 'Dome of Heaven'." *Source* 1 (Spring, 1982): 12-16.

Mazar, B. *The Mountain of the Lord*, 38. Garden City, NJ and New York: Doubleday & Co., 1975.

McCane, B. "Jews, Christians, and Burial in Roman Palestine (Israel)." Ph.D. diss., Duke University, 1992.

McLean Harper Jr., G. "Village Administration in the Roman Province of Syria." *Yale Classical Studies* 1 (1928): 107-68.

Mendels, D. *The Rise and Fall of Jewish Nationalism*. New York: Doubleday, 1992.

Meshel, Z. "Siege Complexes in the Days of the Hasmonaeans." Z. *Vilnay Book* I (1984): 254-58 [Hebrew].

Meshorer, Y. *Ancient Jewish Coinage. Vol. II: Herod the Great through Bar Cochba*. New York: Amphora Books, 1982.

Meshorer, Y. "Ancient Jewish Coinage Addendum I." *The Israel Numismatic Journal*, vol. 11 (1990-91): 104-132.

Meyers, C. *Discovering Eve: Ancient Israelite Women in Context*. New York: Oxford University Press, 1988.

Meyers, E. "Galilean Regionalism as a Factor in Historical Reconstruction." *Bulletin of the American Schools of Oriental Research* 221 (1976): 93-101.

Meyers, E. "Preliminary Report on the Joint Jericho Excavation Project." *Bulletin of the American Schools of Oriental Research* 228 (1977): 15-27.

Meyers. E. "The Cultural Setting of Galilee: The Case of Early Judaism." *Aufstieg und Neidergang der römischen Welt* 2.19.1 (Berlin: Walter DeGruyter, 1979): 686-701.

Meyers, E. "The Bible and Archaeology." *Biblical Archaeologist* 47 (1984): 36-40.

Meyers. E. "Galilean Regionalism: A Reappraisal." In *Approaches to Ancient Judaism*, vol. V, ed. W.S. Green, 115-31. Atlanta: Scholars Press, 1985.

Meyers, E. "The Challenge of Hellenism for Early Judaism and Christianity." *Biblical Archaeologist* 55/2 (1992): 84-91.

Meyers, E. "Roman Sepphoris in Light of New Archaeological Evidence and Recent Research." In *The Galilee in Late Antiquity*, ed. L. Levine, 321-338. New York and Jerusalem: The Jewish Theological Seminary of America, 1992.

Meyers, E. "Roman Sepphoris in the Light of Recent Archaeology." In *Early Christianity in Context: Monuments and Documents*, ed. F. Manns and E. Alliata, 84-91. Testa Festschrift. Collectio Maior vol. 38. Jerusalem, Franciscan Printing Press, 1993.

Meyers, E. "Second Temple Studies in the Light of Recent Archaeology: Part I: The Persian and Hellenistic Periods." *Currents in Research* 2 (1994): 25-42.

Meyers, E. "An Archaeological Response to a New Testament Scholar." *Bulletin of the American Schools of Oriental Research* 295 (1995): 17-26.

Meyers, E., A. Lynd-Porter, M. Aubin, and M. Chancy. "Part II: The Roman Period: A Bibliography." *Currents in Research* 3 (1995): 129-152.

Meyers, E. and C. Meyers. "Expanding the Frontiers of Biblical Archaeology." *Eretz Israel* 20 (1989) : 140-147.

Meyers E. and C. Meyers. "Sepphoris." In *The Oxford Encyclopedia of Archaeology in the Near East*, 4: 527-536. New York: Oxford University Press, 1996.

Meyers, E., A. Kraabel and J. Strange. "Archaeology and Rabbinic Tradition at Khirbet Shema' 1970 and 1971 Campaigns." *Biblical Archaeologist* 35 (1972): 21-25.

Meyers, E., A. Kraabel and J. Strange. *Ancient Synagogue Excavations at Khirbet Shema^c, AASOR* 42. Durham: Duke University Press, 1976.

Meyers, E., C. Meyers, and J. Strange. *Excavations at Ancient Meiron, Upper Galilee, Israel 1971-72, 74-75, 1977*, Meiron Excavation Project 3. Cambridge, MA: *American Schools of Oriental Research*, 1981.

Meyers, E., C. Meyers, and J. Strange. *Excavations at the Ancient Synagogue of Gush Halav*. Winona Lake, IN: Eisenbraun's for the American Schools of Oriental Research, 1990.

Meyers, E., E. Netzer, C. L. Meyers. "Sepphoris. 'Ornament of All Galilee' ." *Biblical Archaeologist* 49 (1986): 4-19.

Meyers, E., E. Netzer, and C. Meyers. "Artistry in Stone: The Mosaics of Ancient Sepphoris." *Biblical Archaeologist* 50 (1987): 223-31.

Meyers, E., E. Netzer, and C. Meyers. "A Mansion in the Sepphoris Acropolis and Its Splendid Mosaic." *Qadmoniot* 21 (1988): 87-92.

Meyers, E., E. Netzer, and C. Meyers. *Sepphoris*. Winona Lake, IN: Eisenbrauns, 1992.

Meyers, E. and J. Strange. *Archaeology, the Rabbis & Early Christianity*. Nashville: Abingdon, 1981.

Meyers, E., J. Strange, and D. Groh. "The Meiron Excavation Project: Survey in Galilee and Golan, 1976." *Bulletin of the American Schools of Oriental Research* 230 (1978): 1-24.

Meyers, E., J. Strange, C. Meyers, "Second Preliminary Report on the 1981 Excavations at en-Nabratein, Israel." *Bulletin of the American Schools of Oriental Research* (1982): 33-54.

Meyers, E., J. Strange, C. Meyers, J. Raynor. "Preliminary Report on the 1980 Excavations at en-Nabratein, Israel." *Bulletin of the American Schools of Oriental Research* 244 (1981): 1-25.

Mienis, H. "Marine molluscs from the Epipaleolithic Natufian and Harifian of the Har Harif, Central Negev, Israel." In *Prehistory and Paleoenvironments in the Central Negev, Israel*, Vol. 2, ed. A. E. Marks, 347-353. Dallas, Texas: Southern Methodist University Press, 1977.

Mienis, H. "Molluscs from the Prehistoric Sites of Abou Gosh and Beisamoun, Israel." *Memoires et travaux centre recherche prehistorique francais Jerusalem* 2 (1978): 269-272.

Mienis, H. "Notes on the Shells from the Bronze Age Strata from Tel Mevorakh." In *Excavations at Tel Mevorakh (1973-1976). Part Two: The Bronze Age*, ed. E. Stern. Qedem, Monographs of the Institute of Archaeology, No. 18, 106-108. Jerusalem: The Hebrew University of Jerusalem, 1984.

Mienis, H. The Molluscs of the Excavation of the Early Arabic Site of Sde Boqer: Some Further Remarks." *Levantina* 60 (1986): 657-662.

Mienis, H. "A Second Collection of Shells from Neolithic Abou Gosh." *Levantina* 66 (1987): 695-702.

Mienis, H. "Molluscs from the Excavation of Mallaha (Eynan)." *Memoires et travaux centre recherche prehistorique francais Jerusalem* 4 (1987): 157-178.

Mienis, H. "Nahal Hemar Cave: The Marine Molluscs." *'Atiqot* (English Series) 18 (1988): 47-49.

Mienis, H. "2. Molluscs." In *Excavations at the City of David 1978-1985*, Vol. 3, ed. A. DeGroot and D. Ariel. Qedem, Monographs of the Institute of Archaeology, No. 33, 122-130. Jerusalem: The Hebrew University of Jerusalem. 1992.

Mienis, H. "Molluscs from the Excavation of a Byzantine Church at Pisgat Ze'ev, Jerusalem, Israel." *Soosiana* 20 (1992): 21-24.

Mienis, H. "The Archaeomalacological Material Recovered During the Second Season of the Excavation of Tel Harisim." In *The Third Season of Excavation at "Tel Harasim" 1992. Preliminary report 3*, ed. S. Givon, 28-38. Tel Aviv: Tel Aviv University, 1993.

Mienis, H. "The Molluscs of the Excavation of the Early Arabic site of Yotvata, Arava Valley, Israel." *Soosiana* 21/22 (1994): 22-28.

Mildenberg, L. *The Coinage of the Bar-Kokhba War*, ed. P. Mottahedeh. Arrau/Frankfurt-am-Main/Salzburg: Sauerlander Verlag, 1984.

Miller, S. *Studies in the History and Traditions of Sepphoris*. Leiden: E.J. Brill, 1984.

Miller, S. "Intercity Relations in Roman Palestine: The Case of Sepphoris and Tiberias." *AJA Review* 12 (1987): 1-24.

Miller, S. "Sepphoris the Well Remembered City." *Biblical Archaeologist* 55 (1992): 74-83.

Miller, S. "The *Minim* of Sepphoris Reconsidered." Harvard Theological Review 86/4 (1993): 377-402.

Morgan M. *Sepher Ha-Razim. The Book of the Mysteries.* Society of Biblical Literature. Texts and Pseudepigraphia Series 11. Chico, Ca.: Scholars Press, 1983.

Nathanson, B. "The Fourth Century Jewish Revolt During the Reign of Gallus." Ph.D. diss., Duke University, 1981.

Nathanson, B.G. "Jews, Christians, and the Gallus Revolt in Fourth-century Palestine," *Biblical Archaeologist* 49 (1986): 26-36.

Naveh, J. and S. Shaked. *Amulets and Magic Bowls.* Winona Lake: Eisenbrauns, 1987.

Naveh, J. and S. Shaked. *Magic Spells and Formulae.* Winona Lake: Eisenbrauns, 1993.

Naveh, Y. *On Mosaic and Stone.* Jerusalem: Israel Exploration Society, 1978.

Neeman, Y. *Sepphoris in the Period of the Second Temple, the Mishna and Talmud.* Jerusalem: Shem, 1993.

Ness, L. "Astrology and Judaism in Late Antiquity." Ph.D. diss., Miami University, 1990.

Ness, L. "Astrology." *Archaeology in the Biblical World* 2 (1992): 44-54.

Netzer, E. "The Winter Palaces of the Judaean Kings at Jericho at the End of the Second Temple Period." *Bulletin of the American Schools of Oriental Research* 228 (1977): 1-13.

Netzer, E. *Greater Herodium.* Jerusalem: Institute of Archaeology, Hebrew University, 1981: 10-30.

Netzer, E. "Ancient Ritual Baths (Miqvaot) in Jericho." *Jerusalem Cathedra* 2 (1982): 106-119.

Netzer, E. *Masada III, The Yigael Yadin Excavations 1963-1965, Final Report: The Buildings Stratigraphy and Architecture.* Jerusalem: Israel Exploration Society, 1991.

Netzer E. and Z. Weiss. "Byzantine Mosaics at Sepphoris: New Finds." *Israel Museum Journal* 10 (1992): 75-80.

Netzer E. and Z. Weiss. *Zippori.* Jerusalem: Israel Exploration Society, 1994.

Netzer E. and Z. Weiss. "New Evidence for Late-Roman and Byzantine Sepphoris." In *The Roman and Byzantine Near East: Some Recent Archaeological Research*, ed. J. Humphrey, Supplemental Series Number 14, 164-176. Ann Arbor, MI: Journal of Roman Archaeology, 1995.

Neusner, J. *Rabbinic Traditions about the Pharisees Before 70*, vols. 1-3 (Leiden: E. J. Brill, 1971).

Neusner, J. *The Peripatetic Saying: The Problem of the Thrice-Told Tale in Talmudic Literature.* (Chico: Scholars Press for Brown Judaic Studies, 1985).

Neusner, J. *From Tradition to Imitation. The Plan and Program of Pesiqta deRab Khana and Pesiqta Rabbati.* Atlanta: Scholars Press for Brown Judaic Studies, 1987.

Neusner, J. *The Formation of the Jewish Intellect. Making Connections and Drawing Conclusions in the Traditional System of Judaism.* Atlanta: Scholars Press for Brown Judaic Studies, 1988.

Neusner, J. *The Economics of the Mishnah.* Chicago: University of Chicago Press, 1990.

Neusner, J. *Introduction to Rabbinic Literature.* New York: Doubleday, 1994

Neusner, J. *The Documentary Foundation of Rabbinic Culture. Mopping Up after Debates with Gerald L. Bruns, S. J. D. Cohen, Arnold Maria Goldberg, Susan Handelman, Christine Hayes, James Kugel, Peter Schäfer,*

Eliezer Segal, E. P. Sanders, and Lawrence H. Schiffman. Atlanta: Scholars Press for South Florida Studies in the History of Judaism, 1995.

Neusner, J. *The Initial Phases of the Talmud's Judaism.* Atlanta: Scholars Press for South Florida Studies in the History of Judaism, 1995.

Neyrey, J. "Josephus' *Vita* and the Encomium: A Native Model of Personality." *Journal for the Study of Judaism* 25 (1994): 177-206.

O'Connor, C. *Roman Bridges.* New York: Cambridge University Press, 1993.

Oppenheimer, A. *Galilee in the Mishnaic Period.* Jerusalem: Merkaz Zalman Shazar, 1991.

Overman, J. "Who Were the First Urban Christians? Urbanization in Galilee in the First Century." *Society of Biblical Literature: 1988 Seminar Papers*, 160-168.

Parlasca, K. *Die römischen Mosaiken in Deutschland.* Berlin, Römisch-germanische, 1959.

Patrik, L. "Is There an Archaeological Record?" *Advances in Archaeological Method and Theory* 8 (1985): 27-62.

Peskowitz, M. "'Family/ies' in Antiquity: Evidence from Tannaitic Literature and Roman Galilean Architecture." In *The Jewish Family in Antiquity*, Brown Judaic Studies, ed. S. Cohen, 9-36. Atlanta: Scholars Press, 1993.

Peskowitz, M. "'The Work of Her Hands': Gendering Everyday Life in Roman-Period Judaism in Palestine (70-250 CE), Using Textile Production as a Case Study." Ph.D. diss., Duke University, 1993.

Poole, J. and A. Holladay. "Thucydides and the Plague of Athens." *Classical Quarterly* 29(ns) (1979): 282-300.

Potter, P. "Critical Archaeology: In the Ground and on the Street." *Historical Archaeology* 26 (1992): 117-29.

Pratt, M. *Imperial Eyes: Travel Writing and Transculturation.* London: Routledge, 1992.

Pruckner, H. and S. Storz. "Beobachtungen im Oktagon der Domus Aurea." *Römische Mitteilungen* 81 (1974): 324-339.

Pucci, G. "Pottery and Trade in the Roman Period." In *Trade in the Ancient Economy*, ed. P. Garnsey, K. Hopkins, and C. Whittaker, 105-117. Berkeley: University of California Press, 1983.

Redfield, R. and M. Singer. "The Cultural Role of Cities." *Economic Change and Social Development* 3 (1954): 57-73.

Reed, J. "Places in Early Christianity: Galilee, Archaeology, Urbanization, and Q." Ph.D. diss., Claremont University, 1993.

Reese, D., H. Mienis, and F. Woodward. "On the Trade of Shells and Fish from the Nile River." *Bulletin of the American Schools of Oriental Research* 264 (1986): 79-84.

Reich, R. "Mishnah, Sheqalim 8:2 and the Archaeological Evidence." In *Jerusalem in the Second Temple Period: Abraham Schalit Memorial Volume*, ed. A. Oppenheimer, U. Rappaport and M. Stern, 225-256. Jerusalem: Yad Yzhak Ben Zvi, 1980.

Reich, R. "Archaeological Evidence of the Jewish Population at Hasmonean Gezer." *Israel Exploration Journal* 31 (1981): 48-52.

Reich, R. "A *Miqweh* at 'Isawiya near Jerusalem." *Israel Exploration Journal* 34 (1984): 220-223.

Reich, R. "*Miqvaot* (Jewish Ritual Immersion Baths) in Eretz-Israel in the Second Temple and the Mishnah and Talmudic Periods." Ph.D. diss., Hebrew University, Jerusalem, 1990 (in Hebrew).

Reich, R. "The Great Mikveh Debate." *Biblical Archaeology Review* 19/2 (1993): 52-59.

Renfrew, A. and P. Bahn. *Archaeology: Theories, Methods, and Practices.* New York: Thames and Hudson, 1991.

Renov, I. "Some Problems of Synagogal Archaeology." Ph.D. diss., Hebrew Union College-Jewish Institute of Religion, New York, 1952.

Roll, I. and E. Ayalon. "The Market Street at Apollonia-Arsuf." *Bulletin of the American Schools of Oriental Research* 267 (1982): 61-76.

Rosenberger, M. *City Coins of Palestine.* Vol. III. Hippos-Sussita, Neapolis, Nicopolis, Nysa-Scythopolis, Caesarea-Panias, Pelusium, Raphia, Sebaste, Sepphoris-Diocaesarea, Tiberias. Jerusalem, 1977.

Rostovtzeff, M. "Les classes rurales et les classes citadines dans le haut empire romain." In *Melanges offerts a Henri Pirenne* 2: 419-34. Bruxelles: Vromant & Co., 1926.

Rostovtzeff, M. *The Social and Economic History of the Roman Empire,* 2 vols., second edition revised by R. M. Fraser. Oxford: Clarendon Press, 1957.

Rouché, C. *Aphrodisias in Late Antiquity.* Journal of Roman Studies Monographs, no. 5. London: Society for the Promotion of Roman Studies, 1989.

Russell, K. "The Earthquake Chronology of Palestine and Northwest Arabia From the Second Through the Mid-eighth Century." *Bulletin of the American Schools of Oriental Research* 260 (1985): 37-59.

Rutgers, L. "Archaeological Evidence for the Interaction of Jews and Non-Jews in Late Antiquity." *American Journal of Archaeology* 96 (1992): 101-18.

Safrai, S. "The Jewish Community in the Galilee and Golan in the Third and Fourth Centuries." *Eretz Israel from the Destruction of the Second Temple to the Muslim Conquest,* ed. Z. Baras et. al., 145-158 (Hebrew). Jerusalem: Yad Izhak Ben Zvi, 1982.

Safrai, Z. "The Roman Army in Galilee." In *Galilee in Late Antiquity,* ed. L. Levine, 103-114. New York and Jerusalem: The Jewish Theological Seminary of America, 1992.

Safrai, Z. *The Economy of Roman Palestine.* London and New York: Routledge, 1994.

Salzmann, M. *On Roman Time.* Berkeley and Los Angeles: University of California Press, 1990.

Sanders, D. "Behavioral Conventions and Archaeology: Methods for the Analysis of Ancient Architecture." In *Domestic Architecture and the Use of Space: An Interdisciplinary Cross-Cultural Approach,*" ed. S. Kent, 43-72. New York: Cambridge University Press, 1990.

Sanders, E. *Jewish Law from Jesus to the Mishnah.* London and Philadelphia: SCM Press and Trinity Press International, 1990.

Sasel, J. "Trajan's Canal at the Iron Gate." *Journal of Roman Studies* 63 (1973): 80-5.

Sawicki, M. "Archaeology as Space Technology: Digging for Gender and Class in Holy Land." *Method & Theory in the Study of Religion* 6 (1994): 319-48.

Sawicki, M. "Caste and Contact in the Galilee of Jesus: Research Beyond Positivism and Constructivism." In *Galilean Archaeology and the Historical Jesus: The Integration of Material and Textual Remains*, ed. R. Horsley and J. Overman (forthcoming).

Scarry, E. *The Body in Pain: The Making and Unmaking of the World.* New York: Oxford University Press, 1985.

Schaefer, J. "Der Aufstand gegen Gallus Caesar." In *Tradition and Interpretation in Jewish and Christian Literature: Essays in Honor of Jürgen C. H. Lebram*, Studia Post-Biblica 36, ed. J. W. van Henten et. al., 184-201. Leiden: Brill, 1986.

Schaefer, P. "Jewish Magic Literature in Late Antiquity and Early Middle Ages." *Journal of Jewish Studies* 41 (1990): 75-91.

Schiffman, L. and M. Swartz. *Hebrew and Aramaic Incantation Texts from the Cairo Geniza.* Sheffield: JSOT Press, 1992.

Schoellgen, G. *Ecclesia Sordida Zur Frage der sozialen Schichtung frühchristlicher Gemeinden am Beispeil Karthagos zur Zeit Terullianus,* Jahrbuch für Antike und Christentum Ergänzungsband 12, 70-88. Münster Westfalen: Aschendorffsche Verlagsbuchandlung, 1984.

Schrire, T. *Hebrew Amulets.* London: Routledge & K. Paul, 1966.

Schürer, E. *The History of the Jewish People in the Age of Jesus Christ,* 4 vols., rev. by G. Vermes, F. Millar, and M. Black. Edinburgh: T and T Clark, 1973-84.

Segal, A. "Theatres in Eretz-Israel in the Roman Period." In *Greece and Rome in Eretz-Israel*, ed. A Kasher, et al., 532 (in Hebrew). Jerusalem: Yad Izhak Ben Zvi, 1989.

Segal, A. *Theatres in Roman Palestine & Provincia Arabia.* In *Mnemosyne: Bibliotheca Classica Batava.* Supplementum 140. Leiden, New York, Köln: E.J. Brill, 1995.

Shackel, P. and B. Little. "Post-Processual Approaches to Meanings and Uses of Material Culture in Historical Archaeology." *Historical Archaeology* 26 (1992): 5-11.

Shatzman, I. "Stone-Balls from Tel Dor and the Artillery of the Hellenistic World." *SCI* 16 (1995): 52-72.

Shiloh, Y. *Excavations at the City of David, I, 1978-1982. Interim Report of the First Five Seasons*, Qedem 19. Jerusalem: The Institute of Archaeology, The Hebrew University of Jerusalem, 1984.

Small, D. "Late Hellenistic Baths in Palestine." *Bulletin of the American Schools of Oriental Research* 266 (1987): 59-74.

Spatharakis, I. "Some Observations on the Ptolemy Ms. Vat. Gr. 1291: Its Date and the Two Initial Miniatures." *Byzantinische Zeitschrift* 71 (1978): 41-49.

Spector, J. "Male/Female Task Differentiation Among the Hidatsa: Toward the Development of an Archaeological Approach to Gender." In *The Hidden Half: Studies of Plains Indian Women*, ed. P. Albers and B. Medicine, 77-99. Washington: University Press of America.

Sperber, D. *Roman Palestine 200-400: The Land. Crisis and Change in Agrarian Society as Reflected in Rabbinic Sources.* Ramat-Gan: Bar-Ilan University, 1978.

Sperber, D. *Roman Palestine 200-400: Money and Prices*, 2nd ed. Ramat-Gan: Bar-Ilan University, 1991.

Stern, E. "The Wall of Tel Dor." *Israel Exploration Journal* 38 (1988): 6-14.

Stern, E. ed. *The New Encyclopedia of Archaeological Excavations in the Holy Land*. Jerusalem: The Israel Exploration Society & Carta; New York: Simon & Schuster, 1993.

Strange, J. "Recent Computer Applications in ANE Archaeology." In *The Answers Lie Below: Essays in Honor of Lawrence Edmund Toombs*, ed. H.O. Thompson, 129-146. Landham, MD: University Press of America, 1984.

Strange, J. "Six Campaigns at Sepphoris: The University of South Florida Excavations, 1983-1989." In *Galilee in Late Antiquity*, ed. L. Levine, 339-55. New York and Jerusalem: The Jewish Theological Seminary of America, 1992.

Strange, J. "Some Implications of Archaeology for New Testament Studies." In *What Has Archaeology to Do with Faith?*, ed. J. Charlesworth and W. Weaver, 23-59. Philadelphia: Trinity Press International, 1992.

Strange, J. "Archaeology and the Social Order." In *Religion and the Social Order: What Kinds of Lessons Does History Teach?*, ed. J. Neusner, 155-174. Atlanta: Scholars Press, 1994.

Strange, J. "The Art and Archaeology of Judaism." In *Judaism in Late Antiquity. Part One. The Literary and Archaeological Sources*, ed. J. Neusner, 64-114. Leiden/New York/ Koeln: E. J. Brill, 1995.

Strange, J., D. Groh, and T. Longstaff. "University of South Florida Excavations at Sepphoris: The Location and Identification of Shikhin. Part I." *Israel Exploration Journal* 44 (1994): 216-27.

Strange, J., D. Groh, and T. Longstaff. "The Location and Identification of Ancient Shikhin (Asochis). Part II." *Israel Exploration Journal* 45 (1995): 171-87.

Sukenik, E. "The Ancient Synagogue at Yafia." *Rabinowitz Bull.* 2 (1951): 6-24.

Sundberg, Jr., A. "Josephus' Galilee Revisited: Akbara, Yodefat, Gamla." In *explor. A Journal of Theology* 3 (1) (1977): 46-51.

Sussman, V. *Ornamental Jewish Oil Lamps From the Destruction of the Second Temple Through the Bar-Kokhba Revolt*. Warminster, Eng.: Aris & Philips and the Israel Exploration Society, 1972.

Syon, D. "Gamla, Portrait of a Rebellion." *Biblical Archaeology Review* 18 (1992): 21-37.

Talgam R. and Z. Weiss. "The Life of Dionysos in the Mosaic Floor of Sepphoris." *Qadmoniot* 21 (1988): 93-99.

Tambiah, S. "The Magical Power of Words." *Man* 3 (1968): 177-206.

Tcherikover, A. "Was Jerusalem a *Polis*?" *Israel Exploration Journal* 14 (1964): 61-78.

Thebert, Y. "Private Life and Domestic Architecture in Roman Africa." In *A History of Private Life, from Pagan Rome to Byzantine*, ed. P. V. Veyne, 353-409. Cambridge, Mass: Harvard University Press, 1987.

Thomsen, P. "Die romischen Meilensteine der Provinzen Syria, Arabia und Palestine." *Zeitschrift des Deutschen Palestine-Vereins* 40 (1917): 1-103.

Trewavas, E. "The Cichlid Fishes of Syria and Palestine." *Annals and Magazine of Natural History* 9 (1942): 526-536.

Tsafrir, Y. and L. Di Segni. Map: "Eretz Israel during the Hellenistic, Roman, and Byzantine Periods, 1:250,000" with Israel Roll. Jerusalem: Israel Academy of Sciences and Humanities, 1993.

Tsafrir, Y., L. Di Segni, and J. Green. *Tabula Imperii Romani: Iudaea, Palestina: Eretz Israel in the Hellenistic, Roman and Byzantine Periods. Maps and Gazetteer. Union Academique Internationale.* Jerusalem: Israel Academy of Sciences and Humanities, 1993.

Tsuk, T. *Sepphoris and Its Site.* Tel Aviv: Society for the Preservation of Nature, 1987.

Tsuk, T. "The Aqueducts to Sepphoris." In *The Aqueducts of Ancient Palestine: Collected Essays*, ed. D. Amit, Y. Hirschfeld, and J. Patrick, 101-8. Jerusalem: Yad Izhak Ben-Zvi, 1989.

Urman, D. and P. Flesher. *Ancient Synagogues. Historical Analyses & Archaeological Discovery*, 2 vols. Leiden: E.J. Brill,1995.

Urman, D. *The Golan. A Profile of a Region During the Roman and Byzantine Periods.* Biblical Archaeology Review International Series 269. Oxford: Biblical Archaeology Review, 1985.

Urman, D. "The House of Assembly and the House of Study: Are They One and the Same?" *Journal of Jewish Studies* 44 (1993) 236-57; reprinted in *Ancient Synagogues: Historical Analysis and Archaeological Discovery*, Studia Post-Biblica 47/1, ed. D. Urman and P. Flesher, 232-55. Leiden: E.J. Brill, 1995.

Vermes, G. *Jesus the Jew.* Philadelphia: Fortress Press, 1972.

Villeneuve, F. "L'economie Rurale et la Vie des Campagnes dans le Hauran Antique." In *Recherches Archéologiques sur la Syrie du Sud à L'Époque Hellenistique et Romaine*, ed. J.-M. Dentzer, 63-129. Paris: Librairie Orientaliste Paul Geuthner, 1986.

Von Hagen, V. *The Roads That Led to Rome.* New York: World Publishing Company, 1967.

Von Szalay, A. and F. Bohringer. "Die Artillery von Pergamon." *Altertumer von Pergamon X* (1937): 48-54.

von Gonzenbach, V. *Die römischen Mosaiken der Schweiz.* Basel Komission, 1961.

Wasserfall, R. "Menstruation and Identity: The Meaning of Niddah for Moroccan Women Immigrants to Israel." In *People of the Body: Jews and Judaism from an Embodied Perspective*, ed. H. Eilberg-Schwartz, 309-27. Albany: State University of New York Press, 1992.

Waterman, L, et al. *Preliminary Report of the University of Michigan Excavations at Sepphoris, Palestine, in 1931.* Ann Arbor: The University of Michigan Press, 1937.

Watson, G. *The Roman Soldier.* Ithaca, NY: Cornell University Press, 1969.

Watson, P. *Explanation in Archaeology.* New York: Columbia University Press, 1971.

Wegner, J. *Chattel or Person? The Status of Women in the Mishnah.* New York: Oxford University Press, 1988.

Weinstein-Evron, M. "Pollen Spectra from the Achulean Site of Mitzpeh Yrion, Israel: A Cautionary Tale." *Pollen et Spores* 28 (2 1986): 157-166.

Weiss, Z. "Sepphoris." In *The New Encyclopedia of Archaeological Excavations in the Holy Land*, ed. E. Stern, 4: 1324-28. Jerusalem: The Israel Exploration Society & Carta; New York: Simon & Schuster, 1993.

Weiss, Z. "Roman Leisure Culture and Its Influence upon the Jewish Population in the Land of Israel." *Qadmoniot* 109 (1995): 2-19.

Weiss, Z. and E. Netzer. *Promise and Redemption: A Synagogue Mosaic from Sepphoris.* Jerusalem: The Israel Museum, 1996.

Whitting, P. *Byzantine Coins.* New York: G. P. Putnam's Sons, 1973.

Wilkinson, J. *Jerusalem Pilgrims Before the Crusades.* Warminster: Aris & Phillips, 1977.

Wood, B. "To Dip or Sprinkle? The Qumran Cistern in Perspective." *Bulletin of the American Schools of Oriental Research* 256: 45-60.

Yadin, Y. *Masada: Herod's Fortress and the Zealots' Last Stand.* Weidenfeld and Nicolson: London, 1966.

Yadin, Y. *Bar-Kokhba. The Rediscovery of the Legendary Hero of the Second Jewish Revolt Against Rome.* New York: Random House, 1971.

Yadin, Y. *Jerusalem Revealed. Archaeology in the Holy City 1968-1974.* Jerusalem: The Israel Exploration Society, 1975.

Yegül, F. *Baths and Bathing in Classical Antiquity.* New York: The Architectural History Foundation, 1992.

Yentsch, A. "Engendering Visible and Invisible Ceramic Artifacts." *Historical Archaeology* 25 (1991): 132-55.

Zohary, M. *Plant Life of Palestine.* New York: Ronald Press Company, 1962.

Zori, N. "An Ancient Synagogue at Beth Shean." *Eretz Israel* 8 (1967): 149-167 (Hebrew).

Index

Author

Subject

South Florida Studies in the History of Judaism

South Florida Academic Commentary Series

243001	The Talmud of Babylonia, An Academic Commentary, Volume XI, Bavli Tractate Moed Qatan	Neusner
243002	The Talmud of Babylonia, An Academic Commentary, Volume XXXIV, Bavli Tractate Keritot	Neusner
243003	The Talmud of Babylonia, An Academic Commentary, Volume XVII, Bavli Tractate Sotah	Neusner
243004	The Talmud of Babylonia, An Academic Commentary, Volume XXIV, Bavli Tractate Makkot	Neusner
243005	The Talmud of Babylonia, An Academic Commentary, Volume XXXII, Bavli Tractate Arakhin	Neusner
243006	The Talmud of Babylonia, An Academic Commentary, Volume VI, Bavli Tractate Sukkah	Neusner
243007	The Talmud of Babylonia, An Academic Commentary, Volume XII, Bavli Tractate Hagigah	Neusner
243008	The Talmud of Babylonia, An Academic Commentary, Volume XXVI, Bavli Tractate Horayot	Neusner
243009	The Talmud of Babylonia, An Academic Commentary, Volume XXVII, Bavli Tractate Shebuot	Neusner
243010	The Talmud of Babylonia, An Academic Commentary, Volume XXXIII, Bavli Tractate Temurah	Neusner
243011	The Talmud of Babylonia, An Academic Commentary, Volume XXXV, Bavli Tractates Meilah and Tamid	Neusner
243012	The Talmud of Babylonia, An Academic Commentary, Volume VIII, Bavli Tractate Rosh Hashanah	Neusner
243013	The Talmud of Babylonia, An Academic Commentary, Volume V, Bavli Tractate Yoma	Neusner
243014	The Talmud of Babylonia, An Academic Commentary, Volume XXXVI, Bavli Tractate Niddah	Neusner
243015	The Talmud of Babylonia, An Academic Commentary, Volume XX, Bavli Tractate Baba Qamma	Neusner
243016	The Talmud of Babylonia, An Academic Commentary, Volume XXXI, Bavli Tractate Bekhorot	Neusner
243017	The Talmud of Babylonia, An Academic Commentary, Volume XXX, Bavli Tractate Hullin	Neusner
243018	The Talmud of Babylonia, An Academic Commentary, Volume VII, Bavli Tractate Besah	Neusner
243019	The Talmud of Babylonia, An Academic Commentary, Volume X, Bavli Tractate Megillah	Neusner
243020	The Talmud of Babylonia, An Academic Commentary, Volume XXVIII, Bavli Tractate Zebahim A. Chapters I through VII	Neusner
243021	The Talmud of Babylonia, An Academic Commentary, Volume XXI, Bavli Tractate Baba Mesia, A. Chapters I through VI	Neusner
243022	The Talmud of Babylonia, An Academic Commentary, Volume XXII, Bavli Tractate Baba Batra, A. Chapters I through VI	Neusner
243023	The Talmud of Babylonia, An Academic Commentary, Volume XXIX, Bavli Tractate Menahot, A. Chapters I through VI	Neusner
243024	The Talmud of Babylonia, An Academic Commentary, Volume I, Bavli Tractate Berakhot	Neusner
243025	The Talmud of Babylonia, An Academic Commentary, Volume XXV, Bavli Tractate Abodah Zarah	Neusner
243026	The Talmud of Babylonia, An Academic Commentary,Volume XXIII, Bavli Tractate Sanhedrin, A. Chapters I through VII	Neusner
243027	The Talmud of Babylonia, A Complete Outline, Part IV, The Division of Holy Things; A: From Tractate Zabahim through Tractate Hullin	Neusner
243028	The Talmud of Babylonia, An Academic Commentary, Volume XIV, Bavli Tractate Ketubot, A. Chapters I through VI	Neusner
243029	The Talmud of Babylonia, An Academic Commentary, Volume IV, Bavli Tractate Pesahim, A. Chapters I through VII	Neusner
243030	The Talmud of Babylonia, An Academic Commentary, Volume III, Bavli Tractate Erubin, A. Chapters I through V	Neusner
243031	The Talmud of Babylonia, A Complete Outline, Part III, The Division of Damages; A: From Tractate Baba Qamma through Tractate Baba Batra	Neusner
243032	The Talmud of Babylonia, An Academic Commentary, Volume II, Bavli Tractate Shabbat, Volume A, Chapters One through Twelve	Neusner
243033	The Talmud of Babylonia, An Academic Commentary, Volume II, Bavli Tractate Shabbat, Volume B, Chapters Thirteen through Twenty-four	Neusner
243034	The Talmud of Babylonia, An Academic Commentary, Volume XV, Bavli Tractate Nedarim	Neusner
243035	The Talmud of Babylonia, An Academic Commentary, Volume XVIII, Bavli Tractate Gittin	Neusner
243036	The Talmud of Babylonia, An Academic Commentary, Volume XIX, Bavli Tractate Qiddushin	Neusner
243037	The Talmud of Babylonia, A Complete Outline, Part IV, The Division of Holy Things; B: From Tractate Berakot through Tractate Niddah	Neusner
243038	The Talmud of Babylonia, A Complete Outline, Part III, The Division of Damages; B: From Tractate Sanhedrin through Tractate Shebuot	Neusner
243039	The Talmud of Babylonia, A Complete Outline, Part I, Tractate Berakhot and the Division of Appointed TimesA: From Tractate Berakhot through Tractate Pesahim	Neusner
243040	The Talmud of Babylonia, A Complete Outline, Part I, Tractate Berakhot and the Division of Appointed Times B: From Tractate Yoma through Tractate Hagigah	Neusner
243041	The Talmud of Babylonia, A Complete Outline, Part II, The Division of Women; A: From Tractate Yebamot through Tractate Ketubot	Neusner
243042	The Talmud of Babylonia, A Complete Outline, Part II, The Division of Women; B: From Tractate Nedarim through Tractate Qiddushin	Neusner

South Florida-Rochester-Saint Louis
Studies on Religion and the Social Order

South Florida International Studies in
Formative Christianity and Judaism